Strategic Human Resources Planning

Monica Belcourt, Ph.D.
Kenneth McBey, Ph.D.

Nelson
Thomson Learning

Australia • Canada • Denmark • Japan • Mexico • New Zealand • Philippines
Puerto Rico • Singapore • South Africa • Spain • United Kingdom • United States

1120 Birchmount Road
Scarborough, Ontario M1K 5G4
www.nelson.com
www.thomson.com

Canadian Cataloguing in Publication Data

Belcourt, Monica Laura, date
        Strategic human resources planning

(Nelson series in human resources management)
Includes bibliographical references and index.
ISBN 0-17-604893-6

1. Manpower planning. I. McBey, Kenneth James, date- . II. Title.
III. Series.

HF5549.5.M3B45 1999   658.3'01   C99-930893-9

Editorial Director	Michael Young
Acquisitions Editor	Tim Sellers
Marketing Manager	David Tonen
Project Editor	Mike Thompson
Production Editors	Rosalyn Steiner and Tracy Bordian
Copy Editor	Sarah Weber
Proofreader	Erika Krolman
Art Director	Angela Cluer
Composition Analyst	Anita Macklin
Printer	Webcom

Printed and bound in Canada
1   2   3   4   03 02 01 00

To my son Marc, with love and
appreciation for his wit and
calm support.

M.B.

With love to Robert, June, Roderick,
and Donald: Nulli Secundus!

K.M.

Brief Contents

Detailed Contents

About the Series

More than ever, HRM professionals need the knowledge and skills to design HRM practices that not only meet legal requirements but also are effective in supporting organizational strategy. The books in the *Nelson Series in Human Resources Management* are the best source in Canada for reliable, valid, and current knowledge about practices in HRM.

The texts in this series include:

- *Managing Human Resources through Training and Development*
- *Occupational Health and Safety*
- *Human Resources Management Systems*
- *Recruitment and Selection in Canada*
- *Compensation in Canada: Strategy, Practice, and Issues*

The *Nelson Series in Human Resources Management* represents a significant development in the field of HRM for many reasons. Each book in the series (except for *Compensation in Canada*) is the first Canadian text in its area of specialization. HR professionals in Canada must work with Canadian laws, statistics, policies, and values. This series serves their needs. It also represents the first time that students and practitioners have access to a complete set of HRM books, standardized in presentation, that enables them to access information quickly across may HRM disciplines. This one-stop resource will prove useful to anyone looking for solutions for the effective management of people.

The publication of this series signals that the field of human resources management has advanced to the stage where theory and applied research guide practice. The books in the series present the best and most current research in the functional areas of HRM. Research is supplemented with examples of the best practices used by Canadian companies who are leaders in HRM. Each text begins with a general model of the discipline, then describes the implementation of effective strategies. Thus, the books serve as an introduction to the functional area for the new student of HR and as a validation source for the more experienced HRM practitioner. Cases, exercises, and references provide opportunities for further discussion and analysis.

As you read and consult the books in this series, I hope you share my excitement in being involved in the development of a profession that has such a significant impact on the workforce and our in professional lives.

Monica Belcourt
SERIES EDITOR
AUGUST 1999

About the Authors

Monica Belcourt

Monica Belcourt is a professor of Human Resources Management at York University. Her research work is grounded in the experience she gained as director of personnel at CP Rail, director of Employee Development at the National Film Board, and as a functional HR specialist for other organizations. Dr. Belcourt alternated working in HRM with graduate school, earning an M.A. in psychology, an M.Ed. in adult education, and a Ph.D. in management. She also holds the designation of Certified Human Resource Professional (CHRP). She has taught HRM at Concordia University, Université du Québec à Montréal (UQUAM), McGill University, and York University. At the latter, she founded and managed the largest undergraduate program in HRM in Canada.

Dr. Belcourt is the founding director of the Human Resources Research Institute (HRRI), in association with the Human Resources Professionals Association of Ontario, which is dedicated to promoting and disseminating research-based HRM knowledge. Under her leadership, HRRI has launched The Research Forum, a column in the *Human Resources Professional;* The Applied Research Stream at the annual conference; the *HRM Research Quarterly;* and the best theses awards program.

Active in many professional associations and not-for-profit organizations, Professor Belcourt is currently on the board of CIBC Insurance and the Human Resources Professionals Association of Ontario. She is a frequent commentator on HRM issues for CTV's *Canada AM*, CBC, *The Globe and Mail*, and other media.

Professor Belcourt is series editor for the *Nelson Series in Human Resource Management*, which includes six texts to date: *Performance Management through Training and Development, Occupational Health and Safety, Human Resources Management Systems, Recruitment and Selection in Canada, Compensation in Canada*, and this text.

Kenneth McBey

Kenneth McBey is a professor of Human Resources Management at York University. His research and teaching draw on his career as an infantry officer in the Canadian army where he rose to the rank of Lieutenant-Colonel and commanding officer of the 48th Highlanders of Canada. Throughout his military career, Dr. McBey held a wide variety of command and staff appointments including those in human-resource related areas such as recruiting, operations and training, personnel officer (adjutant), and compensation. This real-life testing of HR theories has proved of invaluable assistance to his second career in the academic world. Professor McBey earned an Honours B.A. in political economy and a B.Ed. from the University of Toronto, and an M.B.A. and Ph.D. in administrative studies from York University.

Dr. McBey is the coordinator of York University's Human Resources Management program, and he teaches a wide variety of courses including Human Resources Planning, Managerial and Interpersonal Skills, Recruitment, Selection and Performance Appraisal, Organizational Behaviour, and Organizational Theory.

Professor McBey is very active in community and voluntary associations, and he is on the board of directors of St. John Ambulance, Canadian Infantry Association, Army Cadet League of Canada, Fergus Highland Games, and the Ennotville Historical Library (established in 1847). Dr. McBey's honours and awards include the J. Reginald Adams Gold Medal from the University of Toronto, the Canada 125th Anniversary Medal for outstanding service to Canada, the Canadian Forces Decoration (C.D.), and appointment to the Order of St. John by Her Majesty Queen Elizabeth II. His current research interests include leadership and managerial competencies, turnover among part-time workers, the effect of humour on group dynamics, and gender relations in organizations.

Acknowledgments

The authors wish to acknowledge the contributions of three of Canada's experts in HRM: Professor Naresh Agarwal of McMaster University, Professor Terry Wagar of Saint Mary's University, and Professor Sharon Leiba-O'Sullivan of Concordia University. Each drew on personal research and experience to write outstanding chapters in their areas of expertise. We thank Dr. Agarwal for his chapter, "Managing a Diverse Workforce," Professor Wagar for his chapter, "Restructuring," and Professor Leiba-O'Sullivan for her chapter, "International HR: Strategic Issues and Decisions."

The authors wish to thank the following reviewers who made helpful comments on earlier drafts: Jed Fisher, University of Alberta; Linda Piper, Nipissing University/Canadore College; Andrew Templer, University of Windsor; and Jim McVittie, Centennial College. The team at Nelson—Tim Sellers, Mike Thompson, Rosalyn Steiner—contributed enormously through their professionalism and dedication.

Above all, we wish to thank our colleagues across Canada who have supported the HRM Series by contributing their research, their experience, and their input to enable HRM students to read about the HRM landscape in this country.

Finally, we continue to owe much of our career success to the support of our families. I, Monica, thank Michael, my husband, and my sons, Marc and Brooker, who provide the affection and humour that vitalize a project like this. I, Kenneth, acknowledge the loving support of my family and the active interest and involvement of students in my 3430 Human Resources Planning course for the evolution of this text.

Monica Belcourt
Kenneth McBey
YORK UNIVERSITY

Preface

The fundamental premise of this text is that different organizational strategies require different human resources management (HRM) policies and practices. *Strategic Human Resources Planning* is designed to help human resources (HR) managers plan and make decisions about the allocation of resources for the effective management of people in organizations, within a given strategy.

There is a growing perception that human resource planning should be more than just demand and supply forecasting. HR professionals should be business partners in strategy formulation and implementation and should be concerned with the implications of strategic decisions on HRM practices. A decision to expand internationally affects selection, compensation and other functional areas. Strategic decisions to merge or downsize have HR implications beyond simple forecasting ones. All of these strategic options will lead to questions about the best types of compensation, selection, and training to ensure the success of the chosen strategy. This text attempts to answer these questions, without neglecting traditional and important HR forecasting processes. It provides tools for HR planning and forecasting and tries to match corporate strategies with specific HR practices.

Structure of the Text

The text is organized to introduce the reader to the concepts of strategy formulation and implementation, within an HR context. Part I lays the groundwork by embedding HRM strategy in organizational strategy and the environment. A review of the concepts of strategy and the relationship with human resources strategy are introduced in Chapter 1. We spend some time explaining strategic choices, because it is imperative that, as HR managers become business partners, they understand commonly used business terms. This will help them to participate fully in strategic discussions, and to explain the impact of their HR programs on the organization. A model of strategic HR planning is introduced in the first chapter to orient the reader and to provide the structure for the text.

The environmental factors that influence strategic choice, particularly within a HR context, are discussed in Chapter 2. We look at the sources of information about the environment and the methods HR strategists use to scan the environment.

Part II focuses on the more traditional aspects of HR planning: forecasting supply and demand. A critical component of strategy is matching employee capabilities with organizational objectives. The ability to assess current skills is a fundamental part of strategic planning for human resources. Part II provides a comprehensive set of tools that enables the HR professional to develop the numbers and methods needed to support organizational objectives. The critical role of job analysis within a planning context is discussed in Chapter 3, and the use of systems to manage data are outlined in Chapter 4. Chapter 5 explains the techniques used to forecast demand for human resources. Chapter 6 focuses on the use of methods for analyzing demand, while Chapter 7 looks at the methods used for determining supply. Chapter 8, written by Professor Naresh Agarwal of McMaster University, is devoted to managing the stock and flow of a diverse workforce. Managerial succession planning and career development, discussed in Chapter 9, are important considerations for ensuring that the organization has a stock of replacements for its leaders.

Part III examines the types of strategic orientations that firms may choose. Company-wide strategies, sometimes referred to as corporate strategies, are focused on overall strategy for the company and its businesses or interests. Examples of corporate strategies include decisions to merge or to establish the organization in international markets. Strategies at this level are usually also focused on long-term growth and survival goals. In Part III we will discuss three types of corporate strategies: restructuring, international operations, and mergers, and two business-level strategies: low-cost providers and differentiators.

Chapter 10, written by Professor Terry Wagar of Saint Mary's University, discusses restructuring and downsizing. We then turn to an area of increasing importance in the strategies of organizations—growth through international initiatives. In Chapter 11, Sharon Leiba-O'Sullivan of Concordia University discusses the growth option of seeking new customers or markets by locating internationally. HR managers state that globalization of their businesses is the number-one trend impacting their organizations. Operating a business in a foreign country, particularly one that is not North American or European, poses singular problems for the Western HR manager.

In Chapter 12, we examine another high-growth area—mergers and acquisitions. An acquisition occurs when one company acquires another, whereas a merger is typically seen as two organizations merging to achieve economies of scale. Both acquisitions and mergers lead to issues of integration of common functions, elimination of duplication or underproductive units, and a meshing of cultures and practices.

Strategy seems to imply that only corporatewide plans are made, and these are used to manage and control the various units that exist within an organization. But many large organizations operate several businesses, each with its own strategy. For example, Bata operates two "divisions" or businesses, one that focuses on production and the other on retailing. Each has a different business strategy, although the overall corporate strategy is growth. Two types of business-level strategies are discussed in Chapter 13. HRM issues such as HR planning, compensation, selection, training, performance evaluation, and labour relations are discussed within the overall strategies of restructuring, international initiatives, and mergers. By the end of Part III, readers will have an understanding of how specific strategies can be matched with HR policies and practices.

Part IV consists of Chapter 14, which looks back to see how we can measure HR activities, and Chapter 15, which looks ahead to future issues. A critical part of strategic planning is the ability to measure results and to determine if goals have been met. The critical issue for all HR professionals is identifying those HRM activities that add value. Chapter 14 provides a framework for understanding how HR processes, practices, and policies can affect organizational outcomes. It also provides the tools for measuring HRM outcomes.

Chapter 15 examines emerging issues that are starting to influence the field of strategic HR planning. We have addressed the changing nature of jobs, careers in the millennium, outsourcing, and retention of high-skill employees.

Monica Belcourt
Kenneth McBey
MARCH 1999

Introduction

Concepts of Strategy and Planning

A coach of a basketball team has one objective: to win. There are three strategies that this basketball coach can use to win: (1) the *speed* strategy, which relies on an up-tempo, fast-breaking offence and a full-court, pressing defence; (2) the *power* strategy, which makes the best use of offence and defence inside the free-throw area, using shorter, higher percentage shots; and (3) the *finesse* strategy, which focuses on a structured, patterned offence relying on well-designed plays and outside shooting.

Obviously, every basketball coach uses each of these strategies sometimes, but most coaches favour one over the other. Each strategy requires different skills from the players. The coach must choose a strategy and then match human resource skills to the strategy. The coach needs to select, train, and develop players who can play according to the chosen strategy and thus enable the team to win. In this organization (the basketball team), the match between the players' capability and the coach's strategy determines team performance. It is the match between strategy and skills (not technology or equipment) that will make the difference in team performance. Sometimes, player capabilities determine the coach's strategy. The coach may have to change the strategy based on the players' skills, just like the real world.[1]

This sports example demonstrates the link between strategy and human resources. Strategies determine human resource requirements, and sometimes the types of skills available determine strategy. This book will introduce you to the field of strategic HR (Human Resources) planning, in which executives are faced with the same challenges as the basketball coach. We will examine different strategies and learn methods to determine the number and type of people needed to help implement those strategies. We start, in this chapter, by establishing a common understanding of strategy, its importance, and its link to HRM (Human Resources Management).

After reading this chapter you should be able to do the following:

1. Discuss why managers need to examine the human resource implications of their organizational strategies.

2. Define and describe organizational strategies, including restructuring, growth, maintenance, and business strategies.

3. Describe strategic HRM, including its importance and the risks involved.

4. Delineate several approaches to linking HRM strategy with corporate strategy.

5. Outline the characteristics of an effective strategic HR planning process.

6. Describe the strategic HR planning model.

◆ ◆ ◆
A NEED FOR STRATEGIC HRM

Read any Canadian newspaper and you will see stories such as these:

■ IBM and Apple established a joint venture to develop an object-oriented operating system to compete with Microsoft. The social engineering challenge (to get two cultures working together) was greater than the technical engineering challenge.

■ The cities of Toronto, East York, Etobicoke, York, North York, and Scarborough merged into one megacity (called Toronto). The new city's HR managers phoned the authors asking for advice on how to merge the workforces of all these cities.

■ A survey revealed that 80 percent of all managers thought that they would have to compete globally. Most had no idea of how to recruit, compensate, train, and evaluate in an international environment.

■ The federal government laid off 20,000 employees. The government found that too many employees accepted the severance package and had to rehire some to get the work done. Some employees were rehired as consultants, doing the same work for double the pay.

What is the common theme in these stories? All these organizations had adopted a strategy but had problems with the HRM implications. In most cases, unless the HRM strategy is appropriately formulated and skillfully implemented, the success of the chosen organizational strategy is at risk.

We have written this book with the hope that we can provide some answers to those executives who are asking questions about the proper alignment of human resources policies with organizational strategies. Managers who have implemented any kind of change within their organizations realize the importance of matching the HRM practices with organizational goals. There is a growing acknowledgment that the strategic management of people within organizations affects important organizational outcomes such as survival, profitability, customer satisfaction levels, and employee performance. Our goal is to help readers understand strategy and the HRM programs and policies that enable organizations to achieve that strategy. We discuss strategy at some length because HR professionals have been criticized for not understanding and using the language of business when discussing the value of HR programs. HR managers have to use strategy terms to show how their HR practices support organizational strategies. The next sections present a discussion of strategy and outline the types of strategies most frequently used by organizations.

◆ ◆ ◆
STRATEGY

Executives, consultants, and business school professors all agree that business strategy is now the single most important management issue (Byrne, 1996). *Strategy* is the formulation of organization missions, goals, and objectives, as well as action plans for achievement, that explicitly recognize the competition and the impact of outside environmental forces (Anthony et al., 1993).

Strategy has many definitions. We present a sampling of these definitions in Box 1.1.

Mintzberg (1988) has developed a useful framework for understanding strategy, which incorporates many of the meanings found in Box 1.1. The five Ps of strategy that he described are as follows:

Plan: an intended course of action a firm has selected to deal with a situation

Purpose: a consistent stream of actions that sometimes are the result of a deliberate plan and sometimes the result of emergent actions based on reactions to environmental changes or shifting of assumptions

Ploy: a specific manoeuvre at the tactical level with a short time horizon

Position: the location of an organization relative to its competitor and other environmental factors

Perspective: the gestalt or personality of the organization

In this text, we consider strategy as both a purpose and a plan. This perspective views strategy as a rational process in which ends are defined in mea-

BOX 1.1 DESCRIPTIONS OF STRATEGY

Concepts of strategy can be confusing. Here is a guide to some common terms used throughout the text and in the organizations where you work:

Strategy: a declaration of intent.

Strategic intent: a tangible corporate goal, a point of view about the competitive positions a company hopes to build over a decade.

Strategic planning: the systematic determination of goals and the plans to achieve them.

Strategy formulation: the entire process of conceptualizing the mission of an organization, identifying the strategy, and developing long-range performance goals.

Strategy implementation: those activities that employees and managers of an orgainzation undertake to enact the strategic plan, to achieve the performance goals.

Objectives: the end, the goals.

Plans: the product of strategy, the means to the end.

Strategic plan: a written statement that outlines the future goals of an organization, including long-term performance goals.

Policies: broad guidelines to action, which establish the parameters or rules.

surable terms and resources are allocated to achieving those ends. In this context, organizations would set objectives such as "achieve 25 percent market share by 2004" or "be the best health care facility in the province." The organization then develops plans, which include HRM programs, to achieve those goals. These objectives are usually set by senior management, approved by the board, and negotiated and revised as they filter down through the organization. The top management team determines these objectives through a process of environmental analysis (discussed in Chapter 2) and discussions.

Execution of strategy is as important as the careful crafting of strategy. Strategy formulation and implementation achieve the following:[2]

1. Define the vision, and thus provide the organization with a sense of purpose, a mission, and a clear direction.
2. Convert this vision into measurable objectives and performance targets.
3. Determine the plan to achieve the strategy.
4. Implement the plan in ways that are both effective and efficient.
5. Measure the results against goals and revise plans in light of actual experience, changing conditions, new ideas, and new opportunities.

Strategic planning requires thinking about the future. In a perfect world, the strategic planner would establish an objective for five to ten years and then formulate plans for achieving the goals. Other experts do not perceive strategy in such a simplistic, linear fashion. They assert that the future is not that predictable. Planning for the long-term future (i.e., more than ten years) is difficult and would be more appropriately judged as a best guess.

So, many planners look at a relatively shorter period of time, a more predictable term of three to five years. Because of the uncertainty, these plans are somewhat flexible, responding to changes in the environment. Thus, strategic planning must be viewed as a dynamic process, moving and shifting and evolving as conditions warrant changes. The process of subtly redirecting strategy to accommodate these changes is called *logical incrementalism* (Quinn, 1980). Rather than calling for a straight path to the goal, this strategy calls for a series of actions to react to changes in competitor actions or new legislation. Firms can wait passively for these changes to occur and then react, or they can anticipate these moves and adopt a proactive stance.

Writers on strategy sometimes distinguish between intended strategy and realized strategy. The *intended strategy* is the one that was formulated at the beginning of the period. The *realized strategy* is, of course, what actually happened.

You may be asking yourself, Why develop a strategy if the organization must continually change it to accommodate unforeseen changes? Think of strategy as a game plan or a flight plan. A pilot's flight plan appears relatively simple: fly from Toronto to Edmonton. However, the pilot, before departure, is aware of the environment and the capacities (or competencies) of the plane. Based on these external and internal factors, the pilot develops a strategy for a safe flight. While on the voyage, however, environmental changes, such as strong winds or a blizzard, may require the pilot to modify the plan. Even internal factors, such as a passenger suffering a heart attack, may necessitate changes to the plan. But the plane and/or its passengers will somehow, at some time, arrive in Edmonton. This is what is meant by incremental adjustments to the strategy, which do not require changing the focus of the desired result. There is no strategy so finely crafted that adjustments aren't needed. The general rule is that, unless there is a crisis, quantum leaps in strategies should not have to be made. Thus, these strategies should withstand the time test and be durable for several years.

A good strategy recognizes the complexity of these realities. To be effective, strategic management anticipates future problems, provides an alignment with external contingencies and internal competencies, recognizes multiple stakeholders, and is concerned with measurable performance (Lengnick-Hall and Lengnick-Hall, 1990). Just like the flight plan.

The fundamental premise of this book is that different organizational strategies demand different human resource policies and practices. Therefore, before we can discuss HRM strategies, the reader needs to understand the different types of strategies that organizations formulate and implement.

◆ ◆ ◆
STRATEGIC TYPES

Strategies are not idiosyncratic, that is, unique to each organization that develops one. Many executives and senior managers put in an incredible number of hours forging the strategy for the firm, and so they are led to believe that the strategy that they developed, with much sweat and tears, is unique to their organizations. Do pure, unique, organizational strategies exist? In one sense, yes, because organizations are extremely complex and no two are identical. In another sense, no, because unique strategies do not exist and because it is possible to group strategies into categories or generic types. In the same way that we can group our friends into personality categories of passive and active, or introvert and extrovert, we can group organizations by strategy. By their simplicity, these typologies aid our understanding. The more we attempt to add variables to approximate the reality of an organization, the more the typology becomes unwieldy (Duane, 1996). Organizational theorists use classification schemes, or typologies, not only to help us understand how organizations work, but also to enable us to test the concepts, leading us to better information about how to manage.

These identifiable, basic strategies can be classified into corporate strategies and business strategies.

CORPORATE STRATEGIES

Company-wide strategies, sometimes referred to as corporate strategies, are focused on overall strategy for the company and its businesses or interests. Examples of corporate strategies include decisions to compete internationally or to merge with other companies. Strategies at this level are usually focused on long-term growth and survival goals and will include major decisions such as the decision to acquire another company.

Grouped within corporate strategies are three options: restructuring, growth, and maintenance.

RESTRUCTURING STRATEGIES

When an organization is not achieving its goals, whether these goals are business goals of profitability or social goals of helping rehabilitate prisoners, corporate strategy becomes one of trying to deal with the problem. Restructuring options include turnaround, divestiture, liquidation, and bankruptcies.

Turnaround A turnaround strategy is one in which the managers try to restore money-losing businesses to healthy profitability, or government agencies to viability. Sometimes this is done by reducing the number of business units or programs, or restructuring them.

Divestiture This term refers to spinning off a business as a financially and managerially independent company, or selling it outright (Thompson and Strickland, 1995). Sometimes fit is the problem, not finances. One pharmaceutical company divested a cosmetics business. The scientists in the pharmaceutical company had no respect for the frivolous cosmetic unit because they had been trained to apply their scientific training to discover miracle drugs, not make pretty faces (ibid.).

Liquidation The least attractive alternative is liquidation, in which plants are closed, employees are released, and goods are auctioned off. There is little return to shareholders under this option. But an early liquidation may allow some resources (including human resources) to be salvaged, whereas a bankruptcy does not.

Bankruptcy This occurs when a company can no longer pay its creditors, and, usually, one of them calls a loan. The company ceases to exist, and all its assets are divided among its creditors. Confederation Life is a very public example of a company that went bankrupt, owing its creditors $740 million.

Restructuring strategies, like growth strategies, have profound effects on human resource issues. Restructuring strategies demand HR strategies that include managed turnover, selective layoffs, transfers, increased demands on remaining employees, and renegotiated labour contracts. These are described in Chapter 10.

GROWTH STRATEGIES

Many organizations in the private sector target growth as their number one strategy. By this they mean growth in revenues, sales, market share, customers, orders, and so on. To a large extent, the implications of a growth strategy for HR practices are profound. A firm in a growth stage is engaged in job creation, aggressive recruitment and selection, rapidly rising wages, and expanded orientation and training budgets, depending on how the organization chooses to grow.

Growth can be achieved in several ways: incrementally, internationally, or by mergers and acquisitions.

Incremental Growth Such growth can be attained by expanding the client base, by increasing the products or services, by changing the distribution networks, or by using technology. Procter & Gamble uses all these methods. They expand the client base (by introducing skin care lotion or hair conditioner for babies), increase the products (by adding Pringles potato chips to a product mix of cleaning and health care products), change the distribution networks (by adding drug stores to grocery stores), or use technology to manage just-in-time customer purchasing. These are incremental ways of achieving growth.

International Growth Seeking new customers or markets by locating internationally is another growth option. A recent survey of HR managers indicated that globalization of their businesses is the number one trend affecting their organizations (Eichinger and Ulrich, 1995). Managers in Canada would benefit from an understanding of the different HR practices in non-Western countries. Operating a business in a foreign country, particularly one that is not in North America or Europe, poses singular problems for the Western HR manager. The HR implications for an international strategy are described in Chapter 11.

Mergers and Acquisitions Quantum leaps in growth can be achieved through acquisitions, mergers, or joint ventures. An acquisition occurs when one company acquires another, whereas a merger typically is seen as two organizations merging to achieve economies of scale. Acquisitions and mergers have an obvious impact on HR: they eliminate the duplication of functions, meld benefits and labour relations practices, and, most importantly, create common culture. The complexity of merging two companies is outlined in Chapter 12.

MAINTENANCE STRATEGIES

For many reasons, there are executives who wish to maintain the status quo. They do not wish to grow their companies. The executive team is content to keep market share, doing what it has always been doing (a neutral or even a do-nothing strategy). HRM practices remain constant, as they are assumed to be effective for current strategy. Thus, we have not included chapters on the maintenance strategy because the HRM issues would, by definition, be subsumed under another generic strategy.

Executives in other companies, recognizing that the current profitable situation will not last forever, choose to milk the investment. This *harvest* strategy can also be seen as a retrenchment strategy because no investment or efforts will be made to grow the business; therefore, the goal will be restructuring.

BUSINESS STRATEGIES

Strategy, as discussed, seems to imply that only corporate-wide plans are made and these are used to manage and control the various units that exist within an organization. But many large organizations operate several businesses under the same or different names. Each of these businesses within the organization might have its own strategy. For example, Alcan Aluminum Ltd. operates two "divisions" or businesses, one that focuses on primary metals and the other on fabrication. Each has a different business strategy, although the overall corporate strategy is growth.

Business strategy focuses on one line of business (in a diversified company or public organization). While corporate strategy examines questions about which competitive strategy to choose, business-level strategy concerns itself with how to build a strong competitive position. Organizations try to become (or remain) competitive based on a core competence, which can be defined as a specialized expertise that rivals don't have and cannot easily match. As Thompson and Strickland (1995) note, business strategy is the action plan for managing a single line of business. Business strategy is concerned with competitive position. Various business strategies, along with their HRM implications, are discussed in Chapter 13.

While managers recognize implicitly that marketing strategy must support the business strategy, there is not the same sense among managers that HR programs can be designed to support the organizational strategy. We hope that, by the end of this book, you will understand that HRM strategy must match the business strategy. But first, let us try to understand what we mean by HRM strategy.

◆ ◆ ◆
STRATEGIC HRM

Human resources management can be viewed as an umbrella term that encompasses the following:

- Specific HR *practices*, such as recruitment, selection, and appraisal
- Formal HR *policies* that direct and partially constrain the development of specific practices
- Overarching HR *philosophies*, which specify the values that inform an organization's policies and practices

Strategic HRM is a set of distinct but interrelated practices, policies, and philosophies whose goal is to enable the achievement of the organizational strategy. Ideally, these practices, policies, and philosophies form a system that attracts, develops, motivates, and trains employees who ensure the effective functioning and survival of the organization and its members (Jackson and Schuler, 1995). *Attraction* consists of identifying the job requirements through strategic and job analysis, and determining the number of people and requisite skills necessary to do the job and meet organization goals. *Selection* consists of the process of choosing the people who are best qualified to do the tasks necessary to meet the goals, while ensuring there are equal opportunities. The purpose of *training and development* is to ensure that critical competencies are not only preserved but also enhanced. Employee training and development is accomplished through continual assessment of employees to ensure that their behaviours and attitudes are relevant to strategic goals. *Maintenance and retention* activities consist of the reward systems for those who perform their jobs effectively, the maintenance of a healthy and safe work environment, and the compliance with laws governing the employee-employee relationship. These activities should support an organization's strategy.

HR planning can be broadly defined as anticipating the future business and environmental demands of an organization and then developing a blueprint to meet the personnel requirements dictated by these conditions (Cascio, 1987). Think of this as the four Rs: the right people with the right skills in the right place at the right time.

A more traditional perspective of the HR planning concept implies that the organization is concerned only with possible problems of labour surpluses and shortages. The goal was to determine the knowledge, skills, and abilities (KSAs) required within broad organizational outcomes such as growth or decline. Much emphasis was placed on the statistical techniques for analyzing resource supply and demand forecasting while ignoring managerial realities and support for the process (Zedeck and Cascio, 1984). This is a narrow, linear approach to HR planning.

Despite the apparent link between planning and strategy, there is some concern that HR planning has been preoccupied with resource supply and demand forecasting without considering the different HR practices required by fundamentally different strategies. For example, a company that decides to grow through the development of international businesses has different personnel requirements than a company that decides to grow through mergers and acquisitions. Under traditional HR planning models, both strategies would indicate rapid hiring, but the prescriptions for supplying labour effectively would differ radically depending on the strategy. Thus HRM programs would differ fundamentally by strategy.

In this book, we are suggesting an approach that calls for matching specific strategic choices with human resource policies and practices tailored to the strategic needs of the future. Some writers have recognized the need to do this in specific functional areas, such as matching compensation strategies to the different phases of a business (Milkovich and Newman, 1987). However, there is overall a disturbing lack of understanding of the need to match all HR functional practices with corporate strategy.

The litany of bankruptcies, mergers, restructuring, and global competition, now familiar refrains, has affected our view of employees in a profound way. We recognize the need for the strategic input of HR professionals. The next section explains why HR strategy is so important to the achievement of organizational strategies.

◆ ◆ ◆

THE IMPORTANCE OF STRATEGIC HR PLANNING

Executives are demanding that the HR department move from articulating perceived value ("training builds employee skills") to demonstrating real value (an external client can see the economic value). As a game player on the corporate team, HR's focus must be on scoring points, not just coaching, training, or counting the number of players. HR value consists of aligning the HR tool kit to deliver the behaviours needed to enable strategy. There are at least two reasons why strategic HR planning is so important. Employees enable an organization to achieve success because they are strategic resources. The planning process results in improved goal attainment.

EMPLOYEES AS STRATEGIC RESOURCES

Michael Porter (1985) has argued strongly that an organization's employees can provide a firm with a competitive advantage. Employees who provide superior performance because of their skills or flexibility will enable a company to beat its competitors through superior service or the development of unique products. This is a resource-based view of the organization. Classical economists describe three types of resources or inputs used in the production of goods and services: land, capital, and labour. Labour, or human capital, can be described as the mental and physical talents of employees. Other terms to describe these talents include KSAs, competencies, or human assets. The advantages of an organization with effective HR practices may come not from having better resources but from making better use of these resources by achieving higher productivity per worker and by matching the capabilities of employees with the strategy (Wright et al., 1995). HR programs represent an investment in human capital.

This human capital is difficult to duplicate or imitate. Let us explain how this works. If IBM introduces a new software package in January, Microsoft can probably imitate or duplicate this package by February of the same year. However, if IBM technical support people are trained and motivated to provide "knock-your-socks-off-service," then Microsoft will have a difficult time imitating this by February of the next year. Indeed, Porter estimates that it takes approximately seven years to duplicate a competitive edge from human resources. The less a resource can be imitated, the more durable the source of competitive advantage. HRM offers this kind of durable, competitive advantage. The competition can't just buy these human resources because their effectiveness is embedded in the systems and culture that allow them to work productively (Amit and Belcourt, 1999). The HRM process that creates this human capital can't be bought or imitated.

Like other resources, human resources can deteriorate. Skills and knowledge can become obsolete unless either the individual or the employer invest in further education and training. If these investments in training are not made, and the skills become obsolete, then the value of that company's human resources is decreased. Higher investments in training result in higher-value human capital. Thus, human capital has to be replenished.

The value of employees as a resource must be placed within a strategic framework. In other words, a strategy can become obsolete, thus making current employee skills obsolete. Suppose, for example, the current workforce is valuable because of manual skills, but the market for the company's manufactured products is declining. Environmental analyses suggest that the corporation enter the high tech field, with its demand for flexible, knowledgeable workers. By changing the strategy, the "value" of the current workforce is diminished. A corollary to this is that employees can expect to face different HRM practices throughout their lifetimes, and even within a single organization. Employees may be asked to exhibit different behaviours, depending on strategic goals, and these behaviours will be aroused by different HRM practices (Schuler and Jackson, 1989). Organizations with different business units can be expected to have different HRM policies to optimize their employee performance.

To summarize, human assets offer organizations a competitive advantage. These assets must be managed and must be matched to the organizational strategy. An organization that manages its human resources strategically is more likely to survive and profit. A second advantage of managing human resources strategically is increasing the possibility that organization goals are achieved.

IMPROVED GOAL ATTAINMENT

Strategic HRM can improve organization performance (Wright et al., 1995). The goals of these HRM strategies are to shape employee behaviour so that it is consistent with strategic direction. Correct alignment with overall strategy ensures that employees are skilled and committed to achieving these organization goals. Organizations with clear strategies provide direction and meaning to employees and mitigate the need for control by substituting a consistency of purpose, a mission. This provision of vision for the future may result in a more effective organization through increased motivation and performance, lowered absenteeism and turnover, and heightened stability, satisfaction, and involvement (King, 1995).

To summarize, strategy formulation is important to the attainment of organizational goals in order to align all HR functional strategies with overall strategy and to focus employees on important missions and goals of the organization. Research and observations have demonstrated that developing HR practices that support the strategy leads to improved strategy implementation (Lengnick-Hall and Lengnick-Hall, 1990). Is there a downside to strategic HR planning?

◆ ◆ ◆

THE RISKS

The strategic management of human resources seems beneficial, but some researchers point out that there are costs (Lengnick-Hall and Lengnick-Hall, 1988). Their summary of the research shows that these costs include additional decision complexity, greater potential for information overload, impossible commitments to employees, and an overconcern with employee reactions that may be incompatible with industry conditions. In other words, the strategic management of employees is hard work. As anyone who has gone through the strategy formulation and implementation process understands, the strategy formulation phase is relatively easy. Motivating employees to commit to the strategy and implement it is far more difficult, and this text offers guidelines on how to do this. A further difficulty is that any HR plan for the future may raise employees' expectations that they have jobs for life and will be trained for those jobs. The reality is that conditions change, and the plan may be changed, resulting in job losses.

Another problem, some would argue, is that organizations that commit to one strategy become blinded to changes in the environment, and lose their flexibility. However, as we have seen, incremental adjustments based on environmental scanning are part of strategy implementation. The risk of not having a strategy seems greater.

There are risks to not developing a strategy. Organizations that do not actively scan the environment (methods for doing so are discussed in Chapter 2) face the danger of being out of touch with reality. Today's operating decisions may be based on yesterday's conditions. Comfortable with past success, the managers in these organizations focus on resolving internal problems, such as making better horse carriages when automobiles are on the horizon.

An example of a company that was not in touch with reality was Consumers Distributing. Consumers Distributing did not develop a strategy to match or surpass the changing distribution networks and customer-service levels of their competitors. This company, now bankrupt, continued to require customers to come to the stores and stand in line, often for out-of-stock items. Meanwhile, their competitors were offering electronic purchasing from the home or were providing greeters at the door of the store who helped the customer find anything, all of this for a competitive price. MacMillan (1983) argues that those firms that develop strategies gain a strategic advantage and control their own destinies. An apt cliché is "an organization that fails to plan, plans to fail."

Therefore, strategic HR planning is important to optimize the use of the organization's human resources and to focus behaviour on the important goals of the organization.

◆ ◆ ◆
LINKING HR PROCESSES TO STRATEGY

Strategic HRM must facilitate the formulation and implementation of corporate and business-level strategies. Senior managers must focus on issues such as these: What are the HR implications of adopting a strategy? What are the internal and external constraints and opportunities? Exactly what policies, practices, and philosophies contribute to the successful implementation of the strategy?

The basic premise is that every HR policy and practice must directly support the organization's strategy and objectives (Anderson, 1997). This does not happen as frequently as it should. In the worst-case scenario, in many companies, HR plans are developed as an afterthought and separately from organizational strategy. They are not relevant to the business and are owned only by the HR people. No other unit or level is committed to these plans.

While it has long been recognized that HR polices and practices must be linked to overall firm strategy, there has been little research that offers prescriptions on exactly how to do this. Aligning HR strategy with business strategy can be done in these ways:

1. Start with organizational strategy and then create HR strategy.
2. Start with HR competencies and then craft corporate strategies based on these competencies.
3. Do a combination of both in a form of reciprocal relationship.

   Let us examine each approach.

CORPORATE STRATEGY ⟶ HR STRATEGY

A traditional perspective of HR planning views HRM programs as flowing from corporate strategy. Corporate strategy drives HR strategy. In other words, personnel needs are based on corporate plans. The basketball coach decides on the strategy and then selects or develops players who can play to that strategy. If a firm decides to compete on the basis of offering low-cost products, then HR policies and practices must align and be based on low labour costs. McDonald's is a good example of a firm that follows this strategy. This model assumes that people are more adaptable than strategy and that cause and effect relationships are unidirectional (Lengnick-Hall and Lengnick-Hall, 1986). Square workers are forced to fit into round holes, with little consideration for their ability to adjust. If the workers can't adjust to a new strategy, they are terminated in a massive restructuring.

Given their investment in thousands of employees, larger organizations seem to prefer this approach (making the resources fit the strategy), despite the literature on the difficulty and time-consuming nature of organizational change. Within this approach, employees are considered means to an end, not part of the strategy formulation equation.

But another perspective reverses this view, suggesting that employee competencies determine the end.

HR COMPETENCIES ⟶ BUSINESS STRATEGY

A competing view states that an organization cannot implement a strategy if it does not have the human resources necessary to implement a preferred strategy (Cappelli and Singh, 1992). The basketball coach has players with the skills to achieve, for example, the finesse strategy. The coach would then capitalize on the players' skills, rather than attempt to use the team to try to win based on a power strategy, for which their skills are weak.

The critical question is, Is it easier to change HR to fit the strategy or change the strategy to fit the human resource pool? Small businesses seem to choose the latter. The owners of very small businesses are nimble and quickly recognize that, if an employee has a certain capability, it can be exploited to develop new products or services. Diversity management efforts are currently building on this theme. For example, if the number of employees who speak Mandarin reaches a critical mass within an organization, the observant executive will start to explore Asian markets. But it is not just small organizations that buy into this attitude of "skills determine strategy."

High tech firms assume that intellectual capabilities are internal to employees, and thus if different ideas are necessary, then employees are replaced. If some employees have unique skills, these are exploited to open new markets.

This outlook relies too heavily on employee capabilities and not enough on environmental analysis. Nor is consideration given to changing HR practices in training or compensation to facilitate this change in strategy.

These perspectives represent two extremes on a continuum between organizational strategy and HR practices. The reality is closer to the concept of reciprocal interdependencies (Lengnick-Hall and Lengnick Hall, 1988).

CORPORATE STRATEGY ◄────► HR STRATEGY

An emerging perspective sees HR strategy as contributing to business-level strategy, and vice versa. Increasingly in large firms, senior HR vice-presidents are asked not only to review business plans to ensure consistency with HR strategy, but also to provide input to this strategy based on HR strengths and weaknesses.

In this context, an organization chooses a business strategy, such as being a leader in innovative products based on its in-house, highly educated, trained employees who have been socialized to value creativity. Simply phrased, an organization develops its employees and then capitalizes on employees' skills; the employees then learn new skills, and round and round. Corel is a good example. Their HR strategy is to hire the best, invest heavily in training, and socialize employees to value productivity and creativity. In many ways, HR strategy drives business strategy, and business strategy determines HR strategy. This concept of reciprocal interdependence is widely accepted in the HR strategy literature (Bamberger and Fiegenbaum, 1996).

HR BECOMES A BUSINESS PARTNER

The key point here is the concept of *concurrent strategy formulation*. Strategy development, based on environmental analysis, is conducted at the same time that HRM issues are considered. HR issues do not solely determine strategy, nor does strategy unilaterally determine HR practices. The HR senior management team moves from outsider status to insider status. The implications are not trivial. HR managers must understand the numbers language of business or the outcome expectations of nonprofit organizations. They must be able to understand analyses presented by marketing, financial, and operational managers. Cost–benefit assessments of options within the HR domain will have to be prepared and defended. Entrepreneurial instincts will have to be sharpened, as HR managers will be expected to engage in scanning human resource capabilities for business opportunities in this two-way approach to strategic HR planning. Alternative solutions to problems have to be generated. For example, if the low-cost strategy depends on hiring personnel at minimum wage, then HR managers have to develop strategies to deal with rapid training and high turnover rates. This option will have to be compared with outsourcing, robotization, or even increasing wages to reduce the costs of turnover. The HR manager is no longer the auditor, but a partner and problem solver. Linkages, both formal and informal, ensure that this partnership role is enacted. One HR manager describes her perspective on concurrent strategy formulation in Box 1.2.

BOX 1.2 THE NEW APPROACH TO HR STRATEGY

Bonnie Hathcock is the chief HR officer for Siemans Rolm Communications. She claims that a revolution in approaches to human resource management (HRM) is needed for the challenges of the 21st century. "The 21st-century human resource imperative is to raise the company's human capital to sophisticated levels which produce competitive advantages for the enterprise," Hathcock asserts. This requires a shakedown for those in "personnel" who prefer to remain quietly on the sidelines administering employee requests.

The revolution begins with identifying the company's strategy and aligning HR work with strategic imperatives. Hathcock sees HR strategy as a planned response to corporate strategy. The HR role is to enhance the capabilities of the enterprise to execute its business strategies. Hathcock sees herself as a master calibrator, and as the leader of the crusade to maximize human assets. Employees are not commodities to be treated as if they are expendable. The raison d'être for HR is to be the catalyst for human asset capability and commitment. Both dimensions are important: 1) building human commitment through culture management and 2) building human asset capability through competency development. Hancock continues: "If the HR department is to achieve parity with other functions, then they must not just serve and support but must integrate fully with management in achieving business results."

Hathcock's efforts at Sieman's have won her the Optimas Award for Human Resource Excellence in managing change in 1996.

Source: Adapted from Hathcock, B.C. 1996. "The New Breed Approach to 21st Century Human Resources." *Human Resource Management*, Summer, 35, no. 2: 243–250.

STRATEGIC PARTNERING

Human resource professionals recognize the need to play more of a strategic role within the organization. One-third of Canadian HR executives surveyed spoke of the need to operate more as a business partner. They defined their new role as one blending their HR technical skills with an in-depth understanding of the business and its goals (Kulig, 1998). They are addressing the concerns that Rothwell and Kazanas (1988) have identified as obstacles to strategic HR planning:

■ Top managers don't see a need.

■ HR personnel are seen as personnel experts, not experts in the business.

■ HR information generated is useful to HR but incompatible with business needs.

These attitudes are changing as organizations realize the impact that HRM strategy can have on organizational effectiveness and as HR managers develop the linkages to ensure that the strategy is effective.

There are formal mechanisms to ensure that HR is a partner in this process.

Membership in the Executive Team

An obvious one is to ensure that the person responsible for HRM be part of the executive team, occupying a position at the vice-presidential level. Most large organizations now have the most senior HR person at the executive vice-president level.

Review/React Linkage

Another option is a review/react linkage, proposed by Cascio (1991). In this scenario, HR managers have the opportunity to review strategic plans, before they are implemented. They can then approve or modify them.

However, this control or veto option is too passive and reactionary for significant input about a critical resource. Linkages have to be made at earlier stages. HR managers should be supplying information about employee capabilities, be part of the strategic planning committee, and be documenting implications of strategic thrusts (Cascio, 1991).

Integrative Linkage

In a truly integrative linkage, as exhibited in some companies, the interaction between the members of the executive committee and the HR director are frequent, and the HR director is involved in strategic decisions, even when the HR implications are not readily apparent (Buller, 1996). The HR credibility in these organizations is so high that the CEO, vice chair, and other top officials have all held the position of HR director as part of their career development.

Organizations are more responsive to integrative linkages when the environment is turbulent (increased competition, rapid technological change, and changing labour market demographics), resulting in difficulties recruiting the right kinds of people. Organizations with multiple divisions demanding different types of strategies, and therefore different HR practices for each division, also tend to elevate the role of HR. A culture or CEO with a strong belief in the asset value of employees will also result in more attempts at linking HR strategies with corporate strategies. The credibility of the HR director also influences the probability of a linkage. HR managers who were able to deliver information about labour supply, or critical personnel capabilities, in a quantifiable way were deemed more credible. If HR directors are responsible for bottom line results and are measured on these, they become more focused on delivering programs that make a difference. One organization tied 40 percent of the HR manager's compensation (pay at risk) to company performance.

Crises are often an opportunity to establish a linkage. If a company is experiencing high turnover and is unable to meet production quotas, or if a key executive departs and there is no groomed successor, then many HR directors use this as an opportunity to promote the importance of HR strategic planning.

Changes in the environment overall can sometimes increase the attractiveness of HR strategy. Globalization, for example, forces managers to examine the cost–benefit of using national or international labour pools to attain desired cost and quality objectives. Either choice implicates strategic HR planning.

For all these reasons, most organizations have accepted the importance of including the HR director as part of the strategy formulation team. We offer guidelines to the development of an effective HR strategy in the next section.

CHARACTERISTICS OF AN EFFECTIVE HRM STRATEGY

The purpose of HR strategy is to capitalize on the distinctive competencies of the organization and add value through the effective use of human resources (Cooke and Armstrong, 1990). HR strategy is about designing organizational strategy based on HR strengths and weaknesses and making organizational strategies work.

Based on extensive observations by key players in the HR strategic planning process, it appears that effective HRM strategies include the following dimensions: external and internal fit and a focus on results.

External and Internal Fit

Fit and complementariness are important considerations when designing HR programs. We look at two types of fit that are important: fitting HR strategy to organizational strategy (external fit) and linking the various HR programs to other functional areas and to each other (internal fit).

External Fit HR programs must align with or fit the strategy. If the business strategy of the organization is to differentiate itself from its competitors based on superior service, then selection and training programs should be developed to hire and train people in the skills and attitudes necessary to deliver superior service. Fit with other functional strategies is as important as fit with corporate strategies. The consideration of human resource capabilities must be included at all stages of the strategic planning process (Guest, 1990). Integration assures that employees are considered in corporate strategy as an important factor in organizational competence. HR senior management must be included in strategy discussions.

Internal Fit We look at two types of internal fit: a fit with other functional areas, such as marketing, and a fit among all HR programs. Fit with other functional areas is important. If marketing is developing an advertising plan that promises 24-hour access to customer service representatives, and the HR plan does not include compensation differentials for shift work, then the overall marketing strategy might fail.

As HR programs must fit with other functional areas, so they too have to be consistent with each other. That is, training, selection, and appraisal must work in conjunction to support a strategy. If the training department decides to teach employees to use the Internet to handle customer service, then the staffing function must hire people who either are computer literate or who have the kinds of intelligence that enable them to learn computer skills rapidly. This is commonly referred to as bundling HR practices.

Consistent, cross-functional practices are critical to the achievement of an organization's goals. Imagine if the business strategy depended on exemplary customer service as its principal competitive advantage, but untrained employees were incapable of providing customer service. The bundling of HR practices is necessary to ensure that the overall strategy is implemented consistently (Belcourt, 1996).

Focus on Results

The hard work of strategy is not the formulation but the implementation and the tracking of results. Many HR managers do not have the resources or skills to measure programs to see if the goals have been achieved. Unless the strategy contains performance measures, that is, is results oriented, it will be difficult to know how successfully the strategy was implemented. Chapter 14 presents various methods for evaluating programs. As James Harrington says, "Measurements are key. If you cannot measure it, you cannot control it. If you cannot control it, then you cannot manage it" (1991, p. 28).

To summarize, an effective HRM strategy is aligned with organizational strategy, is integrated with other departmental and HR functional area goals, and is focused on results that are measured. Furthermore, HR strategy must explicitly recognize the dynamics of the external environment (including the competition and labour markets) and work within a long-range focus of three to five years.

The final section in this chapter outlines the strategic HR planning model and sets the stage for the rest of the material in the book.

◆ ◆ ◆
THE STRATEGIC HR PLANNING MODEL

The model we are using is based on generic corporate and business strategies linked with complex, bundled HR policies and practices. Our perspective builds on earlier HR planning models (right numbers in the right places at the right times). Our search for a strategic HR planning model was triggered by practitioner needs for information. Most requests we receive from CEOs and executive vice-presidents of HR are of this nature: "Our organization is merging with another. How will this affect HR? What changes in our HR policies and practices do we need to make?" We have tried to provide answers for these managers.

Our model of strategic HR planning is presented in Figure 1.1. The numbers in parentheses refer to the chapters where each of the topics is discussed.

FIGURE 1.1 The Strategic HR Planning Model

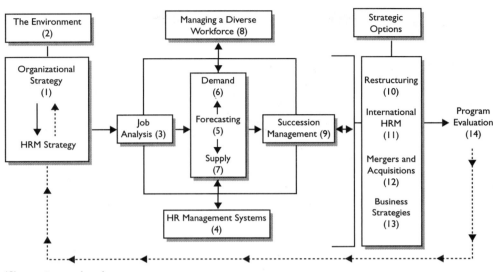

(Chapters in parentheses)

This approach is different from classic approaches to HR planning but builds on their tools. Strategic HR planning complements the traditional approach to HR planning (forecasting supply and demand) but adds more strategic choices.

So, under the strategic HR planning model, the steps become these:

1. Monitor, identify, and analyze external environmental factors influencing issues for the organization in order to develop strategies. Included in this are those factors that influence an organization's human resource capabilities.

2. Develop a tentative corporate or business strategy.

3. Assess the relative strengths and weaknesses of the organization's human resources, using forecasting and analysis techniques. Determine the KSAs of an organization and the capacity to learn and change. Identify the competitive advantages of the HR department.

4. Develop strategic plans for each division that are consistent with overall strategic thrust and that ensure a fit with related components across functional areas.

5. Identify HR policies and practices that will increase the likelihood of achieving the strategy and implement them.

6. Measure results and modify plans as necessary.

Thus, at the most senior levels of the corporation, HR professionals move from a policing role to the role of strategic partner. They need to understand strategies and business needs, and create the kind of human resource competencies that build competitive advantage. Our approach not only serves as a strategic planning model, but also as the structure for the text.

◆ ◆ ◆
SUMMARY

This chapter started with a description of real organizations facing strategic challenges. Concepts of strategy were introduced and generic types of corporate and business strategy were discussed. HRM strategy was described, and its impact on organizational effectiveness was explained. The alignment of HR strategy with corporate strategy was examined from three perspectives, concluding with an outline of effective HRM strategy characteristics. Various approaches to linking HRM strategies to organizational strategies were proposed, with an emphasis on the business partner role. Finally, a model of strategic HR planning was drawn to serve as a map for understanding the ground of the rest of the book.

EXERCISES

1. Discuss the reasons why strategic HR planning is important. What value does it add? List the risks of trying a strategic HRM approach and the risks of not doing so.

2. Visit three large companies from three different sectors. Try a hospitality sector (hotels, fast food, etc.), a high tech sector, and a manufacturing sector. Talk with a senior HR manager, and see if you can determine how such managers work with executives on strategy for-

mulation and development. What is their role in the process?

3. The emphasis in this chapter was on private companies because much of the research in strategy has been done with for-profit organizations. But many of us work for public companies, that is, for nonprofit organizations. Does strategic HRM make any sense for these companies? Explain your answer, discussing organizational strategies for public companies.

ENDNOTES

1. Adapted from Wright et al., 1995.
2. Adapted from Thompson and Strickland, 1995.

References

Amit, R., and M. Belcourt. 1999. "Human Resources Processes as a Source of Competitive Advantage." *European Management Journal* 17, no. 2 (April).

Anderson, W. 1997. "The Future of Human Resources: Forging Ahead or Falling Behind?" *Human Resource Management* 36, no. 1 (Spring): 17–22.

Anthony, W.P., P.L. Perrewe, and K.M. Kacmar. 1993. *Strategic Human Resource Management.* Fort Worth, Tex.: Harcourt Brace Jovanovich.

Bamberger, P., and A. Fiegenbaum. 1996. "The Role of Strategic Reference Points in Explaining the Nature and Consequences of Human Resources Strategy." *Academy of Management Review* 21, no.4 (October): 926–958.

Belcourt, M. 1996. "What Gets Measured, Gets Managed." *Human Resource Professional*, The Research Forum (April): 10–11.

Buller, P.F. 1996. "Successful Partnerships: HR and Strategic Planning at Eight Top Firms." *Organizational Dynamics:* 27–43.

Byrne, J. 1996. "Strategic Planning." *Business Week* (August 26): 46–52.

Cappelli, P., and H. Singh. 1992. "Integrating Strategic Human Resources and Strategic Management." In D. Lewin, O.S. Mitchell, and P. Sherer, eds. *Research Frontiers in IR and HR.* Madison, Wis.: IRRA.

Cascio, W. 1991. *Applied Psychology in Personnel Management*, 4th ed. Englewood Cliffs, N.J.: Prentice-Hall.

_____. 1987. *Applied Psychology in Personnel Management*, 3rd ed. Englewood Cliffs, N.J.: Prentice-Hall.

Cooke, R., and M. Armstrong. 1990. "The Search for Strategic HRM." *Personnel Management* (December): 30–33.

Duane, M.J. 1996. *Customized Human Resource Planning.* Westport, Conn.: Quorum Books.

Eichinger, B., and D. Ulrich. 1995. "Are You Future Agile?" *Human Resource Planning* 18, no. 4: 30–41.

Guest, D. 1990. "Personnel and HRM: Can You Tell the Difference?" *Personnel Management* (January).

Harrington, J. 1991. *Business Process Improvement*. New York: McGraw-Hill.

Jackson, S.E., and R.S. Schuler. 1995. "Understanding Human Resource Management in the Context of Organizations and Their Environments." *Annual Review of Psychology* 46: 237–264.

King, A.S. 1995. "Multi-Phase Progression of Organizational Ideology: Commitment." *Mid-Atlantic Journal* 31, no. 2: 143–160.

Kulig, P. 1998. "Top Human Resource Leaders Pursuing Boardroom Partnerships." *Canadian HR Reporter* (November 30): 3, 11.

Lengnick-Hall, C., and M. Lengnick-Hall. 1990. *Interactive Human Resource Management and Strategic Planning*. New York: Quorum Books.

_____. 1988. "Strategic Human Resources Management: A Review of the Literature and a Proposed Typology." *Academy of Management Review* 13, no. 3: 454–470.

MacMillan, I.C. 1983. "Seizing Competitive Initiative." *Journal of Business Strategy:* 43–57.

Milkovich, G.T., and J.M. Newman. 1987. *Compensation*, 2nd ed. Dallas: BPI.

Mintzberg, H. 1988. *In the Strategy Process*. Englewood Cliffs, N.J.: Prentice-Hall.

Porter, M.E. 1985. *Competitive Advantage*. New York: Free Press.

Quinn, J.B. 1980. *Strategies for Change: Logical Incrementalism*. Homewood, Ill.: Richard D. Irwin.

Rothwell, W.J., and H.C. Kazanas. 1988. *Strategic Human Resources Planning and Management*. Englewood Cliffs, N.J.: Prentice-Hall.

Schuler, R.S., and S.E. Jackson. 1989. "Determinants of Human Resource Management Priorities and Implications for Industrial Relations." *Journal of Management* 15, no. 1: 89–99.

Thompson, A.A., and A.J. Strickland III. 1995. *Crafting and Implementing Strategy*, 6th ed. Chicago: Irwin.

Wright, P.M., D.L. Smart, and G.C. McMahan. 1995. "Matches between Human Resources and Strategy among NCAA Basketball Teams." *Academy of Management Journal* 38, no. 4: 1052–1074.

Zedeck, S., and W.F. Cascio. 1984. "Psychological Issues in Personnel Decisions." *Annual Review of Psychology* 35: 461–518.

2

Environmental Influences on HRM

◆ ◆ ◆
CHAPTER GOALS

To understand strategic HR planning, we must understand how HRM is affected by the environment in which it operates. Most HR managers actively scan their surroundings, looking at cultural changes or laws or technologies that might affect the way that HR is practised. HR planners want to track trends in the environment that influence the way in which employees can be managed. HR strategists need information about the environment in order to exploit the opportunities or cope with the threats.

After reading this chapter, you should be able to do the following:

1. Identify the sources (publications, associations, conferences, and futurists) that HR planners use to keep current with business and HR trends.
2. List several of the methods, including trend analysis, Delphi techniques, and impact analyses, used to predict future trends.
3. Discuss the challenges in scanning the environment.
4. Delineate the environmental factors, such as the economic climate, the labour force, the political and regulatory context, and the social and cultural climate, that influence HRM.
5. Describe the role of the stakeholder, and list several examples.
6. Understand how environmental scanning is practised.

We will look first at the sources and methods HR planners use to track these trends.

◆ ◆ ◆
ENVIRONMENTAL SCANNING SOURCES AND METHODS

Managers have to develop strategies and keep a keen eye on what is happening in the world outside the organization. *Environmental scanning* is the systematic monitoring of the major factors influencing the organization. The goal of scanning the environment is to identify trends that might affect the formulation and implementation of both organizational and HR strategies.

"Environment" is a fuzzy term. It means anything outside organizational boundaries. Even talking about an environment suggests that the environment is different, not part of the organization. But the organization and the environment are tightly bound. For example, managers are themselves influenced by the culture in which they operate, that is, they are not independent of the environment. Rather than attempt a definition of the word "environment," we will simply list the methods used to scan the environment and the environmental factors that seem to influence HRM strategy formulation.

In the past, HR managers monitored changes that might affect their programs and policies by reading newspapers or trade publications. They would keep informed of any particular issues regarding employment laws by subscribing to particular news services, or perhaps by keeping in touch with their networks. The scanning method was not perfect, but no one can accurately predict all the forces that will shape the future workplace and the workforce. However, we do have sources of information and scanning methods that we can use to help us. The next section describes the sources that HR professionals might use to monitor trends in the environment.

◆ ◆ ◆
SOURCES OF INFORMATION

When developing strategies and determining their likely impact on an organization, HR professionals rely on many sources of information. These include publications, professional associations, conferences, and professional consultants.

PUBLICATIONS

HR professionals actively scan Canadian newspapers, business publications, and HR magazines, journals, and newsletters. We are fortunate to have access not only to a wide range of Canadian sources of information but also to the extensive publication network originating in the United States. The authors' experiences suggest that Canadian HR trends lag U.S. trends by a year or two. For example, workplace violence and employee retention were hot issues in the United States three years before they became important in Canada. Thus, reading U.S. publications acts as an early warning signal for Canadian HR professionals. HR practitioners subscribe to many of the publications listed in Box 2.1.

BOX 2.1 PUBLICATIONS OF INTEREST TO HR PROFESSIONALS

Canadian

Canadian Business
Canadian Compensation News
Canadian HR Reporter
Canadian Journal of Learning
Globe and Mail Report on Business
HR Professional
Ivey Business Quarterly

U.S.

Business Week
Fortune
HR Focus
HR Magazine
HR News
People Management
Training
Work Week

Research Journals

Academy of Management Executive
Academy of Management Review
Benefits Canada
Business Horizons
Business Quarterly

California Management Review
Canadian Journal of Administrative Studies
Canadian Labour Law Reporter
Compensation
Compensation and Benefits Review
European Management Journal
Harvard Business Review
Human Resource Management
HR Research Quarterly
Journal of Applied Psychology
Journal of Business Ethics
Journal of Labour Research
Journal of Management
Journal of Staffing and Recruitment
Labour Studies Journal
Management Review
Occupational Outlook Quarterly
Organizational Behaviour and Human
   Performance
Personnel
Personnel Journal
Personnel Psychology
Public Personnel Management
Training and Development Journal

PROFESSIONAL ASSOCIATIONS

Canadian HR professionals and executives belong to a number of organizations that publish newsletters and updates on current events. Many of these organizations, like the Human Resources Professionals Association of Ontario, have committees that actively scan the regulatory scene for upcoming changes. Some, like the Conference Board of Canada, regularly conduct research with their members to track trends. Relevant associations are listed in Box 2.2.

BOX 2.2 ASSOCIATIONS OF INTEREST TO HR PROFESSIONALS

Administrative Sciences Association of Canada (HR division)

BC Human Resources Management Association

Canadian Compensation Association

Canadian Council of Human Resource Associations

Canadian Industrial Relations Association

Canadian Payroll Association

Canadian Public Personnel Managers Association

Conference Board of Canada

Greater Victoria Human Resources Management Association

Human Resource Planning Society

Human Resources Association of Nova Scotia

Human Resources Institute of Alberta

Human Resources Management Association of Manitoba

Human Resources Professionals Association of Ontario

International Association for Human Resources Information Management Association

L'ordre des conseillers en relations industrielles du Québec

New Brunswick Human Resources Association

North American Human Resources Management Association

Ontario Society for Training and Development

Saskatchewan Council of Human Resource Associations

Society for Industrial and Organizational Psychology

Note: The current Web sites for all of these organizations can be found at www.hrm.nelson.com.

CONFERENCES AND SEMINARS

Most professionals keep current and even ahead of emerging trends by attending conferences, seminars, and workshops in Canada and the United States. Most provincial HR associations hold annual conferences. The Human Resources Professionals Association of Ontario, for example, attracts over 1000 participants to its conference each February. Such events, including those sponsored by private organizations, are widely publicized in HR publications such as those listed in Box 2.1.

PROFESSIONAL CONSULTANTS

Organizations that have an active interest in understanding the influence of potential trends often hire consultants to research or interpret these trends for them. Companies that specialize in this form of consulting include the Hudson Institute and most consulting firms. Most organizations have a person on staff, often the librarian, whose job is to bring information to the consultants' attention by actively scanning multiple sources. Box 2.3 contains a description of how one consulting company, Watson Wyatt Worldwide, keeps informed about trends.

◆ ◆ ◆

TECHNIQUES FOR SCANNING

There are several methods that HR professionals can use to generate predictions about the future or extrapolate from current events to determine their impact on HR practices. These include trend analysis, the Delphi technique, and impact analysis.

TREND ANALYSIS

Trend analysis is a quantitative approach that attempts to forecast future personnel needs based on extrapolating from historical changes in an organizational index. This method relies on a single index such as sales, while modelling or multiple predictive techniques (used by professional planners) rely on the combination of several factors. These methods are described in Chapter 5.

DELPHI TECHNIQUE

The Delphi technique is a process in which the forecasts and judgments of a selected group of experts are solicited and summarized in an attempt to

---

BOX 2.3 SCANNING AT WATSON WYATT WORLDWIDE

At Watson Wyatt Worldwide, the function of the Canadian Research and Information Centre (CRIC) is to keep pension and benefits consultants apprised of changes in legislation or regulations. CRIC scans the media and identifies articles of interest to the consultants. These scans are available daily on the company's intranet. Various journals and magazines (e.g., *HR Reporter, Benefits Canada, Harvard Business Review*) are circulated to consultants who have expressed an interest in reading them. CRIC also produces its own publication, the *Wyatt Memorandum*, to highlight relevant HR issues. Watson Wyatt Worldwide consultants are expected to track trends through reading, association membership, and conference attendance.

Source: Correspondence with Owen Parker, Research Associate, Watson Wyatt Worldwide, November 1998.

determine the future of employment. This method, too, is described in Chapter 5. Box 2.4 describes a Delphi round conducted by the Society for Human Resources Management in 1997.

IMPACT ANALYSIS

This method, too, looks backward in order to look forward. Past trends are analyzed. A panel of experts then attempts to identify future probable events and study their effects on the extrapolated trend (Burack and Mathys, 1987).

Other methods for assessing the future include the nominal group technique, critical incident approach, scenarios, and questionnaires, all discussed in Chapter 5.

An excellent evaluation of all these approaches can be found in Rothwell and Kazanas (1988). Readers are invited to experience a nominal group technique as part of a group exercise at the end of this chapter.

We have described rear-view mirror ways of scanning the environment. If you examine studies or articles that are supposed to predict the future, you will see that they contain, for the most part, simple extensions of present trends. We assume that tomorrow will be much like yesterday, with minor variations. HR planners recognize that there are problems with these attempts to interpret the environment.

BOX 2.4 THE EXPERTS PREDICT THE FUTURE OF HRM

In the fall of 1997, experts in a variety of fields provided written input to a series of questions developed by the Society for Human Resources Management. Thought leaders in HR were asked about business conditions and their implications for HRM. For example, one question was "How will businesses utilize employee resources in the future?"

The experts agreed that the primary employment model would be one of self-employed individuals who form ad hoc virtual services companies. A small number of core employees would remain part of the formal organization. The workforce would continue to become bipolar, with skilled workers having significant employment advantages over unskilled workers. Contingent workers would be treated better than they are now, and would gain benefits. Security would be based on performance contracts in contrast to the present system of tenure or service years.

Source: Adapted from M. Minehan. 1998. "SHRM: Futurist Task Force." *HR Magazine* 43, no. 3: 77–84.

◆ ◆ ◆
CHALLENGES IN ENVIRONMENTAL SCANNING

There are problems in scanning the environment. These include our inability to accurately predict the future and to isolate what really is important to HR. The 21st century has arrived. Can we say what the world will look like in 2050? In 1900, could those working in HRM have predicted what it would look like in the year 2000? Not likely, because the field of HRM did not exist then. One hundred years ago, there were no payroll and benefits clerks. Even twenty years ago, it would have been difficult to forecast the flattening of organizations, downsizing, the impact of technology, outsourcing, telecommuting, and a range of other changes we now live with. Most HR strategists limit themselves to a two- to three-year time frame, and extrapolate from current trends.

ISOLATING THE CRITICAL FROM THE INSIGNIFICANT

So much change is happening in so many arenas that scanners have trouble picking out the truly important events. As we enter the new millennium, we cannot determine which current issues are important enough to cause a shift in the way we practise HR. For example, which of these HR issues, which are headlines in HR publications as this text is being written, are critical and which will prove insignificant: Increasing workplace violence? Rising compensation at the executive levels? The brain drain to the United States?

HR planners do not only react to current events. Sometimes they attempt to shape the issues that will impact their practice.

A PROACTIVE APPROACH

Some HR managers do not like passively observing the game through their windows. They want to go outside and influence how the game is played. Thus, we find most professional associations have a group that lobbies for legislation that will favour the association membership. Most have public relations firms that try to shape the perception of the profession and its goals (thus influencing public opinion favourably toward regulations). For example, the Human Resources Professionals Association of Ontario attempted to influence the provincial government as it undertook a review of the Workers Compensation Board.

Box 2.5 outlines how one company scans the environment and links its observations with its planning.

Despite the challenges of environmental scanning, most HR strategists do monitor the environment and look for changes that may affect HR. We will now examine the major areas that these strategists typically scan.

◆ ◆ ◆

ENVIRONMENTAL FACTORS

Nearly everything, from birth rates to pollution levels, could be said to influence organizational and HR strategies. However, there are a number of factors that HR strategists monitor more closely because these factors seem more closely related to HRM. Following this tradition, we have included factors such as the economic climate, the labour force, the political and regulatory context, issues related to technology, and social values and norms. For each factor we have provided some current (i.e., 1999) examples of such forces, keeping in mind that such examples quickly lose their relevance.

ECONOMIC CLIMATE

The economic indices that we are so familiar with from the media are also important to HR strategists. Let us provide a few examples of how these indices influence HR managers who are

- concerned with the unemployment rate because it affects their ability to recruit;

- worried about the value of the Canadian dollar because it affects the company's ability to sell products internationally, and thus affects employment levels;

- troubled by the amount of public debt because it affects business taxes, and, therefore, a company's ability to survive and grow; and

- anxious about interest rates because they affect how much a company is willing to borrow to grow its business and invest in employees.

It could be argued that anything to do with the economy touches the management of human resources. However, it is impossible to deal with every economic indicator and change. We will provide two examples: the economic shift from hand work (manual production) to head work (the use of mental processes) and globalization.

BOX 2.5 STRATEGIC HR PLANNING AT SUN LIFE OF CANADA

Wendy Yule, director of organizational development for Sun Life of Canada, is continually involved in strategic planning of human resources. "Having the right resources in place to make change happen is the key. We are constantly looking at how our business is changing and at ongoing trends. We want to ensure that we can anticipate the human resource needs of our business," says Yule. She belongs to professional associations, such as the Human Resources Planning Society, that provide her with information that assists with the forecasting challenge. "We are constantly reading about new issues and trends, attending seminars and breakfast meetings. We listen to our business units to hear how their businesses are changing and jointly seek strategies to meet their needs."

Sun Life of Canada integrates its HR planning process very tightly with overall strategic planning. Each July, all vice-presidents, including the vice-president of HR, meet to develop the strategic plan. Collectively they develop an issue and response list, based on short- and long-term business needs. Each business unit is responsible for developing its own plan. An HR consultant reports directly to the vice-president of each business unit, and there is a dotted line relationship to the vice-president of HR. One part of the planning process is succession planning, that is, insuring that the right resources are in place to achieve company objectives. The plan is then sent to the executive office for review and final approval in January.

A very difficult task is predicting what the organizational changes will be. "We are currently working on some very precise business systems changes that have required us to hire more staff," says Yule. "But in two or three years from now, what will we do with that staff? We are starting to plan now and to identify other possible opportunities for those people.

"Key to our success in HR planning is our conservative approach. We are able to evolve because we avoid fads. Questions like 'What are our needs?' and 'What can we learn from this trend?' are considered before we do anything. It has to work in our culture."

Source: Interview, May 1995.

From the Industrial Revolution to the Knowledge Revolution

The economy is shifting from one based on the production of goods to one in which services are delivered. The number of workers in the service sector has increased from 40 percent of the workforce in 1945 to 75 percent in 1995 (Lowe, 1998). These services may be "hard," such as the kinds of services a hair stylist offers, or "soft," such as the selling of information. The types of employees needed by the diminishing industrial sector are different from those needed by the service sector.

We are facing a paradox as the century closes. On one hand, companies are downsizing and outsourcing. On the other, they are claiming that employees are a source of strategic advantage, and they are facing recruitment and retention problems with employees. Thus, for some types of jobs (low skilled), the economic climate consists of part-time workers, contract workers, and those working for outsourcing organizations. For jobs requiring scientific and technological competencies there is high demand, and organizations must compete on compensation, culture, and benefits. These issues are discussed in Chapter 15.

Globalization

Another trend to watch is increasing globalization. About three-quarters of Canadian companies are affected by international competition, and many are using the low dollar (of 1999) to export goods and services. HR managers will need to develop international competencies, as is discussed in Chapter 11.

THE LABOUR MARKET

A *labour market* is the area from which an organization recruits its employees. Such an area may be metropolitan, regional, provincial, national, or international. The number of people available for work depends on factors such as the unemployment rate, geographic migration, graduation rates from educational institutions, and so on.

The labour market influences an organization's ability to implement strategy. An organization may decide to enter the high tech playing field, only to discover itself unable to recruit enough electrical engineers to meet its personnel requirements, and so must abandon this particular strategy. This example is not hypothetical. A skills gap exists. Companies wishing to grow are facing problems in recruiting and retaining qualified scientists and technologists. There is a growing concern with the division of labour in Canada: the *shortage* of people with the right skills who can earn good money and expect benefits, and the *surplus* of people available to work in McJobs. These "ground workers" have little education, or low math and science skills, and can expect short-term work contracts and few benefits.

Other issues such as the aging baby boomers, increasing diversity, and working women are covered in Chapter 8.

POLITICAL AND LEGISLATIVE FACTORS

Governments, both provincial and federal, can influence the business environment through political programs that result in changes to laws and regulations. For example, governments that wish to improve the climate for job creation emphasize tax cuts, legislate tax incentives to develop jobs, increase job-training opportunities, and create balanced labour legislation. Governments can spur economic growth by reducing the public debt, balancing the budget, and cutting taxes. Such measures encourage businesses to invest in that province (or Canada) and encourage consumers to spend, resulting in more jobs.

The employer–employee relationship is governed by a legal framework that includes common law (judicial precedents that do not derive from specific laws), constitutional law (e.g., the Charter of Rights and Freedoms, acts of federal and provincial parliaments), and contract law (e.g., collective agreements). You are probably familiar with some of these laws. For example, each province has employment standards that establish the maximum number of hours to be worked each day and human rights legislation that prohibits discrimination on the basis of sex, race, and so on.

Organizational actions have to be legal, and the law is relatively clear. A company may be competing on a low-cost strategy and be able to find people willing to work for $3 an hour. The employment standards legislation in each province, however, governs the minimum wage, and in no province is it as low as $3 an hour. Therefore, cost savings have to be achieved elsewhere in order to implement this low-cost strategy.

It is worth observing the regulatory issues that are dominating the U.S. environment, as these often influence Canadian issues. Legal issues currently facing U.S. employers are affirmative action, family and medical leave issues, privacy, sexual harassment, temporary workers, and workforce reductions, which result in violence, severance pay issues, increased stress, and harassment of older workers to retire to save the jobs of younger workers (Nobile, 1997).

The decisions that are not governed by law are usually governed by morals or an ethical code. Less clear is the concept of ethics. Ethical and moral decisions and practices go beyond the law, from "you must" to "you should." An employer can require an employee to work overtime and not pay him or her overtime rates (as required by the law). How? The employer gives the employee the title of "manager" (a category exempted from overtime regulations), even when the employee has no managerial responsibilities. Legal? Maybe, but not ethical.

Ethical issues are sometimes raised and resolved by employees, and sometimes organizations have official policies on ethics. For example, most organizations have explicit guidelines on the kinds of "gifts" (kickbacks) that employees may accept from suppliers. But most HRM ethical decisions are much more complicated. Should a company produce goods in a country that employs child labour? Should an organization eliminate one unit (laying off the staff in the process) only to subcontract the work to an outside supplier that employs workers at one-half the compensation rates? Obviously, these ethical decisions affect strategy formulation and implementation.

TECHNOLOGICAL FACTORS

You, as a consumer, are very aware of how technology used by companies is affecting the way business is done. Whenever you want to interact with any organization, you are led into a series of technical experiences, from voice-mail systems moving you through a customer service "experience" to automated machines controlling your access to your money.

Technology is having a large impact on human resources and is predicted to continue to do so. Every HR function has the potential to become managed electronically. The trend started with payroll and benefits. Now software is used to manage training data and succession management information. On-line counselling for managers is available. Managers can complete performance appraisals interactively. Job candidates apply for positions and are interviewed by a computer. As the hardware becomes smaller and the software becomes smarter, we can expect most HR functions to be managed electronically.

There are related issues. There is a blurring of the line between personal and professional lives as employees answer e-mail on vacation and use the phone to telecommute. Issues of privacy, the protection of intellectual property, and the safeguarding of company secrets are made more difficult because of the ease of transferring information by means of technology (Minehan, 1997).

SOCIAL AND CULTURAL FACTORS

Society can express its intent through laws and regulations. However, society can also exert pressure on HR in less formal ways. The public comments on the way employers treat employees. Employees are shaped by the norms and values of the society in which they live. One issue that is receiving increasing public attention is the right to privacy. Does the employer have a moral (and legal) right to monitor employee activities through video surveillance cameras or reading e-mail? Does the employee have a right to see his or her personnel records?

Another issue is the employee's attempt to balance a personal life with an ever more encompassing work life. Many employees face the challenges of trying to spend quality time with their families while vigorously pursuing a career. They are in a timing bind. People are generally most active in moving forward in their careers between the ages of 25 and 45, exactly the same stage at which most people raise their children. Both roles are demanding. Both require long hours, during the same period (6 a.m. to 10 p.m.). Organizations respond to this issue by increasing workplace flexibility. Some options include flextime, part-time work, job sharing, telecommuting, elder care, and child care.

Environmental factors influence the adoption and implementation of specific HRM strategies. The stakeholders are another major source of influence on HR strategy.

◆ ◆ ◆
STAKEHOLDERS

When discussing HR strategy, the natural tendency is to think only about the organization under consideration and its managers and employees. However, there is a call for an expansion of these boundaries. Many groups have an influence on the organization's strategy. These groups can be referred to as the *stakeholders*.

Stakeholders are groups of people who have an interest or claim on the organization. Sometimes called *constituent groups*, they follow the actions of the organization and lobby to have their interests satisfied. These stakeholders affect strategy formulation. Employees want more wages and job security; suppliers want longer-term relationships, customers want faster service, and shareholders want more dividends and higher stock prices. Organizations will often adapt their strategies to accommodate powerful stakeholders such as unions or regulatory agencies or customers. Let us look at some of these stakeholders.

SHAREHOLDERS

For private organizations, the primary stakeholder is the owner or those who hold shares: the shareholders. Public organizations are accountable to the taxpayer (the shareholder) through a complex system of departmental hierarchies and political webs. Most CEOs interviewed on television about some major change, such as a downsizing, will reply that their responsibility is not to the employee or the public but to the shareholder.

CUSTOMERS

A second stakeholder is the customer or client. Organizations have a moral duty to provide safe, hazard-free products. This appears relatively simple to do. However, if a provider knows that a product has an infinitesimal probability of being unsafe, the costs of withdrawing the product are often weighed against the costs of litigation. Car manufacturers make this kind of decision frequently. They will absorb the liability costs of an automobile that is unsafe under atypical conditions because these costs are less than the costs of redesign, remanufacture, or recall. Another example occurs when a powerful customer demands changes from its suppliers. Clients can influence the skill level of their suppliers. Wal-Mart will train their suppliers' employees in just-in-time order processing and deal (electronically) only with those suppliers. This forces suppliers to change systems to match Wal-Mart's system. The suppliers then have to select and train people to handle these systems in order to meet Wal-Mart's demands.

SUPPLIERS

Suppliers can influence the skill level of their clients' employees. Polo Ralph Lauren Canada sends its own skilled staff to Eaton's and the Bay to help these companies merchandise the supplier's clothing, and in doing so raises the skill level of retail clerks in these chain stores.

GOVERNMENTS

The federal government gives extensive assistance with implementing employment equity programs in federally regulated corporations, thus encouraging sensitivity, training, and skill development not only in equity matters but also generally in management of change programs.

THE PUBLIC

An increasingly important stakeholder is the community at large. This is evident where a company is the sole or largest employer in a small community. In this situation, the company would be influenced in its strategic decisions by the need to keep the community alive, the people employed, and the environment healthy in the long term. Another example occurs with the production and distribution of products such as alcohol or with gambling casinos, which cause great hardship and upheaval to some individuals but result in programs and services that would not necessarily be affordable under normal taxation efforts.

The public expects very large organizations to be more socially responsible. Size matters, as can be seen by the research presented in Box 2.6.

UNIONS

The presence of unions in the environment will affect HRM strategy for firms entering new sectors with high unionization rates. Employees who are currently unionized within an organization can influence strategy in two ways. One is a restrictive way, in which the collective agreement limits an organization's ability to make drastic changes in working methods or jobs to accommodate changes in strategic direction. A second way is that unions now play a larger role and are more cooperative than adversarial in terms of HR practices such as gain sharing, plant locations, selection procedures, and quality improvement (Jackson and Schuler, 1995).

BOX 2.6 SIZE MATTERS

Larger organizations adopt more sophisticated HR practices partly because acceptable economies of scale are achieved in organizations with thousands of employees. Furthermore, large organizations are more visible and subject to pressures to engage in legitimate state-of-the-art HRM practices. Compared to small organizations, larger organizations are more likely to adopt employee involvement programs, use sophisticated staffing and training practices, and pay employees more, but put more pay at risk through bonuses and long-term incentives and have more highly developed internal labour markets.

Source: Jackson, S.E., and R.S. Schuler. 1995. "Understanding Human Resource Management in the Context of Organizations and Their Environments." *Annual Review of Psychology* 46: 237–264.

The degree of unionization in the sector also affects HR planning. When entering a new business sector, an organization can assume that if most of the competition is unionized, then union activity will be a large part of the HR strategy. Although the rate of unionization in the United States is dropping, Canadian rates are steady at around 33 percent (Belcourt et al., 1999). Unionized employees receive higher wages and have better working conditions than their nonunion counterparts (Lawler and Mohram, 1987).

EMPLOYEES

As indicated earlier, sometimes an organization's strategy is influenced by the kinds of competencies it already possesses. If employees are motivated, committed, and flexible, then an organization might be more willing to grow rapidly through numerous product introductions. If the workforce is unusually multilingual, then the possibility of growing through international markets becomes more attractive. Likewise, the strengths can reside in the HR department itself. If the HR department has excelled in its ability to ramp up rapidly by attracting, hiring, and orienting highly qualified candidates, then corporate venturing or a joint venture becomes an attainable goal. If culture management is the HR department's strength, then mergers and acquisitions can be considered as a strategic option.

TOP MANAGEMENT

Much of the research on HR planning recognizes the powerful influence of the CEO on the organization's ability to attain its goals. The concept of the rational manager is well embedded in our business psyche. We assume that the head of an organization carefully analyzes the environment—looking at competitors' actions and technological changes—and then decides the best strategy to take advantage of opportunities and corporate strengths. But hearts may be as influential as heads. Managers are more than rational actors: they have personal values, ethics, attitudes toward risk, and ambition (Guth and Tagiuri, 1965).

Research has shown that different types of strategies require different types of managers and executives. Studies of these managerial elites have indeed found that managers with certain personalities, for example, those with a tolerance for ambiguity, managed firms with a build strategy more successfully than those with a harvest strategy (Gupta and Govindarajan, 1984). Let's take just one of these managerial traits—attitude toward risk.

From readings on corporate strategy, we know that managers who are risk avoiders will take the conservative, cautious approach with an eye on "guaranteed," short-term profits. Risk takers will be willing to sacrifice short-term gains, to "gamble" on long-term bigger payoffs. But these studies fail to recognize that the entire employee pool must have the necessary skills and attributes to carry out the strategy.

The purpose of this section was to demonstrate that stakeholders can have a powerful influence on the choice of strategy. Before this, you have learned about the methods HR strategists use to scan the environment and the areas they are concerned with. We turn now to an illustration of how this process works.

◆ ◆ ◆
ENVIRONMENT SCANNING: A CASE APPLICATION

Scanning must have a purpose. It must not be the collection of information just to have reports gathering dust on executive bookshelves. The information must be analyzed for its impact on the organization, and particularly for its implications for the organization's HR strategy.

In Table 2.1, we describe how this might be done by imagining how an HR planner working for a large retailer in the Canadian market would use environmental information to determine how the HR practices in a retail environment might be affected.

◆ ◆ ◆
SUMMARY

HRM strategy is determined primarily by organizational strategy. However, there are environmental factors that shape HRM strategy, so HR managers and planners must continually monitor the environment. Typically, they scan by reading publications, retaining memberships in professional associations, attending conferences, or using professional scanners. A number of methods, such as trend and impact analyses and the Delphi technique, are used to identify future trends. The environmental factors that are monitored include the economic climate, the labour market, the political and regulatory climate, and social norms. Stakeholders such as shareholders, unions, customers, and executives contribute strongly to the formulation and implementation of strategy.

TABLE 2.1 TRENDS AND HR IMPLICATIONS

TREND	HR IMPLICATIONS
Economic	
High unemployment rates	Low consumer spending, fewer staff needed
Global competition	Internationalization, possible domestic downsizing
Labour Market	
Outsourcing	Less job security, lower spending, fewer staff
Aging workforce/consumers	Changing spending patterns
Flexible work arrangements	More day clients, changing staff distribution
	Less work clothing needed, more home office leisure clothes
Globalization	Outsourcing to low-wage countries
	Need for managers with global competencies
Regulatory	
Pay equity	Need to review systems, allow contingency funds
Workforce rights	More complex terminations; privacy issues
Part-time benefits legislation	Increased costs of part-time employees
Technological	
E-mail commerce	Increased need for employees with technological skills
Computerization of work	Increased telecommuting, nontraditional offices
	Need for results appraisals (not face-time judgments)
Social	
Workplace violence	Development of HR policies on safety; provision of secure environment
Retirement trends	Retiring of bulk of boomers, fighting for jobs
Work–family issues	Problems recruiting nontraditional shifts
Diversity	Workforce reflecting customer demographic
Stakeholders	
Union	Increasing move to nonadversarial arrangements
Public	Demands for socially responsible corporation
	Demands for excellent customer service, therefore need to train and upgrade sales skills
Customers	Few large customers control type of jobs and skills
Suppliers	Demand for seamless connections, need for employees
Top management	Move to recruit global executives

EXERCISES

1. Scan the most recent copies of the publications listed in Box 2.1. Try to determine current trends in HRM. Compare your list to the trends identified in Chapter 15. How much have issues changed?

2. Read what futurists such as David Foot and Faith Popcorn have to say about our future. Try, using impact analysis, to predict what impact these trends will have on the workplace.

3. Study an organization in which you or a close friend works. For each environmental factor, consider what the HRM implication for that organization could be. Factors such as technology, international conditions, and demographics should be particularly relevant.

Group Exercise: The Nominal Group Technique

1. Form a group of about four to six people. If you are working with a group of students, then you will be discussing the future of the student role, or "job." If you are working with a group of people in the same occupation or job, then your group will be discussing the future of that occupation or job. Appoint a group leader.

2. Ask everyone to list the trends that may change, at some likely future time, the work methods or work outcomes for the "job" under consideration. Try a time span of three, five, or ten years. (Allow fifteen minutes for this step.)

3. Each person then states the first item on his or her list and records this item on a flip chart or green board so that others can see it.

4. Each person, in turn, continues to state items until all are listed. If an item is mentioned more than once, then the group leader asks for the number of people who listed this item. That number is then recorded beside the item.

5. Ask each person to discuss the relevance of his or her item to the job.

6. Ask each person to assign a rating from 1 to 10 to each item on the flip chart, 1 being the most important influence on the job and 10 being the least important.

7. Analyze the results.

8. Use these results to prepare a group report on the future of the job.

9. Present this report to the class.

After the presentations, discuss the challenges of predicting the future in this manner. Should HR planners not scan the environment because of these problems? Is there a better way?

(Note that many of these steps can be done with group software, such as Lotus Notes.)

References

Belcourt, M., A.W. Sherman, G.W. Bohlander, and S.A. Snell. 1999. *Managing Human Resources*, 2nd Canadian ed. Toronto, Ont.: ITP Nelson.

Burack, E.H., and N.J. Mathys. 1987. *Human Resource Planning: A Pragmatic Approach to Manpower Staffing and Development*, 2nd ed. Lake Forest, Ill.: Brace-Park Press.

Gupta, A., and V. Govindarajan. 1984. "Business Unit Strategy Managerial Characteristics, and Business Unit Effectiveness at Strategy Implementation." *Academy of Management Journal* 27: 25–41.

Guth, W.D., and Tagiuri, R. 1965. "Personal Values and Corporate Strategy." *Harvard Business Review* 43, no. 5 (September–October): 123–132.

Jackson, S.E., and R.S. Schuler. 1995. "Understanding Human Resource Management in the Context of Organizations and Their Environments." *Annual Review of Psychology* 46: 237–264.

Lawler, E.E., and S.A. Mohram. 1987. "Unions and the New Management." *Academy of Management Executives* 1: 293–300.

Lowe, G. 1998. "The Future of Work." *Industrial Relations* 53, no. 2 (Spring): 235–257.

Minehan, M. 1997. "Technology's Increasing Impact on the Workplace." *HR Magazine* 42, no. 12 (December).

Nobile, R.J. 1997. "HR's Top Ten Legal Issues." *HR Focus* 74, no. 4 (April): 19–20.

Rothwell, W.J., and H.C. Kazanas. 1988. *Strategic Human Resources Planning and Management*. Englewood Cliffs, N.J.: Prentice-Hall.

II

HR Planning

3

Job Analysis

◆ ◆ ◆
CHAPTER GOALS

An organization's mission statement presents the guiding rationale for the activities of all subunits and employees. As we move down the organizational hierarchy from the executive suites to the production floor, corporate and divisional strategic goals are subdivided and allocated to various units as their operational goals. To attain the strategic and operational goals, it is necessary to develop short-run production and operational budgets, as well as to specify the division of labour, commonly referred to as partitioning the work process into manageable units called jobs. A *job* can be defined as a grouping of related duties, tasks, and behaviours performed by an individual, namely the jobholder. The analysis of subdivided work in the organization, both at the level of the individual job and for the entire flow of the production process, is referred to as *job analysis* and is the focus of this chapter. As HR planners, it is essential that we are knowledgeable about the nature of work and its overall contribution toward the attainment of the organization's mission. It is important for us to see how each individual job, when aggregated with others in a process referred to as departmentalization, contributes to the performance of essential organizational tasks without unnecessary duplication or redundancy. Furthermore, as HR planners, we are responsible for determining the demand for and supply of personnel in the organization. In order to do this we must have detailed knowledge about working conditions, employee qualifications, and the educational training and skill requirements of each job, as well as the nature of the organization's work process itself. For these reasons, knowledge of the job analysis process and methods of evaluating jobs are essential components in the formulation of the successful HR planning system (Walker, 1994; Schuler and Walker, 1990).

In this chapter, we will discuss the importance of job analysis, examine the process underlying a successful job analysis, and explore specific methods used by organizations to attain successful levels of performance.

After you have completed reading this chapter, you should be able to do the following:

1. Understand the central role played by job analysis in all HR activities, and especially in the effective conduct of HR planning.

2. Comprehend the two essential elements of any job: methods and time standards.

3. Explain common problems associated with the job analysis process.

4. Identify the five steps of the job analysis process.

5. Employ criteria to select job analysis methods that are best suited to the organizational jobs being examined.

6. Develop analytical questions that will permit an in-depth examination of the knowledge, skills, abilities, and other attributes required for successful evaluation of jobs.

7. Analyze the advantages and disadvantages of the most common methods of job analysis.

◆ ◆ ◆
JOB ANALYSIS

Job analysis can be defined as an examination of the jobs in an organization with a view to documenting the knowledge, skills, and abilities (KSAs, e.g., experience) associated with successful performance of those jobs. The written outcomes of this process are referred to either as a *job description* or a *job specification*. The difference between the two documents centres on whether the emphasis is on the duties or tasks to be carried out on the job (i.e., the job description) or on the competencies or KSAs the jobholder must possess to be a successful performer in a specific job (i.e., the job specification). KSAs are defined as follows:

> *Knowledge:* Knowledge is the body of information, usually of a factual or procedural nature, that allows an individual to perform a task successfully:

> *Skill:* Skill is the individual's level of proficiency or competency in performing a specific task. Level of competency is typically expressed in numerical terms.

Ability: Ability is a more general, enduring trait or capability an individual possesses at the time when he or she first begins to perform a task (Gatewood and Field, 1990).

Other attributes: Other attributes include work experience.

HR practitioners refer to job analysis as the foundation for all HR activities, and there are extremely valid reasons for this assertion. Before we can meaningfully advertise jobs and recruit individuals to fill job vacancies identified by the HR planning process, to attract the desired applicants we must be able to specify the individual competencies that we are looking for. Once we have developed a pool of high-quality job applicants, the selection process will incorporate employment tests and interview questions based on the need to choose the individual who best meets the formal requirements for success identified by our job analysis process. The selection criteria that flow out of the job analysis process are also used in succession planning to appraise the organization's internal candidates for possible transfer or promotion to management or executive jobs. Once we have selected an individual to fill a job, he or she should be given a copy of the job description or specification for the job, which provides specific guidance on how to perform the job in accordance with the wishes of the organization. The performance appraisal process compares the individual's accomplishments over a predetermined period with the desired standards specified in the job description or specification. If the performance appraisal process reveals that the individual has deficiencies that can be rectified by training and development, specific programs or courses can be instigated to help the individual reach the desired standards. Furthermore, compensation systems in organizations typically use a classification process based on skills, effort, responsibility, and working conditions, the four compensable factors of the job that are explicitly noted and formalized by the job analysis process (Risher, 1989).

Finally, successful career planning programs also draw heavily on the front-end requirement of a comprehensive job analysis. In planning future career moves, the individual and the organization note the employee's current KSAs and level of performance and compare these to the KSAs required in various target jobs for which the employee would like to apply. Once this information is provided by job analysis, the employee is informed of the explicit education and skills development that will be required prior to being considered for the target jobs. Job analysis, therefore, is not only a critical requirement for the proper implementation and operation of the HR planning process, as examined in this book, but is also an essential prerequisite for the success of virtually all other HR functions (Walker, 1980).

Job analysis has a long history within the HR field. Fred Taylor's scientific management studies were key contributions to the evolution of contemporary job analysis methods (McBey and Hammah, 1990). Taylor's industrial engineering approach was focused on reducing costs and improving the efficiency of the manufacturing worker. In particular, his analysis process concentrated on finding the "one best way" to do any job. This approach, still a central feature of present-day job analyses, examines two main aspects of each job in the organization: (1) the *methods employed* and (2) the *time measurement* for task completion.

The first aspect is concerned with how the job incumbent performs the job, that is, with the minimum requirements for success in the job. These requirements include (a) the individual's knowledge of production techniques and processes (e.g., raw materials and other inputs, machinery, tools), cognitive (mental) abilities, mechanical abilities (e.g., principles and spatial relationships), and psychomotor abilities and (b) the working conditions in which the job is performed (e.g., whether the work is done by the individual alone or in conjunction with other members of a team).

The second aspect common to all job analyses is time measurement, or the cycle/production time required to produce the good or service to the performance standards of the organization. This time standard is completely dependent on the first aspect, which is concerned with the methods employed (or how the job is performed). Obviously, changing the process from individual to team-based production and modifying the number of raw material inputs or steps in the production process will substantially change the output or number of items that can be produced on a time basis per hour, shift, or day.

◆ ◆ ◆

PROBLEMS ASSOCIATED WITH JOB ANALYSIS

Having noted the importance of job analysis and its two constituent elements of methods and time, let's now turn to an examination of frequent problems associated with job analysis.

1. Job Analysis That Is neither Updated nor Reviewed

One has only to consider the topic of computer technology to recognize the impact that an extremely rapid rate of change has on how work is being performed. Job analyses must be reviewed on a regular basis by incumbents, supervisors, HR staff, and so on to ensure that the written job requirements reflect the reality of contemporary job performance. Recent changes in technology, materials, and processes must be incorporated into the amended job description or specification. Obsolete job descriptions not only fail to provide job incumbents with meaningful guidance as to their required performance levels but also mean that the HR planning process is attempting to match individuals to jobs based on information that is no longer valid.

2. Job Description or Specification That Is Too Vague

If job analysis is to provide important information to allow us to select the individual who best meets job requirements, we must be specific as to what those exact requirements are. For example, organizations often specify that applicants must have a certain number of years' experience in a certain functional area instead of specifying the exact skills or competencies the applicant should have learned over that period. Without this specific information, experience or time spent on the job has little relevance for selection. Similarly, organizations may mistakenly include elements such as "dependability" as one of their job requirements without giving specific examples of what constitutes dependable behaviour (e.g., the individual arrives on time

---

BOX 3.1 THE IMPORTANCE OF KEEPING JOB INFORMATION CURRENT

Despite the fact that skilled labour is still in hot demand, people with the most current skills and qualifications may not be matched with jobs offered by potential employers due to the fact that the *National Occupational Classification* has not been updated. The Canadian federal government's employment database, the *National Occupational Classification* or NOC, is based upon data gathered during the late 1980s and early 1990s and it lists 25,000 job titles according to skill level and employer requirements. However, Human Resources Development Canada (HRDC) and Statistics Canada officials concede that thousands of jobs are not contained in the occupational database, the most noteworthy being new jobs created by technology over the past decade. The importance of having timely and current information on jobs in order to match individual and organizational requirements is clearly highlighted by this situation.

Adapted from: Matheson, K. 1997. "Job Killer." *Canadian Business* 70, no. 12 (September 26): 18–20.

for meetings with all preparatory work properly completed). To be an effective component of HR planning, the job analysis process must produce detailed, specific behavioural examples of successful job performance for each job in the work process.

3. Contamination and Deficiency

Although brevity and clarity are definite virtues with respect to job analysis (a short, clear job description is of great use to both job incumbents and the HR staff), taken to an extreme these characteristics may cause problems during job analysis efforts. If our job description or specification fails to incorporate important aspects of the job that are required for success, this error of omission is referred to as *deficiency*. Conversely, if we include peripheral, unimportant aspects of a job in the formal job description, we run the risk of contaminating it by diverting attention from valid, important correlates of success. *Contamination* of our job analysis process may also lead to legal consequences if we use the information to select individuals based on factors not related to the job that are discriminatory under provincial or Canadian human rights legislation. For job analysis, therefore, we should try to be as brief and clear as possible but not at the expense of excluding any important behavioural or performance element of the job.

4. Time and Costs of Job Analysis

Some organizations are deterred from conducting job analyses due to the significant time and start-up costs perceived to be associated with the process. Typical costs include consulting fees for job analysts (if the organization does not have in-house HR staff with relevant qualifications); licensing fees associated with usage of copyrighted job analysis methods; the costs of lost production (or overtime) involved with interviewing and surveying job incumbents, managers, and so on; and the administrative costs involved with codifying, analyzing, drafting, revising, and disseminating the information that results from the process. However, many organizations that bemoan the large time and cost expenditures associated with job analysis do so only because they have not conducted a proper cost–benefit analysis with respect to this decision. For example, organizations should also consider the time and cost savings that result from the following: (1) better matching of individual skills to organizational requirements (e.g., reduced costs, and often lower absenteeism and turnover, associated with training and development) (McBey,

1996), (2) incorporation of the benefits of organizational learning with respect to product and process improvements, (3) reduced job ambiguity and wastage, (4) clarification of operating procedures and job relationships, (5) explicit definition of performance expectations for individuals and teams, and (6) facilitation of other HR programs. If organizations consider the full costs and benefits associated with entering into the job analysis process, the decision to proceed is invariably very clear!

◆ ◆ ◆
THE PROCESS OF JOB ANALYSIS

The process of job analysis involves following five steps to maximize the potential for success. We now examine each of the five steps in turn, noting the actions required at each stage.

I. DETERMINE THE JOB OR PROCESS TO BE ANALYZED

Although the desired outcome of a job analysis is to have a comprehensive record of all organizational jobs and their associated duties, skill requirements, working conditions, and so on, reality dictates that organizations normally select certain well-defined jobs common throughout the industry that can be benchmarked externally, that is, the analysis commences with these well-known jobs first. Some of the factors that determine whether job analysis will be concurrent (all jobs analyzed at approximately the same time) or sequential (job analyses conducted in different stages over time) include (1) the degree to which the selected job is central or critical, (2) the availability of job analysts and other resources, and (3) the availability of external performance benchmarks for organizational jobs.

In the first instance, the more critical or central the job or process, the greater the tendency to analyze it and to defer examination of less central jobs or processes to a future time. The number and availability of job analysts, be they external consultants or internal HR specialists, are key factors influencing whether an organization is able to conduct concurrent job analysis or is forced to do it sequentially by stages.

Finally, the Canadian government's *National Occupational Classification* (NOC), which contains standardized job descriptions on approximately

25,000 jobs, facilitates external benchmarking for the job analyst (Employment and Immigration Canada, 1993). The NOC and its U.S. counterpart, the *Dictionary of Occupational Titles* (DOT), provide information on the main duties and employment requirements of each classified job, along with a listing of other job classifications that are similar to the one being analyzed (United States Department of Labor, 1994). This information is invaluable as it facilitates comparison to similar jobs in other organizations with respect to required applicant specifications and performance standards for key duties and tasks.

2. DETERMINE METHODS AND ANALYZE THE JOB OR PROCESS

The second step in the job analysis process involves an appraisal of the most appropriate method(s) to use to study and record job-related behaviours. Selection criteria for job analysis methods include the following:

Cost: Cost includes licence fees for such things as copyrighted questionnaires, training, and administration.

Time: Time includes that spent on survey and interview training and assessment, data coding and analysis, and so on.

Flexibility of Methods: This criterion has to do with whether the method is appropriate for the particular circumstances (e.g., clerical service jobs as opposed to those in manufacturing).

Validity and Reliability: These criteria relate to whether the job analysis methods have been tested and found to be accurate measures of the job's essential elements and whether the results of these methods show a consistent pattern over repeated usage.

Acceptance: Some job analysis methods, such as direct observation and videotaping of work performance, may be considered intrusive by the workforce and, therefore, may be met with resistance (Jenkins, 1975). Other methods, such as questionnaires and interviews, might be deemed more acceptable by the workers, who would then cooperate in providing information to the job analysts (Gael, 1988; Ghorpade, 1988; Prien and Ronan, 1971).

The aforementioned selection criteria are used to evaluate the following common methods of job analysis.

Interviews

To gather information about a job, a job analyst may interview job incumbents, as well as co-workers, supervisors, suppliers, clients, and subordinates. This type of all-round analysis of a job is referred to as *360-degree evaluation*, as the job analyst has input from individuals who are in the job under evaluation and in other jobs that relate to it.

Observation

Observation of a job can be either direct or indirect. In *direct observation*, analysts observe the production line for worker behaviours and the skills required for job success. Recording of the number and duration of individual behaviours is normally captured on a standardized recording sheet (Jenkins, 1975). *Indirect observation* can incorporate a variety of means, such as a videotaped recording of the job being performed, for subsequent analysis by the analyst.

Questionnaires

Numerous standardized questionnaires are used for job analysis. Some of the more frequently used instruments include: (1) the *Position Description Questionnaire* (Denton, 1975), (2) the *Functional Job Analysis* (Fine and Wiley, 1971; Fine 1974), (3) the *Job Diagnostic Survey* (Hackman and Oldham, 1974, 1975), (4) the *Dimensions of Executive Positions* (Hemphill, 1960), and (5) the *Position Analysis Questionnaire* (McCormick et al., 1972). These survey instruments are normally completed by jobholders, their supervisors, and people who work in other jobs that are related to the specific job being investigated. The questionnaires vary substantially, but common elements are questions concerning the following:

a. Education, training, and skill requirements to be successful in the job

b. Responsibility or accountability (e.g., in terms of budgets, specific duties and tasks performed, number and type of people supervised, etc.)

c. Effort, that is, the cognitive and physical demands placed on the individual

d. Working conditions, for example, whether the work is done by an individual or team, the equipment or materials used, the job context or the environmental conditions of work (e.g., telephone line repairperson), the work shifts or hours of work, the potential health hazards, and so on

BOX 3.2 RATING JOBS AGAINST NEW VALUES

Bayer Group AG, headquartered in Leverkusen, Germany, reorganized its three U.S. companies into one entity and in so doing revised their job analysis/evaluation processes. The new system was designed to meet the vision, culture, and goals of the unified company and to identify and measure competencies required for future organizational success. The existing Hay Guide Chart–Profile Method used previously was used as a starting point for the new system, although the language describing each work-value cluster was changed. Each of the following work-value clusters is matched to a numerical scale to enable Bayer to ensure internal equity through usage of point-based evaluation. Bayer's work-value dimensions are as follows:

1. *Improvement Opportunity:* "Describes the requirement for and assesses the ability to improve performance within the context of assigned roles and rate of change in the work environment."
2. *Contribution:* "Describes the requirement for and ability to achieve results that improve performance and define success."
3. *Capability:* "Describes the total of proficiencies and competencies required to support effectiveness and progress."

Each of these three work-value clusters also incorporates various sub-elements, such as the following components of the capability cluster:

a. *Expertise and Complexity:* "Measures the depth and breadth of specific technical and professional proficiencies and competencies required for expected individual and team performance."
b. *Leadership and Integration:* "Measures the ability to manage, coordinate, integrate, and provide leadership for diverse people, processes, and organizational resources to achieve common goals and objectives."
c. *Relationship-Building Skills:* "Measures the requirements for meeting internal and external customers' needs through effective listening, understanding, sensitivity, and analytical abilities. This capability also measures the requirements for proactive persuasiveness, organizational awareness, and collaborative influencing skills necessary to effect desired change and build effective, enduring relationships."

Source: Laabs, J. 1997. "Rating Jobs against New Values." *Workforce* 76, no. 5 (May): 38–49. Used with permission of ACC Communication/*Workforce,* Costa Mesa, CA. All rights reserved.

Journals and Diaries

This method of job analysis asks jobholders to maintain a written record of their job activities, and associated time expenditures, for a preset period that typically ranges from a complete work cycle or typical week to up to a month. Although the information can be useful in discovering actual time expenditures and activities—for example, it was a vital component of the Mintzberg (1973) research investigation into the nature of managerial work—there can be the problem of selective reporting and bias as the respondent is fully aware that his or her time and activities are being monitored.

Output and Production Analysis

Machine-generated output reports, as well as production reporting procedures, can obtain information about the job and its normal and peak levels of production. Although these techniques reveal little about the qualitative or process aspects of the job, they are useful in determining appropriate performance standards for output.

Current Job Descriptions and Specifications

In the quest for information about the job, a useful starting point, if a previous job analysis has been performed, is an examination of the existing job descriptions and specifications. Although the information contained in these documents is already dated, it is advantageous to see how the job in question has evolved and whether its component duties, tasks, and employee specifications, as well as the authority and status the job is accorded, have increased or diminished over time.

Despite Fred Taylor's best efforts, in fact there is no one best way to analyze a job, so most contemporary job analyses employ a combination of the aforementioned methods. This multi-method approach not only provides a more comprehensive examination of the job but also enables quantitative aspects (e.g., production reports, questionnaires, observation) as well as qualitative aspects (e.g., interviews, journals, observation) of each job to be recorded (Schuler and Walker, 1990; Godet, 1983; Mahmoud, 1984).

3. EXAMINE THE RECORDED DATA ON THE JOB OR PROCESS

Having selected the most appropriate methods to analyze the job, job analysts record the knowledge, skills and abilities, job-related behaviours, duties, tasks, responsibilities, and working conditions of the job. The next step is to examine this data from a variety of perspectives to get a detailed profile of the current job. Some of the questions involved in the examination are as follows:

a. What is the purpose of this job? Why does it exist?

b. Where is the job physically performed? Are there compelling reasons why the job must be performed there?

c. What is the sequence of behaviours required for successful job performance? Are there ways to modify the methods and process to improve the job both qualitatively (e.g., worker and client satisfaction, worker motivation) and quantitatively (e.g., output)?

d. Who performs the job? What constitutes the employee specifications (e.g., education, training, skills, etc.) required for job success? Are these specifications optimal, or are they the minimum standards required for success on the job?

e. What are the means of performing the job? Are the materials, machines, group processes (if applicable) and operating procedures congruent with effective performance of the job?

After addressing all these issues, the job analysts start to form a clearer picture of the present job profile. This information is used to draft the job description or specification, which should be reviewed not only by the job incumbents but also by their supervisors. Reference is also made to the NOC, which provides an external comparison for the validity of the emerging job documentation. Any inconsistencies or discrepancies in the findings are examined by all the job analysts and are taken back to the jobholders and supervisors for further feedback and elaboration.

BOX 3.3 JOB DESCRIPTIONS AT THE CLICK OF A MOUSE

KnowledgePoint, an HR software company, has launched a fee-based Internet Web site that enables downloading of thousands of job descriptions. The Web site (www.jobdescription.com), entitled "Descriptions Now! Direct," contains job descriptions, which can be either automatically e-mailed to the user or downloaded by the client him/herself. The benefits of this service are not only speed and convenience, but also that you can customize the job descriptions, which are kept current by the site provider.

Adapted from: Frost, M. 1997. "Descriptions Now!" *HR Magazine* 42, no. 8 (August): 28.

4. DEFINE AND FORMALIZE NEW METHODS AND PERFORMANCE STANDARDS FOR THE JOB OR PROCESS

To this point in the process, the analysts have (a) examined existing descriptions and specifications for the job (if previous analyses have been conducted), (b) analyzed data on the job as it is presently performed by the jobholder(s), and (c) compared (a) and (b) to the job classification in the NOC and current practices in competitive firms. At this stage, the job analysts attempt to improve on current practices by recommending new methods and performance standards for the job. To do this, analysts must present the following questions to the incumbents and managers:

a.   Would you recommend any changes to materials, machinery, behavioural sequencing, training, or procedures to improve performance on the job?

b.   Are there any duties or tasks that should be added to or deleted from the job?

c.   Would you recommend any changes in the specifications (e.g., knowledge, skills, or abilities) for individuals selected to perform this job?

d.   What changes in working conditions would you recommend to improve performance on this job?

e.   What is your rationale for these recommended changes?

Having gleaned the collective wisdom of all relevant parties regarding the performance of the job under examination, the HR specialists or job analysts write the new description or specification. This will incorporate improvements in how the job is performed (i.e., methods) as well as revisions to performance and output standards (i.e., time). These changes are formalized into written documents—either a job description or a job specification.

A job description is job focused as it concentrates on the duties or tasks, responsibilities, and specific behaviours that are required to be a successful performer. These duties are listed in order of importance to the organization, with the most critical ones listed first. It is also common practice for job descriptions to indicate the amount or percentage of work time devoted to the performance of each job task. While this information is undoubtedly useful for the jobholder, it is important to remember that time-consuming tasks are not necessarily highly valuable or critical to the organization's success! Due to its emphasis on tasks, the job description is best employed for assessing individual performance.

Job specifications are person focused as they detail the profile of the individuals who are best suited to perform the job. They concentrate on the knowledge, skills, abilities, experience, and physical capabilities required for job performance (e.g., the ability to clearly express ideas in oral communication) and are used by HR planners for recruitment and selection.

Both job descriptions and specifications contain the following information: (a) the job title, (b) the job code or classification number, (c) the compensation category, (d) the department or subunit, (e) the supervising job title (the title of the person to whom one reports), (f) the date of the approved description or specification, and (g) the name of the job analyst. This information facilitates quick access to the information by HR planners.

BOX 3.4 WHY JOB DESCRIPTIONS ARE NOT USED MORE

Despite the fact that job descriptions have a wide variety of uses in the organizational context—one study uncovered 132 uses for them—most managers use them infrequently and only for two or three purposes. Most often they are used for recruiting staff, designing the content of jobs, and occasionally for orientation processes. Dr. Philip Grant investigated why job descriptions were fulfilling only a small part of their potential utility for organizations. He found that the most common reason provided by managers to explain the limited usage of job descriptions was that their organization did not unify or assemble all job descriptions into a well-organized, bound volume that was linked to the organizational chart and made available to all managers. Other reasons for their limited usage included:

1. Managers do not know for what or how to use job descriptions.
2. Job descriptions are perceived to be lacking in sufficient detail and comprehensiveness.
3. Job descriptions are perceived to be inaccurate.
4. Managers are not motivated to use job descriptions.
5. Managers do not know what job descriptions are.
6. Job descriptions are not structured well.
7. The job is perceived to "escape definition," or it changes too often.
8. Jobs are not standardized in format.

Adapted from: Grant, P. 1998. "Why Job Descriptions Are Not Used More." *Supervision* 59, no. 4 (April): 10–13. Reprinted by permission of © National Research Bureau, P.O. Box 1, Burlington, Iowa 52601-0001.

5. MAINTAIN NEW METHODS AND PERFORMANCE STANDARDS FOR THE JOB OR PROCESS

It is one thing to have formal written documents specifying the duties, tasks, and KSAs required for job success, but it is quite another to ensure that these new methods and standards for performance are put into practice. There are four main methods to help ensure usage of the new techniques and to prevent relapses to the old, comfortable ways of performing on the job: (1) communication and training, (2) supervisory reinforcement, (3) employee feedback, and (4) reward systems.

As soon as the job description or specification with its new methods and standards has received final approval, the affected jobholders must be given a copy of the revised job description or specification. The process of formally communicating the job changes must also provide sufficient time for questions and answers to ensure workers are clear on the new expectations for their job performance. Training and development programs may have to be instituted if there are significant changes in methods, materials, or the sequencing of behaviours required on the job.

After being formally notified of the changes, supervisors must spend considerable time ensuring that workers are, in fact, behaving in accordance with the new job procedures. (In a unionized environment, of course, the procedure for job reclassification will be specified under the terms of the collective agreement.) Coaching, modelling the desired behaviours, and reinforcing successful performance of the new methods are all effective techniques supervisors can employ to prevent relapses to the outdated, yet habitual, methods of performing the job.

Feedback is critical to the success of the job analysis process. We have already seen that all parties to the process must be consulted on an ongoing basis for their valuable input. Even after the written job analysis documents have been prepared, feedback is essential in ensuring the process has been successful. Employees must be given the freedom to express suggested improvements or concerns with respect to methods, performance standards, and so on if we expect them to become motivated and committed to their jobs. It is important to bear in mind that job analysis is a never-ending process of data gathering, coding, interpreting, and refining job methods and standards. Even if we "get it right" today, changes in technology, competitive practices, economic circumstances, and so on will ensure that we must change to reflect the realities of tomorrow. Besides, who is better able to provide valid feedback about the circumstances of the job than the actual jobholder?

A common downfall of work redesign and job analysis efforts is that although the job methods and standards have changed, the organizational reward system has not been altered, and it reinforces the undesirable old job behaviours (Kerr, 1975). Even if workers have been trained on the new methods of the job and have been provided with a written copy of their revised job description and with ample supervisory coaching, actual worker actions may be very different from formal requirements. For example, if the revised work process is team based, but the compensation system conflicts with job descriptions by being disproportionately weighted toward evaluation of individual performance, we can expect to see unplanned, dysfunctional behaviours and conduct from members of the team. In this instance, worker demeanour may be dysfunctional from the perspective of the organization or the team, but extremely functional and rewarding from the individual's point of view! The oft-repeated dictum "what gets measured, gets done" comes to mind, and if workers are still rewarded for their individual actions and not for their contributions to team success, conflicting organizational systems will ensure we do not get the desired results from the job analysis process.

◆ ◆ ◆
SPECIFIC JOB ANALYSIS TECHNIQUES

The final section of this chapter is devoted to an examination of specific job analysis techniques that are widespread in contemporary organizational usage. We will present five well-known and widely utilized techniques.

I. CRITICAL INCIDENTS TECHNIQUE

The Critical Incidents Technique is a qualitative process of job analysis that produces behavioural statements along a range from superior to ineffective performance for a specific job (Flanagan, 1954; Ghorpade, 1988). Several experts, normally trained jobholders with considerable experience in the job that is being examined, are asked to identify the key dimensions of their job. Subsequently they describe for the analyst, in writing or verbally, specific critical incidents that relate to success, as well as those that would lead to job failure. Once these critical incidents have been described, they are ranked with respect to their importance to success on the job. The behavioural statements are then used to provide specific guidance for HR planners in refining employee specifications for the job in question.

2. BEHAVIOURALLY ANCHORED RATING SCALES

Behaviourally Anchored Rating Scales (BARS) are used by organizations for appraisal of employees' performance and for job analysis purposes. In essence, each job is examined and divided into a small number of key dimensions (e.g., customer relations). Next, behavioural statements are developed for each dimension on a continuum ranging from examples of superior performance to examples of unsuccessful performance. In this aspect, BARS is quite similar in its approach to the Critical Incidents Technique. The next step involves anchoring the behavioural statements by assigning numerical values to them, with perhaps a value of 7 being allocated to a behavioural example of superior performance and a value of 1 to an example of an unsuccessful behaviour. This BARS analysis provides a qualitative and quantitative comparison of jobs based on the derived behavioural statements and numerical values generated by the process. (Campbell et al., 1973; Hom et al., 1982; Jacobs et al., 1980; Kingstrom and Bass, 1981).

3. POSITION ANALYSIS QUESTIONNAIRE

The Position Analysis Questionnaire (PAQ) (McCormick et al., 1972) is a structured job analysis checklist that includes 194 items or job elements that are used to rate a job. These job elements are incorporated into the following six different dimensions:

i. *Information input:* How and where the worker obtains necessary information for job functioning

ii. *Mental processes:* The types of planning, reasoning, and decision-making processes required by the job

iii. *Work output:* The specific items produced by the worker and the tools he or she employs to produce them

iv. *Relationships with other workers:* Important interpersonal contacts for the jobholder

v. *Job context and work satisfaction:* The physical and social working environments

vi. *Other job characteristics:* Elements of the job that do not fall into the other five dimensions. (McCormick, 1976)

Although the job incumbent can complete the PAQ, typically a job analyst will interview the incumbent prior to directly observing his or her actions in fulfilling the performance requirements of the job. This enables the job analyst to score each of the 194 items on several five-point scales such as frequency of usage, importance to the specific job, and so on. The resultant quantitative score enables the comparison of jobs throughout the organization and for those jobs to be grouped according to similar scores on the six different dimensions.

4. FUNCTIONAL JOB ANALYSIS

Functional Job Analysis (FJA) was used to establish the U.S. government's DOT and had a strong formative influence on Canada's NOC (Fine and Wiley, 1971; Fine 1974). The FJA employs a series of written task statements, each containing four essential elements: (1) a verb related to the task action being performed by the worker, (2) an object that refers to what is being acted on, (3) a description of equipment, tools, aids, and processes required for successful completion of the task, and (4) the outputs or results of task completion (Fine 1974; Levine 1983). A compendium of various task statements covers all necessary tasks of the job and, although brevity and concise written statements are the norm, some analysts have devised as many as 100 statements for a job (Levine 1983). The completed task statements are used to describe any job in terms of three essential elements: (1) people (important interpersonal relationships on the job), (2) data (obtaining, using, and transforming data in aid of job performance), and (3) things (physical machinery, resources, and the environment). Each of these three dimensions is then rated in terms of level of complexity and importance with respect to the job being analyzed. The result of the rating is a quantitative score that can be used to compare various jobs.

5. THE HAY SYSTEM

Edward Hay and Associates have developed a system of job analysis that is used extensively for their consulting work in compensation and organizational analysis. The Hay system uses three key factors to analyze each job: (1) know-how (the specific knowledge and skills required to perform the job), (2) problem solving (the decisions and problems that must be successfully handled on the job), and (3) accountability (the jobholder's responsibilities for critical task completion and for organizational resources, budgets, supervision of people, etc.) (Henderson, 1993). Points are assigned to each factor for (1) levels of knowledge (job depth) and (2) breadth of knowledge required to perform the job (job scope). The sum of the points assigned to the job locates it in an overall compensation scheme that provides higher remuneration to those jobholders whose jobs were rated higher by the job analysis.

◆ ◆ ◆
SUMMARY

In this chapter, we have examined a number of important aspects of the job analysis process in preparation for the next chapter's presentation on human resources management systems (HRMS). We have noted how an organization's work process is subdivided into meaningful units of work called jobs, and how the analysis of these jobs can take many forms, such as interviews, observation, and questionnaires. The investigation of jobs focuses on two specific aspects, namely, the methods employed to perform the job and the time standards for work completion. Once job information has been collected and analyzed, it is stored in the HRMS or database to be used in the HR planning process. This stored job analysis information will be combined with personal information on the workforce employees to enable the best possible match to be made between individual needs for fulfilling and rewarding work and the organization's requirements for specific work competencies. We now turn to our examination of the HRMS.

EXERCISES

1. One of the common reasons advanced for not conducting job analyses is the substantial cost that can be associated with such an undertaking. Present a more balanced perspective by identifying both the various benefits of conducting job analyses and the incremental costs that may occur if the process is not instigated.

2. In this chapter, it was stressed that effective job analysis incorporates qualitative and quantitative aspects, as well as a multi-method approach. Why is this additional complexity an important component of an effective job analysis intervention?

3. Jobs and the nature of work itself are dramatically changing in our information-based, global economy. How will the emerging patterns of work affect the nature of organizational participation, the nature of our jobs, and the process we employ to conduct job analyses in the future?

References

Burack, E. 1995. *Creative Human Resource Planning and Applications: A Strategic Approach*. Englewood Cliffs, N.J.: Prentice-Hall.

Burack, E.H., and N.J. Mathys. 1996. *Human Resource Planning: A Pragmatic Approach to Manpower Staffing and Development*, 3rd ed. Northbrook, Ill.:Brace Park.

Campbell, J., M. Dunnette, R. Arvey, and L. Hellervik. 1973. "The Development and Evaluation of Behaviorally Based Rating Scales." *Journal of Applied Psychology* 57, no. 1 (February): 15–22.

Denton, J.C. 1975. The Position Description Questionnaire. Cleveland, Ohio: Psychological Business Research.

Dunham, R., R. Aldag, and A. Brief. 1977. "Dimensionality of Task Design as Measured by the Job Diagnostic Survey." *Academy of Management Journal* 20, no. 2: 209–233.

Employment and Immigration Canada. 1993. *National Occupational Classification*. Cat. no. MP 53-25-1-1993E. Ottawa: Minister of Supply and Services.

Fine, S. 1974. "Functional Job Analysis: An Approach to a Technology for Manpower Planning." *Personnel Journal* (November): 813–818.

Fine, S., and W.W. Wiley. 1971. *An Introduction to Functional Job Analysis*. Kalamazoo, Mich.: Upjohn Institute for Employment Research.

Flanagan, J.C. 1954. "The Critical Incidents Technique." *Psychological Bulletin* 51: 327–358.

Gael, S. 1988. *The Job Analysis Handbook for Business, Industry, and Government*. New York: John Wiley.

Gatewood, R.D., and H.S. Field. 1990. *Human Resources Selection*, 2nd ed. New York: Dryden Press.

Ghorpade, J.V. 1988. *Job Analysis: A Handbook for the Human Resource Director.* Englewood Cliffs, N.J.: Prentice-Hall.

Godet, M. 1983. "Reducing the Blunders in Forecasting." *Futures* 15, no. 3 (June): 181–192.

Grant, P. 1997. "Job Descriptions: What's Missing." *Industrial Management* 39, no. 6 (December): 9–13

Hackman, R., and G. Oldham. 1975. "Development of the Job Diagnostic Survey." *Journal of Applied Psychology* 60: 159–170.

____. 1974. *The Job Diagnostic Survey: An Instrument for the Diagnosis of Jobs and the Evaluation of Job Redesign Projects.* Springfield, Ill.: National Technical Information Service.

Hemphill, J.K. 1960. *Dimensions of Executive Positions.* Columbus, Ohio: Ohio State University.

Henderson, R. 1993. *Compensation Management*, 6th ed. Reston, Va.: Reston Publishing.

Hom, P. W., A.S. DeNisis, A.J. Kinicki, and B. Bannister. 1982. "Effectiveness of Performance Feedback from Behaviorally Anchored Rating Scales." *Journal of Applied Psychology* 67, no. 5 (October): 568–576.

Jacobs, R., D. Kafry, and S. Zedeck. 1980. "Expectations of Behaviorally Anchored Rating Scales." *Personnel Psychology* 33, no. 3 (Autumn): 595–640.

Jenkins, G.D. 1975. "Standardized Observations: An Approach to Measuring the Nature of Jobs." *Journal of Applied Psychology* (April): 171–181.

Kerr, S. 1975. "On the Folly of Rewarding A, While Hoping for B." *Academy of Management Journal* (December): 769–783.

Kingstrom, P., and A. Bass. 1981. "A Critical Analysis of Studies Comparing Behaviorally Anchored Rating Scales and Other Rating Formats." *Personnel Psychology* 34, no. 2 (Summer): 263–289.

Levine, E.L. 1983. *Everything You Always Wanted to Know about Job Analysis.* Tampa, Fla.: Mariner Publishing.

Mahmoud, E. 1984. "Accuracy in Forecasting: A Survey." *Journal of Forecasting* 3, no. 2 (April): 139–159.

McBey, K.J. 1996. "Exploring the Role of Individual Job Performance within a Multivariate Investigation into Part-time Turnover Processes." *Psychological Reports* 78: 223–233.

McBey, K., and C. Hammah. 1990. "The Evolution of Managerial and Organizational Thought." In L. Allan, ed. *Introduction to Canadian Business.* Toronto: McGraw-Hill Ryerson.

McCormick, E.J. 1976. "Job and Task Analysis." In M.C. Dunnette, ed. *Handbook of Industrial and Organizational Psychology*. New York: Rand McNally.

McCormick, E.J., P.R. Jeanneret, and R.C. Meecham. 1972. "A Study of Job Characteristics and Job Dimensions as Based on the PAQ." *Journal of Applied Psychology* 56, no. 4 (August): 347–368.

Mintzberg, H. 1973. *The Nature of Managerial Work*. New York: Harper and Row.

Prien, E., and W.W. Ronan. 1971. "Job Analysis: A Review of Research Findings." *Personnel Psychology* 24: 371–396.

Risher, H.W. 1989. "Job Evaluation: Validity and Reliability." *Compensation and Benefits Review* 21, no. 1 (January): 32–33.

Schuler, R.S., and J.W. Walker. 1990. "Human Resources Strategy: Focusing on Issues and Actions." *Organizational Dynamics:* 5–19.

United States Department of Labor. 1994. *Handbook for Analyzing Jobs*. Washington, D.C.: U.S. Government Printing Office.

Walker, J.W. 1994. "Integrating the Human Resource Function with the Business." *Human Resource Planning* 17, no. 2: 59–77.

_____. 1980. *Human Resource Planning*. New York: McGraw-Hill.

4

HR Management Systems

◆ ◆ ◆
CHAPTER GOALS

To become effective HR planners, it is essential that we have current, relevant information readily available for our planning purposes. Specifically, to correctly calculate personnel demand and supply levels, we must have access to information on the numbers, availability, skill qualification levels, performance evaluation results, career development plans, succession/replacement scenarios, training needs, and so on of our entire workforce. It is to these elements of information, among many others, that we devote the present chapter on Human Resources Management Systems (HRMS), also known as Human Resources Information Systems (HRIS). The HRMS constitutes the database that is essential to permit high-quality, informed HR planning decisions to be made.

After reading this chapter you should be able to do the following:

1. Understand the critical importance of the HRMS to the HR planning process.
2. Appreciate the increasing complexity associated with the normal three-stage evolution of HRMS.
3. Use selection and design criteria that will allow you to evaluate various HRMS as to their degree of fit with specific organizational configurations.
4. Evaluate specific data elements, which are inputs to the HRMS, and evaluate their utility based on selection criteria.
5. Comprehend the necessity for operating restrictions and safeguards on the access and usage of data contained in the HRMS.
6. Discuss the importance of various reports that can be developed as output formats from the HRMS, and evaluate their relative utility to a specific organization.

In Chapter 3, we noted that the job analysis process identifies the employee specifications (KSAs) required to successfully perform the duties and tasks of the various jobs in an organization. This information is stored on a computer database to enable matching comparisons to be conducted between the organizational requirements, as identified by the job analysis process, and the current state of our employee competencies. The degree of congruence between the two is the key factor in instigating HR programs such as training and development, work redesign, re-evaluation of compensation (e.g., pay for performance, skill-based pay, merit pay) and other terms of employment, as well as various staffing initiatives (e.g., recruiting, layoffs, hiring freezes, attrition).

The information contained in the HRMS is critical to effective HR planning, so it is essential that it be accurate, up to date, relevant and of high quality, and in sufficient quantity to make effective decisions. HRMS data is used to make policy decisions that affect a variety of different areas including the following: (1) legal compliance, (2) absenteeism and turnover reports, (3) the organization's demographic composition, (4) performance appraisal rating history, (5) succession/replacement plans, (6) compensation reviews, (7) assessment of training and development needs, (8) career counselling and planning, (9) matching of individual and organizational needs, (10) work redesign and restructuring planning, and (11) assessment centre/potential ratings (Bechet and Walker, 1993).

BOX 4.1 TOP TEN CALCULATIONS FOR YOUR HRIS

Human resource information/management systems have been central in converting traditional personnel administration into today's strategic human resources planning systems. *HR Focus* interviewed Dr. Jac Fitz-Enz on the topic of the top 10 calculations that an organization can run on its HRIS. He identified the following ten elements:

1. Healthcare cost per employee
2. Pay and benefits as a percentage of operating expense
3. Cost per hire
4. Return on training
5. Voluntary turnover rate
6. Total turnover costs (including vacancy and learning curve costs)
7. Time to fill jobs
8. Return on human capital invested (adjusted profit/pay and benefits)
9. Profit per full-time employee (human value-added)
10. That which impresses the CEO the most!

Source: Fitz-Enz, J. 1998. "Top 10 Calculations for Your HRIS." *HR Focus* 75, no. 4 (April): S3. Copyright © 1998 American Management Association International. Reprinted by permission. All rights reserved. http://www.amanet.org

◆ ◆ ◆
THREE STAGES OF HRMS DEVELOPMENT

Having noted the requirement to match the needs of both the individual employee and the organization, we now turn to a discussion of the organizational evolution of HRMS. Generally, we can classify an organization as being in one of three stages of development with respect to their HRMS. The three stages are discussed below.[1]

I. BASIC PERSONNEL SYSTEM

A number of Canadian companies are still operating at stage one with a basic personnel system. This bare bones approach to an HRMS incorporates databases that often mix written records on file with other data elements stored on computer database. The data maintained by this type of system focuses on the following areas: (1) employee records (e.g., individual profile, personal information sheet, application form, orientation acknowledgment, employment agreement or contract); (2) payroll (wage or salary, attendance and vacation entries, and pension and benefit data); (3) staffing (job descriptions for executive and key organizational jobs only); and (4) basic data required for compliance with pertinent labour legislation (Bassett, 1973). This information is used almost exclusively by HR staff in stand-alone applications. The focus is on correct record keeping of the organization's personnel activities, so the system is oriented toward the past. Due to this situation, the basic personnel system is reactive in nature and of limited usage for HR policy decision making and strategic HR planning.

2. AUGMENTED HR SYSTEM

Movement to the second stage, an augmented HR system, occurs when the organization decides to commit the resources to become more proactive with respect to HR policy decisions. A stage two setup requires the HRMS to move beyond the basic record keeping function of a stage one system. In stage two, the HRMS becomes entirely computer based, and the data elements in stage one typically are augmented by a variety of information determined by a needs analysis. Given the increasing memory and data processing capabilities of present-day computers, there are almost limitless possibilities for data inclusion. As we shall see later in this chapter, the organization must give priority to the addition of data that is of greatest relevance to its operations. If, for example, absenteeism and turnover have been noted as problems, the augmented HR system can track individual absences or separations by a variety of combinations of worker classification, geographical location, authority level, and so on. This enables HR planners to identify more readily developing problem areas or trends and thereby be proactive in developing or modifying personnel policies to effectively deal with such problems.

3. COMPREHENSIVE AND INTERACTIVE HRMS

Relatively few companies have evolved to the stage three setup of a comprehensive and interactive HRMS (Burack and Mathys, 1996). This type of HRMS configuration enables the HR planning staff to run future *"what if"* *scenarios* to determine the best future policy alternatives given a range of possible outcomes (Mason, 1994). Also, *relational databases* enable the user to customize the HR data to be investigated, thereby offering a wide variety of searches and analyses to be conducted. A typical example would be the use of such a system to develop a candidate list for attendance at an assessment centre and for future management development programs. In such an instance, the computer search could select candidates who had (1) performance appraisal ratings of "above average" or higher over the past five years, (2) successfully completed a graduate degree (preferably an MBA), and (3) a minimum of five years' seniority in the organization. The program coordinator of management development could then review the list produced by the database search, using input from senior managers and executives, to decide who to include or exclude from the list. Although the list would undoubtedly be modified through the review by HR staff and managers, using the HRMS would save considerable time and expense in developing a comprehensive list of management trainees. This list would then form the basis for comment and review.

Although a comprehensive and interactive HRMS is the goal of many organizational HR planning systems, especially due to its orientation toward analysis of future scenarios and decision-making options, it is not necessarily optimal for all organizations. Only very large multinational and governmental organizations, particularly those operating in the transportation, communications, and utilities industries, tend to use complex, integrated statistical systems for their HRMS and forecasting procedures (Stone and Fiorito,

1986). Furthermore, it is reported that many firms, despite having the financial resources to afford sophisticated systems, had, in fact, reverted to relatively simple systems due to ease of use and environmental stability. Therefore, although there is support for the three-stage evolution of an HRMS, a contrasting view is that many organizations opt for simplicity or concurrently use sophisticated and primitive forecasting techniques (Stone and Fiorito, 1986; Fiorito et al., 1985). A variety of factors have to be weighed to determine the right system configuration for each organization. We now turn to an analysis of a few of these factors.

◆ ◆ ◆
SELECTION AND DESIGN CRITERIA FOR HRMS

1. SYSTEM SECURITY AND ACCESS CONTROL

Given that the HRMS contains sensitive personal information on the workforce, as well as planning scenarios for such things as replacement and succession, it is vital that proper attention be given to controlling access to this information (Adams, 1992). This is especially important in those organizations that are devolving or decentralizing HR functions to the operational line managers. Access should be granted only on a "need-to-know" basis, with passwords, personal identification numbers (PINs), and codes serving as entry barriers prohibiting unauthorized access to other data elements that are not required by the legitimate work requirements of a particular jobholder. Some HRMS also offer data encryption options to ensure that confidential data cannot be viewed or altered by non-authorized personnel. Second, access requirements should be reviewed on a regular basis to determine if continued access to the specific data elements is still valid; if not, the job incumbent should be denied entry to the confidential database. A third element with respect to access concerns the individual employee's right to examine his or her personal record to ensure that it is accurate and contains only job-related information. This right of access is upheld by the Canadian Privacy Act to prevent discriminatory material or information that is not related to the job from entering into selection and employment decisions, which are regulated by federal and provincial human rights legislation.

BOX 4.2 TIPS FOR DATA SECURITY

The financial and legal implications of poor data security can be enormous. Fraud, loss of proprietary information, sabotage, and breach of personal, privileged information all can result from improperly secured data. *Workforce* recently presented some helpful advice on ways to enhance data security. As the biggest security threat is normally from inside the organization, that is, current members of the workforce, it is essential that the organization train and educate workers on data handling, storage, and usage considerations, and have explicit, well-communicated security policies in place. Procedures to enhance security of data include the usage of PINs and passwords, the usage of encryption devices or software when sending sensitive e-mail, providing regular, ongoing education and reinforcement of clearly defined organizational policies, and turning off systems when they are not in use.

Source: Adapted from Greengard, S. 1998b. "How Secure Is Your Data?" *Workforce* 77, no. 5 (May): 52–60.

2. USER FRIENDLINESS OF THE HRMS

HRMS software varies substantially with respect to the training time and ease of use for HR staff. Systems that build on common HR terminology and are designed to run in conjunction with other widespread computer operating systems (e.g., Microsoft's Windows and MS DOS, UNIX, etc.), will require less preparatory training of staff than would very specialized HRMS applications. Second, HRMS vary substantially as to the degree to which they can be customized to meet user requirements. Users should consider explicitly the degree to which the selected system will allow customization of HR forms and reports to meet actual operating requirements. The wise purchaser will note that many HRMS are not configured to enable end-user modification of the HRMS. Therefore, the formats are as delivered by the vendor's assessment of your needs, which may be very different from your actual requirements now and especially in the future (Mathys and La Van, 1984).

3. FLEXIBILITY AND INTERFACE WITH OTHER ORGANIZATIONAL SYSTEMS

When purchasing HRMS software, the organization must consider the linkage between existing computer hardware and the proposed software system as well as staff computer literacy with the various systems (Mathys and La Van, 1984). It is important to ensure that there is a smooth interface between hardware and software, thereby minimizing the errors or bugs occurring as a result of the joint operation of the two (Brooker, 1992). In addition to close scrutiny of operational requirements and programming sequences, smart purchasers will ask for demonstrations and a trial period of operating the HRMS to ensure successful and problem-free operation of the system before a purchase commitment is made.

4. APPROPRIATENESS FOR MEETING ORGANIZATIONAL NEEDS

Some companies make the mistake of purchasing HRMS software because of beneficial features in one specific area (e.g., compensation). Vendors naturally are delighted to expound on all the nifty features of their particular HRMS system. The wise purchaser will take time to identify and rank the organization's HR goals for the HRMS. Doing so will lead to search behaviour that is focused on the "must haves" and will lessen the purchaser's distraction by peripheral options that are only "nice to have" (Diers, 1992).

With respect to the vendor, it is important to research the wide variety of HRMS software vendors offering products. A comprehensive and comparative analysis, such as that provided by *HR_Matrix* (HRMS Directions Inc., 1995), can facilitate intelligent comparison of vendors. One must consider not only the price (annual licensing fee), but also a variety of factors such as (1) the number of years the software company has been in existence (incorporated), (2) whether the vendor specializes in HRMS or whether they are only a peripheral sideline for its other information system activities, (3) post-purchase service support packages, (4) the number of clients in Canada , (5) the number of actual installations in Canada (which can be dramatically different from the number of clients!) and, of course, (6) the vendor's reputation for reliability in the industry (HRMS Directions Inc., 1995).

5. SYSTEM COSTS AND SERVICE SUPPORT

With respect to HRMS implementation costs, organizational purchasers sometimes forget to factor in the training expense of converting HR and other staff users to operating the new system. Furthermore, some purchasers take a very myopic approach to cost analysis because they consider only the annual licensing fee for the HRMS (which can vary from several hundred dollars to several hundred thousand dollars per year, depending on the size and complexity of the HRMS). However, in addition to this annual licensing fee, one has to consider the ongoing costs of providing assistance, technical support, and upgrades to the newly established system. Vendors vary widely as to the post-purchase support they offer to clients, and the supplemental costs to clients for these services typically runs in the range of 15 percent to 25 percent of annual licensing fees (HRMS Directions Inc., 1995). For this money, you might receive a combination of user training, use of a 1-800 telephone help line, e-mail help through the Internet, installation of HRMS upgrades, newsletters. and so on. The wise customer shops carefully to get the specific vendor support required and does not pay extra for superfluous assistance that can be provided by in-house organizational resources.

Speaking of organizational staff, the HR and management information system (MIS) or decision support system (DSS) staff must be involved in developing the HRMS decision criteria and selecting the final system because these people will be the primary source of on-site expertise and assistance once the system is running successfully. It is absolutely essential that the selected HRMS build on this staff's knowledge of computer operating systems and software so that the system can be improved as time goes on. Programming development for HRMS uses a wide variety of languages, depending on the particular system purchased. Some systems use C, PASCAL, or ORACLE, as well as more traditional programming languages such as COBOL and BASIC. Ensure the HRMS purchased either can use a variety of different programming languages or, at the bare minimum, operates those developmental procedures that are established and well known by your HR and MIS/DSS staff.

BOX 4.3 THE NEW HRIS: GOOD DEAL OR $6-MILLION PAPERWEIGHT?

The successful implementation of a new HRIS depends on consideration of technological, people, and process issues. With regard to technology, it is important that the HRIS dovetails with the organization's current and future requirements for technology. The biggest issues concern people, including the requirement for top management support for the system, consideration of ways to get end-users to use system features, and ensuring that in-house systems/DSS (decision support system) personnel have the proper skills to implement and support the HRIS. With respect to process, there is a requirement for either a customized HRIS to fit existing processes or modifications to existing organizational processes to conform to the off-the-shelf HRIS configuration.

Adapted from: Roberts, B. 1998. "The New HRIS: Good Deal or $6-Million Paperweight?" *HR Magazine* 43, no. 2 (February): 40–46.

6. HRMS FUTURE EXPANSION

Given the considerable time expenditures and costs associated with implementing an HRMS, paying the ongoing annual licence and service-support fees, training the organizational staff, and, of course, the critical informational outputs of the HRMS, it is hoped that our selected system, like our new car, will stand us in good stead well into the future. Accordingly, we must buy now with an eye to probable future requirements for our HRMS (O'Connell, 1994).

Currently, there are over 75 integrated and specialist HRMS available to the Canadian business organization (HRMS Directions Inc., 1995). *Integrated systems* are those that offer a variety of HR record and decision-making functions, whereas *specialist programs* are tailored to servicing customer needs in one or two narrowly defined areas (e.g., compensation, that is, payroll plus benefits). The individual components contained in a basic integrated system differ substantially among vendors. Typically, we see record keeping, payroll and compensation, time and attendance tracking protocols, and elements for job analysis information, as well as for performance appraisal, contained in the basic package. Irrespective of the integrated system obtained, it is wise to inquire about vendor options or modules, which can be added to the current HRMS to expand its capability at a future date. As we move from the augmented to a more comprehensive and interactive HRMS, we must always consider not only current organizational requirements, but also future needs. Notwithstanding the benefits of any one HR component, if the HRMS system cannot provide modular add-ons to the existing database, then it will probably be of limited value in terms of meeting your future organizational needs.

Typical modules that can be added to an HRMS include the following: (1) performance appraisal, (2) employment equity, (3) replacement/succession and career planning, (4) accounts receivable (e.g., for employee pay advances), (5) accounts payable (e.g., for training program costs), (6) pension administration, (7) job applicant and résumé tracking, (8) occupational health and safety, (9) job analysis and evaluation, (10) compensation (payroll and benefits), (11) staff scheduling (attendance and time, including flextime program options), (12) training and development, (13) severance and termination, (14) adherence to legislation, (15) labour relations (e.g., discipline and grievances), (16) multinational staffing planner, and (17) accounting and billing (Anthony, 1977; Berry, 1993; Braderich and Bourdreau, 1991;

Johnson et al., 1983; Kossek et al., 1994). The degree to which various vendors have developed these modules and their associated costs, as well as your in-house capability to develop local procedures, must all be considered with respect to future use of the HRMS. Finally, as we have noted earlier, a stage three comprehensive and interactive HRMS should be able to conduct HR research by offering a relational database with a variety of flexible search options and capabilities. These should include methods of portraying research results, including graphic protocols such as scatter plots, bar charts, graphs, and so on; the ability to run mathematical and statistical procedures, such as multiple regressions and linear programming; and the ability to create succession charts and vacancy models used in HR forecasting.

◆ ◆ ◆
CRITERIA FOR DATA INCLUSION IN THE HRMS

There are countless elements of data that could be entered into an organization's HRMS. The key aspect with respect to data inclusion is not how much data is collected and stored but how useful the data will be for HR staff and organizational decision makers (Anthony, 1977; Diers, 1992; McBeath, 1992). In particular, we should remember the old computer programmer's maxim "GIGO": if you put Garbage In, invariably you will get Garbage Out! Paying attention to the specific data requirements of your organization will help minimize the time-consuming and expensive labour costs associated

---

BOX 4.4 HRMS FACILITATES STRATEGIC HR PLANNING

With the increasing importance of knowledge capital in today's global economy, the HRMS is an important factor in facilitating effective strategic planning and decision making. Many companies, such as Fluor Daniel Inc. and National Semiconductor Corporation, utilize the information technology of the HRMS for services such as on-line résumé scanning for recruitment, interview question databases based on job requirements, e-mail, and corporate intranets. Furthermore, the existence of the HRMS enables administrative elements of HR to be centralized, while concurrently enabling HR field personnel to concentrate on the provision of services to line management and employees, such as training and development interventions.

Adapted from: James, G. 1997. "IT Helps HR Become Strategic." *Datamation* 43, no. 4 (April): 110–114.

with the entry and updating of personal data into the HRMS. Before the data fields are established for the HRMS, it is important to conduct a needs analysis that explicitly identifies why the data is required and provides a justification for its collection and updating (e.g., justification related to legalities, accounting and compensation, career development, and job assignment). Furthermore, the needs analysis will estimate the frequency of access for each element of data (per day, week, or month), identify the jobholders who will be permitted to have access to and use of the data, estimate the memory storage requirements, and develop the data access safeguards, and so on.

Databases that contain substantial personal and confidential data, for example, Revenue Canada's taxation data and Statistics Canada's census data, require very extensive user safeguards to restrict access to information and prevent its use for reasons other than those explicitly stated in the HRMS objective statements. As mentioned earlier in the text, data encryption, passwords, personnel security clearances, and so on are vital elements linked to the appropriate employment of personal, privileged information.

Given the legal penalties and adverse public relations outcomes that may arise if we fail to comply with Canadian and provincial human rights acts, control of data collection and data access is absolutely critical. Although we can legitimately include in our HRMS entries age, marital status, and employee dependents for medical and health care benefit purposes, if this data from the HRMS is used inappropriately, for example, for selection purposes where decisions based on marital status and age are considered discriminatory, the organization would be in contravention of federal and provincial human rights legislation and would be legally liable to provide redress to the individual.

Notwithstanding the above, there are some data elements that are common to most organizational HRMS databases. It is to these core data elements that we now turn our attention.

◆ ◆ ◆

CORE HRMS DATA ENTRIES[2]

I. IDENTIFICATION AND PERSONAL RECORD

The following are some common elements of the identification and personal record:

- Surname, first and middle names, previous names

- Address (including postal code), telephone numbers (residence, office, and mobile), e-mail address
- Next of kin (including address and telephone number)
- Gender
- Date of birth
- Marital status, dependents
- Nationality, work permit number
- Designated group membership or race (for employment equity purposes)
- Social insurance number, health card number, employee number, union membership

2. WORK HISTORY

Work histories often include the following elements:

- Date of hire
- Employment status (full-time, part-time, contract, etc.)
- Current job title, manning number, authority level or classification, location of employee (department or division)
- Length of time in current job
- Previous job titles in the organization and dates of service for each
- Work history prior to joining the company (including employers, positions held, dates of service, etc.)

3. CAREER AND COMPETENCIES

Most HRMS databases typically include the following types of data on career and competencies:

- Employee's desired future positions, target positions recommended by employee's supervisors
- Individual performance appraisal data; assessment centre and appraisals tests results and ratings regarding potential, promotability, and readiness for movement

- Specific skills and competencies, licences
- Certificates, diplomas, and degrees, each listed with the granting educational institution, date of completion, and field of study (major)
- Recent training activities
- Hobbies and interests
- Community and volunteer activities
- Professional or trade association memberships
- Geographical location preferences
- Foreign language competencies
- Honours and awards, publications

4. ACCOUNTING AND COMPENSATION DATA

Accounting and compensation data usually include the following types of information:

- Gross compensation (salary, hourly wage)
- Compensation band and location on the salary range
- Hours/shifts worked per week
- Overtime and bonuses
- Merit or incentive plan membership
- Date of the last salary or wage change
- History of compensation changes: amounts and dates, planned date and amount of next change
- Vacation taken or banked
- Benefit package selected
- Life insurance
- Medical and dental coverage
- Deductions (e.g., pension plan contributions, parking, union dues, income tax, unemployment insurance)
- Leaves of absence

FIGURE 4.1 **Sample Skills Inventory**

Malachi Marine Adventures

NAME: _____   CURRENT DATE: _____

CURRENT POSITION: _____   DATE OF HIRE: _____

EMPLOYEE NUMBER: _____   DEPARTMENT: _____

Education and Training Qualifications:
Please list licences, certificates, diplomas, degrees, and other training qualifications, along with the year of graduation and the relevant training institution.

_____

_____

_____

Honours, Awards, and Professional Memberships/Responsibilities:

_____

_____

_____

Previous Work Experience: (Malachi Marine and other work experience):
Please provide the job title and code, key responsibilities, dates held, location, and company name (list chronologically, most recent job first).

_____

_____

_____

Hobbies and Interests, Community and Volunteer Activities:

_____

_____

_____

Career Plans:

_____

_____

_____

Performance Summary (strengths, development needs):

_____

_____

_____

Current Performance Rating, Present Job (scale 1 to 7): _____

Date of Commencement of Present Job: _____

Promotability Readiness Code: _____
(a = now, b = 1 year, c = 2 years, d = review/not yet determined)
Potential Rating Code: _____
(++ = promotable 2 levels, + = promotable 1 level, ~ = suited current level, ? = review/not
yet determined. Include date and name of assessor/s.)

Targeted Positions:

_____
_____
_____

Development Plan:

_____
_____
_____

General Commentary:

_____
_____
_____

Signature: _____   Date: _____

Review and Approval: _____   Date: _____

CONFIDENTIAL (when completed)

Once all of this data is transferred from the skill and management inventories (Grabosky and Rosenbloom, 1975; Kaumeyer, 1979; Martin, 1967; Seamans, 1978) into the HRMS, a wide variety of reports and output formats can be produced and analyzed, including the following:[3]

1. Employee rosters

2. Actual versus authorized staffing

3. Analyses of gender, age, designated group membership, seniority, salaries, pay equity, full- and part-time distributions

4. Performance appraisals

5. Position tenure and movement, blockages

6. Vacant positions

7. New hires and cohort analysis

8. Attrition through voluntary turnover and termination

9. Absenteeism

10. Job transfers and reassignments

11. Job reclassifications

12. Succession short lists

◆ ◆ ◆
SUMMARY

The HRMS is an essential element of a properly functioning HR planning process. In this chapter we have presented information relating to the normal three-stage evolution of the HRMS, along with the associated changes in capability that are linked to each step in the process. We discussed criteria that can be used for system design and stressed that the HRMS must be selected based on explicit, previously established operating requirements and organizational goals. Skills and management inventories provide input to the HRMS, and our discussion made it clear that identifying the specific rationale for including each type of data is required to prevent unfocused, costly, and time-wasting database management. Given that the HRMS uses sensitive personal information, we presented various options for operating restrictions and safeguards to ensure that access to and use of data is restricted to approved users engaged in operations required by the organization. Finally, we discussed a wide variety of output formats and reports that can be generated by the HRMS, which are of use not only to the HR planning staff but also to line managers and individual workers. We now turn to a presentation of the HR forecasting process, which integrates information about the job, as revealed by means of the job analysis process, with personal and organizational data elements contained in the HRMS database.

E X E R C I S E S

1. An HRMS is essential for conducting effective HR planning. Define HRMS, and identify various data elements that act as inputs to the system. Discuss the various output formats that could be of use to HR planning staff.

2. Identify the criteria that should be used when selecting an HRMS for an organization. Rank these system selection criteria. Are they a universal set of criteria that apply to all organizations?

3. The HRMS contains a wide variety of personal and sensitive data that necessitates security, privacy, and usage policies to be set by the organization. What are some of the safeguards, operating restrictions, and policies that should be developed for users of an HRMS?

E N D N O T E S

1. Adapted from Braderich and Bourdreau, 1991; Burack and Mathys, 1996; Greiner, 1972; Stone and Fiorito, 1986; Walker, 1989.

2. Adapted from McBeath, 1992; Anthony, 1977; Burack and Mathys, 1996.

3. Adapted from McBeath, 1992; Walker, 1980.

References

Adams, L. 1992. "Securing Your HRIS in a Microcomputer Environment." *Human Resource Management* (Fall): 56–61.

Anthony, W. 1977. "Get to Know Your Employees: The Human Resource Information System." *Personnel Journal* (April): 179–186.

Bassett, G.A. 1973. "Elements of Manpower Forecasting and Scheduling." *Human Resources Management* (Fall): 35–43.

Bechet, T.P., and J.W. Walker. 1993. "Aligning Staffing with Business Strategy." *Human Resource Planning* 16, no. 2: 1–16.

Berry, W. 1993. "HRIS Can Improve Performance, Empower and Motivate 'Knowledge Workers.'" *Employment Relations Today* (Autumn): 297–303.

Braderich, R., and J. Bourdreau. 1991. "The Evolution of Computer Use in Human Resource Management: Interviews with Ten Leaders." *Human Resource Management* 30, no. 4: 485–508.

Brooker, R. 1992. "What Hardware Means to the HRIS." *Personnel Journal* (May): 122–138.

Burack, E.H., and N.J. Mathys. 1996. *Human Resource Planning: A Pragmatic Approach to Manpower Staffing and Development*, 3rd ed. Northbrook, Ill.: Brace Park.

Diers, C. 1992. "Common Mistakes in Implementing an HRIS." *Employment Relations Today* (Autumn): 265–271.

Fiorito, J., T.H. Stones, and C.R. Greer. 1985. "Factors Affecting Choice of Human Resource Forecasting Techniques." *Human Resource Planning* 8, no. 1: 1–17.

Grabosky, P., and D. Rosenbloom. 1975. "Racial and Ethnic Integration in the Federal Service." *Social Science Quarterly* 56, no. 1 (June): 71–84.

HRMS Directions Inc. 1995. *HR Matrix.* Mississauga, Ont.: HRMS Directions.

———. 1997. "Harness the Power of HRMS: The Wild Ride, but Worth It." *Workforce* 76, no. 6 (June): 28–33.

Greiner, L. 1988. *Power and Organizational Development: Mobilizing Power to Implement Change.* Reading, Mass.: Addison-Wesley.

Johnson, B., G. Moorhead, and R. Griffin. 1983. "Human Resource

Information Systems and Job Design."
Human Resource Planning 6, no. 1
(March): 35–40.

Kaumeyer, R.H. 1979. *Planning and
Using Skills Inventory Systems.* New York:
Van Nostrand Reinhold.

Kossek, E.E., W. Young, and D. Gash.
1994. "Waiting for Innovation in the
Human Resources Department: Godot
Implements a Human Resource
Information System." *Human Resource
Management* 33, no. 1: 135–159.

Martin, R. 1967. "Skills Inventories."
Personnel Journal (January): 28–83.

Mason, D. 1994. "Scenario-Based
Planning: Decision Model for the
Learning Organization." *Planning
Review*: 6–11.

Mathys, N., and H. La Van. 1984. "Issues
in Purchasing and Implementing HRIS
Software. *HR Magazine* 29, no. 8
(August): 91–97.

McBeath, G. 1992. *The Handbook of
Human Resource Planning: Practical
Manpower Analysis Techniques for HR
Professionals.* Oxford: Blackwell.

O'Connell, S. 1994. "Planning and
Setting Up a New HRIS." *HR Magazine*
(February: 36–39.

Seamans, L. 1978. "What's Lacking in
Most Skills Inventories." *Personnel
Journal* (March).

Stone, T., and J. Fiorito. 1986. "A
Perceived Uncertainty Model of Human
Resource Forecasting Technique Use."
Academy of Management Review 11, no.
3: 635–642.

Walker, J.W. 1989. "Human Resource
Roles for the '90s." *Human Resource
Planning* 12, no. 1: 55–61.

____. 1980. *Human Resource Planning.*
New York: McGraw-Hill.

5

The HR Forecasting Process

CHAPTER GOALS

HR forecasting, which constitutes the heart of the HR planning process, can be defined as ascertaining the net requirement for personnel by determining the demand for and supply of human resources now and for the future. After determining the demand for and supply of workers, the organization's HR staff develop specific programs to reconcile the differences between the requirement for labour in various employment categories and its availability, both internally and in the organization's environment. Programs in such areas as training and development, career planning, recruitment and selection, managerial appraisal, and so on are all stimulated by means of the HR forecasting process.

After completing this chapter you should be able to do the following:

1. Recognize the three different categories of HR forecasting activity and their relationship to the HR planning process.

2. Understand the considerable advantages that accrue to organizations from instituting effective HR forecasting procedures.

3. Discuss the rationale for giving special attention to specialist, technical, and executive personnel groups in the HR forecasting process.

4. Comprehend the impact of environmental and organizational variables on the accuracy and time horizon of estimates derived from future estimates of HR demand and supply.

5. Identify the various stages in the process of determining net HR requirements.

6. Understand the policy and program implications of an HR deficit or an HR surplus.

◆ ◆ ◆

FORECASTING ACTIVITY CATEGORIES

Forecasting activity can be subdivided into three categories: (1) transaction-based forecasting, (2) event-based forecasting, and (3) process-based forecasting (Atwater, 1995). Transaction-based analyses focus on tracking internal change instituted by the organization's managers, while event-based forecasting is concerned with change in the external environment. Process-based forecasting is not focused on a specific internal organizational event but on the flow or sequencing of several work activities (e.g., the warehousing shipping process). All three categories are important if we are to have a comprehensive method for ascertaining our HR requirements.

Forecasting is only an approximation of possible future states and is an activity that strongly favours quantitative and easily codified techniques. As such, it is important that an explicit effort be made to obtain and incorporate qualitative data into our analyses (Godet, 1983). Furthermore, not only are more successful HR forecasting processes those which use both qualitative and quantitative data, but also a number of studies have clearly shown that accuracy of prediction improves significantly when we use multiple forecasting techniques (Hogan, 1987; Mahmoud, 1984). Effective forecasting also hinges on obtaining a fine balance between global and local control of the process. A study of multinational corporations operating in Ireland showed that most of the firms that were analyzed adopted a local approach to forecasting, with the (global) headquarters maintaining a vigilant yet loose monitoring of financial costs and other performance criteria (Monks, 1996).

BOX 5.1 HR FORECASTING IN A GLOBAL ECONOMY

Organizations that operate globally face additional challenges to their effective and efficient usage of human resources. For starters, differences in time zones and the vast geographic dispersion of operational units and workforces can be problematic. Technology can help these companies, such as Arthur Andersen and Nortel, through use of the Internet, organizational intranets, as well as e-mail and video conferencing systems. Global HR planning managers should encourage employee collaboration through (1) maximizing use of technology such as e-mail, (2) explicitly scheduling work to take advantage of time zone differences that can be used to the company's advantage (e.g., preparation of a contract by employees in an advanced time zone, which can then be sent to a client firm which is in a time zone several hours behind that of the preparing unit), and (3) eliminating of redundant costs through centralizing of data in the HRMS.

Adapted From: Solomon, C. 1998. "Sharing Information Across Borders and Time Zones." *Workforce* 3, no. 2 (March): 12–18.

BOX 5.2 FACTORS IN SUCCESSFUL IMPLEMENTATION OF AN HR SYSTEM

With an ever increasingly competitive global marketplace, organizations are turning their attention to strengthening the linkage between individual performance and organizational profitability. To tighten up organizational work processes, HR systems should be implemented with the following guidelines in mind:

- Integrate re-engineering and system implementation efforts.
- Get senior leadership involved early and often.
- Involve employees in the effort.
- Be sure the system's design supports the organization's business strategy.
- Consider an organizational readiness assessment.

Adapted from: Horney, N., and I. Ruddle. 1998. "All Systems Go?" *Bank Marketing* 30, no. 1 (January): 20–26.

◆ ◆ ◆
BENEFITS OF HR FORECASTING

A great number of important benefits accrue to organizations that take the time to institute effective HR forecasting processes, and the forecasting techniques employed do not have to be sophisticated to be of value to the firm (Stone and Fiorito, 1986; Meehan and Ahmed, 1990). A few of the more important advantages of HR forecasting are discussed below.

1. REDUCES HR COSTS

Effective HR forecasting focuses on a comparison between the organization's present stock of workforce KSAs (e.g., experience) and the numbers, skill competencies, and so on desired in the workforce of the future. This inherent comparison facilitates a proactive, sequential approach to developing internal workers and is concurrent with activities focused on obtaining the best external recruits from competitors, universities, and training programs (Walker, 1980). In this manner, organizations can reduce their HR costs as they take a long-run planning approach to HR issues. This means that organizations will be less likely to have to react in a costly last-minute crisis mode to unexpected developments in the internal or external labour markets.

2. INCREASES ORGANIZATIONAL FLEXIBILITY

An oft-cited advantage of HR forecasting is that its proactive process increases the number of viable policy options available to the organization, thereby enhancing flexibility (Beck, 1991; Schuler, 1989). In terms of labour supply considerations, forecasting processes develop program options that can determine whether it is more advantageous and cost effective to retrain present members of the workforce to fill anticipated job openings or fill these openings with external recruits who are already in possession of the required competencies and skills. Given that HR forecasting is predicated on trends, assumptions, scenarios, and various planning time horizons, the process itself encourages the development of a wide range of possible policy options and programs from which the HR staff can select. Furthermore, each of the various HR programming options are ranked, subjected to cost–benefit analyses, and allocated organizational resources after being carefully examined as part of the HR forecasting process.

3. ENSURES A CLOSE LINKAGE TO THE MACRO BUSINESS FORECASTING PROCESS

A serious problem develops in some organizations when the personnel planning process becomes divorced and disconnected from the overall business goals of the organization (Fulmer, 1990). The implementation of an HR forecasting process helps to eliminate the possibility that personnel policies will veer away from the overall operating and production policies of the organization. First, HR forecasting, although an ongoing process, takes its lead from specific production, market share, profitability, and operational objectives set by the organization's top management. These objectives have been established through proactive internal and environmental scans of market and competitor strengths, weaknesses, opportunities, threats, resources, and policy actions (McEnery and Lifter, 1987). Once these have been established, spe-

---

BOX 5.3 WHY HR SYSTEM IMPLEMENTATION EFFORTS FAIL

1. The organization's top management has not communicated the need to implement new technology or new systems.
2. People resist change efforts because they are not asked to help develop new business strategies, solutions, and plans.
3. Organizations underestimate the time, energy, budget, and planning required to successfully implement new technology.
4. Different groups within an organization either cannot agree on what a system needs to do or overburden it with too many requirements.

Adapted from: Horney, N., and I. Ruddle. 1998. "Why HR System Implementation Efforts Fail." *Bank Marketing* 30, no. 1 (January): 24.

cific HR forecasting analyses are set in motion to determine the feasibility of the proposed operational objectives with respect to time, cost, resource allocation, and other criteria of program success. The HR analyses are subsequently sent back to top management, and they either confirm the viability of the original business objectives or indicate that changes (e.g., the allocation of additional resources) need to be made to enable the objectives to be met.

The business forecasting process, therefore, establishes overall organizational objectives, which are input into the HR forecasting process (Fulmer, 1990). The HR staff analyze whether the explicit objectives, with their associated specific performance parameters, can be met with the organization's current HR policies and programs or whether specific changes have to be instituted, with their associated costs, to achieve the objectives. These analyses and the subsequent feedback of the HR forecast summaries to senior management help to ensure that the top decision makers in the organization (1) are aware of key HR issues and constraints that might affect organizational plans for success and (2) ensure the HR objectives are closely aligned with the organization's operational business objectives (Schuler and Walker, 1990).

4. ENSURES THAT ORGANIZATIONAL REQUIREMENTS TAKE PRECEDENCE OVER ISSUES OF RESOURCE CONSTRAINT AND SCARCITY

As we present each step of the HR forecasting process in sequence throughout this text, it will quickly become evident that the first step in the process is the calculation of organizational requirements or *demand* for human resources. Determining the source of personnel, that is, the availability or *supply* of workers, is only done once the process of evaluating personnel requirements for present and future time horizons has been finalized. This sequence is not accidental, and it reinforces the fact that attainment of desired organizational goals and objectives must take priority over all issues concerning resource scarcity and other implementation issues.

◆ ◆ ◆

KEY PERSONNEL ANALYSES CONDUCTED BY HR FORECASTERS

Although the forecasting process for personnel in an organization is conducted to determine the number of employees and the skill competencies required by subunits, as well as the entire organization, a number of personnel categories typically are given greater than average attention in the forecasting process. These categories are discussed below.[1]

1. SPECIALIST/TECHNICAL/ PROFESSIONAL PERSONNEL

Workers holding trade qualifications that are in high demand or that require lengthy preparatory training for attainment of skill competency constitute a key area of focus for HR forecasting. In our increasingly global economy, these workers will be in high demand by competitive firms both in Canada and abroad, which means we will have to give special attention to programs to induce these workers to join our organization. Furthermore, we must give attention to benchmarking compensation schemes to meet or lead industry standards so as to attract and retain people who perform well in these categories. With respect to supply issues, a longer lead time is often required to recruit technicians and professionals due to the need for a more comprehensive and larger geographic search for this specialist talent pool.

2. EMPLOYMENT EQUITY DESIGNATED GROUP MEMBERSHIP

Provincial and federal governments in Canada have enacted employment equity legislation and guidelines in response to public pressure for employment practices that reflect the rapidly changing face of Canadian society. In particular, four main groups are designated for special attention with respect to their degree of use or equitable employment in organizations: (1) people of aboriginal descent, (2) women, (3) people with disabilities, and (4) members of visible minorities. Particular attention must be paid to monitoring members of these designated groups with respect to the opportunities they receive for employment, promotion, training, and so on as compared to those received by the dominant population of the organization (Grabosky, 1975). Furthermore, the composition of the organizational workforce should reflect the underlying characteristics of the society in which it is embedded, so the supply issue, as it relates to proportional representation of designated groups in the organization, is a key area for HR forecasting.

3. MANAGERIAL AND EXECUTIVE PERSONNEL

To be successful, any organization must ensure that its executives and managers possess the skills required for success in their specific environmental niche. Executives (CEO, president, vice-presidents, etc.) interact with key environmental stakeholder groups on behalf of the organization and are responsible for setting the goals for the organization's future direction. Managers, acting as the supervisory layer of authority between executives and the operating shop-floor level, are responsible for coaching, directing, and controlling worker behaviours to achieve the goals established by the executive group. Although there is no shortage of managers and executives who can function effectively in relatively benign, predictable, environmental situations, researchers believe that organizational leaders who are able to transform organizational culture and anticipate external change, and who possess the dynamic personal attributes necessary to unify the organization, are very rare indeed in most public and private sector organizational settings (Zaleznik, 1977). For this reason, not only must greater attention be paid to identifying leadership talent within the organization, but also assessment or appraisal centres must be conducted to match the "right person to the right job at the right time" (Bucalo, 1974). The organization's survival and future success depend directly on succession and replacement planning!

BOX 5.4 PROFITABLE PERSONNEL

Critics have applied the sarcastic label "big hat, no cattle" to HR managers who have little effect on the performance of the organization. The United Kingdom's Sheffield Effectiveness Program disputes this assertion because its research discovered that not only was "people management" critical to business performance, but it far outstripped the emphasis on quality, technology, competitive strategy, or research and development in its influence on the organization's bottom-line performance. Although research findings with respect to the relationship between individual satisfaction and job performance have been mixed, the Sheffield research found that at the macro level, satisfaction of the work group across a wide range of areas, for example, developing skills, creativity, and recognition processes, was critical to organizational productivity.

Adapted from: West, M., and M. Patterson. 1998. "Profitable Personnel." *People Management* 4, no. 1 (January):

---

4. RECRUITS

As was the case with succession and replacement planning, recruiting trainees is extremely important to the success of the organization's overall HR policies. When determining whether to obtain trainees from the internal workforce or externally, a wide variety of factors must be considered. For example, selecting current employees to attend training courses leading to promotion rewards loyalty and past performance and simultaneously diminishes the need for the organizational socialization of newcomers from outside. However, current employees may be very comfortable with the status quo and existing methods of organizational operation, and, therefore, may not be well suited for employment on novel, creative work processes that differ substantially from established practices. Furthermore, new entrants can bring the organization insights into how competitors structure and operate their business and may, as well, bring with them the latest trends and practices taught in universities and specialist training agencies. The relative balance of internal to external personnel to be selected for training courses is a key factor in the HR forecasting and programming operations of many organizations.

The goal of HR forecasting is to obtain sufficient numbers of trained personnel who will be able perform successfully in jobs when those jobs need to be filled. To do this, the forecasting process has five stages:[2]

1. Identify organizational goals, objectives, and plans.
2. Determine overall demand requirements for personnel.
3. Assess in-house skills and other internal supply characteristics.
4. Determine the net demand requirements that must be met from external, environmental supply sources.
5. Develop HR plans and programs to ensure that the right people are in the right place.

Before turning to aspects concerned with determining personnel demand, we will examine the effects of environmental uncertainty and of planning time horizons on HR forecasting.

◆ ◆ ◆

ENVIRONMENTAL AND ORGANIZATIONAL FACTORS AFFECTING HR FORECASTING

The HR forecasting process is extremely complex, requiring specific numerical and skill competency targets for personnel to be met despite operating in circumstances of high uncertainty (Beck, 1991). This uncertainty arises from both external environmental factors and from inside the organization itself. Given this uncertainty and the natural rate of change resulting from operating in a turbulent, global economy, the key factor for HR forecasters is to incorporate flexibility into the program responses associated with demand and supply forecasts (McEnery and Lifter, 1987; Schuler, 1989). When considering the following discussion of environmental and organizational factors, it is important to remember that these factors may affect the forecasting of demand, supply, or both of these key planning variables.

◆ ◆ ◆
HR FORECASTING TIME HORIZONS

As we have discussed in Chapter 2, environmental and organizational factors increase uncertainty for HR forecasters and necessitate flexibility in the programs they devise to balance personnel demand and supply. The key point to consider from an analysis of environmental and organizational factors is that uncertainty decreases our confidence in our ability to predict the future accurately and hence reduces the HR forecasting time horizon (Beck 1991; Butinsky and Harari, 1983). Large organizations with substantial resources and sizeable numbers of well-trained personnel who perform well may be better able to weather the storms of future change in environmental, economic, technological, and competitive market factors. If this is the case, they

TABLE 5.1 SELECTED FACTORS AFFECTING THE HR FORECASTING PROCESS	
Internal/Organizational	**External/Environmental**
Corporate mission statement, strategic goals	Economic situation
Operational goals, production budgets	Labour markets and unions
HR policies (e.g., compensation, succession)	Governmental laws and regulations
Organizational structure, restructuring, mergers, etcetera	Industry and product life cycles
Worker KSAs/competencies and expectations	Technological changes
HRMS level of development	Competitor labour usage
Organizational culture and internal communications	Global market for skilled labour
Job analysis: workforce coverage, current data	Demographic changes

will be able to extend their HR forecasting process further into the future with greater confidence in the accuracy of their predictions. Irrespective of their situation with regard to environmental and internal factors, organizational forecasters use several different time horizons for forecasting. Although there are variations among organizations with respect to how they define their specific time parameters, the typical HR forecasting time horizons are as follows:[3]

1. *Current forecast:* The current forecast is the one being used to meet the immediate operational needs of the organization. The associated time frame is up to the end of the current operating cycle, or a maximum of one year into the future.

2. *Short-run forecast:* The short-run forecast extends forward from the current forecast and states the HR requirements for the next one- to two-year period beyond the current operational requirements.

3. *Medium-run forecast:* Most organizations define the medium-run forecast as the one that identifies requirements for two to five years into the future.

4. *Long-run forecast:* Due to uncertainty and the significant number and types of changes that can affect the organization's operations, the long-run forecast is by necessity extremely flexible and is a statement of probable requirements given a set of current assumptions. The typical long-run forecast extends five or more years ahead of the current operational period.

The outcome of forecasts derived from these four time horizons leads to predictions and projections. A *prediction* is a single numerical estimate of HR requirements associated with a specific time horizon and set of assumptions, whereas a *projection* incorporates several HR estimates based on a variety of assumptions (Burack and Mathys, 1996). The forecasting term *envelope* is synonymous with projection as one can easily visualize the four corners of an envelope, with each corner containing a specific prediction; for example, corner 1 contains an optimistic sales assumption (time 1), corner 2 contains a pessimistic sales assumption (time 1), corner 3 contains an optimistic sales assumption (time 2), and corner 4 contains a pessimistic sales assumption (time 2). The four corner predictions serve to anchor the envelope, which may also contain a number of other specific predictions (e.g., the most likely assumption, which may be to maintain the current sales level). The use of a combination of predictions and projections provides the necessary forecasting flexibility required to cope with the uncertainty and change associated with the environmental and organizational factors described previously.

HR forecasters therefore devise a set of alternative *scenarios*, each with its own set of assumptions and program details associated with HR functions such as training and development, staffing (advertisement, recruiting, and selection), and succession/replacement planning (Mason, 1994). Naturally, organizations must also conduct *contingency planning* to have HR policy responses ready if substantive unanticipated changes occur. Contingency plans are brought into action when severe, unanticipated changes to organizational or environmental factors completely negate the usefulness of the existing HR forecasting predictions or projections (e.g., a substantial drop in consumer demand occurs due to adverse public relations, as was seen in the Classic Coke and Tylenol cases).

◆ ◆ ◆
DETERMINING NET HR REQUIREMENTS

Thus far we have discussed the importance of HR forecasting, key personnel groups targeted for special attention, environmental and organizational factors influencing supply and demand of personnel, and forecasting time horizons. The final part of this chapter addresses the process of determining net HR requirements. The next two chapters will be devoted to an examination of specific methods used to calculate HR demand (Chapter 6) and supply (Chapter 7), but, for the present, we will lay the foundation for these chapters by examining the overall process.

I. DETERMINE HR DEMAND

As we mentioned briefly previously, it is essential that we calculate our requirement or demand for personnel in terms of numbers and obligatory skill competencies before we consider how we will meet those requirements (i.e., what supply or source of personnel to use). In determining demand, a variety of factors have to be considered. First, each organizational subunit has to submit its net personnel requirement to the corporate forecasting unit, based on future needs for labour required to meet the agreed on corporate and subunit objectives (e.g., market share, production levels, size or expansion, etc). It is critical to note that this HR demand figure must incorporate the individuals needed to maintain or replace the current personnel who retire, die, are fired or otherwise terminated, or take long-term leave (e.g., for reasons such as disability, training courses, etc.), as well as the replacements for individuals who are promoted or transferred out of the department. All these elements must be included in the calculation of departmental or subunit HR demand. These subunit labour demands are then aggregated and used as the starting point for the HR demand forecasts.

Next, planned future changes in organizational design or in restructuring (e.g., expansion of certain departments, downsizing of mid-level management, planned redundancy and elimination of specific jobs), with their associated increases or decreases in staffing levels, must be incorporated into the equation to revise the aggregated net departmental demand requirements. Furthermore, forecasters have to consider how to replace nonproductive paid time (e.g., vacation and sick days) either by increasing demand for full- or part-time personnel (i.e., slack resources [Thompson, 1967]) or perhaps by using overtime with the existing set of current employees to prevent loss of productive capacity and required level of service to organizational clients. Finally, consideration of all these issues leads us to the *net HR demand*, broken down into the forecasting time horizons mentioned previously and containing (1) the number of employees required by each subunit and by the organization in total and (2) the employee skill sets, competencies, or specifications required for each of the positions. Finally, we conduct a cost estimate (HR budget) for the net HR demand figure as a reality check to determine whether our forecasts are realistic, given financial resource considerations. Often, at this stage, subunits are asked to rank their HR demand, identifying jobs that are most critical to the achievement of their departmental objectives (Burack, 1995).

2. ASCERTAIN HR SUPPLY

Step one produced an estimate of personnel requirements or demand. Step two examines exactly how we plan to fill the anticipated future requirements for personnel. In essence, there are two supply options: (1) *internal supply*, which refers to current members of the organizational workforce who can be retrained, promoted, transferred, and so on to fill anticipated future HR requirements, and (2) *external supply*, which refers to potential employees who are currently undergoing training (e.g., university students) or working for competitors, or who are members of unions or professional associations, or currently in a transitional stage between jobs or unemployed. Typically, most organizations use a mix of both internal and external supply, rewarding loyal employees who perform well with promotion and advancement possibilities and recruiting outside individuals who possess competencies not held by the present workforce.

With respect to internal supply, the ability to meet HR demand hinges on the size of the current workforce and especially its level of or ability to perform certain jobs. The number and the KSAs of the workforce are analyzed using the HRMS (as described in Chapter 4), which contains a *personal record* or *inventory* of each member of the workforce. Included in the inventory (see Figure 4.1) are items such as employee name, seniority, classification, part- or full-time work status, work history and record of jobs held in the organization, education, training, skill competencies, history of performance appraisals, and future jobs desired by or recommended for the individual, as well as hobbies and interests that may be useful for organizational planning (Martin, 1967; Kaumeyer, 1979; Seamans, 1978). For example, a computer search of the HRMS database could enable us to quickly determine the numbers, names, and employment status of, and performance records for, all employees who have successfully completed a graduate degree in statistics. If the search procedure fails to find a sufficient number of employees with the necessary KSAs to meet HR demand, then the policy options would be either to identify and retrain employees with related KSAs who perform well or to turn to external sources for personnel.

Although some organizations hire recruits externally only when their internal searches and job posting or bidding process fail to identify sufficient numbers of high-quality internal candidates (Connolly, 1975), there are several other reasons why many organizations use external labour to meet their HR demand. First, and most obviously, if it is necessary to expand our operations without increasing labour efficiency or implementing labour-saving technology, we might have to increase the size of the workforce by hiring externally. Second, internal employees are socialized and may be comfortable in their modus operandi, whereas external applicants can introduce to the organization competitive insights and highly creative novel operational techniques recently learned in external institutions. Third, an internal candidate may be considerably more expensive (due to collective agreement provisions relating compensation to seniority) than an individual who is recruited from outside the organization. Finally, if organizational objectives require a shift in operating techniques, culture, and past practices, then hiring external candidates is often desirable for shaking up the organization!

Irrespective of the reasons why organizations seek external recruits, the key factor in determining whether the organization will be effective in meeting HR requirements from external supply sources is an analysis of how HR policies are perceived by individuals who are potential employees. By benchmarking competitor practices with respect to compensation, it is possible to examine staffing and compensation policies to make them more attractive to high-quality applicants. An organization's ability to attract the "cream of the crop" will be substantially enhanced if the organization is perceived as being the industry leader with respect to compensation, rather than just meeting or lagging behind (following) its competitors. Also, recruiting policies must be fine-tuned to ensure communication is established with the appropriate labour markets. For example, it might be possible to fill many production jobs from local labour market sources, but specialized technicians and professionals may require external recruiting, which is national, if not international, in scope. In this case, additional resources, time, and effort may be required if we are expected to fully meet the numerical and KSA requirements specified by our HR demand process. Finally, obtaining external applicants requires not only identifying where these individuals live and work, but also ascertaining the most appropriate media to use to contact and attract them. These media may include job fairs, open houses, and career days, as well as advertising in industry and professional association journals, publications, newspapers, and Web sites read by potential external applicants who are trained in the skills needed.

3. DETERMINE NET HR REQUIREMENTS

The third step in the process involves the determination of net HR requirements. From steps one and two above, the following equations are derived:

HR demand = external supply + internal supply

HR demand − internal supply = external supply

Personnel who can fill organizational HR demand requirements must be found from either the current internal workforce supply or from external environmental sources. As explained above, if we are unable to meet the numerical and KSA demands for personnel from internal sources, either because of the qualification or performance deficiencies of present workers or because of an explicit organizational decision to recruit new blood, then the residual supply not met through current employees must come from outside:

external supply requirements = replacement + change supply components

replacement supply = hiring to replace all normal losses

(Normal losses are those that result from retirements, terminations, voluntary turnover, promotions, transfers, and leaves, and these losses must be replaced to keep the workforce size at the current level.)

change supply = hiring to increase (or decrease) the overall staffing level

Recall from our earlier discussion of HR demand that future personnel requirements must not only replace the current workforce employees (in terms of numbers and skill competencies), but also reflect desired future changes to staffing levels. Therefore, the first element in deriving our external supply calculation is to meet our replacement needs, that is, to maintain operations at the current level by hiring new employees to replace workers who have left due to firing, transfers, retirements, promotions, leaves, and so on. Next, if we are to increase or decrease our staffing levels, based on organizational and subunit objectives, then we have to consider the change component that moves the overall size of the workforce to its new future level. This process can be represented by the following equation:

external supply = current workforce size × (replacement % per year + change % per year)

Using the example of an organization with a current workforce size of 1000 workers, an annual historical replacement/loss rate of 11 percent, and a desired future growth rate of 7 percent, the net external supply requirement is that 180 individuals be hired per year:

external supply = 1000 (.11 + .07) = 110 + 70 = 180

Of the new hires, 110 people are allocated strictly to replacement of departing workers, and the other 70 individuals constitute the change requirement for new growth.

Another organization with a workforce of 450, which has a historical annual replacement/loss rate of 8 percent and a corporate downsizing policy that will reduce overall staffing levels by 9.5 percent, has the following supply requirement:

external supply = 450 (.08 + [-.095]) = 36 − 43 = -7

(In the equation above, note that the figure 43 was rounded up from 42.75.) In this case, the annual replacement/loss rate is insufficient on its own to reduce the size of the organization's workforce to the desired lower staffing level. The result is *a net HR surplus*, and the organization must not only institute a freeze on external hiring but also further reduce the current internal workforce complement by seven positions to meet the mandated downsizing policy!

In many cases, the existence of a collective agreement between the management and the union representing the employees may result in the organization not being able to specify which workers are to be terminated due to seniority and layoff articles in the agreement.

4. INSTITUTE HR PROGRAMS: HR DEFICIT AND HR SURPLUS

When a forecast of HR demand is reconciled with the current workforce supply of personnel (i.e., HR internal supply), the result is the net HR requirement, which will be either a deficit or a surplus (unless we are exceedingly lucky and achieve parity with an exact balance of the two!).

HR deficit = HR demand > HR internal supply

Simply stated, an *HR deficit* means that forecasted HR demand requirements cannot be entirely satisfied solely by use of the current internal workforce supply of employees. Therefore, policy options focus on external supply considerations of recruitment, selection, and compensation schemes to attract new employees. It might be possible to hire part-time employees, full-time employees, or a combination of both in an attempt to address the deficit. Similarly, it might be possible to recall any workers (depending on their KSAs and training) who were laid off due to past lower levels of HR demand. Also, retired employees might be enticed back to work on at least a part-time basis by means of attractive flexible work schedules. The use of temporary workers also can help the organization meet a short-run HR deficit, although in the long run, further attention to providing promotion and transfer opportunities for internal workers by means of training and development programs usually proves more advantageous.

HR surplus = HR demand < HR internal supply

An *HR surplus* occurs when the internal workforce supply exceeds the organization's requirement or demand for personnel. In this instance, a number of policy options can be considered. Employees might be laid off to reduce the excess labour supply to a level equal to the demand requirements. Alternatively, employers might terminate employees if certain jobs are considered redundant and the skill sets associated with these jobs will not be required in the future. Job sharing occurs when two or more employees perform the duties of one full-time position, each sharing the work activities on a part-time basis. This policy option is gaining strength in Canadian industry as it allows the company to retain valued employees, albeit with reduced hours and lower income levels, with the hope of reinstating them to full-time status once HR demand levels increase at some time in the future.

Other programs for addressing an HR surplus include reducing the number of hours, shifts, or days worked by each worker so that all workers can be retained, while reducing overall work hours to the level required by operational demand imperatives. Secondments or leaves occur when the organization lends some of its excess workforce to community groups or permits those surplus workers to take educational leave or training away from the operational workplace. Attrition is the process of reducing an HR surplus by allowing the size of the workforce to decline naturally due to the normal pattern of losses associated with retirements, deaths, voluntary turnover, and so on. This decrease of internal supply over time can be accentuated by a hiring freeze, which is a prohibition of all external recruiting activities. Early retirement packages attempt to induce surplus workers to leave the organization when granted severance benefits and outplacement assistance. Finally, if internal supply exceeds HR demand for specific positions, organizational retraining and development, and assistance with the expenses associated with moving to a better labour market (geographic mobility), as well as transfer and demotion, can also be considered as possible policy options for the organization's affected personnel (McLaughlin, 1975).

◆ ◆ ◆
SUMMARY

This chapter has examined a wide variety of aspects associated with HR forecasting. The advantages of instituting effective forecasting procedures were discussed, as were the different groups (e.g., executives, specialist/technical personnel) that attract special attention in the HR demand and supply reconciliation process. Both environmental and organizational factors have tremendous impact on various forecasting procedures, and many of these factors have to be addressed explicitly in HR forecasting procedures. The latter part of the chapter was devoted to the various stages associated with the HR forecasting process, specifically the sequence of activities involved in determining net HR requirements. Finally, we discussed the policy implications of reconciling HR demand and supply, ending up with either an HR deficit or surplus, and the various programs that may have to be instituted by organizations to address these varying situations.

The next two chapters are devoted to an examination of specific techniques used by organizations to calculate HR demand and supply. Chapter 6 presents specific techniques employed by organizations to derive HR demand forecasts.

EXERCISES

1. Conduct a comprehensive analysis of the various stakeholders involved in an organization with which you are familiar. From this analysis, ascertain the key uncertainties that would be associated with the HR forecasting process for this organization. Based on the material in this chapter and your own knowledge, how would you address these environmental and organizational uncertainties in your modifications to the HR forecasting process?

2. Over the past decade, there have been dramatic employment shifts in many industries due to product life cycles and technological change, as well as general changes in demand for workers with specific KSAs, for example, in computer and systems engineering. Select a particular industry and conduct a literature review and Internet search for business and labour employment statistics related to its operations (access the Internet Web sites for Industry Associations and Statistics Canada). Based on this historical review and your knowledge of current business trends, forecast possible employment shifts for the specific industry you have selected. How would you use this information as an HR planner?

3. A wide range of HR programming options is available to address either an HR deficit or an HR surplus. However, these programs have widely divergent consequences for the workforce, service to clients, and the local labour market, as well as for the organization's financial bottom line. Identify specific criteria to evaluate and differentiate the effectiveness of the various HR program options.

1. Adapted from Burack and Mathys (1996).
2. Adapted from Schuler and Walker (1990).
3. Adapted from Bechet and Walker, 1993; Walker, 1980.

References

Atwater, D.M. 1995. "Workforce Forecasting." *Human Resource Planning* 18, no. 4:50-53.

Bechet, T.P., and J.W. Walker. 1993. "Aligning Staffing with Business Strategy." *Human Resource Planning* 16, no. 2: 1–16.

Beck, B.M. 1991. "Forecasting Environmental Change." *Journal of Forecasting* 10, no. 1: 3–19.

Bucalo, J. 1974. "The Assessment Center: A More Specified Approach. *Human Resource Management* (Fall): 2–12.

Burack, E. 1995. *Creative Human Resource Planning and Applications: A Strategic Approach.* Englewood Cliffs, N.J.: Prentice Hall.

Burack, E.J., and N.J. Mathys. 1996. *Human Resource Planning: A Pragmatic Approach to Manpower Staffing and Development*, 3rd ed. Northbrook, Ill.: Brace Park.

Butinsky, C.F. and O. Harari. 1983. "Models vs. Reality: An Analysis of 12 Human Resource Planning Systems." *Human Resource Planning* 6, no. 1: 11–20.

Connolly, S. 1975. "Job Posting." *Personnel Journal* (May): 295–299.

Fulmer, W. 1990. "Human Resource Management: The Right Hand of Strategy Implementation." *Human Resource Planning* 12, no. 4:1–11.

Godet, M. 1983. "Reducing the Blunders in Forecasting." *Futures* 15, no. 3 (June): 181–192.

Grabosky, P., and D. Rosenbloom. 1975. "Racial and Ethnic Integration in the Federal Service." *Social Science Quarterly* 56, no. 1 (June): 71–84.

Hogan, A. 1987. "Combining Forecasts: Some Managerial Experiences with Extrapolation." *Socio-Economic Planning Sciences* 2, no. 3: 205–211.

Kaumeyer, R.H. 1979. New York: Van Nostrand Reinhold.

Mahmoud, E. 1984. "Accuracy in Forecasting: A Survey." *Journal of Forecasting* 3, no. 2 (April): 139–159.

Martin, R. 1967. "Skills Inventories." *Personnel Journal* (January): 28–83.

Mason, D.H. 1994. "Scenario-Based Planning: Decision Model for the Learning Organization." *Planning Review:* 6–11.

McEnery, J., and M. Lifter. 1987. "Demands for Change: Interfacing Environmental Pressures and the Personnel Process." *Public Personnel Management* 16, no. 1 (Spring): 61–87.

McLaughlin, G. 1975. "A Professional Supply and Demand Analysis." *Educational Record* 56, no. 3 (Summer): 196–200.

Meehan, R., and B.S. Ahmed. 1990. "Forecasting Human Resources Requirements: A Demand Model." *Human Resource Planning* 13, no. 4: 297–307.

Monks, K. 1996. "Global or Local? HRM in the Multinational Company: The Irish Experience." *International Journal of Human Resource Management* 7, no. 3 (September): 721–735.

Schuler, R.S. 1989. "Scanning the Environment: Planning for Human Resource Management and Organizational Change." *Human Resource Planning* 12, no. 4.

Schuler, R.S., and J.W. Walker. 1990. "Human Resources Strategy: Focusing on Issues and Actions." *Organizational Dynamics* (Summer): 4–19.

Seamans, L. 1978. "What's Lacking in Most Skills Inventories." *Personnel Journal* (March).

Stone, T., and J. Fiorito. 1986. "A Perceived Uncertainty Model of Human Resource Forecasting Technique Use." *Academy of Management Review* 11, no. 3: 635–642.

Thompson, J. 1967. *Organizations in Action*. New York: McGraw Hill.

Walker, J.W. 1980. *Human Resource Planning*. New York: McGraw-Hill.

Zaleznik, A. 1977. "Managers and Leaders: Are They Different?" *Harvard Business Review* 55, no. 3 (May): 67–78.

6

HR Demand

CHAPTER GOALS

T his chapter is devoted to a presentation and examination of various real-world techniques used by organizations to forecast their HR demand. As we progress through the chapter, you will note that the techniques presented vary according to their forecasting time horizon and that these techniques tend to be either qualitative or quantitative. Successful organizations combine statistically driven quantitative forecasts with more qualitative expert processes to achieve the most comprehensive demand forecasts possible (Schuler and Walker, 1990). Also, organizations must consider demand for personnel not only for the current operational period, but also well into the future to ensure the right numbers of workers with the requisite skills and competencies are ready and available to work when the organization requires them.

After reading this chapter, you should be able to do the following:

1. Understand the importance of demand forecasting in the HR planning process.
2. Recognize the linkages between the HR plan, labour demand forecasting techniques, and the subsequent supply stage.
3. Compare and contrast the advantages and disadvantages of various demand forecasting techniques: index/trend analysis, expert forecasts, the Delphi technique, the nominal group technique, HR budgets (staffing/manning tables), envelope/scenario forecasting, and regression analysis.

◆ ◆ ◆

INDEX/TREND ANALYSIS

Examining the relationship over time between an operational business index, such as level of sales, and the demand for labour (as reflected by the number of employees in the workforce) is a relatively straightforward quantitative demand forecasting technique commonly employed by many organizations (see Table 6.1) (Cascio, 1991; Ward, 1996). This technique, also known as *trend analysis*, reveals the historical relationship between the operational *index* and the number of employees required by the organization (demand for labour) (McLaughlin, 1975). Although sales level is probably the most common index used by organizations, other operational indices include (1) the number of units produced, (2) the number of clients serviced, and (3) the production (i.e., direct labour) hours. Similarly, although the relationship between the operational index and workforce size (number of employees) can be calculated for the entire organization, as well as for the department or operational subunit, some organizations use trend analysis to ascertain demand requirements for (1) direct labour and (2) indirect labour (e.g., staff such as HR staff).

There are five steps to conducting an effective index/trend analysis.[1]

1. SELECT THE APPROPRIATE BUSINESS/OPERATIONAL INDEX

The HR forecaster must select a readily available business index, such as sales level, that is (a) known to have a direct influence on the organizational

TABLE 6.1 INDEX/TREND ANALYSIS

Puslinch Pottery

Year	Sales ($ Thousands)	# of Employees	Index (Sales per Employee)
1997	$2,800	155	18.06
1998	3,050	171	17.83
1999	3,195	166	19.25
2000	3,300	177	18.64
2001	3,500[a]	188[b]	18.64[c]
2002	3,600[a]	193[b]	18.64[c]
2003	3,850[a]	207[b]	18.64[c]

[a] Time now is the year 2000. We are forecasting labour demand for 2001, 2002, and 2003, and therefore sales figures for those years are future estimates.

[b] Employee numbers are historical, except for the figures for 2001, 2002, and 2003, which are our future HR demand forecasts.

[c] The index used to calculate future demand (number of employees) can be the most recent figure, or an average of the up-to-date period (e.g., the past four years, for which the average is 18.44). In this trend analysis, the most recent index (18.64) for the year 2000 was used for forecasting.

demand for labour, and (b) subjected to future forecasting as a result of the normal business planning process.

2. TRACK THE BUSINESS INDEX OVER TIME

Once the index has been selected, it is necessary to go back in time for at least the four or five most recent years, but preferably for a decade or more, to record the quantitative/numerical levels of the index over time.

3. TRACK THE WORKFORCE SIZE OVER TIME

Record the historical figures of the total number of employees, or, alternatively, the amount of direct and indirect labour (see above) for exactly the same period used for the business index in step 2.

4. CALCULATE THE AVERAGE RATIO OF THE BUSINESS INDEX TO THE WORKFORCE SIZE

In this step, a ratio of the number of employees required for each thousand dollars of sales (e.g., for each automobile produced) is obtained by dividing each year's number of employees by the level of sales (e.g., the number of automobiles produced). This *employee requirement ratio* is calculated for each year over the period of analysis so an average ratio describing the relationship between the two variables over time can be determined.

5. CALCULATE THE FORECASTED DEMAND FOR LABOUR

Multiply the annual forecast for the business index times the average employee requirement ratio for each future year to arrive at forecasted annual demand for labour. For example, obtain future sales forecast figures for the next five years. For each of the years, multiply the level of sales by the average employee requirement ratio to obtain the forecasted numerical demand for labour for each future year.

Although employment of index/trend analysis is widespread due to its ease of use, it is important to remember that the analysis incorporates only the relationship between a single business variable and demand for labour (workforce size). By design, any single-variable relationship provides a simplistic forecast for demand. For more comprehensive analyses that reflect a variety of factors affecting business operations, such as interest rates, level of unemployment, consumer disposable income, and so on, the quantitative techniques normally employed are multivariate regression or other similar modelling/programming models (Meehan and Ahmed, 1990). Although these sophisticated, multiple-predictor techniques require detailed knowledge of statistics and systems programming, we will present an example of simple regression later in the chapter.

◆ ◆ ◆
EXPERT FORECASTS

Direct managerial input is the most commonly used method for determining workforce requirements (Ward, 1996). Using experts to arrive at a numerical estimate of future labour demand is considered to be a qualitative process for determining future labour requirements because it is a detailed process of stating assumptions, considering potential organizational and environmental changes, and deriving a rationale to support the numerical estimate derived.

A wide variety of individuals may be considered experts for their knowledge of organizational operations, competitive HR practices, international trends in the labour markets, and so on (Gatewood and Gatewood, 1983). First and foremost, the organization's own line managers, who each have detailed knowledge of workload, responsibilities, and overall task responsibilities for his or her own department, are in possession of important insights into how future demand for labour should or might change in their own areas of responsibility. Second, the organization's HR and business planning staffs certainly have critical information that can enable them to provide wise guidance in forecasting future levels of labour demand. For example, the planning staff may use econometric and strategic models to predict future level of sales of or demand for the organization's goods and services, as well as provide important insights into future economic indicators affecting labour demand such as interest rates, change in gross national product, level of consumer disposable income, savings, and so on. The HR staff, whether they are HR generalists or a team of HR planning specialists, are able to draw up a detailed set of assumptions with respect to industry, local, and international labour market trends that have an impact on how the organization organizes and employs its own workforce. Third, business consultants, financial analysts, university researchers, union staff members, industry spokespersons, and so on possess detailed knowledge of specific industries or types of organizational activity and are able to give rich, detailed, and largely impartial judgments on future labour demand because of their external perspective relative to the organization. Finally, but not exclusively, federal, provincial, and local governmental staff and officials are important individuals to consult because they possess knowledge of future environmental changes in labour and business legislation that can dramatically change labour demand not only for a specific organization, but also for the industry in general. For example, pending legislation to ban the use of certain materials in product manufacturing might cause a substantial drop in demand for these products and hence an associated reduction in demand for employees who are involved in their manufacture.

Governmental ministries and departments, most specifically those devoted to labour, human resources, and economic development, and, of course, the highly regarded Statistics Canada at the federal level can all provide expert information for our labour demand forecasting process. Irrespective of which experts we select, a number of options are available for obtaining labour demand estimates and assumptions from those concerned. Interviews, questionnaires (conducted in person or by mail or e-mail), and telephone conference calls are some of these options, but other techniques can be employed to maximize the benefit of each expert's contributions in specific circumstances. We now turn our attention to two of these methods of facilitating high-quality labour demand forecasts, namely, the Delphi technique and the nominal group technique.

◆ ◆ ◆
DELPHI TECHNIQUE

The Delphi technique, which was named after the Greek oracle at Delphi, was developed by N.C. Dalkey and his associates at the Rand Corporation in 1950 and is an especially useful qualitative method for deriving detailed assumptions on long-run HR demand (Luthans, 1992). A key feature of this demand forecasting technique is that once a group of experts are selected, they do not meet face to face (Fusgeld, 1971). Instead, a project coordinator canvasses them individually for their input and forecasts by means of a progressively more focused series of questionnaires. The advantage of the Delphi technique is that it avoids many of the problems associated with face-to-face groups, namely, reluctance by individual experts to participate due to

(1) shyness, (2) perceived lower status or authority, (3) perceived communication deficiencies, (4) issues of individual dominance and groupthink (i.e., group conformity pressures: Janis 1972), and so on (Hampton et al., 1987; Milkovich et al., 1972; Milkovich and Mahoney, 1978). Because the Delphi technique does not employ face-to-face meetings, it can serve as a great equalizer and can elicit valid feedback from all expert members.

There are disadvantages associated with the Delphi technique, as indeed there are with all forecasting techniques. In particular, due to the series of questionnaires administered to derive a forecast, the time and costs incurred when using the Delphi technique can be higher than those incurred when using alternative forecasting methods. Another deficiency is that obviously the results cannot be validated statistically and are greatly dependent on the individual knowledge and commitment of each of the contributing experts (Meehan and Ahmed, 1990).

There are six steps associated with using the Delphi technique for HR demand forecasting.

1. DEFINE AND REFINE THE ISSUE OR QUESTION

During this stage, a project coordinator is assigned, and he or she works with the HR staff to determine the specific personnel category or activity that will be the focus of the Delphi technique. It is essential that the group targeted for HR forecasting be defined in detail so that relevant, focused, and detailed feedback based on a minimum of assumptions (redundant assumptions are associated with loss of the experts' time) can be derived.

2. IDENTIFY THE EXPERTS, TERMS, AND TIME HORIZON

The project coordinator, normally in conjunction with the HR staff, identifies and selects a team of individuals who are deemed to be experts with respect to the specific personnel grouping that requires a forecast. Next, given that in many cases the group of experts will include individuals who are not members of the organization, it is important to set the context and to be explicit with definitions. For example, the team of experts must be absolutely clear as to which jobs constitute "production workers" if those experts are being asked to derive a demand forecast for this category.

Similarly, the exact time horizon(s) must be specified for the personnel category being analyzed.

3. ORIENT THE EXPERTS

In addition to identifying the relevant time horizon(s) and clarifying which personnel groups are of interest, the orientation process for experts includes an overview of the demand forecasting decision process (which is very similar to the structural framework in which you are now engaged!). The experts are told either that there will be a predetermined number of questionnaire iterations or that the sequence will continue until a majority opinion exists among the experts.

4. ISSUE THE FIRST-ROUND QUESTIONNAIRE

The project coordinator sends each expert the questionnaire by hand, mail, or e-mail and includes a time frame for completing and returning it. Typically, this first questionnaire is focused on defining both the explicit assumptions made by each of the experts and the background rationale supporting their own particular demand estimate.

5. ISSUE THE FIRST-ROUND QUESTIONNAIRE SUMMARY AND THE SECOND ROUND OF QUESTIONNAIRES

Following the completion of the first questionnaire, the project coordinator sends the second and subsequent rounds of questionnaires to the experts with a written summary of the findings from the first round. The aim of the subsequent questionnaires is to focus the experts' initial assumptions and estimates by providing summarized feedback from all members of the group. Points of commonality and conflict are identified in the summary, as is the need to clarify specific assumptions identified by the responses to the previous round.

6. CONTINUE ISSUING QUESTIONNAIRES

The project coordinator continues to issue questionnaires until either all the predetermined questionnaire stages have been completed and summarized or the group reaches a clear majority decision. In either case, the majority or nth-round summary comprises the experts' future demand estimate for the HR category under analysis.

NOMINAL GROUP TECHNIQUE

Although the nominal group technique is also a long-run, qualitative demand forecasting method, it differs from the Delphi technique in several important respects. First, unlike in the Delphi technique, the group does, in fact, meet face to face and interact, but only after individual written preparatory work has been done and all the demand estimates (idea generation) have been publicly tabled, or written on a flip chart, without discussion (Van de Ven, 1974). Second, each demand estimate is considered to be the property of the entire group and to be impersonal in nature, which minimizes the potential for dominance, personal attacks, and defensive behaviour in support of estimates presented in the group forum (Rohrbaugh, 1981). Finally, the expert forecast is determined by a secret vote of all group members on their choice of the tabled demand forecasts. The estimate receiving the highest ranking or rating during the voting process is deemed to be the group's forecast (Delbecq et al., 1975; Green, 1975).

There are seven steps associated with implementing the nominal group technique.

I. DEFINE AND REFINE THE ISSUE OR QUESTION AND THE RELEVANT TIME HORIZON

This step is similar to the first step of the Delphi technique. The HR forecasting staff or coordinator is responsible for identifying the specific personnel category or activity that will be the focus for the nominal group technique. The more refined the problem definition is, the more likely it is that relevant, focused, detailed feedback will be derived with a minimum of redundant assumptions. Second, it is essential that the time horizon(s) of interest for the demand estimate be clearly specified. Overall, the issue is often phrased as a question: "What will ABC Corporation's demand for production workers be in the year 2005 (or in five years from the present)? Please provide your demand estimate and the explicit assumptions and rationale supporting your forecast."

2. SELECT THE EXPERTS

In the second step, the coordinator or HR forecasting staff select the individuals who have expert knowledge of the specific personnel group being analyzed. Experts are then contacted to confirm their participation in the process and to schedule the time for the face-to-face meeting.

3. ISSUE THE HR DEMAND STATEMENT TO THE EXPERTS

During the third step, the coordinator for the nominal group process sends each of the experts a concise statement of the HR demand they are being asked to address. As stated in the first step, the issue is normally framed as a question that the experts are being asked to answer, and an accompanying sheet of terms, definitions, and assumptions may accompany the question or issue statement.

4. APPLY EXPERT KNOWLEDGE, STATE ASSUMPTIONS, AND PREPARE AN ESTIMATE

Having received the issue or question posed by the coordinator on behalf of the organization, each expert now considers his or her specific knowledge of the particular personnel group that is the subject of the demand estimate. In particular, experts will undoubtedly have personal insights or insider information not available to other members of the group and should explicitly state the various assumptions that arise from this information, as well as the numerical estimate of demand. In this way, once the nominal group meets face to face, the supporting rationale for what may be widely divergent demand estimates quickly becomes apparent to the group as a whole.

5. MEET FACE TO FACE

Having prepared their individual assumptions and a numerical estimate of demand, the experts then meet face to face. The first item of business will be a brief presentation of each expert's demand estimate with the associated supporting assumptions. Individual interaction and discussion is strictly forbidden so as not to stifle creativity. The coordinator will arrange for individual introductions and ice-breakers to facilitate group interaction only after all estimates have been tabled. He or she will also specify the process for the nominal group's subsequent actions.

6. DISCUSS THE DEMAND ESTIMATES AND ASSUMPTIONS

After each expert has presented his or her demand estimate, the process shifts to detailed analyses and group discussion of the estimates and their assumptions. To minimize individual defensiveness and personal ownership of estimates, group members are asked to focus on ascertaining supportive information for estimate assumptions and to avoid attacks on the soundness of any specific estimate. The question, answer, and discussion session continues until all pertinent information affecting the HR demand estimates has been presented to the satisfaction of the experts in attendance, or at least to the point where all positions and assumptions are clear to group members.

7. VOTE SECRETLY TO DETERMINE THE EXPERT DEMAND ASSESSMENT

A secret vote is taken, and the estimate drawing the highest ranking or number of votes from the experts is selected to be the group's HR demand estimate solution to the question posed in the first step.

◆ ◆ ◆
HR BUDGETS: STAFFING/MANNING TABLE

HR budgets are quantitative, operational, or short-run, demand estimates that contain the number and types of personnel (i.e., personnel classes, such as bank clerks, loans officers, branch managers) required by the organization as a whole and for each subunit, division, or department (see Table 6.2) (McBeath, 1992). These HR budgets are prepared by the HR staff in conjunction with line managers and take into consideration information from historical company staffing trends, competitor staffing practices, industry and professional associations, and Statistics Canada.

The HR budget process produces what is referred to as a *staffing* or *manning table*, which contains information related to a specific set of operational assumptions or levels of activity (e.g., maintain the current organization structure; increase the sales level by 5% over last year's level). The staffing/manning table presents the total HR demand requirement, as well as the number of personnel required, by level (e.g., vice-presidents) and function (e.g., marketing personnel).

In this way, HR planners can determine short-run future demand requirements for subunits and the organization as a whole. This enables budgeting processes to incorporate changes in compensation costs linked to the level of future personnel demand.

◆ ◆ ◆
ENVELOPE/SCENARIO FORECASTING

Previously, we noted that an HR budget is focused on deriving short-run operational HR demand and a staffing/manning table for each organizational department, as well as for the entire organization, assuming a specific future outcome (e.g., a constant level of sales). This constitutes a *prediction* or single estimate of future HR demand. If, however, we wish to conduct much more comprehensive future planning of operational and short-run HR demand, we should instigate *envelope/scenario forecasting*. Simply put, enve-

TABLE 6.2 STAFFING TABLE/HR BUDGET

Ennotville Eateries

Staff Demand Requirements
(Sales $ Millions)

	$1–10	>$10–25	>$25–50	>$50–75
Administrative Positions				
President	1	1	1	1
Vice-presidents	1	1	2	3
Marketing managers	1	1	2	2
Sales staff	4	7	10	18
HR staff	2	4	5	7
Treasurer	1	1	1	2
Financial staff	3	5	7	9
Clerical and general staff	5	8	12	14
Production Positions				
Executive chef	1	1	1	1
Chef	2	4	5	6
Cook	8	15	25	35
Haggis helper	10	20	30	40
Saucier	1	3	5	6

lope/scenario forecasts are projections, or multiple-predictor estimates, of future demand for personnel predicated on a variety of differing assumptions on how future organizational events will unfold (Mason, 1994; Bechet and Walker, 1993; Burack and Mathys, 1996).

> *Scenarios are developed by having brainstorming sessions with line managers and human resource managers, developing their view of the workforce five years or more in the future, and then working backwards to identify key change points. (Ward, 1996, p. 55)*

Figure 6.1 illustrates envelope/scenario forecasting.

This flexible demand forecasting process is much more useful for incorporating the effects of uncertainty and change into our strategic HR planning process than is consideration of the single assumption of an HR budget. Each of the scenarios or predicted future states contains its own set of assumptions, resulting in an entirely different estimate presented in *a single staffing/manning table for each specific course of action.* In this way, an organization's HR staff are able to develop, with the associated staffing tables, future scenarios that are optimistic (e.g., sales levels will increase by 10% to 15%), realistic or most likely (e.g., sales levels will increase by 5% to 10%), or pessimistic (e.g., sales levels will remain constant or increase by less than 5%). Furthermore, as we consider the optimistic, realistic or most likely, and

FIGURE 6.1   **Envelope/Scenario Forecasting**

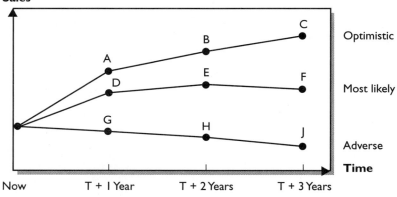

Note that A=Staffing table A; B=Staffing table B, etc.

pessimistic scenarios extended into the future, the impact of the time horizon (e.g., year 1, year 2, year 3, year 4, and year 5) forms the shape of a letter envelope. The optimistic and pessimistic scenarios, and their associated staffing tables, constitute the four corners of the envelope from the initial time period to the final time period being forecasted. Other scenarios are plotted as midpoints on the envelope. By means of this comprehensive, explicit set of staffing tables, which reflect a wide variety of future organizational circumstances, the scenario/envelope technique allows us to have ready access to flexible, preplanned demand estimates when future circumstances change in rapid fashion.

◆ ◆ ◆
REGRESSION ANALYSIS

The final demand forecasting technique to be discussed in this chapter is regression analysis (Drui, 1963). Regression/analysis is a very effective quantitative forecasting technique for short-, medium- and long-range time horizons and can be easily updated and changed (Georgoff and Murdick, 1986; Meehan and Ahmed, 1990). This section presupposes that readers possess a basic knowledge of statistical techniques as instruction in statistics is not the focus of this book. The section will enable HR practitioners to understand the essence of what regression can do for them (Tullar, 1991) but will not get involved in the mathematical derivation of the regression equation from first principles. Individuals who would like more information about such statistical methods should refer to any one of a number of high-quality statistical textbooks. Regression is such a powerful technique for forecasting demand, however, that we will present a brief and simple explanation of the underlying rationale and basic principles behind its use in HR planning.

Simply put, regression analysis presupposes that a *linear relationship* exists between one or more *causal independent variables*, which are predicted to affect the *dependent target variable*, in our instance, future HR demand for personnel (i.e., the number of personnel required). Based on logic similar to that used in trend analysis, regression projects into the future based on the past historical relationship between the independent and dependent variables. *Linearity* refers to the observed relationship between the independent and dependent variables. For example, if a per unit increase or decrease in the level of sales and the market rate of interest, respectively, result in a concurrent associated change in HR demand (the dependent variable), then the assumption of linearity might be met and regression analysis could be used for our demand forecasting. If, however, the relationship between the independent and dependent variables was random or nonlinear, the use of regression to forecast future demand would not be valid. If there are several causal or independent variables, such as the market interest rate (i.e., the cost of capital), the unemployment rate, the organization's sales level, and so on, then the analysis is referred to as a *multivariate regression analysis*. Due to the complexity of the calculations, such multiple regressions are inevitably carried out by statistical software programs such as SPSS (Statistical Program for the Social Sciences) or the SAS Programming Language. For our purposes, we will present an example of what is referred to as *simple regression:* a prediction model based on the impact on HR demand (the dependent variable) of a single causal independent variable.

SIMPLE REGRESSION PREDICTION MODEL

The simple regression prediction model is as follows:

$$Y = A + BX$$

Y = the *dependent variable* (HR demand/number of
    personnel required)
A = constant (intercept)
B = the slope of the linear relationship between X and Y
X = the *independent/causal variable* (e.g., level of sales,
    production output)

where

$$B = \frac{\Sigma XY - N(\bar{X})(\bar{Y})}{\Sigma(X^2) - N(X)}$$

$$A = \bar{Y} - B\bar{X}$$

In other words, the predicted value for HR demand (Y) will be a function of a constant starting point (A) (i.e., the value of Y when X = 0) plus the interaction between the value of the causal/independent variable (X) multiplied by a slope factor (B). Let's turn to a specific example to make sense of it all!

Regression Question

As HR planning manager for Keele Kontainers Ltd., a dynamic, fast-growing company located in Wawanesa, Manitoba, you have an important task to fulfil. To continue the company's history of successful growth, you need to forecast the number of marketing personnel required for $8 million and $10 million of sales activity. You have the following historical information available to guide your regression analysis and HR demand forecast:

X Sales Level ($ Millions)	Y Number of Marketing Personnel
2.0	20
3.5	32
4.5	42
6.0	55
7.0	66

Note that the above information represents five sets of observations for both the independent (X) and dependent (Y) variables: set 1 (2.0; 20), set 2 (3.5; 32), set 3 (4.5; 42), and so on. Record that $N =$ *the number of sets of observations*, in this instance, five.

There are five steps to conducting the regression analysis:

1. *Calculate XY, X^2, average X ($\bar{X}$), and average Y ($\bar{Y}$):* We can do this by extending the two columns shown above to a four column set. XY is simply the result of multiplying each observation set's X level by the associated Y level, and X^2 is determined by multiplying the X value by itself:

X Sales Level ($ Millions)	Y Number of Marketing Personnel	XY	X^2
2.0	20	40	4.00
3.5	32	112	12.25
4.5	42	189	20.25
6.0	55	330	36.00
7.0	66	462	49.00
23.0	215	1133	121.50

Average X or $\bar{X}$ = 23/5 = 4.6
Average Y or $\bar{Y}$ = 215/5 = 43.0
Recall N = 5, and Y = A + BX

2. *Calculate the value of B (slope of the linear relationship between X and Y):*

$$B = \frac{\Sigma XY - N(\bar{X})(\bar{Y})}{\Sigma(X^2) - N(X)}$$

Plug in the values calculated in step 1; therefore

$$B = \frac{1133 - (5)(4.6)(43)}{121.5 - (5)(4.6)}$$

$$B = \frac{1133 - 989}{121.5 - 105.8} = 9.17$$

3. *Calculate A (constant or intercept):* Recall that

$$Y = A + BX$$

Then

$$A = \bar{Y} - B\bar{X}$$

Plug in the values calculated in step one; therefore

$$A = 43 - (9.17)(4.6) = 0.82$$

4. *Determine the regression prediction equation:* We know that the general prediction model for regression is

$$Y = A + BX$$

For our specific problem, we have calculated A and B, so we insert these values into the equation, which will be used to calculate our HR demand (Y) as follows:

$$Y = 0.82 + (9.17)(X)$$

What does this mean? For our comparison between the level of sales (the independent/causal variable represented by X) and the predicted HR demand for marketing personnel (the dependent variable represented by Y), even when level of sales is at a zero level (i.e., less than \$1 million of sales), the A value (the constant/intercept) shows that we have one marketing person (0.82 of a person rounds to 1.0). Furthermore, the prediction model shows that for every one unit (\$1 million) increase in the level of sales (the independent variable X), there is a predicted increase of 9.17 marketing staff (Y) associated with that change.

5. *Calculate predicted HR demand (Y) by inserting values for X:* To predict our HR demand for marketing personnel at $8 million and $10 million of sales, as has been asked of us, we simply plug these levels into the values of X as follows:

$$\text{For \$8 million of sales } (X = 8)$$
$$Y = A + BX = 0.82 + (9.17)(8) = 74.18$$
$$\text{or 74 marketing staff are required}$$

$$\text{For \$10 million of sales } (X = 10)$$
$$Y = A + BX = 0.82 + (9.17)(10) = 92.52$$
$$\text{or 93 marketing staff are required}$$

As we can see, regression models can be extremely valuable tools for the HR planner. In our calculation of the simple regression problem above, we used five years/sets of observed historical data for our organization with respect to matching levels of sales and their relationship to levels of marketing personnel (HR demand). Most recent sales levels of $7 million of sales were associated with a marketing staff size of 66 personnel. We wish to predict into the future what our personnel requirements for $8 million and $10 million of sales will be. Our calculations of the regression equation noted that for every $1-million increase in sales, our marketing staff increased by approximately 9 (9.17) personnel, indicating the linear relationship between the two variables. Furthermore, we now know that for $8 million and $10 million of sales, we require 74 and 93 marketing staff respectively. This valuable forecasting technique enables us to plan and execute recruitment, selection, training, and development programs in a planned, proactive fashion to ensure the trained marketing staff are on hand exactly when required by the organization.

◆ ◆ ◆
SUMMARY

In this chapter we examined various techniques that are used by organizations to forecast future requirements for HR demand. We noted that index/trend analysis examines the historical relationship between workforce size and a measure of operational efficiency, such as sales, to determine the ratio between the two measures for forecasting purposes. Expert forecasts revealed that there are a number of individuals, not necessarily just those who are HR staff, who have valid information on organizational policies, procedures, and planned future changes. This information can have a dramatic impact on deriving accurate forecasts of numbers and types of employees required for the organization's workforce of the future.

With respect to experts, we saw that the Delphi technique and the nominal group technique can be used effectively to obtain demand estimates from individuals while minimizing the time wastage and interpersonal dominance that often occurs in group settings. The HR budget process produces staffing/manning tables that are concerned with short-run operational time horizons in planning HR demand. Specifically, the staffing table presents a prediction of the number of personnel required by authority or functional level, given a specific set of assumptions regarding the future organizational activity. Plotting a wide variety of possible future scenarios produces what is referred to as envelope forecasting of HR demand, in which each corner of the envelope has its own specific staffing table.

Finally, we demonstrated the tremendous usefulness of the regression analysis technique in determining future workforce requirements. Our example of simple regression revealed how this statistical technique can enable us to be proactive with respect to determining future HR requirements and planning and programming to fulfil those requirements.

We have examined specific techniques associated with the first element of HR forecasting, that is, the calculation of demand or requirement for personnel. In Chapter 7, we look at specific methods used to ascertain personnel supply. The sources of labour supply will derive from either the current organization (internal workforce) or from the external environment.

E X E R C I S E S

1. The Delphi technique and the nominal group technique are often used to facilitate creative and innovative solutions to HR demand issues. List the conditions associated with successful employment of each of these two demand forecasting techniques.

2. Index or trend analysis can be a very effective method for determining HR demand. Identify a wide variety of relevant indices that can be used for this demand forecasting technique in different organizational contexts including public nonprofit organizations, as well as in diverse industrial settings in the private sector.

3. As HR forecasting manager for the Downsview University Dating Service,

you have been faced with a tremendous increase in customer demand over the company's five years of operations. As a result, you are using regression analysis to ascertain future requirements for staff to handle customer inquiries. In particular, you need to forecast the number of customer service representatives required for 5000 and for 7000 dating contracts. The following information will help guide your regression analysis:

X Dating Contracts (Thousands)	Y Customer Service Representatives	XY	X²
1.5	9		
2.0	14		
3.0	21		
3.8	25		
4.2	27		

ENDNOTES

1. Adapted from Hughes (1995) and Cascio (1991).

References

Bechet, T.P., and J.W. Walker. 1993. "Aligning Staffing with Business Strategy." *Human Resource Planning* 16, no. 2: 1–16.

Burack, E.H., and N.J. Mathys. 1996. *Human Resource Planning: A Pragmatic Approach to Manpower Staffing and Development*, 3rd ed. Northbrook, Ill.: Brace Park.

Cascio, W.F. 1991. *Applied Psychology in Personnel Management*, 4th ed. Englewood Cliffs, N.J.: Prentice-Hall.

Delbecq, A.L., A.H. Van de Ven, and D.H. Gustafson. 1975. *Group Techniques for Program Planning.* Glenview, Ill.: Scott Foresman.

Drui, A.B. 1963. "The Use of Regression Equations to Predict Manpower Requirements." *Management Science* 9, no. 4 (July): 669–677.

Fusgeld, A.R., and R.N. Foster. 1971. "The Delphi Technique: Survey and Comment." *Business Horizons* (June).

Gatewood, R.D., and E.J. Gatewood. 1983. "The Use of Expert Data in Human Resource Planning: Guidelines from Strategic Forecasting." *Human Resource Planning* 6, no. 2 (June): 83–94.

Georgoff, D.M., and R.G. Murdick. 1986. "Manager's Guide to Forecasting." *Harvard Business Review* 64, no. 1.

Green, T.B. 1975. "An Empirical Analysis of Nominal and Interacting Groups." *Academy of Management Journal* (March): 63–73.

Hampton, D.R., C.E. Summer, and R.A. Webber. 1987. *Organizational Behavior and the Practice of Management*, 5th ed. Glenview, Ill.: Scott Foresman.

Hughes, C. 1995. "Four Steps for Accurate Call-Center Staffing." *HR Magazine* (April): 87–89.

Janis, I.L. 1972. *Victims of Groupthink.* Boston: Houghton Mifflin.

Luthans, F. 1992. *Organizational Behavior,* 6th ed. New York: McGraw Hill.

Mason, D.H. 1994. "Scenario-Based Planning: Decision Model for the Learning Organization." *Planning Review*: 6–11.

McBeath, G. 1992. *The Handbook of Human Resource Planning: Practical Manpower Analysis Techniques for HR Professionals.* Oxford: Blackwell.

McLaughlin, G. 1975. "A Professional Supply and Demand Analysis." *Educational Record* 56, no. 3 (Summer): 196–200.

Meehan, R., and B.S. Ahmed. 1990. "Forecasting Human Resources Requirements: A Demand Model." *Human Resource Planning* 13, no. 4: 297–307.

Milkovich, G., A. Annoni, and T. Mahoney. 1972. "The Use of Delphi Procedures in Manpower Forecasting." *Management Science* 19, no. 4 (December): 381–388.

Milkovich, G.T., and T.A. Mahoney. 1978. "Human Resource Planning Models: A Perspective." *Human Resource Planning* 1, no.1.

Rohrbaugh, J. 1981. "Improving the Quality of Group Judgement: Social Judgement Analysis and the Nominal Group Technique." *Organizational Behavior and Human Performance* (October): 272–288.

Schuler, R.S., and J.W. Walker. 1990. "Human Resources Strategy: Focusing on Issues and Actions." *Organizational Dynamics* (Summer): 5–19.

Tullar, W. 1991. "Theory Development in Human Resource Management." *Human Resource Management Review* 1, no. 4 (Winter): 317–323.

Van de Ven, A.H. 1974. *Group Decision-Making Effectiveness.* Kent, Ohio: Kent State University Center for Business and Economic Research Press.

Ward, D. 1996. "Workforce Demand Forecasting Techniques." *Human Resource Planning* 19, no. 1: 54–55.

7

Ascertaining HR Supply

♦ ♦ ♦
CHAPTER GOALS

n the preceding chapter, we examined a variety of methods that are used in the process of forecasting HR demand. Many of these procedures (e.g,. the Delphi technique, the nominal group technique, index/trend analysis) can also be used to determine personnel supply.

After you having finished reading this chapter, you should be able to do the following:

1. Understand the relationship between demand and supply forecasting techniques in the HR planning process.

2. Recognize the importance of the HRMS in implementing effective supply forecasting procedures.

3. Comprehend the critical relationship between supply forecasting and succession planning.

4. Discuss and evaluate the advantages and disadvantages of the following specific methods of determining external and internal supply of an organization's personnel:

    a. Skills and management inventories
    b. Succession/replacement analysis
    c. Markov models
    d. Linear programming
    e. Movement analysis
    f. Vacancy/renewal models

When considering the issue of supplying personnel to meet organizational demand, one aspect of the analysis is quite simple. Our personnel must be obtained from a source that is either *internal* (present employees) or *external* (individuals currently not employed by the organization) or, more commonly, some combination of these. Many organizations give preference to internal supply because selecting these individuals for training and development, and subsequent promotion, enables the organization to reinforce employee loyalty and performance. Other reasons for giving preferential consideration to your own workforce to fill job openings include the following: (1) your employees are already socialized to the norms, rules, and procedures of your organization, (2) employee motivation and commitment to the organization may increase when you reinforce their past loyalty and performance, and (3) you possess knowledge (e.g., HRMS files) on their performance and KSAs (e.g., work history and experience). We now turn our attention to this latter point concerning organizational databases on current workforce members, namely, skills and management inventories.

◆ ◆ ◆
SKILLS AND MANAGEMENT INVENTORIES

A good first step in the supply analysis is an examination of the number and capabilities of our present employees. Individual records on the HRMS database are called inventories, of which there are two types, skills inventories and management inventories (Martin, 1967; Kaumeyer, 1979). A *skills inventory* is an individualized personnel record held on each employee except those currently in management or professional positions. Typically, a skills inventory contains information for each individual on the following areas: (1) personal information (e.g., name, employee number, job classification and compensation band, emergency notification, and telephone number), (2) education, training, and skill competencies (e.g., certificates, licences, and diplomas or degrees completed, including the area of specialization, dates of attendance, and names of the institutions attended), (3) work history (e.g., date of hire, seniority, current job and supervisor, and previous jobs held in the organization and the dates associated with them), (4) performance appraisals (i.e., a numerical score of the employee's history of performance in jobs in the organization), (5) career information (e.g., future jobs desired by employee and those recommended by supervisors), and (6) hobbies and interests (including community and volunteer associations) (Martin, 1967; Seamans, 1978). This skills inventory record is entered into the HRMS database and can be searched when we are looking for people with the skills and competencies required by a specific job. For this reason, skills inventories must be kept current, and employees should be given frequent opportunities to update or correct their personal entries; otherwise, an employee may not be considered for a job that he or she could fill successfully.

Management inventories can be considered to be enhanced skills inventories because they contain all the above information and the following: (1) a history of management or professional jobs held, (2) a record of management/professional training courses and their dates of completion, (3) key accountabilities for the current job (i.e., organizational resources, including the size of the budget controlled, the number of subordinates, important organizational outcomes for which the incumbent is primarily responsible), (4) assessment centre and appraisal data, and (5) professional and industry association memberships. Only when an organization has a properly functioning HRMS, complete with the skills and management inventories described above, is it really able to assess correctly the numbers and competency levels of its current workforce. In this way, HR planners can determine the organization's workforce strengths and weaknesses and plan training and development courses accordingly, while noting which job openings must be filled from external sources because current employees lack the skill competencies required.

◆ ◆ ◆
SUCCESSION/REPLACEMENT ANALYSIS

Succession planning for key organizational positions is critical to effective organizational functioning (Cooke, 1995). There are two aspects to succession planning: (1) *long-term succession*, which is a process of training and work experience to enable individuals to assume higher-level job appointments in the future and (2) *short-term emergency replacement* of individuals who have quit, been terminated due to performance problems, have died, and so on. Succession planning can help the organization be more effective in filling vacant positions.

There are several reasons why succession planning is critical for effective HR planning:[1]

1. Succession planning enables an organization to respond appropriately and stay on track when inevitable and unpredictable changes occur. It provides for continuity and future direction even in the turmoil of change.

2. It helps develop people as they prepare for new experiences and jobs, and this development can also help improve their performance in present positions.

3. When succession planning takes into account employees' performance and promotes them for it, employees are positively motivated.

4. It supports new organizational structures and flexibility by explicitly providing backups to various positions, thereby reducing organizational dependency on any one employee.

5. It saves time and money by having plans already in place to enable smooth internal employee movement and continuity, and therefore external hiring is an exception to the process.

It should come as no great surprise that the skills and management inventories described in the previous section are extremely useful information for succession and replacement planning. Furthermore, they are important for matching an individual's qualifications to the requirements of a specific job in the organization (e.g., those needed by the HR planning manager) and for identifying possible successors for specific positions. The key requirement for succession and replacement planning to function effectively is that supervisors, in conjunction with the HR staff, must develop *succession/replacement charts* and *tables* for key executive, managerial, and professional jobs in the organization (see Tables 7.1 and 7.2). The information that fuels this process is derived not only from current managerial assessments of subordinates, but also from information contained in the inventories con-

---

BOX 7.1 TAKE STEPS TO KEEP BUSINESS ALL IN THE FAMILY

A study by Deloitte & Touche states that the majority of Canada's family businesses are facing a leadership crisis due to a lack of succession planning. John Bowey, a Deloitte & Touche partner, states that family businesses in Canada account for 4.7 million full-time jobs, 1.3 million part-time jobs, and $1.3 trillion dollars in annual sales. Furthermore, customers often prefer these businesses due to the personal contact and perceived high standards of credibility and quality. However, a full 75 percent of family business owners believe that the future success of their business depends wholly on them, reflecting a failure to develop future leaders and a neglect of the succession/replacement planning process. Almost half (44%) of these same business owners doubt their businesses will survive once they bow out of the operations. To cast further dire light on the situation, 27 percent of the family business owners plan to retire within five years, a further 29 percent in six to ten years, and 22 percent in eleven to fifteen years.

Adapted from: Harvey, I. 1999. "Be Careful to Keep Biz All in the Family." *Toronto Sun* (January 19): 27.

cerning education, training, and skills, as well as historical records of each potential successor's performance appraisals. Obviously, given the large amount of personal information used and the sensitive nature of the information, succession planning documents are highly confidential. Access to the succession/replacement charts and tables, and to their supporting documentation, must be strictly controlled and limited on a "need-to-know" basis to such people as the CEO, vice-president of HR, HR planning staff, and divisional executives. Access by the latter should be restricted solely to their own area of responsibility (Cooke, 1995). Although a manager should naturally consider his or her current subordinates in the process of developing succession plans, the skills and management inventories are important to ensure that other employees who have been transferred, seconded to other divisions, or are working in areas different from those for which they received functional training will not be overlooked. In fact, such employees will be identified by the search capabilities of the HRMS.

The first type of document used in succession planning is referred to as a succession/replacement chart. As you will notice from Table 7.1, it closely

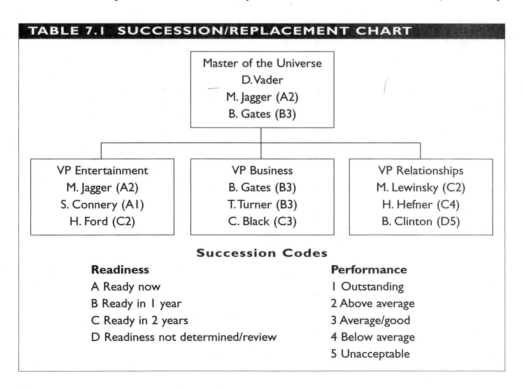

TABLE 7.1 SUCCESSION/REPLACEMENT CHART

Master of the Universe
D. Vader
M. Jagger (A2)
B. Gates (B3)

VP Entertainment	VP Business	VP Relationships
M. Jagger (A2)	B. Gates (B3)	M. Lewinsky (C2)
S. Connery (A1)	T. Turner (B3)	H. Hefner (C4)
H. Ford (C2)	C. Black (C3)	B. Clinton (D5)

Succession Codes

Readiness

A Ready now
B Ready in 1 year
C Ready in 2 years
D Readiness not determined/review

Performance

1 Outstanding
2 Above average
3 Average/good
4 Below average
5 Unacceptable

resembles a typical organizational chart in that it represents the organizational hierarchy and the key jobs with their inherent reporting relationships. However, on closer inspection, the succession/replacement chart provides more detailed information on each job, specifically, the name of the current job incumbent and a short list (determined by managers in conjunction with the HR staff) of the top internal candidates who might replace the incumbent if he or she left the job.

An important aspect of the succession/replacement chart is the *succession readiness code*, which is listed next to the names of all employees. This code contains two elements of information essential for succession planning: (1) the employee's level of performance in the current job (e.g., represented by a value on a five-point scale ranging from 1 to 5, where 1 = outstanding and 5 = unacceptable) and (2) the employee's readiness for movement or promotion (e.g., A = ready now, B = probably ready within 1 year, C = needs development [i.e., probably ready in 2 years], D = not suitable for this job). By including the two elements of the succession code next to the name of each employee on the succession chart (e.g., Mary Bloggins B2), we are able to get an accurate, although admittedly incomplete, picture of the state of succession readiness for each department and for the entire organization.

Although we will have to refer back to specific inventories, performance appraisal records, and assessment centre reports to get further information on potential successors, the key benefit of a succession/replacement chart is that it allows us to identify what are referred to as *ripple* or *chain effects*: one promotion in the organization can cause several movements in the organization as a series of subordinates are promoted to fill the sequential openings (White, 1970b). This is referred to as a ripple effect, as it is similar to the effect that a fish jumping out of the water in one part of a lake has on other remote bays of the same lake—the waves ripple away from the site of the original movement. The chain metaphor is also appropriate because the departure of a high-level employee (e.g., through retirement or termination) causes a series of successors each to move up one link (i.e., by being promoted) in the organization's hierarchical chain. Therefore, use of the succession/replacement chart, with its graphic illustration of ripple or chain effects, allows us to determine HR blockages or problem areas (Foot and Venne, 1990). For example, the organization may not be able to immediately promote a top performing potential successor to a particular jobholder because no subordinates to the potential successor are trained and ready to

BOX 7.2 CAR DEALERS STEER CLEAR OF SUCCESSION

According to a survey by Coopers & Lybrand and DesRosiers Automotive Consultants Inc., a great many of Canada's more than 3400 new car retailers/dealerships have a looming succession problem. The study found that more than 80 percent of dealers plan to retire or be semiretired within ten years. Yet almost half of the dealers who responded to the survey did not have a succession plan, including a full third of those older than 55 years of age. Approximately 70 percent of dealers would like to keep their dealerships within their families, but less than half (44%) think that will actually happen. Dealers are facing this succession problem due to their short-run orientation on selling cars today, without considering the costs and implications of not planning for the future.

Adapted from: Keenan G. 1998. "Car Dealers Steer Clear of Succession." *Globe and Mail* (June 16): B14.

replace him or her. The successor who was rated second, who has ensured that his or her departmental subordinates have been properly trained by being exposed to increasingly more challenging job assignments and thereby are ready to be promoted themselves, may be chosen by the organization to replace the jobholder who is leaving.

The second document that is produced for succession/replacement planning is referred to as a succession/replacement table (see Table 7.2). We have seen how the succession/replacement chart gives an important yet incomplete pictorial representation of the state of succession readiness throughout a department or the entire organization. The succession/replacement table complements the succession/replacement chart in that it provides additional information on each specific job, the incumbent jobholder, and all potential internal successors.

A succession/replacement table is prepared for each key job in the organization. In considering a replacement for the HR planning manager, for example, although the succession/replacement chart provides us with the top two or three candidates and their succession codes, all it may indicate is that promoting any of these individuals may be problematic for a variety of reasons (e.g., because of their performance or lack of training). By turning to the succession/replacement table, we get a list of *all* potential internal successors, not just the short list or top three individuals, as well as a very detailed information code for each candidate. Typically, a series of alphanumerical code combinations will provide us with important information not presented on the succession/replacement chart due to space limitations. Succession/replacement table codes summarize information on personal

TABLE 7.2 SUCCESSION/REPLACEMENT TABLE

Keith Kiltmakers
Chief Executive Officer (Position A11)

Incumbent	Employee Number	Current Appointment and Tenure[a]	Expected Date of Movement
Robert James	060422	CEO	06 April 2004

Potential Successor			Succession Codes
June Catharine	070121	VP Operations (A21)/61	T, O, P
Roderick Alexander	010753	VP Legal (B24)/52	A, T, B, O, Y
Kenneth James	010956	VP HR (D19)/48	D, O, G
Donald Martin	290959	VP Systems (C24)/16	J, N, R

[a]The tenure of the current appointment is listed in number of months duration.

career and training preferences, long-run historical data on performance appraisal, family and geographical posting preferences, and so on, all of which may affect movement or promotion and are not included on the succession/replacement chart.

The succession/replacement tables and charts are very useful tools for HR planners analyzing the state of the current workforce. Once we have used these two instruments of succession/replacement analysis, other details concerning specific job blockages or problems with our current internal workforce and the resultant requirement to process new hires from external sources become much more clear (Foot and Venne, 1990). We may find that a perceived shortage of labour is the result of specific personnel policies concerning how we use our workforce and is not due to any shortage in the actual number of workers (Lewin and Keith, 1976). Chapter 9 contains further detailed information on succession planning.

◆ ◆ ◆

MARKOV MODELS

Markov models are the most popular technique used for contemporary supply-side HR planning applications (Bechet and Maki, 1987; Konda and Stewman, 1980; Weigel and Wilcox, 1993). These models are widely used in both educational and personnel planning processes (Bartholomew, 1973; Law, 1977). Furthermore, they have been found to be more accurate than regression models when used in HR planning systems (Venezia and Shapira, 1978). Markov models, also referred to as *probabilistic* (using probabilities of various movement options) or *stochastic models* (Meehan and Ahmed, 1990), determine the pattern of employee movement throughout an organization's system of jobs (Heneman and Sandiver, 1977; Vassiliou, 1976). Markov analysis produces a series of matrices that detail the various patterns of movement to and from the wide variety of jobs in the organization. When considering employee movement patterns in the organization, there are five possible options for an employee: (1) remaining in the current job , (2) promotion to a higher classified job, (3) a lateral transfer to a job with a similar classification level, (4) exit from the job (e.g., termination, layoff, voluntary leaving by the employee), and (5) demotion (which is relatively rare) (Bechet and Maki, 1987). Probabilistic or Markov models do not examine individual employees but instead examine overall rates of movement between various job levels, and this movement between jobs is based on historical movement patterns (Blakely, 1970). It is normally assumed, for calculation purposes, that the pattern of employee movement is relatively stable over time. If this is not the case, then adjustments have to be made to the historical data to allow it to be used for HR planning in the present day. However, it is important to note that Markov techniques depend on stable transition probabilities, so dynamic and unstable environmental scenarios may preclude the effective usage of Markov models (Stone and Fiorito, 1986).

There are three main steps to using a Markov model for HR planning purposes (Zeffane and Mayo, 1995). First, we must collect historical data on mobility rates between jobs in the organization. Second, based on this data we develop matrices to forecast future personnel movement between jobs. Third, we use the forecasts of the model to analyze our HR policies and programs and instigate the necessary adaptive measures (Zeffane and Mayo, 1995).

By using employee movement data from the past five years or so, we are able to calculate *transitional probabilities*, or the likelihood that an individual in a specific job will exhibit one of the five aforementioned movement behaviours, normally one year into the future. By multiplying the total number of employees or positions in a particular job (e.g., eighteen managers) by the associated probabilities for each of the five possible movement scenarios, the HR planner derives numerical data on employee flow patterns throughout the organization, and between various job levels (see Table 7.3).

TABLE 7.3 MARKOV MODEL

Ottermere Outbound Adventures

		Year 2002[b]			
		Chief Outfitter	Outfitter	Guide	Exit
Year 2001[a]	Chief Outfitter (n=4)	3 (.75)	—	—	1 (.25)
	Outfitter (n=12)	1 (.08)[c]	9 (.75)[a]	—	2 (.17)[c]
	Guide (n=16)	—	3 (.19)	9 (.56)	4 (.25)
	Supply=32	*4*	*12*	*9*	*7*

[a] The current year is shown on the vertical axis.

[b] The future year is shown on the horizontal axis.

[c] The probabilities of movement (percentages) are expressed horizontally and sum to 1 (100%).

The sequences of movements between various job states are referred to as *Markov chains* (Neilsen and Young, 1973). Detailed examination of the Markov model enables us to determine the number of external recruits required at various levels of the organizational hierarchy to fill openings caused by turnover, termination, promotion, and so on. Furthermore, we earlier made reference to blockages or problems in succession planning, and these problems become readily apparent when we use this supply model based on historical trends of movement probability. The Markov model enables us to determine the specific number of replacements/successors required for any job family annually, as well as for specified future planning periods (based on normal attrition assumptions), and this can help us to be more proactive in our external recruitment programs. Additionally, we can calculate the chain of movement from an entry-level job all the way to the CEO appointment, along with forecast times of arrival, stay, and departure, in conjunction with breaks in career progression along the way. In fact, White (1970 a,b) refers to the length of a vacancy chain as its *multiplier effect*, and his study of U.S. churches showed that for any one retiring minister, a chain of movement for five subsequent ministers was created (White, 1970a). The length of an average chain is approximately three (Stone and Fiorito, 1986).

Apart from its obvious appeal for the career planning of individuals who have upward aspirations in the organization (Gridley, 1986), we can use the derived information to plan when training and development courses, job rotations, and so on should be conducted for a specific group of employees, based on predicted time to move from their present jobs to target jobs several levels higher in the organization's hierarchy (Sandefur, 1981; Bartholomew, 1996). Therefore, the use of a Markov model has great value for determining (1) the number of personnel who move annually, and over specified time periods, between various job levels; (2) the number of external hires that are required by the organization, and the specific jobs where they are needed; (3) the movement patterns and expected duration in specified jobs associated with patterns of career progression for employees in the organization (i.e., career paths) (Tuma, 1976); and (4) the number and percentage of all starters at a particular job level who will successfully attain a future target job level by a specified time period (Rowland and Sovereign, 1969; Glen, 1977). All of this information provides us with important insights in calculating the most appropriate balance between training and promoting internal employees on the one hand, and external recruiting on the other. All in all, the Markov model is a very useful tool for analyzing HR supply.

BOX 7.3 MANAGING THE FIRM'S INTERNAL LABOUR MARKET: LESSONS FROM THE FIELD

Professors at Simon Fraser University's Faculty of Business Administration have uncovered four lessons in properly using internal labour markets to supply the organization's staffing requirements based on their study of a large manufacturing firm. The lessons are:

1. Managers should recognize that there are often *multiple internal labour markets* typically operating in one firm.
2. Managers should conceptualize their staffing task as managing a system of human resource *flows*.
3. Managers need to develop an appreciation for the *temporal and situational contexts* within which staffing decisions are made.
4. Staffing decisions themselves can be appropriately viewed as garbage-can models in which *multiple issues* and *multiple criteria* are typically invoked in matching individuals and jobs.

Adapted from: Pinfield, L., and V. Bushe. 1992. "Managing the Firm's Internal Labour Market: Lessons from the Field." Burnaby, B.C.: Faculty of Business Administration, Simon Fraser University. Paper presented at the Western Academy of Management Annual Meeting, Spokane (April).

◆ ◆ ◆
LINEAR PROGRAMMING

Linear programming is a mathematical procedure commonly used for project analysis in engineering and business applications. It has utility for HR planners because it allows us to determine the future supply of personnel based on achieving the best staffing outcome while minimizing constraints such as labour costs (Weigel and Wilcox, 1993). Furthermore, conditions such as desired staffing ratios (e.g., the internal/external mix of employees) can be programmed into the equation for determining HR supply. The optimum or best supply mix solution is provided by the model, and the best conditions obviously vary among organizations (Patz, 1970). Some companies may seek to minimize turnover or total labour costs, while others may seek to achieve an optimum level of staffing with respect to designated groups (e.g., visible minorities, women, aboriginal people, people with disabilities) in all job levels throughout the organization (Walker, 1980). By providing the level of personnel supply that is best with respect to explicitly defined constraints or criteria, linear programming enables us to calculate "what if" scenarios by changing or relaxing various model assumptions in order to determine the impact these changes will have on final numerical requirements for supply, both internal and external. To use linear programming, our assumptions must be similar to those used in regression analysis (discussed in Chapter 6), namely, that the mathematical model must contain variables that have *linear relationships* among the various constituent elements. If this situation does not hold, then we have to employ nonlinear or quadratic programming techniques to determine supply requirements. As linear programming is a relatively complex mathematical procedure normally performed on a computer, a detailed presentation on this technique is beyond the scope of this book. For further information, see the References section.

◆ ◆ ◆
MOVEMENT ANALYSIS

Movement analysis is a technique used to analyze personnel supply, specifically the chain or ripple effect that promotions or job losses have on the movements of other personnel in an organization (Bartholomew, 1982; Bartholomew, 1996; Burack and Mathys, 1996; White, 1970). Specifically, we are able to identify the total number of vacant or open positions in the organization or department, as well as the total number of personnel movements that are caused by replacing and filling these vacant positions. The total numbers of personnel movements are always greater than or equal to the number of vacant positions to be filled. If we rely solely on external personnel, the number of vacant positions to be filled is exactly equal to the number of new hires obtained by the organization, as there are no internal promotions of current employees to replace the losses. Conversely, if we rely heavily on current employees (i.e., internal supply) to fill position openings, then the total number of personnel movements will be greatly in excess of the number of open positions because any one opening (e.g., due to a promotion or termination) will result in a whole chain of subordinates sequentially moving up one authority level to fill the gaps (White, 1970). Movement analysis enables the HR planner to select the desired mix or percentage of internal/external supply for those positions requiring replacements, ranging from a promote from within policy to the other extreme of replacing losses entirely through hiring personnel from outside the organization.

Movement analysis can be performed for the organization as a whole, although analysts normally find it more useful to conduct separate analyses for each department, division, or functional area (Monks, 1996). The normal planning time horizon is one year, and we start by identifying the number of personnel in each authority or compensation band level at the start of the forecasting period. Next, we consider changes in the level of staffing for the department, that is, whether we are going to increase the number of jobs in some or all authority levels or downsize to reduce the total number of employees in the department. Having increased or decreased the personnel requirement from that which was was forecast at the start of the period, we now turn to calculating the losses requiring replacement for each authority level of the department. We are interested only in losses (e.g., because of promotions, transfers out of the department, voluntary turnover, termination) that need to be *replaced;* therefore, it is important that we not "double-count" positions that have already been incorporated into the staffing changes column! Changes in staffing level are added to personnel losses requiring replacement to give us the total number of positions requiring replacement. At this stage, having determined the total number of positions to be filled, the actual number of personnel movements, as briefly described previously, can vary widely depending on our organization or department's desired policy concerning the supply mix of internal and external replacements. To demonstrate, we now turn to a practical example of a movement analysis.

MOVEMENT ANALYSIS QUESTION

As HR forecasting manager of Keele Kontainers Ltd., your focus of interest is the organization's finance department. You wish to determine (a) the total number of positions requiring replacements over the next one-year period, and, equally important, (b) the impact these openings will have on the current employees' movements throughout the department. Keele Kontainers has a policy of "promote from within" for all authority levels above the basic entry level (level 9), which obviously must be filled externally with new recruits. The finance department does not have any personnel in authority levels 1 to 3 inclusive (i.e., president, senior vice-president, vice-president); the senior appointment is a level 4 (senior manager) position. Based on historical trends and information provided by the strategic planning cell, you know the following:

1. A 5 percent staffing (position) increase for each of authority levels 6 to 9 inclusive will be required to meet additional financial processing activity in the department; one additional senior manager (level 4) will be required, as management wants one senior manager to handle financial forecasting while one senior manager is responsible for financial claims (i.e., current operations); six additional managers (level 5) will be required to supervise the financial analysts and clerks (i.e., the increases in levels 6 to 9 mentioned above) added over the course of the year.

2. Historical annual loss rates include the following:

   a. Retirements (requiring replacements): 2 positions for level 5, 15% of current positions for levels 6 to 9 inclusive

   b. Turnover = resignations (voluntary) + terminations (involuntary):

      Levels 5 and 6 = 10% of positions at start of period

      Level 7 = 15% of positions at start of period

      Level 8 = 20% of positions at start of period

      Level 9 = 25% of positions at start of period

   Note: The loss rates can be grouped into one column or broken into individual components (e.g., terminations, retirements).

3. The number of personnel/positions at the start of the year are as follows:

   Level 4 (senior manager) = 1

   Level 5 (manager) = 6

Level 6 (senior analyst) = 20

Level 7 (analyst) = 32

Level 8 (clerk) = 40

Level 9 (clerical assistant) = 50

In calculating our movement analysis, we construct two separate tables: the first determines the total number of positions to be filled, while the second identifies the internal/external personnel movements required to fill the open positions identified. When conducting a movement analysis, there are two basic rules to follow:

1. Work from the top down: Start at the highest authority or hierarchy level in the organization, since normal personnel movement in organizations is upward as people are promoted to replace higher level losses.

2. Calculate the movement figures for one authority or compensation level at a time.

Let's construct a movement analysis table, shown in Table 7.4, and use historical information to calculate position replacement requirements or positions to be filled.

By using historical information, we are able to determine that the finance department, with 149 positions at the start of the year, requires 68 positions to be filled over the year. These positions are needed because of a planned staffing increase of 15 positions and because 53 individuals are required to replace personnel losses (i.e., losses due to retirements, resigna-

TABLE 7.4 NUMBER OF POSITIONS TO BE FILLED

Authority Level	Number of Positions at Start of Period	Staffing Changes		Personnel Losses		Positions to Be Filled
4	1	1	+	0	=	1
5	6	6		3		9
6	20	1		5		6
7	32	2		10		12
8	40	2		14		16
9	50	3		21		24
	149	15		53		68

Source: Adapted from Burack, E.H., and N.J. Mathys. 1996. *Human Resource Planning: A Pragmatic Approach to Manpower Staffing and Development*, 3rd ed. Northbrook, Ill.: Brace Park.

tions, and terminations). The calculations to arrive at these numbers are straightforward. For example, the increased staffing requirement for level 7 is determined by multiplying the original number of positions at that level by the percentage increase (i.e., $32 \times 0.05 = 1.6$ positions), and since we don't normally hire fractions of people, the requirement is for two new positions! Similarly, total personnel losses for level 8 consist of fourteen positions, which is the sum of six retirements (i.e., 40 starting positions times 15%) plus eight turnover losses (i.e., 40 starting positions times 20%).

Starting with the "Positions to Be Filled" column from Table 7.4, we construct a second table, Table 7.5, that reveals the employee movement at all levels of the finance department caused by promotions to fill the identified vacancies.

What does this all mean? Overall, to fill the 68 positions that require replacements over the next year, a total of 167 movements will occur in the finance department due to the ripple or chain effect on promotions. In Table 7.5, note that for level 5, although we start off with having to find replacements for nine open positions, we also have to promote one individual from level 5 to fill the requirement for an additional senior manager at level 4. Therefore, the total number of individual movements at level 5 is ten although only nine open positions had to be filled at that level. Similarly, at level 6, in addition to having to fill six open positions, we also have to promote nine individuals to fill the openings one level higher at level 5, and one individual must be promoted to replace the level 5 individual who was promoted to level 4. Although there were only six open positions at level 6, the

TABLE 7.5 PERSONNEL MOVEMENT

Positions to Be Filled	Ripple or Chain Movement						Total Personnel Movement
1	–	–	–	–	–		1
9 +	1	–	–	–	–	=	10
6 +	1 +	9	–	–	–	=	16
12 +	1 +	9 +	6	–	–	=	28
16 +	1 +	9 +	6 +	12	–	=	44
24 +	1 +	9 +	6 +	12 +	16	=	68
68	5	36	18	24	16	=	167

Source: Adapted from Burack, E.H., and N.J. Mathys. 1996. *Human Resource Planning: A Pragmatic Approach to Manpower Staffing and Development*, 3rd ed. Northbrook, Ill.: Brace Park.

ripple or chain effect of sequential movement means that sixteen individuals had to move to fill the organizational job openings. Furthermore, our assumption that we promote from within means that all 68 new hires originate from outside (i.e., from an external supply) at the entry level of clerical assistant (level 9). All other vacancies are filled by upward movement of current employees. Additionally, 99 promotions occur for current employees (i.e., internal supply) as is reflected in the ripple or chain effect matrix (i.e., 99 promotions = 5 + 36 + 18 + 24 + 16). In other words, movement analysis has allowed us to identify that for this year's need to fill 68 position vacancies, a total of 167 individual moves will be required due to extensive promotion from within. If we were to balance external and internal supply, the only adjustment would be that fewer individuals would be promoted from within the organization. This would lead to a decrease in the individual moves to a number closer to the number of open positions to be filled.

◆ ◆ ◆
VACANCY MODEL

The vacancy model, sometimes referred to as a renewal or sequencing model, analyzes flows of personnel throughout the organization by examining inputs and outputs at each authority or compensation level (White, 1970a,b;

BOX 7.4 HELP WANTED

Matrox Electronic Systems Ltd. is one of Montreal's high tech success stories, yet its staffing shortages are preventing it from achieving full performance potential. With 1997 revenues of almost $1 billion, and revenue growth of more than 800 percent in just three years, Matrox is poised for future success with its video imaging and graphics products, yet it can't attract enough trained engineers to work in Quebec. Although Matrox hired 300 people last year for a total of 1440 worldwide, that figure is well short of demand requirements, and president Lorne Trottier would hire 30 engineers on the spot if they were available. In addition to high worldwide demand for high tech engineering and systems staff, Trottier blames the Parti Québécois government's language policies and a high personal income tax rate as major causal factors in his company's labour shortage. "There's a lot of things about Montreal that don't appeal to outsiders. There's the political climate. There's the tax climate. There's the climate in the original sense of the word. That makes a lot of negative factors. So there's very little talent that we've been able to bring in from the outside. The problem is likely to get worse before it gets better."

Adapted from: Millan, L. 1998. "Help Wanting." *Canadian Business* (August 14): 72–75.

Bartholomew, 1982, 1996). Vacancy models have been found to have more predictive capacity than Markov models over short- and long-term periods (of three, five, and ten years) (Konda and Stewman, 1980), although the common time frame for this model is one year into the future. It is important that we always calculate our personnel supply requirements one level at a time in a "top down" fashion, beginning at the highest relevant authority level, because the normal direction of personnel movement in the organization is from the bottom to the top. In other words, vacancies at the top are often filled by promoting individuals from lower organizational levels. The underlying rationale behind the vacancy model is simple. Our need for personnel must be met either by external recruiting or by internal promotions of current employees or by some combination of the two. More specifically, the supply needs of each salary level are determined by staffing changes—the number of personnel who are promoted away from the level—and personnel losses (e.g., retirements, departures, terminations).

Organizational policy will determine the extent to which these openings will be filled by internal and external supply. Personnel losses are normally based on historical trends with respect to the percentage of personnel at each level who normally exit from that level annually, while growth estimates are based on the normal business forecasting process. Overall, vacancies in the organization lead to a sequence of internal promotions from lower levels as the open positions are filled by the replacement personnel. The model identifies the specific number of external and internal personnel required at each level and for the organization as a whole. We now turn to an illustrative example of the vacancy model.

VACANCY MODEL QUESTION

Steeles Sinsational Snacks Ltd. offers high-quality, low-cost snacks and meals to budget-conscious students at Moosehead University. Based on the following information, calculate the company's vacancy model for next year's HR supply forecast.

1. Staffing changes: None (i.e., stable size)
2. Personnel losses during the year:

    Level 1 (president)   = 100% (compulsory retirement)
    Level 2 (vice-presidents) = 15%
    Level 3 (managers)   = 17%

Level 4 (team leaders)　　= 20%

Level 5 (associates)　　　= 25%

Level 6 (trainees)　　　　= 50%

3. Personnel replacement policy (% external supply:%internal supply)

Level	% external hiring	% internal promotion
Level 1	0	100
Level 2	10	90
Level 3	20	80
Level 4	30	70
Level 5	55	45
Level 6	100	0

Remember that the key to successful completion of the model is to start your calculations at the top of the organization and work down one level at a time! So let's start our analysis at level 1, the position of the president:

Level	No. of Personnel at Start of Year	Annual Losses	Promotions to Level	Level Outflows	External Hiring
1	1	1	1	1	0

The president of Steeles will be retiring this year, so there will be an annual loss of one person. The company's personnel replacement policy states that for the president's job (level 1), all (100% of) loss replacements will come from internal promotions, in this case, from level 2 below. Therefore, there is one promotion to level 1 (from level 2) with no external hires, and annual losses are exactly equal to outflow at that level. Now consider the situation for level 2:

Level	No. of Personnel at Start of Year	Annual Losses	Promotions to Level	Level Outflows	External Hiring
1	1	1	1	1	0
2	6	1	2	2	0

Having completed level 1, we now calculate the personnel flows one level lower in the organization's authority or compensation system. For level 2, the annual losses are one, consisting of the number of personnel at that level at the start of the year multiplied by the historical loss rate (i.e., 6 × 0.15 = 0.9, rounded to one person). Next, it is crucial to note that the outflows from level 2 are not the same as losses because we must take losses due to termination, retirement, and so on of one person and add to that the one individual who was promoted to level 1 to replace the retiring president. Therefore, our total personnel outflows from level 2 are two people. Total outflows from any organizational level are equal to losses at that level plus promotions to higher levels.

Now we refer to the company's personnel replacement policy, which dictates that we are required to replace the two personnel who left level 2 by 10 percent external hires and 90 percent internal promotions. Naturally, we do not deal in fractions of people, so $2 \times 0.9 = 1.8$, which is rounded to two persons. Both replacements are promoted from level 3, and we do not hire any individuals externally for the level 2 losses. The analysis continues in a like manner until all organizational levels have been completed. The finished vacancy model is as follows:

Level	No. of Personnel at Start of Year	Annual Losses	Promotions to Level	Level Outflows	External Hiring
1	1	1	1	1	0
2	6	1	2	2	0
3	18	3	4	5	1
4	45	9	9	13	4
5	88	22	14	31	17
6	156	78	0	92	92
	314	114	30	144	114

In this instance, our vacancy model meets the specified requirement of a stable workforce size (i.e., no growth) as annual personnel losses of 114 are exactly replaced by 114 new hires from outside the organization. Furthermore, we know that in addition to the 114 annual losses (from a stable organizational workforce of 314), there are 144 total personnel movements, consisting of 114 new hires from external supply sources and 30 internal promotions across all levels. If instead of a no-growth scenario we predict a staffing increase or decrease, the above table is merely revised with the growth percentages (e.g., 5% at level 3, 8% at level 5) multiplied by the original number of personnel in each level to arrive at a column containing the revised (increased or decreased) number of personnel. This adjusted number of personnel is then used as the base point for calculating losses, promotions, and other flows from and to each authority level in the organization. Given the vacancy model information, it is possible to calculate the promotion rate (sometimes called the "upward mobility rate") for each authority level in the organization. For example, the promotion rate for level 4 is 8.8 percent, which is obtained by dividing 4 (the four people who were promoted to level 3) by 45 (the total number of personnel who are in level 4). As we can see, the vacancy model is a very useful tool for ascertaining specific personnel supply requirements for internal promotions of current employees, as well as for specifying the exact number of external new hires required at each level of the organization.

◆ ◆ ◆
SUMMARY

This chapter presented six models or techniques used by organizations to determine future HR supply requirements. Skills and management inventories contain information that enables a detailed analysis of the present workforce to determine whether we can meet the demand for personnel replacement from current employees in the organization. Succession/replacement analysis expands on the inventories approach by using succession/replacement charts and tables to identify specific replacements for key organizational jobs and to examine whether problem areas or blockages would occur if specified individuals were to be promoted or transferred. The Markov model uses historical patterns of individual movement between jobs in the organization and attaches transitional probabilities for promotion, transfer, and remaining in the particular job for an annual or specified future period. In this way, we are able to derive exact numbers of open positions throughout the organization and can track career progression and the time required for individuals to reach specified target jobs. Linear programming uses mathematical equations to determine the optimal or best mix of personnel supply given specified constraints, such as minimizing labour cost or achieving a desired mix of diverse employee group memberships. Movement analysis enables us to identify not only the location and number of open positions that must be filled by the organization, but also the total number of individuals who will be moved to fill these openings. Finally, the vacancy model provides specific information on total personnel flows into and out of each authority or compensation level, as well as for the organization as a whole. Accordingly, we are able to calculate the exact numbers of internal promotions and external recruits that will be required by the organization. Our presentation now turns to the topic of managing a diverse workforce and its relationship to HR planning.

EXERCISES

1. A Markov model provides important information to the HR supply analyst with respect to movement or flows of personnel through various jobs in the organization. Discuss how this supply forecasting technique could also provide useful information to rank and file members (i.e., non-HR staff) of the organization's workforce?

2. Movement analysis analyzes the ripple effects or workforce movements resulting from various supply policy options selected by the organization. Discuss the varying implications of using internal sources of labour (i.e., the current workforce) versus external sources of labour (i.e., recruits) for the supply needs of an organization. What are the advantages, disadvantages, costs, and benefits associated with the different options?

3. Dave's Dumpsters offers a low-cost disposal system for the high-quality campus food served at Moosehead University, as well as for many other institutions of higher learning. The company has retained your services on a lucrative contract to calculate the vacancy model for next year's HR forecast, based on the following assumptions:

A. Workforce complement at beginning of period (i.e., before staffing changes):
Salary level 1 = 1
Salary level 2 = 4
Salary level 3 = 18
Salary level 4 = 40
Salary level 5 = 75
Salary level 6 = 136

B. Organizational growth: 5% increase in each salary level with the exception of salary level 1 (CEO), which remains at one position.

C. HR losses during year:
Salary level 1 = 100%
Salary level 2 = 20%
Salary level 3 = 22%
Salary level 4 = 25%
Salary level 5 = 30%
Salary level 6 = 50%

D. HR supply policy:

	Outside %	Inside %
Salary level 1	0	100
Salary level 2	10	90
Salary level 3	20	80
Salary level 4	30	70
Salary level 5	50	50
Salary level 6	100	0

ENDNOTE

1. Adapted from Cooke (1995).

References

Bartholomew, D. 1996. *Mobility Measurement Revisited in the Statistical Approach to Social Measurement.* San Diego: Academic Press.

Bartholomew, D.J. 1982. *Stochastic Models for the Social Sciences*, 3rd ed. New York: John Wiley.

____. 1973. *Stochastic Models for the Social Sciences.* London: Wiley.

Bechet, T.P., and W.R. Maki. 1987. "Modeling and Forecasting: Focusing on People as a Strategic Resource." *Human Resource Planning* 10, no. 4: 209–217.

Blakely, R. 1970. "Markov Models and Manpower Planning." *Industrial Management Review* (Winter): 39–46.

Burack, E.H., and N.J. Mathys. 1996. *Human Resource Planning: A Pragmatic Approach to Manpower Staffing and Development*, 3rd ed. Northbrook, Ill.: Brace Park.

Cooke, R. 1995. "Succession Planning." *Credit Union Management* (October): 27–28.

Foot, D., and R. Venne. 1990. "Population, Pyramids, and Promotional Prospects." *Canadian Public Policy* 16, no. 4 (December): 387–398.

Glen, J.J. 1977. "Length of Service Distributions in Markov Manpower Models." *Operational Research Quarterly* 28, no. 4: 975–982.

Gridley, J. 1986. "Who Will Be Where When? Forecast the Easy Way." *Personnel Journal* 65, no. 5 (May): 50–58.

Heneman, H.G., and M.G. Sandiver. 1977. "Markov Analysis in Human Resource Administration: Applications and Limitations." *Academy of Management Review* (October): 535–542.

Kaumeyer, R.H. 1979. *Planning and Using Skills Inventory Systems.* New York: Van Nostrand Reinhold.

Konda, S., and S. Stewman. 1980. "An Opportunity Labor Demand Model and Markovian Labor Supply Models: Comparative Tests in an Organization." *American Sociological Review* 45, no. 2 (April): 276–301.

Law, H. 1977. "A Projection Model and a Rational Policy for the Supply and Demand of Human Resources from an Educational Institution." *Applied Mathematical Modeling* 1, no. 5 (June): 269–275.

Lewin, D., and J. Keith. 1976. "Managerial Responses to Perceived

Labor Shortages: The Case of Police."
Criminology 14, no. 1 (May): 65–92.

Martin, R. 1967. "Skills Inventories."
Personnel Journal (January): 28–83.

Meehan, R., and B.S. Ahmed. 1990.
"Forecasting Human Resources
Requirements: A Demand Model."
Human Resource Planning 13, no. 4:
297–307.

Monks, K. 1996. "Global or Local? HRM
in the Multinational Company: The Irish
Experience." *International Journal of
Human Resource Management* 7, no. 3
(September): 721–735.

Nielsen, G.L., and A.R. Young. 1973.
"Manpower Planning: A Markov Chain
Application." *Public Personnel
Management* (March): 133–143.

Patz, A.L. 1970. "Linear Programming
Applied to Manpower Management."
Industrial Management Review 11, no. 2
(Winter): 131–38.

Rowland, K., and M. Sovereign. 1969.
"Markov Chain Analysis of Internal
Manpower Supply." *Industrial Relations*
(October): 88–99.

Sandefur, G. 1981. "Organizational
Boundaries and Upward Job Shifts."
Social Science Research 10, no. 1
(March): 67–82.

Seamans, L. 1978. "What's Lacking in
Most Skills Inventories." *Personnel
Journal* (March).

Stone, T., and J. Fiorito. 1986. "A
Perceived Uncertainty Model of Human

Resource Forecasting Technique Use."
Academy of Management Review 11, no.
3: 635–642.

Tuma, N. 1976. "Rewards, Resources,
and the Rate of Mobility: A
Nonstationary Multivariate Stochastic
Model." *American Sociological Review* 41,
no. 2 (April): 338–360.

Vassiliou, P.C. 1976. "A Markov Chain
Model for Wastage in Manpower
Systems." *Operational Research Quarterly*
27, no. 1: 57–70.

Venezia, I., and Z. Shapira. 1978. "The
Effects of Type of Forecasting Model and
Aggregation Procedure on the Accuracy
of Managerial Manpower Predictions."
Behavioral Science 23, no. 3 (May):
187–194.

Walker, J.W. 1980. *Human Resource
Planning.* New York: McGraw-Hill.

Weigel, H., and S. Wilcox. 1993. "The
Army's Personnel Decision Support
System." *Decision Support Systems* 9, no.
3 (April): 281–306.

White, H. 1970a. *Chains of Opportunity:
System Models of Mobility in
Organizations.* Cambridge, Mass.:
Harvard University Press.

_____. 1970b. "Matching Vacancies and
Mobility." *Journal of Political Economy*
78, no. 1 (January): 97–105.

Zeffane, R., and G. Mayo. 1995. "Human
Resource Planning for Rightsizing: A
Suggested Operational Model."
American Business Review 13, no. 2
(June): 6–17.

8

Managing a Diverse Workforce

This chapter was written by Dr. Naresh C. Agarwal, Professor, Michael de Groote School of Business, McMaster University, Hamilton, Ontario.

◆ ◆ ◆

CHAPTER GOALS

Today's organizations are faced with an increasingly diverse workforce. Such a workforce presents both an opportunity and a challenge to organizations. It presents an opportunity because organizations can draw on this growing resource to achieve their goals. A diverse workforce poses a challenge because its effective use requires organizations to develop innovative and flexible HR policies and substitute these for many long-standing, traditional policies. In this chapter, we examine the definition of and trends in workforce diversity, discuss the reasons why the management of workforce diversity is an important issue for organizations, and provide an overview of policies and measures for effective use of a diverse workforce.

After reading this chapter, you should be able to do the following:

1. Understand the meaning of workforce diversity and its various implications.

2. Appreciate the growing diversity of the Canadian labour force.

3. Discuss why it is important for organizations to focus attention on diversity management.

4. Describe and evaluate strategies for effective use of a diverse workforce.

5. Be familiar with government policy and legislation relating to employment equity and workforce diversity.

◆ ◆ ◆

WORKFORCE DIVERSITY: MEANING AND TRENDS

Diversity can be defined in various ways. The traditional definition of diversity focuses on primary dimensions such as age, gender, race, and ethnicity. Broader definitions of the concept include different physical abilities, religion, language, and sexual orientation. In its broadest definition, diversity encompasses any characteristic used to differentiate one person from others. Defined in this way, diversity becomes an all-inclusive individual differences variable. Consequently, its focus shifts from groups of individuals to separate individuals.

Organizations that have developed formal diversity management policies tend to use varying definitions of diversity. In general, however, they focus on a broader range of human differences than just gender, age, race, and ethnicity. For example, the Pillsbury Company defines diversity as "all the ways in which we differ" (Hayles and Russell, 1997). Similarly, Kaiser Permanente's policy refers to the following specific differences: ethnicity, residence, age/generation, race, tenure, gender, birth order, family structure, education, sexual orientation, religion, marital status, disability, politics, parental status, shift/worksite, personal history, profession or discipline, socioeconomic status, and level in the organization (Wheeler, 1995).

Canada's labour force is becoming increasingly diverse. This is occurring against a backdrop of decelerating labour force growth. Systematic data are collected and published only on certain dimensions of diversity. Based on this data, the key trends in the Canadian labour force and its growing diversity are noted below:[1]

■ *Overall labour force:* The growth in the Canadian labour force has slowed down significantly in recent years. The labour force grew by 24.6 percent over the decade from 1976 to 1985. However, the rate of growth declined by more than half to 11.6 percent over the next decade, 1986 to 1995. The slower rate of growth of the labour force has continued in the post-1995 period as well.

■ *Age distribution:* The Canadian population and labour force are getting older. The median age of the population rose from 26.2 years in 1971 to 33.9 years in 1993 and is expected to rise to 39.5 years by the year 2011. The age distribution of the labour force, too, is changing in favour of older workers. The total number of youth (aged 15–24 years) in the labour force declined by 11 percent during the period from 1976 to 1996. Their proportion in the labour force fell from 26.9 percent in 1976 to 16.1 percent in 1996. Correspondingly, the number of workers aged 25 and over increased by 70.3 percent between 1976 and 1996, and their proportion in the labour force rose from 73.1 percent to 83.9 percent during the same period.

■ *Women:* Census figures show that women comprise slightly over 50 percent of Canada's population. The labour market activity among women has increased significantly over the years and is fast catching up with their relative representation in the population. For example, their relative share in the labour force went up from 37.5 percent in 1976 to 45.2 percent in 1996. Over this period, women accounted for 60.9 percent of the total labour force growth in Canada. These trends have resulted from the rising labour force participation rate among women. This rate was 45.2 percent in 1976; it increased to 57.6 percent in 1996.

■ *Visible minorities:* According to census figures, visible minorities formed 4.7 percent of the population in 1981. This figure rose to 9.4 percent in 1991 and 11.2 percent in 1996. It is projected that by the year 2006, visible minorities will account for 18.3 percent of the population (Heritage Canada projections as reported in Taylor [1995]). These population figures are reflected in the labour market activity among visible minorities. For example, this group formed 4.7 percent of the local employed labour force in Canada in 1981. This figure rose to 9.1 percent in 1991 (Employment and Immigration Canada, 1987, 1994).

■ *Aboriginal peoples:* According to census figures, aboriginal peoples accounted for 2.0 percent of the population in 1981 and 3.8 percent in 1991. Their share in the employed labour force was 1.3 percent and 3.0 percent respectively in these two years (Employment and Immigration Canada, 1987, 1994).

■ *Persons with disabilities:* Very little systemic data is available on persons with disabilities. It is estimated that this group accounted for 1.3 percent of the employed labour force in 1981 and 3.0 percent in 1991 (Employment and Immigration Canada, 1987, 1994).

It is obvious from the data summarized above that labour force growth in Canada has slowed down considerably in recent years. At the same time, the labour force is increasingly becoming older and more diverse. The latter is reflected in the growing share in the labour force of the four designated groups—women, visible minorities, aboriginal peoples, and persons with disabilities. It is expected that by the year 2000, two-thirds of the new entrants to the labour force will come from these four groups (Heritage Canada, 1996). Note that despite their importance in the labour force, these groups continue to be poorly represented in upper level management positions and certain specific occupational categories (Jain and Verma, 1996).

Box 8.1 provides an example of how one Canadian organization has recognized the growing diversity of its workforce in its statement of philosophy.

◆ ◆ ◆
IMPORTANCE OF DIVERSITY MANAGEMENT

If managed effectively, a diverse workforce can provide organizations with many different benefits. These are discussed below.

GROWING DOMESTIC MARKET DIVERSITY

The Canadian marketplace is becoming increasingly more diverse. This reflects the changing demographics of the Canadian population. Economically, the new, diverse segments of consumers present a major marketing opportunity for organizations. Estimates are that, in the U.S. economy, women spend 85 percent of the consumer dollar, older Americans control 50 percent of all discretionary income and spend over $800 billion annually, and African-Americans, Hispanics, and Asian-Americans will have an annual spending power of over $600 billion dollars by the year 2000 (Densford, 1995). Similarly, it is estimated that the visible minority market in Canada is worth $78 billion annually (Heritage Canada, 1995).

Clearly, organizations cannot rely on a simple, homogeneous marketing approach to be successful in the new marketplace. A diverse workforce,

---

BOX 8.1 VALUING DIVERSITY

Early in 1995, Sunnybrook & Women's College Health Sciences Centre began an initiative called Valuing Diversity. The demographic shifts in the population were the driving force behind this initiative as the hospital felt the effects of these shifts in its employee and patient population. The Valuing Diversity initiative has two components, one dealing with patients, called Barrier-Free Services, and the other dealing with employment issues, called Managing Diversity. The latter comprises a comprehensive management attempt to develop employment systems that value a person's contribution and encourage the retention and hiring of the best people, regardless of their race, gender, age, disability, aboriginal status, or any other factor unrelated to job performance.

Source: Adapted from information provided by A. Keogh, specialist, workplace diversity and compensation, Sunnybrook & Women's College Health Sciences Centre, Toronto, March 1999.

---

reflective of the diverse customer population, can prove to be a valuable asset in this context. At the higher decision-making levels, such a workforce can help organizations develop a marketing and sales strategy that is suited to the needs and preferences of a diverse consumer base. This strategy could include, for example, integrating diversity into advertising and promotional campaigns (e.g., using multilingual copy, participating in ethnic trade shows), developing products and services targeted at specific market segments (e.g., Shade of You lipsticks introduced by Maybelline in the early 1990s for women of colour), and developing distribution channels to reach the target markets. At lower management levels, a diverse workforce can help the organization sell products or services more effectively to the "new" customers. "The cultural understanding needed to market to these demographic niches resides most naturally with the marketers with the same cultural background" (Robinson and Dechant, 1997, p.26).

A study by the Conference Board of Canada shows that organizations that have adopted diversity management tend to report an increase in their market share, improvement in customer feedback, and higher profitability (Taylor, 1995). Box 8.2 and Box 8.3 present two specific examples from this same study of how Canadian companies have benefited from a diverse workforce in responding to the new market realities.

GLOBALIZATION

The Canadian economy is heavily dependent on exports. Traditionally, export markets for Canadian organizations have been dominated by three countries, the United States, the United Kingdom, and Japan. The potential for significant growth in these markets is very limited. If we continue to rely on them, our export growth and standard of living "will be relegated to the slow lane of international commerce" (Nevison, 1994)

Canadian organizations have begun to realize the need to diversify their global interests and operations. They have begun looking at the developing economies in Asia and South America as prospects for expanding business. These economies have developmental needs in the areas of transportation, communications, and banking and financial services. Canadian organizations have long-standing expertise in these fields and are well situated to meet these needs. These emerging economies also represent vast purchasing power for many consumer goods that Canadian firms can supply.

BOX 8.2 MANAGING DIVERSITY

At Petro-Canada, the largest Canadian owned oil and gas company, the link between managing diversity and the bottom line was firmly established in 1991 when the company began pursuing a strategy of service excellence. The importance of valuing and managing diversity to this bottom-line success of Petro-Canada's business was clearly demonstrated by the marketing team in metropolitan Vancouver. Managing territory in downtown Vancouver with a large Chinese and East Indian community, Shirley Dickman, territory manager, Retail Marketing, pointed out that her efforts to manage and value the diversity within her team of sales associates were an intuitive part of conducting day-to-day business. According to Ms. Dickman, valuing the team's ethnocultural diversity and making links with the ethnocultural communities they served was the approach chosen to expand the business. "We looked at our customer base and realized we didn't know how to appeal to a more diverse group of customers. We didn't know what they wanted or what attracted them to a particular station."

Together with her team of sales associates, Ms. Dickman began experimenting with ethnoculturally specific marketing activities. For example, at a site in Vancouver's Chinese community, signs were posted in English and Mandarin, the site was officially blessed, a dragon dance was performed, and the associate started bringing touches of Chinese culture onto the site.

These initiatives helped increase the centre's profile within the community. However, the real turning point came when the team realized that attracting new guests wasn't enough—they had to be able to speak their language. Communicating effectively with the new guests was the key to ensuring their loyalty. According to Ms. Dickman, the logical next step was to realign some of the sales associates with distinct ethnocultural communities.

Source: Taylor, C.E. 1995. *Dimensions of Diversity in Canadian Business*, Report No. 143-95. Ottawa: Conference Board of Canada. Reproduced with permission from the Conference Board of Canada.

However, to successfully compete in the more diversified global area, organizations need to overcome some barriers. These barriers result from differences in culture, language, traditions, business practices, and government policies and regulations. Organizations have to be aware of and sensitive to the unique characteristics of countries in which they operate or wish to operate. In this regard, a diverse workforce can prove to be of major advantage. It can help the organization develop cross-cultural awareness and sensitivities. For example, Honeywell has a workforce of 55,000 employees representing 80 languages, 60 national cultures, and 95 customer countries. With the help of such a diversified workforce, the company has been able to set up a series of "global organization development initiatives" (Wheeler,

BOX 8.3 INCREASING CULTURAL AWARENESS

Two years ago, the company [Warner-Lambert Canada Inc.] realized that the majority of its small retailers in Toronto were of Korean ethnic origin. The company had calling cards and promotional material printed in Korean and hired an Asian representative to establish an initial contact with current and potential accounts. By tailoring sales strategies to meet the needs of this culturally distinct market segment, Warner-Lambert estimates that it increased its market penetration by approximately 30 percent. Paul Tepperman, business manager, remarked: "Our approach made business sense. By increasing our cultural awareness we could land more accounts and presumably increase our sales."

Source: Taylor, C.E. 1995. *Dimensions of Diversity in Canadian Business*, Report No. 143-95. Ottawa: Conference Board of Canada. Reproduced with permission from the Conference Board of Canada.

1995). Similarly, Northern Telecom operates in 86 countries. While it has well-established technological expertise, cross-cultural expertise has become an essential resource requirement for success in international projects. "For instance, having technical staff of Asian background has been a significant source of competitive advantage for Northern Telecom in the Asia Pacific region" (Taylor, 1995, p. 6).

ENHANCED CREATIVITY AND PROBLEM SOLVING

Managing and valuing workforce diversity can also contribute to competitive advantage through increased creativity and problem-solving capability. Many research studies show that diverse work teams tend to be more creative and better problem solvers than homogeneous work teams (Cox, 1991; Cox and Blake, 1991; Watson et al., 1993, Moscovici, 1994; Jehn, 1995). This may be because diverse work teams bring together a wider range of talent, experiences, and point of view, all of which can lead such teams to look at a problem from many different perspectives, generate a greater number of alternatives, and subject these alternatives to a more critical evaluation process. For example, minority members with strong opinions may stimulate groups "to take in more information in more divergent ways, to perform better, to think more creatively, and to detect correct solutions that otherwise would have gone undetected" (Nemeth, 1994, p. 11). Diverse groups may initially experience more conflict in agreeing about what is important and difficulty in working as a group. As well, there is some indication that these groups may also exhibit higher levels of dissatisfaction and turnover (Milliken and Martins,

1996). However, ultimately these groups can do a better job of identifying problems and solving them, particularly if minority opinions are encouraged and respected and the group does not get further divided into familial sub-groups (Jackson et al., 1995; Jehn, 1995; Lau and Murnigham, 1998).

COSTS OF IGNORING DIVERSITY MANAGEMENT

The demographic trends outlined earlier in this chapter clearly establish that employers are faced with an increasingly diverse labour force. What's more, this diversity is expected to increase even further in the future. Many traditional HR policies were developed against the backdrop of a homogeneous (i.e., prime age, white, male) workforce. Continued use of such policies in today's context is tantamount to having a policy of ignoring the new realities in the labour market. Such policies can prove to be costly to the organization in two major ways. First, many members of nontraditional labour force groups, who might otherwise be qualified for the job, might not be considered for hiring or promotion due to some traditional notion of what constitutes a suitable candidate. This can result in a situation of self-imposed shortage of labour in which the employer perceives the applicant pool to be smaller than in reality it is. Economic costs associated with such underutilization (including occupational segregation) of many diverse labour force groups have been estimated to be significant (Dunnette and Motowidlo, 1982; Agarwal, 1985; Agarwal, 1998).

Second, failing to manage workforce diversity can be economically costly to the organization in another way. Following equity theory, it can be argued that perceptions of unfair treatment in the workplace can cause the affected employees to exhibit lower productivity and higher turnover and absenteeism rates. Perceived discrimination can also be viewed as a culturally relevant work stressor. The perceived discrimination has been found to adversely affect organizational commitment, job satisfaction, and work tensions (Sanchez and Brock, 1996). These negative employee outcomes in turn can cause poor productivity and high absenteeism and turnover rates among members of the diverse labour force groups. The economic costs associated with these employee behaviours are estimated to be significant for organizations. For example, a Fortune 500 utility company with 27,000 employees found that it was losing $15.3 million per year because of the costs, associated with higher turnover and lower productivity on the part of women, that were caused by systemic gender bias in its HR policies (Stuart, 1992). The perception of lack of opportunity for career advancement and of being unwelcome in the upper management positions has been suggested as a key reason for the higher rate of turnover among women as compared to men. Similar explanations have been put forward for higher turnover rates among members of visible minority groups (McNerney, 1994).

LEGAL COMPLIANCE

Most Western societies have become increasingly committed to democratic principles of equality and freedom. In the workplace, these principles imply that employment decisions affecting individuals ought to be made without any regard to their personal and demographic characteristics. Instead, such decisions should be based on work-related criteria such as bona fide occupational requirements. These equality principles are also enshrined in the Canadian Charter of Rights and Freedoms. The Charter guarantees that "Every individual is equal before and under the law and has the right to the equal protection and equal benefit of the law without discrimination and, in particular, without discrimination based on race, national or ethnic origin, colour, religion, sex, age or mental or physical disability" (section 15). These rights and freedoms are "subject only to such reasonable limits prescribed by law as can be demonstrably justified in a free and democratic society" (section 1). Similar equality rights are also guaranteed under the human rights legislation in various jurisdictions in Canada. Finally, there are two public policy initiatives that apply to organizations in the federal jurisdiction. These are the Employment Equity Act and the Federal Contractors Program for Employment Equity. Both these initiatives are directed at ensuring equal employment opportunities for the traditionally disadvantaged groups in the labour force (i.e., women, visible minorities, aboriginal peoples, and persons with disabilities). These initiatives are discussed in greater detail in a later section in this chapter.

Thus, it is clear that organizations are under legal obligations to develop bias-free, nondiscriminatory employment policies and practices. The cost of noncompliance with legislation can be substantial for organizations. Two decisions of the Canadian human rights tribunals are noteworthy. In a decision that was upheld by the Supreme Court of Canada in 1987, a Canadian human rights tribunal found systemic discrimination against women at the St. Lawrence operations of Canadian National Railways. The tribunal ordered the company to increase to 13 percent the proportion of women working in nontraditional occupations in the regional facility in question. In a more recent case decided in 1997, another Canadian human rights tribunal ordered Health Canada to develop a wide-ranging program including mandatory human rights workshops, management training on employment equity, and bias-free recruitment practices. It also ordered that a specific proportion of visible minorities be promoted within a specified number of years (Jain, 1997). It should be noted here that a new Employment Equity Act passed in 1996 specifically prohibits the imposition of quotas on employers.

OTHER REASONS

The presence of an effective diversity management program can help the organization in two additional ways. First, it can help the organization develop a positive image as an employer, thereby enhancing its ability to attract, retain, and motivate a diverse workforce. Second, the presence of diversity programs can also influence the organization's performance in financial markets. A study by Wright, Ferris, Hiller, and Kroll (1995) examined the relative impact on the stock prices of corporations of announcements of U.S. Department of Labour awards for exemplary affirmative action programs and announcements of damage awards from the settlement of discrimination lawsuits. The findings of this study suggest that announcements of awards may be associated with higher stock valuation and that discrimination-related announcements may be associated with lower stock valuation. These findings should be extendible to the Canadian setting as well. Canadian organizations are subject to significant penalties and negative press if they are found to be in violation of the existing antidiscrimination legislation. They are also eligible for merit awards from Human Resources Development Canada if they develop and implement exemplary employment equity programs (Human Resources Development Canada, 1997).

◆ ◆ ◆
DIVERSITY MANAGEMENT: POLICIES AND PROGRAMS

Organizations can undertake a variety of measures to effectively manage workforce diversity. Some of these measures are mandated by law. Organizations that are covered by such legislation have no choice but to initiate these measures. Other measures are voluntary in nature, and their development is driven by organizational interest in harnessing the benefits of a diverse workforce. Key voluntary measures, as well as those that are legally required, are briefly discussed below.

DEVELOPMENT OF BIAS-FREE HR POLICIES

Most organizations are increasingly faced with a diverse workforce. They should examine carefully their existing HR policies and identify those that discriminate against members of diverse labour force groups. This is critical not only for ethical and legal reasons, but also for organizations' own economic benefit. Bias-free HR policies are needed to ensure full and effective use of the growing pool of diverse workers. Many studies point to the existence of various stereotypes about nontraditional workers. For example, age stereotypes portray older workers as having poorer health, lower productivity, rigid and less creative behaviour, an inability to learn new skills, and higher accident rates (Burack, 1988; Forteza and Prieto, 1994). Similar negative stereotypes may be held about women and visible minority employees, especially in relation to upper-level management positions (Morrison, 1992). There is, however, very little research evidence supporting these stereotypes and generalizations. HR decisions based on such inaccurate beliefs can be economically costly to the organization because, as a result of these beliefs, employers may perceive the pool of "qualified" candidates for available positions to be smaller than it actually is. Organizations should ensure that their HR policies and practices rely on objective, work-related criteria and that these policies and practices are applied consistently across all employees, based on their attributes as related to productivity. Only then can the organization hope to make the most effective use of its diverse workforce.

EXPANDING THE POOL OF QUALIFIED APPLICANTS

To maximize the labour supply available to them, organizations should aggressively recruit qualified women, members of visible minorities, and other nontraditional workers. However, organizations may not be successful in their efforts unless they re-examine the ways in which they advertise and promote themselves to potential recruits. Recruitment advertising must be carefully analyzed to ensure that nontraditional candidates are not discouraged from applying. New recruits may also have quite different expectations. They may want to know if diversity efforts are being initiated and what kind of representation of the diverse labour force exists in the organization, especially at management levels (Wheeler, 1995). Thus, organizations need to promote themselves as valuing diversity and offering equal employment opportunity to all members of the labour force. Networking with women and ethnocultural groups and advertising in their newspapers and magazines can also help in generating more applicants from the nontraditional groups.

TRAINING AND DEVELOPMENT INITIATIVES

These initiatives are important for all employees. If properly developed and implemented, training and development programs can help employees become more valuable to the organization and provide them with new and better career opportunities. There are, however, some training and development programs that may prove to be particularly beneficial to women and members of other minority groups. Technological changes and organizational restructuring often result in the elimination of lower-skilled, administrative jobs in which a greater proportion of the workforce tends to be women and members of other nontraditional groups. Organizations can develop training programs to upgrade and expand the skill base of these employees so that they can become more mobile and marketable as employees. New Brunswick Telephone Co. Ltd. and the International Development Research Centre have targeted clerical workers, a female-dominated occupational group, for such training programs (Human Resources Development Canada, 1997).

Mentoring is another training and development activity that can be of particular benefit to women and minority group members. Research studies show that these workers often make poor career decisions and are less knowledgeable about the inside track on how to get ahead in the organization (Morrison, 1992). Mentoring can be an important vehicle for the development of management and executive succession potential of women and minority group employees. In this program, senior managers serve as coaches and role models for junior employees who are assigned to them as protégés. Mentoring is a key component of the workplace equality programs developed by the Bank of Montreal for its diverse workforce. The first group targeted for the mentoring program was women because they constituted 91 percent of the workforce but held only 9 percent of the executive positions. It was recognized that women were not advancing into the senior management positions because of stereotypical attitudes and myths. The mentoring program at the Bank of Montreal has proved to be a great success (Dreyfus et al., 1995).

An interesting policy question surrounds mentoring programs. There is some indication that protégés in same-race mentoring relationships experience more psychosocial support than those in cross-race relationships, and protégés in same-gender mentoring relationships find more trust and mutuality than those in cross-gender relationships (Thomas, 1990; Ragins, 1997). These findings may lead one to conclude that organizations should attempt to form same-gender or same-race mentoring pairs. However, forming such pairs may not always be possible because there might not be enough women and nonwhite managers in the senior ranks of the organization. Also, it might not even be desirable to establish such a practice because diversified mentoring relationships can have a positive impact on organizational culture (Ibarra, 1995). For example, minority protégés can sensitize majority mentors to diversity issues. Also, to insist that black protégés be paired with black mentors and female protégés be paired with female mentors may run counter to the very spirit of diversity management.

ALTERNATIVE WORK ARRANGEMENTS

Diversity of the workforce implies a diversity of needs and preferences. Flexible work arrangements can satisfy these varying needs and preferences. Such programs allow employees to choose a work arrangement option that is best suited to their specific circumstances. Flexible work arrangements are sometimes referred to as family-friendly employment policies because they enable employees to balance their work and family responsibilities (e.g., child care or elder care responsibilities). These policies can also satisfy personal preferences or needs for more time off from work (i.e., increased leisure time). Flexible work arrangements can include the following programs and policies:

- *Flextime work:* This arrangement involves a full-time, five-days-a-week job. Employees are present for certain core hours (e.g., 10 a.m. to 3 p.m.) each day, but they can vary when their working day begins and ends. In Canada, 16 percent of employees were on flextime in 1991. This number increased to 24 percent in 1995. Employed women with preschool children were slightly more likely to be on flextime.

- *Compressed work:* Employees work full-time hours but over fewer days per week (e.g., 4 days, 10 hours a day).

■ *Part-time work:* Employees work less than 30 hours a week. In 1995, 19 percent of all employees worked part-time (Akyeampong, 1997). In general, women and those with children are more likely to work part-time hours.

■ *Job sharing:* Two employees share one full-time job. Sharing arrangements can vary. For example, one person may work the first half of the day or the week and the other person works the second half. In 1995, 84 percent of the 171,000 job sharers were women (Marshall, 1997).

■ *Telework/working at home:* Employees work at least some or all hours of work at home. This arrangement is also sometimes referred to as flexwork location. In 1995, 9 percent of employees worked at home. Working at home is more prevalent among female workers and workers with children under age 16 (Pérusse, 1998).

Box 8.4 shows the alternative work arrangements program offered by one Canadian organization.

Flexible work arrangements offer advantages to both employees and employers. Employees benefit because they are able to choose a work arrangement that is best suited to their needs. Benefits to employers result from higher worker morale, lower absenteeism, and improved recruitment (Friedman and Galinsky, 1992). However, flexible work arrangements are not free from concerns. From the employer's perspective, these programs may present coordination and supervision problems and involve higher administrative costs (Parker and Hall, 1993; Hammer and Barbera, 1997). From the employee's perspective, flexible work arrangements may mean reduced promotional opportunities (Zeytinoglu, 1996; Marshall, 1997; Pérusse, 1998).

BOX 8.4 ALTERNATIVE WORK ARRANGEMENTS

The Bank of Nova Scotia has a program called Alternate Work Arrangement for its employees. This program includes the following alternative work arrangement (AWA) options: flextime, flexible work weeks, job sharing, and home/telecommuting. All employees with at least a satisfactory performance rating are eligible to apply for an AWA. The employee's manager reviews the application. A preliminary approval is given if the application is judged to make good business sense. The final approval is given after a three-month trial period, at the end of which the new arrangement must be deemed to be working for everyone involved.

Source: *Alternate Work Arrangements.* 1996. Bank of Nova Scotia (June).

FLEXIBLE RETIREMENT OPTIONS

The labour force data presented earlier in this chapter shows that the Canadian labour force is both growing at a slower pace and getting older. Strong evidence indicates that older people as a group are participating less and less actively in the labour market. This is reflected in two trends. First, the labour force participation rate (LFPR) among older people (i.e., among the proportion of older people who remain in the labour force) is declining. For example, the LFPR of those aged 55 to 64 years fell from 53.5 percent in 1976 to 47.9 percent in 1996. The decline in the rate was even sharper for men in this age bracket, from 76.3 percent to 58.3 percent over the same period. Second, older workers are leaving the labour force at an earlier age than before. For example, only 51 percent of those retiring between 1976 and 1980 were under age 65. This figure rose to 71 percent over the period from 1991 to 1995. As a consequence, the median age of retirement fell from 64.9 years in the period from 1976 to 1980 to 62.3 years in the period from 1991 to 1995 (Gower, 1997).

Anticipating these demographic trends about the labour force in general and older workers in particular, the Federal Task Force on Labour Market Developments in the 1980s concluded the following:

> There emerges a pattern of an increasing pool of older persons fully capable of continuing their attachment to the labour force at a time when serious industrial adjustment can be expected to require the skills they have developed ... (Employment and Immigration Canada, 1981, p. 101).

The same conclusions have been drawn for the 1990s in a subsequent study of respondents from over 400 public and private sector organizations in Canada. The study found that even in the midst of widespread downsizing and layoffs, close to 60 percent of the respondents reported current difficulties in recruiting technical or technical support employees, supervisory or managerial employees, and professional employees. An even greater proportion of respondents expected these difficulties to continue or become worse in the coming years. The study observed that in view of these recruiting difficulties, "companies may be missing an opportunity to tap into an already existing and capable resource: their own aging employees" (Towers Perrin and Hudson Institute Canada, 1991, p. 17).

Organizations need to undertake HR planning to determine their own specific situation with regard to current and impending skill shortages and imbalances. Organizations should assess their future HR requirements across occupations and identify areas of expected shortages and surpluses. If an array of imbalances is found, flexible retirement policies may be more appropriate. "Making more selective use of early retirement incentives, as well as implementing delayed retirement incentives ... may help many companies see through the skills and labour shortage crunch in the years ahead" (Towers Perrin and Hudson Institute Canada, 1991, p. 11). Delayed retirement may not appear to make much sense in an environment of downsizing and restructuring. But, if a possibility of future human resource and skill shortages exists in an organization, it is advisable for that organization not to reject such initiatives out of hand. A major advantage in retaining older employees is that their accumulated work experience can be a real asset, particularly in jobs with high levels of complexity (Avolio et al., 1990).

A key issue in retaining older workers is their availability and willingness to continue working. In this context, the traditional standardized work arrangement and fixed-age, mandatory retirement policies are likely to be less effective. Fixed-age, mandatory retirement policies do not guarantee that employees will continue working until they reach the mandatory age of retirement. Employees can, and many do, leave the labour force prior to reaching that age. Many older workers may be willing to prolong working if they are given flexible work and retirement options. They can then choose the option that best suits their needs and preferences. For example, many older workers may prefer more developmental, mentoring, and advisory job responsibilities to exclusively operational or production responsibilities. Similarly, many older workers may prefer phased-in retirement options in which they can gradually reduce the number of hours they work over an extended number of years. If confronted with a choice between "all-or-none hours," these workers may well opt to take early retirement. Under flexible retirement policies, workers who are judged to be competent and performing well in their jobs can continue to work beyond the normal retirement age of 65 years should they choose to do so.

Thus, by developing more flexible work arrangements and flexible retirement options, organizations can better satisfy the needs and preferences of older workers and at the same time make more effective use of this growing workforce (Agarwal, 1998).

MANDATED EMPLOYMENT EQUITY MEASURES

In Canada, there are two public policy initiatives at the federal level that require the affected employers to develop and implement employment equity plans. These are the Employment Equity Act (EEA) and the Federal Contractors Program for Employment Equity. Both these initiatives have been in effect since August 1986. The EEA was subsequently amended and a new EEA incorporating these changes came into effect in October 1996. The act was enacted to improve employment opportunities for traditionally disadvantaged groups: women, members of visible minorities, aboriginal peoples, and persons with disabilities. These are referred to as designated groups under the legislation.

The EEA covers private sector employers and crown corporations that fall under the federal jurisdiction and employ 100 or more workers. Thus, employers in such sectors as banking, communications (e.g., the postal service, telephone companies, and broadcasting organizations), and transportation (e.g., railways, airlines, and interprovincial bus and trucking companies) come under its purview. As of October 1996, the coverage of the EEA was extended to the federal public service as well. The EEA requires the regulated employers to undertake the following specific measures:

- *Workforce survey and analysis:* Employers are required to carry out a workforce survey to collect information on the number of members of designated groups in their workforce. The survey results are then compared to the data on the availability of an external labour supply to determine the underrepresentation of members of designated groups in the organizational workforce.

- *Review of policies and procedures:* Employers are required to conduct a review of their HR system, policies, and practices to identify employment barriers affecting designated group members. These barriers include those requirements that cannot be validated as being necessary for safe and efficient operation of the business and at the same time have an adverse effect on employment opportunities for designated group members.

- *Employment equity plan:* Employers are required to develop an employment equity plan that includes the following: short- and long-term numerical goals for hiring and promoting members of designated groups to correct any underrepresentation; the steps to be taken to remove employment barriers and enact positive policies and practices in the area of hiring, training, promotion and retention; and a timetable for achieving goals and implementing policy initiatives.

It is important to draw attention to certain other provisions of the EEA. First, the act specifically prohibits the imposition of quotas on employers. The numerical goals are set by individual employers, taking into account their particular context and circumstances. These goals should be viewed as flexible planning tools in the same way as are the goals set by employers in other areas such as production, sales, and so on, along with the plan to achieve them. Progress is monitored regularly and the plan is adjusted if needed (Jain, 1997). The EEA also requires employers to make "all reasonable efforts" to achieve the numerical goals and implement the measures and policies set out in the employment equity plan. At the same time, employees are allowed to make adjustments in their employment equity plans if such adjustments appear to be justified and reasonable. Second, the EEA specifically states that employers are not required to hire or promote unqualified persons and disregard the merit principle in employment decisions. Finally, the EEA makes it clear that employers cannot be forced to create new positions to achieve the employment equity goals.

Under the EEA, the legislated employers are required to file an annual report detailing their employment equity plans and the progress made in implementing those plans. In 1996, 330 employers employing 5,679,081 workers were covered under the EEA (Human Resources Development Canada, 1997). The assessment of the annual reports filed by these employers "indicates that, generally speaking, the representation of designated group members in the workforce under the Act is still far from that of the same groups in the Canadian labour force and that segregation of these groups is still present in the workplace. The results also indicate that significant progress could still be achieved by a larger number of employers from year to year" (Human Resources Development Canada, 1997, p. 4). Based on an assessment of their annual reports, employers are also given a rating on a three-point scale for the progress achieved in improving the situation for members of each of the four designated groups. In 1996, the best result, relatively speaking, was achieved for visible minorities—30 percent of the employers receiving the highest rating ("A") and 39 percent receiving the lowest rating ("C"). For the remaining three designated groups, women, aboriginal peoples, and persons with disabilities, the results were much poorer. Only 7 to 11 percent of the employers received an "A" rating while as many as 53 to 60 percent received a "C" rating. Two employers, namely, Canada Post and Rogers Broadcasting, were given merit awards for the special efforts they made to achieve a representative (i.e., diverse) workforce.

The other public policy initiative in the area of labour force diversity is the Federal Contractors Program for Employment Equity (FCP). This is not a law but an administrative directive of the federal Treasury Board. Enacted in 1986, the FCP applies to all Canadian firms with 100 or more workers who bid on federal contracts worth $200,000 or more. Under the FCP, contractors are required to sign a certificate of commitment to develop and implement an employment equity plan. The requirements for this plan are equivalent to those applicable to employers under the EEA. Contractors that do not meet their commitments may be excluded from bidding on future federal contracts.

◆ ◆ ◆
SOME IMPLEMENTATION ISSUES

Successful implementation of workforce diversity programs requires a number of steps. First, it is critical to gain the support and commitment of top leadership for these programs. One way to do so is to integrate workforce diversity objectives into the overall business objectives of the organization. The Bank of Montreal uses such an integrated approach:

> *The cornerstone of this approach is the integration of workplace equality into the bank's business planning process. Goals for workplace equality are set at the same time as other business goals, have a direct relationship to marketing and financial strategies, and are given as much emphasis as financial targets in the performance planning and review process. (Taylor, 1995).*

Second, a detailed workforce diversity arrangement plan should be developed, outlining the underlying goals (in measurable terms), strategies for achieving them, and procedures for assessing the results achieved. The plan can be modified and adjusted over time on an as-needed basis. Third, it is important to establish accountability for implementing the workforce diversity management plan. A possible strategy would be to make this accountability a part of the managerial performance evaluation process. Fourth, individual employers must be closely involved in the development and implementation of initiatives for workforce diversity management. In this regard, individualized HR planning can be a useful tool. Such planning would require, among other things, collecting pertinent information from employees and integrating this information into appropriate HR databases. These databases should cover such areas as training and development needs; career interests, goals, and possibilities; job design and work schedule preferences; and retirement intentions. Individual employees must be active and responsible participants in this planning process. They must gain understanding of their personal needs, preferences, and competencies. To remain current and competitive, they must also be willing to take advantage of relevant developmental opportunities offered to them. Finally, a strategy must be developed to address backlash and negative reaction that might surface among majority group employees toward workforce diversity programs. These feelings may arise, for example, from a perception that less qualified persons are being hired or promoted to achieve the goals of workforce diversity programs. Such a perception can cause resentment among majority workers. It can also damage the self-esteem and confidence of the minority workers. The organization should first confirm that HR decisions are not being made on criteria other than true merit and competence. Such a practice neither makes business sense nor is required by employment equity and human rights legislation. The organization should then communicate to employees its firm commitment to adhere to the principles of merit and competence in making hiring, promotion, and all other HR decisions.

◆ ◆ ◆
SUMMARY

Canada's labour force is becoming more diverse. The proportion of women and other minority groups in the labour force has risen significantly in recent years and is expected to continue growing in the future. There are strong moral and legal reasons, but even stronger economic reasons, why organizations should pay attention to workforce diversity management programs. Some Canadian organizations have made significant progress in developing and implementing them. However, a large number of organizations have a long way to go.

EXERCISES

1. Why should workforce diversity be considered an important business issue? Explain your reasons in detail.

2. Discuss the pros and cons of developing mandatory versus flexible retirement policies.

3. What is meant by a bias-free employment policy? What is involved in developing such a policy?

4. How is employment equity related to workforce diversity? Outline the steps involved in developing an employment equity plan as required by the federal legislation.

5. What are the advantages of implementing flexible work arrangements? Are there any potential problems associated with these arrangements?

ENDNOTES

1. Labour force trends reported here were computed from the following Statistics Canada annual publications for relevant years: *Labour Force Annual Averages*, Cat. No. 71–220–XPB; and *Historical Labour Force Statistics*, Cat. No. 71–201. Data on population and aging of population were adapted from Census of Canada reports and the following publications of Statistics Canada: 1993. *Population Aging and Elderly*, Cat. No. 91–533 E; and 1990. *Population Projections for Canada 1989–2011*, Cat. No. 91–520.

References

Agarwal, N.C. 1998. "Retirement of Older Workers: Issues and Policies." *Human Resource Planning* 21, no. 1: 42–52.

____. 1985. "Economic Cost of Employment Discrimination." *Research Studies:* 401–419. Ottawa: Royal Commission on Equality in Employment.

Akyeampong, E.B. 1997. "Work Arrangements: 1995 Review." *Perspectives on Labour and Income* 9, no. 1: 48–52.

Avolio, B.J., D.A. Waldman, and M.A. McDaniel. 1990. "Age and Work Performance in Nonmanagerial Jobs: The Effects of Experience and Occupational Type." *Academy of Management Journal* 33, no. 2: 407–422.

Burack, E.H., 1988. *Creative Human Resource Planning and Applications*. Englewood Cliffs, N.J.: Prentice-Hall.

Cox, T. Jr. 1991. "The Multicultural Organization." *Academy of Management Executive*. 5, no. 2: 34–47.

Cox, T. Jr., and S. Blake. 1991. "Managing Cultural Diversity: Implications for Organizational Competitiveness. *Academy of Management Executive* 5, no. 3: 45–56.

Densford, L.E. 1995. "Studies Make Economic Case for Diversity." *Workforce Training News* 3, no. 5: 1–6.

Dreyfus, G., M.J. Lee, and J.M. Totta. 1995. "Mentoring at Bank of Montreal." *Human Resource Planning* 18, no. 4: 45–49.

Dunnette, M.D., and S.J. Motowidlo. 1982. "Estimating Benefits and Costs of Anti-Sexist Training Programs in Organizations." In J.J. Bernardin, ed., *Women in the Work Force*. New York: Praeger.

Employment and Immigration Canada. 1994. *Employment Equity Availability Data Report on Designated Groups*. Ottawa: Employment and Immigration Canada.

____. 1987. *Employment Equity Availability Data Report on Designated Groups*. Ottawa: Employment and Immigration Canada.

____. 1981. *Labour Market Development in the 1980s*. Ottawa: Employment and Immigration Canada.

Forteza, J.A., and J.M. Prieto. 1994. "Aging and Work Behavior." In H.C. Triandis, M.D. Dunnette, and L.M. Hugh, eds., *Handbook of Industrial and Organizational Psychology*, 2nd ed. Palo Alto, Ca.: Consulting Psychologists Press Inc.

Friedman, D.E., and E. Galinsky. 1992. "Work and Family Trends." In S. Zedeck, ed., *Work and Family*. San Francisco: Jossey-Bass.

Gower, D. 1997. "Measuring the Age of Retirement." *Perspectives on Labour and Income* 9, no. 2: 11–17.

Hammer, L.B., and K.B. Barbera. 1997. "Toward an Integration of Alternative Work Schedules and Human Resource Systems." *Human Resource Planning* 20, no. 2: 28–36.

Hayles, R., and A. Russell. 1997. *The Diversity Directive*. Chicago: Irwin Publishing.

Heritage Canada. 1996. *Annual Report 1994–1995 on the Operation of the Canadian Multi-culturism Act*. Ottawa: Heritage Canada.

____. 1995. *Ethnocultural Diversity: A Source of Competitive Advantage*, Ottawa: Heritage Canada.

Human Resources Development Canada. 1997. *Annual Report Employment Equity Act 1997*. Ottawa: Human Resources Development Canada.

Ibarra, H. 1995. "Race, Opportunity and Diversity of Social Circles in Managerial Networks." *Academy of Management Journal* 38, no. 3: 673–703.

Jackson, S.E., K.E. May, and K. Whitney. 1995. "Understand the Dynamics of Diversity in Decision Making Teams." In R.A. Guzzo and E. Salas, eds., *Team Executives and Decision Making in Organizations*. San Francisco: Jossey-Bass.

Jain, H.C. 1997. "Human Rights in Employment: Issues in Employment." In N.C Agarwal, A. Allon, K.M. Bullock, D.E. Dimick, H.C. Jain, D.L. McPherson, V.V. Murray, D.M. Robertson, L. Shouldice, and J.T. Wallace, eds., *Human Resources Management in Canada*. Toronto: Carswell.

Jain, H.C., and A. Verma. 1996. "Managing Workforce Diversity for Competitiveness: The Canadian Experience." *International Journal of Manpower* 17, no. 415: 14–29.

Jehn, K.A. 1995. "A Multimethod Examination of the Benefits and Determinants of Intragroup Conflict." *Administrative Science Quarterly* 40, no. 2: 256–282.

Lau, D.C., and J.K. Murnigham. 1998. "Demographic Diversity and Faultiness: The Compositional Dynamics of Organizational Groups." *Academy of Management Review* 23, no. 2: 325–352.

Marshall, K. 1997. "Job Sharing." *Perspectives on Labour and Income* 9, no. 2: 6–10.

McNerney, D. 1994. "The Bottom-Line Value of Diversity." *HR Focus* 71, no. 1: 22–23.

Milliken, F.J., and L.L. Martins. 1996. "Searching for Common Threads: Understanding the Multiple Effects of Diversity in Organizational Groups." *Academy of Management Review* 21, no. 2: 402–433.

Morrison, A. 1992. *The New Leaders: Guidelines on Leadership Diversity in America*. San Francisco: Jossey-Bass.

Moscovici, S. 1994. "Three Concepts: Minority, Conflict and Behavioural Style." In S. Moscovici, A. Mucchi-Fama, and A. Maass, eds., *Minority Influence*. Chicago: Nelson-Hall Publishers.

Nemeth, C.J. 1994. "The Value of a Minority Dissent." In S. Moscovici, A. Mucchi-Fama, and A. Maass, eds., *Minority Influence*. Chicago: Nelson-Hall Publishers.

Nevison, D. 1994. *Profiling in the Pacific Rim: Can Canada Capture Its Share?* Ottawa: Conference Board of Canada.

Parker, V., and D.T. Hall. 1993. "Workplace Diversity: Faddish or Fundamental?" In P.H. Mirvis, ed., *Building the Competitive Workforce*. New York: John Wiley & Sons.

Pérusse, D. 1998. "Working at Home." *Perspectives on Labour and Income* 10, no. 2: 16–23.

Ragins, B.E. 1997. "Diversified Mentoring Relationships in Organizations: A Power Perspective." *Academy of Management Review* 22, no. 2: 482–521.

Robinson, G., and K. Dechant. 1997. "Building a Business Case for Diversity." *Academy of Management Executive* 11, no. 3: 21–31.

Sanchez, J.I., and P. Brock. 1996. "Outcomes of Perceived Discrimination Among Hispanic Employees: Is Diversity Management a Luxury or a Necessity?" *Academy of Management Journal* 39, no. 3: 704–719.

Stuart, P. 1992. "What Does the Glass Ceiling Cost You?" *Personnel Journal* (November): 70–80.

Taylor, C.E. 1995. *Dimensions of Diversity in Canadian Business*, Report No. 143–95. Ottawa: Conference Board of Canada.

Thomas, D. 1990, "The Impact of Race on Managers' Experiences of Developmental Relationships (Mentoring and Sponsorship): An Intra-Organizational Study." *Journal of Organizational Behaviour* 2, no. 2: 479–492.

Towers Perrin and Hudson Institute Canada. 1991.*Workforce 2000*. Ottawa: Ontario.

Watson, W.E., K. Kumar, and L.K. Michaelson. 1993. "Cultural Diversity's Impact on Interaction Process and Performance: Comparing Homogeneous and Diverse Task Groups." *Academy of Management Journal* 36, no. 3: 590–602.

Wheeler, M.L. 1995. *Diversity: Business Rationale and Strategies*, Report No. 1130–95–RR. New York: Conference Board.

Wright, P., S.P. Ferris, J.S. Hiller, and M. Kroll. 1995. "Competitiveness through Management of Diversity: Effects on Stock Price Valuations." *Academy of Management Journal* 38, no. 1: 272–287.

Zeytinoglu, I.U. 1996. "Key Workplace Issues in Telework: An Empirical Study." In *The Globalization of the Economy and the Worker,* Selected Papers from the Annual Conference of Canadian Industrial Relations Association, Montreal.

9

Succession Management

♦ ♦ ♦
CHAPTER GOALS

Executives of any organization must develop the next generation of leaders, just as sports teams need to develop the next generation of players. This chapter starts with a definition of succession management and continues with a discussion of how succession management has evolved from the more traditional succession planning. Next, we move into the main subject of the chapter, the succession management process. This process consists of five steps: aligning succession management with the goals of the organization, identifying the skills needed to meet those goals, identifying employees who have the potential to acquire the needed skills, developing those employees, and tracking the process. Development methods include promotions, job rotations, special assignments, formal training and development, and coaching and mentoring. We then examine the problems associated with succession management, including the creation of "crown princes" and the managerial risks in identifying the top employees and then losing them. We conclude with a discussion of the succession management process at Air Canada.

After reading this chapter you should be able to do the following:

1. Understand why succession management is important.

2. Trace the evolution of succession management from its roots in succession planning, comparing the two models in terms of focus, time, and talent pools.

3. List the steps in the succession management process.

4. Compare and contrast the job-based and competency-based approaches to aligning future needs with strategic objectives.

5. Discuss the four approaches to the identification of managerial talent.

6. Describe several ways to identify high-potential employees.

7. Evaluate the advantages and disadvantages of the five management development methods: promotions, job rotations, special assignments, formal training, and mentoring and coaching.

8. Recognize the difficulties in measuring the success of a management succession plan.

9. Be familiar with the employee's role in the succession management process.

10. Describe the limitations of succession management, and propose some possible solutions to these limitations.

◆ ◆ ◆

IMPORTANCE OF SUCCESSION MANAGEMENT

Succession management refers to the process of ensuring that pools of skilled employees are available to meet the strategic objectives of the organization. Succession management consists of a process of identifying employees who have the potential to assume key positions in the organization and preparing them for these positions. Succession management assures continuity in leadership, and, like any rookie program, develops the next generation of players.

As Peter Drucker says, the ultimate test of good management is succession management, ensuring that there is a replacement for the CEO (Drucker, 1998). Organizations must prepare for expected and unexpected turnover, for key players do die, retire, or quit. The story about the fiery young entrepreneur who builds a hugely successful business only to see it fail in the hands of his untrained children has been repeated thousands of times. Succession management is the great failing of entrepreneurs. Many Canadian dynasties (Eaton's, Woodward's, McCain's) have withered due to this failing. But not only family firms fail at succession management. For example, Goldman Sachs & Co. is an extremely successful investment bank because its president spends much of his day not doing deals as expected but dealing with issues of succession, staffing, and compensation. Getting the right people in place was the key element in ensuring that the company passed successfully to a new generation of partners. The founding partners of Goldman Sachs realized $75 million (US) (when they sold the company) because the president got the people stuff right.

Contrast the Goldman Sachs case to that of Gordon Capital, a company that has been humbled significantly because it suffered from "founders mentality," never nurturing the next generation of leaders. Its executives were working sixteen-hour days because there were no skilled replacements to relieve them. The firm never realized its potential.

Succession management is needed even when retirements and company sellouts are predictable. Texas Instruments CEO Jerry Junkins died of a heart attack at age 56 while visiting customers in Germany. TI had groomed two successors, and so the transition to a new CEO was smooth (Dutton, 1996). An organization that can weather this type of management change will survive. At a minimum, firms need to plan for replacements, and succession planning was the first step in the march toward sophisticated models of succession management. The next section traces this evolution.

◆ ◆ ◆
EVOLUTION OF SUCCESSION MANAGEMENT

Succession planning can be defined as the process of finding replacement employees for key managerial positions: If the CEO dies, who will be prepared to take over that position? Is there a replacement for the vice-president of marketing if she suddenly quits to take another job? Succession planning has existed for over 30 years, and its critics claim that it is not a perfect process. This section examines how succession planning has evolved into succession management by broadening the focus, expanding the time horizon, creating a talent pool of replacements, and improving the evaluation system.

FOCUS

The focus of succession planning was the job and having a replacement ready to fill that job if the incumbent died or quit. This concept of succession planning referred mainly to the succession/replacement charts for the high-level or key positions in the organization. Each key position was represented by a box on the chart, with the name and possible retirement or departure date of the incumbent in the box. Below the box were the names of two or three potential successors, with codes next to their names. These would be, for example, such codes as "PN" for "promotable now" or "RD" for "ready with development." See Table 7.1 for an example of a succession/replacement chart.

In short, replacement planning consisted of a periodically updated table of employees who might be nominated if a need arose. Succession planning focused on the high-potential candidates (replacement track stars), all ready to step into vacant positions and in doing so set off a chain effect throughout the organization. This model assumed that people have single careers within one organization. Thus, replacements were replicas of the current job-holders.

This planning depended on a stable future, where the KSAs of future managers looked pretty much like those of the current managers. Jobs of the next five to ten years were assumed to be identical to jobs today. Organizational structures (i.e., how the organization was set up along divisional lines, product lines, or functional lines) were unchanging, and few new competitors were seen on the horizon. Obviously, this type of scenario just doesn't exist for most companies.

In succession planning, the starting point was the job, whereas in succession management, the starting point is the strategy of the organization. Employees are selected based on long-term goals, and the developmental plans for employees are aligned with strategic plans, not position replacements.

A case might best illustrate how succession management aligns with strategy. Traditionally, the goal of a large utility like Ontario Hydro was to provide safe, reliable energy. Its core competencies were reliability of distribution, measurement of consumption, and the maintenance of its power plant. However, deregulation and a more competitive environment will force Ontario Hydro to compete on price and on bundled services. Sales and marketing are the new competencies needed. The strategy has changed from providing energy to marketing energy. Thus, in the long run, Ontario Hydro must identify or develop managers who have not only sales and marketing abilities, but also the ability to change a production culture to one of marketing. (This example was adapted from Leibman et al., 1996).

TIME HORIZON

The traditional planning approach was concerned with immediate and short-term replacements. What if the CEO were killed in a plane crash? Who would replace him? Or, who is our backup for that vice-president we are planning to promote in six to twelve months? A strategic focus of under one year is a "business as usual" perception, which, if repeated, will not be true over a ten-year period. This short time perspective does not allow for the intake or career management of those with different skills in growth areas.

Succession management looks at a longer term (after ensuring that immediate replacements are in place) and focuses on a future of two years or more. Obviously, this is harder to do, and so rather than identify one replacement, succession managers identify talent pools.

TALENT POOLS

Traditional models of succession planning looked at succession as the passing of the baton to the next capable runner. Managers would identify their top performers, who would be groomed for success. Sometimes two or three successors would be identified, and these would be in a race to the finish line of executive promotion.

As employees cannot trust organizations for lifetime job security, so too, organizations cannot rely on single individuals or a small group of employees for their succession plans. Organizations are trying to identify and develop many employees as possible replacements to insure against employee departures and changing needs for KSAs and to avoid the "crown prince" syndrome.

The organization needs a pool of talent and must mandate the development of many employees with flexible job skills and competencies. "A pool" is a good description of the next generation of talented leadership because the term implies fluidity and responsiveness to the impact of forces. This evolution from succession planning to succession management has led to a model of generating pools of leadership talent within an organizational context of global competition, environmental turbulence, delayered organizations, and new technologies.

Furthermore, a succession management approach should not depend on only internal candidates, but also should track external candidates. Rather than rely on inbred internal managers, the new generation of succession managers tracks high performers in the external market, thus ensuring that new skills and ideas flow into the organization. Large companies like IBM and AT&T have recruited over half their executives from outside the organization to obtain the skills that these megacompanies were unable both to predict they would need and to develop internally.

RATING SYSTEM

Traditional succession planning relied on the identification of the replacement people by a single rater. Previously, only the boss of the high-potential employee supplied information about that employee. The information on which succession plans were based could be both out of date and unreliable. The gathering and recording of these judgments may have been seen as a personnel function, which incorporated little understanding of the real needs of the organization. Thus, managers may not have bought into the process.

In a succession management approach, multiple raters have current evaluations on an employee's performance. The increasing use of 360-degree feedback mechanisms sheds light on multiple aspects of any candidate's style and performance. Table 9.1 compares succession planning and succession management.

◆ ◆ ◆
SUCCESSION MANAGEMENT PROCESS

The succession management process links succession planning and management development. Until recently, in some organizations, succession planners worked with one database, management trainers with another. Now, both databases are integrated, with succession managers working in strategic planning committees, performance management groups, and organizational learning/training functions.

The succession management process is simple to understand but difficult to implement. The process involves five steps, each of which we will now consider in some detail.

TABLE 9.1 COMPARISON OF SUCCESSION PLANNING WITH SUCCESSION MANAGEMENT		
Factors	**Planning**	**Management**
Environment	Stable	Dynamic
Focus	Jobs	Strategy
Time frame	6–12 months	2+ years
Selection criteria	Job experience	Competencies
Appraiser	Immediate manager	360-degree feedback
Selection pool	Internal	Internal and external
Successors	Slated individuals	Talent pools
Development	Limited	Flexible, multiple

I. ALIGN SUCCESSION MANAGEMENT PLANS WITH STRATEGY

Management development has to be linked to business plans and strategies. If the business plan focuses on global markets, then managers have to be formed to manage global businesses. How does this translate into everyday skills? To build global talent, an organization could start by asking these questions: What are the unique skills and perspectives necessary to compete globally? How many managers possess these skills? What percentage of employees could represent the firm to the world? How many could have an extended dinner with key international customers? (Eichlinger and Ulrich, 1996).

The strategic connection is important, and organizations must start with the business plan. Coupled with environmental scanning, managers try to predict where the organization will be in 3 to 5 to 10 years.

2. IDENTIFY THE SKILLS AND COMPETENCIES NEEDED TO MEET STRATEGIC OBJECTIVES

From the strategic plan, managers can then develop a list of the employee skills and competencies needed. There are at least two approaches to identifying the characteristics of successful managers: the job-based and the competency-based approaches.

Job-Based Approach

The first impulse is to start with the job. We know that employees have jobs with duties and responsibilities (discussed under "Job Analysis" in Chapter 3). The job-based approach suggests that employees who have significant experience as managers and have acquired job skills, such as motivating, delegating, marketing, or managing finances, will make successful managers. Additionally, organizations such as Procter & Gamble insist that their leaders understand the marketing of brand names.

Others suggest that this job-based approach to successors is not enough because jobs change rapidly. Furthermore, the increase in knowledge work has led many to search for a different approach to employee development, particularly for those employees at the managerial level. Therefore, many are turning to a competency-based approach in which the capabilities of individuals are the primary focus (Lawler, 1994).

Competency-Based Approach

Core competencies are the capabilities that lead to success. Core competencies are those behaviours that excellent workers demonstrate much more consistently than average performers (Klein, 1996). These competencies are a collection of observable behaviours and can be "hard" or "soft." Hard competencies might be the ability to build new technologies. Soft competencies might be the ability to retain top talent. Given an uncertain future in which skill needs change rapidly, succession management should focus on the development of competencies.

Consulting firms are the perfect example of companies in which the skills and capabilities of individuals drive the business and business opportunities drive the development of new capabilities. Thus, a list of skills (rather than jobs or positions) forms the basis for succession management. Rather than moving *up* a career ladder, individuals move *through* a certification process, developing increasingly complex capabilities along the way. There may be multiple skill acquisition paths, rather than one sure path to the top.

A good place to start preparing a list of competencies is to look at what experts have said about the competencies of successful managers. There are many lists available that outline the kinds of generic skills and competencies that managers should possess. Box 9.1 presents a list of these characteristics.

The lists of skills managers need to possess are endless, and each "expert" develops a preferred list. These lists could be used as a starting point and then be customized to identify and develop managers in any organization. By emphasizing competencies rather than job skills, individuals will be more flexible in adapting to changing organizational needs. Once we know what skills are needed, we can then turn to the identification of employees who might ultimately acquire these skill sets.

BOX 9.1 MANAGERIAL COMPETENCIES

General mobility skills and knowledge: These competencies facilitate re-employment and include effectiveness in group process, communication skills, and flexibility and adaptation.

General managerial core competencies: These competencies were identified by studying successful managers and include "being able to build a cohesive team" and "being able to persuade employees to accept much needed organizational changes."

Detailed, job-specific competencies: Job-specific competencies vary by function, but in HR would include "the ability to implement a change program" and to "identify the best selection tool to identify high-potential candidates." These abilities would vary by level, with a junior manager mastering the ability to identify performance gaps in a subordinate and a senior manager being able to initiate change programs to improve performance.

Source: Adapted from Burach, E.H., W. Hochwarter, and N.J. Mathys. 1997. "The New Management Development Paradigm." *Human Resource Planning*, 20, no. 1: 14–21.

3. IDENTIFY HIGH-POTENTIAL EMPLOYEES

Regularly scheduled discussions about succession force the leaders of the organization to think about the future of the business and the kinds of employee skills needed to facilitate the chosen strategy. By focusing on the future directions of the organization, executives are concerned with the managers who will guide that future. The performance appraisal process becomes meaningful and not just another personnel form to complete. Executives come to own the succession and development plans because they are integral to the success of the organization.

Organizations use several approaches to identify managerial talent (Joinson, 1998), including the following:

1. At the most primitive level, most individual managers will have identified a designated backup and potential successor. This is done in case the manager is away from the office for extended periods (e.g., vacations, training). A manager who fails to pick a successor may never be promoted as no replacements would be ready to succeed him or her.

2. At the next level, some organizations prepare replacement charts with predicted departure dates of the incumbents, along with a short list of possible successors. This is usually done around performance appraisal time, using the performance evaluation data. At Knight Ridder, a handful of senior executives target a diverse list of employees for growth and create annual development plans. These executives stay in touch with each individual assigned to them and become responsible for the development of the leadership competencies of those individuals (Martinez, 1997). Corning Inc. has a list of candidates for each of the top 35 jobs, and this list is reviewed twice a year (Dutton, 1996). The list identifies those candidates who are ready now, those who will be ready in three to five years, and the long shots. These approaches tend to replicate current strengths (and weaknesses) and are not necessarily future oriented, nor are they strategically aligned with the needs of the business. A very sophisticated variation of this approach is to identify the critical competencies for effective performance in specific jobs (Nowack, 1994).

3. A more advanced succession management program exists in an organization that is less inclined simply to replicate existing incumbents but instead identifies the leadership competencies it needs, based on organizational plans. The organization then tries to grow these managers from within. The identification of high-potential people moves beyond the

evaluations conducted by one or two managers. The Public Service Commission of Canada, for example, uses a formal assessment centre to identify those public servants who will become the future executives in the federal public service. Wary of evaluations done by only one individual with one perspective on employee performance, many organizations are moving to a 360-degree evaluation. For many employees, such an evaluation is the first time they have received feedback on how others perceive them. Some employees likened the experience to holding up a mirror, others to a breath of fresh air (Lenz and Wacker, 1997). Employees who had undergone 360-degree feedback reported that they felt that their peers often knew better than their managers how to improve the employees' performance.

All these systems favour the selection of internal candidates. As such, these systems have a motivating impact on employee performance. However, they are limited in their ability to introduce new ways of thinking and working and may not suit the strategic direction of the organization. In the next approach, the managers more actively scan the environment.

4. Managers actively scan the environment (e.g., the actions of their competitors; the actions of the world's best industry leaders in other areas with overlapping functions, such as finance or logistics) looking for external talent. They have developed both internal and external lists of high-potential candidates.

Finally, some companies operate with all four approaches, using replacement planning for highly predictable jobs such as accounting and external scanning for rapid changes in strategic needs.

Assessing employees to identify high-potential candidates must be done both fairly and accurately: fairly so that employees buy into the process and feel that the search for talent pools is an equitable procedure, and accurately so that the selection process is both reliable and valid. Organizations typically use the direct supervisor's informal judgments and formal evaluations such as performance appraisals and assessment centres. (More information can be found in the performance evaluation chapter of any introductory HRM text.) Box 9.2 contains a brief description of common assessment methods.

4. PROVIDE DEVELOPMENTAL OPPORTUNITIES AND EXPERIENCES

Before we discuss the methods used to develop managers, we should first consider two issues:

Are leaders born or made?

Should organizations grow their own managerial talent or buy it on the open market?

Born or made? Many great leaders have had no formal management training. Shouldn't we just select leaders with the inherent qualities of leaders and not try to teach leadership skills to those with no talent?

Peter Drucker, considered by many to be the founder of management as a discipline, is credited with saying, "Most managers are made, not born.

BOX 9.2 TECHNIQUES FOR ASSESSING EMPLOYEE POTENTIAL

Performance appraisals: Managers identify high-potential employees through performance appraisal systems. Raters, who may include the supervisor, colleagues, customers, and subordinates of an employee, evaluate the employee against some predeveloped standards. The goal is to identify and communicate the employee's performance strengths and weaknesses. The information is then used for developmental purposes, so that gaps in performance can be closed. High-potential employees are tracked in this way using a standardized organizational assessment tool. Managers are forced to identify high-potential employees through performance appraisal systems and may be rewarded for developing employees.

Assessment centres: Assessment centres involve a process by which candidates are evaluated as they participate in a series of exercises that closely resemble the situations faced on the job. Trained and experienced managers observe the candidates' behaviour during this process and provide an evaluation of their competence and potential.

HRMS: Large amounts of information about employees' KSAs can be stored in databanks and used to identify employees with needed skills. Employee files can document their experiences, skills, abilities, and performance evaluations. Employees' interests and career objectives may also be recorded. Basic matching to identify high-potential candidates is simplified with an effective HRMS. A useful feature of HRMS is their ability to construct scenarios. Planners can create "what if?" models to determine the effect of employee movements.

There has to be systematic work on the supply, the development, and the skills of tomorrow's management. It cannot be left to chance" (Walter, 1996).

Buy or make? Organizations invest many dollars and other resources to develop managers, but perhaps experienced, trained managers could simply be hired from other organizations.

Some organizations do prefer to pick up their needed executive talent by buying it on the open market. Elliot Whale, president and CEO of Dylex Ltd., had been president of Toys "R" Us (Canada) Ltd. and director of player personnel for the Toronto Blue Jays baseball club before he moved to Dylex. Selecting outsiders allows companies to bring in fresh perspectives, people who can lead the organization through a transformation. By bringing in an outsider, the board of directors sends a strong message to employees and shareholders that the old way of doing things is going to change (Church, 1998). Other organizations feel strongly that they want to indoctrinate and train their own leaders, who then have a deep commitment to the organizational vision.

There are no easy answers to these questions. Organizations may find outstanding leaders by chance, or they may commit to the development process. Some may choose to hire from the outside to obtain fresh approaches; others will commit significant time and money to grow their own managers. However, most large organizations have a policy of "promotion from within." Between 50 percent and 70 percent of organizations replace their senior managers from inside the firm (Dutton, 1996). There are many advantages to this: the organization has accurate records of employees' past performance, and employees understand and are committed to organizational objectives, know the ropes, and know how to get things done. Most large organizations have formal management development programs to ensure a ready supply of "promotables." Let us look at some of the methods such organizations use.

Management Development Methods

In the succession management process, the focus in management development is on the development of competencies, not just on job preparation. Because the goal is to develop multiple skills that may be needed in an uncertain future (in contrast to simply replicating the skills of the present incumbents), management is much more open to various approaches to develop the talent pool. More traditional approaches might have relied on a senior leadership course and one developmental assignment, perhaps mimicking exactly what the current CEO did. The key point is that the approach has changed from one of providing training to fill jobs to one of providing experiences to realize leadership potential. The most common development methods are promotions, job rotations, special assignments and action learning, formal training and education, and coaching and mentoring.

Promotions Promotion refers to an employee's upward advancement in the hierarchy of an organization and usually involves increased responsibilities and compensation. Traditional models of management development saw managers moving up a pyramid, managing larger and larger units until their appointments at the top. Each organization had its favourite route up to the top, some through sales, others through operations. These paths became worn over time, and few succeeded by using other paths, such as an HR track. However, this all changed in the mid-1970s, when the oil crisis made unlimited growth of the pyramid more difficult: the baby boomers were bunching up at the bottom, rough economic times delayered the pyramid, making it shorter, and the development of generalists became more popular, reducing the use of the few footpaths to the top (Peiperl and Baruch, 1997). In flat organizations, where promotions are rare, a preferred developmental method is job rotations—developing managers horizontally rather than vertically.

Job Rotations Job rotations are lateral transfers of employees between jobs in an organization (Campion et al., 1994). Rotations involve a change in job assignments but not necessarily more responsibility or money. For example, one way of orienting a new employee quickly is to place him or her in a new department every few weeks, thus providing the employee an overview of the organization.

Rotations have several motivational benefits for employees, including the reduction of boredom and fatigue. Trying out new jobs also benefits employees who have reached a career plateau. The development of additional skills may increase an employee's job and career prospects. Almost all the research suggests that job rotation makes employees more satisfied, motivated, involved, and committed (Campion et al., 1994).

From the organization's standpoint, rotations are useful for orientation and career development. Rotations allow an employee to increase his or her experience. A common use of job rotation is to take a functional specialist, such as an accountant, and rotate this specialist through both HR and operations in preparation for management positions. As another example, an information technology specialist might try to sell his idea to management by saying "We have to invest in a multiprotocal router," and might be met with complete incomprehension. After a rotation through the sales department, the same specialist might sell the same program by explaining "We're building an infrastructure so salespeople can get access to product or inventory information from anywhere." The technician has learned business skills (Horwitt, 1997).

Besides the additional knowledge of the functional areas, like sales, and management areas, like business knowledge, the rotated employee is making contacts and establishing a network that might prove useful in the future. Learning new ways of doing things, with different co-workers and bosses, also might make employees more adaptable in their managerial jobs. The research shows that rotation improves knowledge of the organization (e.g., of business, strategy, and contacts) and improves the employee's ability to cope with uncertainty. Furthermore, employees who have tried out several jobs gain a better insight into their strengths and weaknesses. Job rotation produces generalists and should be supplemented by training for any specific skills needed.

Of course, the downside of employee rotations includes the increased time needed to learn the new jobs, the cost of errors while learning, and the loss of efficiency that otherwise is gained through repetition and specialization (Horwitt, 1997). In other words, workload may increase for the employee while productivity decreases. The manager and the team into which the employee is rotated experience additional work and stress as they attempt to socialize, orient, and train the newcomer.

At the managerial level, employers should be concerned about producing a short-term orientation in its leadership ranks. Employees in six-month jobs may well do more to create fast results, which might hurt the unit in the long term. For example, employees with a short-run focus may neglect plant safety in a rush to exceed production quotas. Furthermore, the rotation of managers places new expectations on performance, new goals, and reassignment of work, producing stress on the unit managed by rotation (Chereskin and Campion, 1996).

One approach is to give an employee a number of assignments within the company or a related sector. For example, the president of Zellers (now merged with KMart) has worked as president of KMart, at Zellers, at the Hudson's Bay Company (the parent company), and at Woodward's.

Ultimately, managers may be better formed by developing skills horizontally, throughout an organization, rather than by developing specialized skills vertically, up a career ladder.

Special Assignments On-the-job learning is still a favoured path to the development of managerial skills. Most organizations test high-potential employees by giving them an assignment in addition to their regular duties. For example, the manager of corporate banking might be placed on a task force that is considering the acquisition of another bank. In another case, a team of managers might be given a special assignment, such as developing an equity plan for the organization or developing an electronic commerce plan for the company. These types of special projects enable candidates for future executive positions to network and to test their skills in new environments.

Formal Training and Development Management training and education is big business, worth about $45 billion in the United States alone (Fulmer, 1997). Hundreds of thousands of dollars may be spent preparing one executive to become the CEO of the organization. This cost appears relatively minor when it is estimated that the total career investment in an individual employee is 160 times the initial starting salary (Dahl, 1997). In this book, we use the term "management development," but others label a similar process "executive education" or "leadership training" or a combination of any of these words.

According to a study of U.S. organizations, 87 percent offer management development programs that were designed, developed, and delivered in-house (Walter, 1996). Only a small number used external vendors. The majority of companies use traditional and passive instructional techniques and rate them least effective. Most use lectures, seminars, role-playing, and case studies more often than behaviour modelling and experiential learning. (For a fuller discussion of these methods, see Belcourt et al., 1998.) Senior managers need the soft skills of delegation and motivation, rather than hard technical skills such as Web site development or benefits management. Thus, we would recommend that role-playing, case studies, behaviour modelling, and action learning be used as training methods for management development. In most cases, the effectiveness of the training method is evaluated by the smile sheets at the end of the program rather than the application of the learned skills on the job. Techniques for increasing the extent to which training is then applied to and endures in the performance of the job have been described by Belcourt and Saks (1998). Some feel that these training programs teach very specific skills that might not be robust enough to stand the test of time and prepare managers for rapidly changing environments.

Many companies prefer an educational approach that broadens intellectual skills such as the ability to analyze. These companies turn to universities to teach their executives conceptual skills, which would be useful in many situations. Others create their own training centres, which they label corporate universities.

U.S. organizations, more than 1000 of them, have begun opening corporate universities because these organizations view training as a lifelong process, rather than as a course. Most of these universities focus on building competencies and skills that are aligned strategically to meet both employee and corporate needs. These universities offer a wide range of courses, which together constitute something resembling a mini MBA. Through case studies and action learning, these courses offer managers a chance to practise and receive feedback. Unlike professional athletes or musicians, managers seldom get a chance to practise their skills and try out new ideas or methods. Sometimes, these corporate universities have mentors on staff, often with more than twenty years in the business, who coach and assist in the transfer of learning. Such an approach is used by Motorola (Walter, 1996).

The advantage of an off-site location is that it allows managers the freedom to listen, contemplate, and learn in hassle-free surroundings. Some of the corporate university sites have more resources than exist at most regular university campuses. For example, Arthur Andersen operates a centre with 200 educational specialists and 200 support staff, spending about $300 million (US) (7% of Andersen revenues) and serving 60,000 trainees; one-half of them are clients or outside customers. The site has 130 classrooms, six auditoriums, two amphitheatres, five large conference centres, 1000 computer work stations, restaurants, a barber shop, and a bookstore.

Mentoring and Coaching Many very successful managers will explain that their success resulted directly from having been mentored. A senior executive took an interest in them and their careers at a critical time in their lives. Mentors are executives who coach, advise, and encourage junior employees. The mentor takes an active interest in the career advancement and the psychosocial development of the mentee. Career development aspects include examining approaches to assignments and learning how tasks should be handled, which conferences or networks have high career value, and which senior managers to emulate. Psychosocial considerations include building the self-confidence of the mentee, as well as offering counselling and friendship to make him or her aware of the political open doors and open pits of the organization.

Mentoring used to happen informally. Organizations have recognized the value of having a senior manager take a career interest in a junior employee and so have started formal mentoring programs. These programs link executives who have the motivation and time to nurture managerial talent with employees who are motivated to advance quickly.

While it is necessary for discussion purposes to separate management development methods, all companies will use a combination of methods. Some focus on formal programs, such as a three-week leadership course followed by an assignment in a foreign country. Others, such as 3M, allow their employees to choose assignments and to work on ad hoc committees to manage new projects, as well as free time to tinker and play with ideas.

Another reason for using multiple methods is that the development of a senior executive may take 25 years. It is unusual to see a vice-president of a large company who is less than 40 years old. So some companies, such as Wal-Mart, start early, grooming the store managers under a mentoring system to take on more and more responsibility.

5. MONITOR SUCCESSION MANAGEMENT

Some succession plans are placed on an executive's top shelf, ready to be dusted off to prepare for the annual discussion. In no way do they form part of a strategic plan, nor are they used to guide employee development. They are not effective. How do you measure the effectiveness of succession management? Succession planners used to count the number of predicted "high-potential replacements" with the actual number of those placed in the position. If the needs of the business change dramatically, this may be a poor way of measuring. As one expert asked, "If this process worked perfectly and everything happened the way it was supposed to happen, what would the results look like?" (Borwick, 1993).

The answer? Employees would receive regular feedback based on the assessment process and would participate in development plans. The best result would be an organization prepared with skilled employees to contribute to the goals of the organization under changing conditions.

Until this point, we have examined succession management from the organizational perspective. No consideration has been given to the employee perspective.

◆ ◆ ◆
EMPLOYEE ROLE IN SUCCESSION MANAGEMENT

A top-down, organization-directed approach to succession management assumes that employees are ready and willing to be prepared for the next generation of leadership. A top-down approach treats employees as pieces in a chess game. But employees are not pawns. Their voices need to be heard.

The first consideration is that an employee's relationship with any organization is not permanent. The employee can quit, or the employer can terminate him or her. The new employment contract does not guarantee jobs to anyone, even to those performing competently. The former contract was built on an implied promise of a long-term, mutually satisfying relationship. However, market forces create turbulence that sometimes causes companies to restructure or fail. The employer cannot guarantee jobs, and the employee cannot guarantee loyalty.

Today's career model may be perceived as a transactional one in which benefits and contributions are exchanged for a short period (Hall and Moss, 1998). (For a fuller discussion of careers, see Chapter 15.) This transactional view of employer–employee relationships suggests that, as organizations develop employees, they must take into consideration employee aspirations and goals. Employees will participate in management development programs more eagerly if their goals match the succession plans of the company. Employees will enthusiastically engage in self-development if they are aware of the strategic goals of a company, thus enhancing their own job security or marketability. If employees of the *Globe and Mail* knew that the company was changing from a newspaper publishing business to an international information marketing business, then employees would undertake, on their own time and at their own expense, to study languages or marketing. Managerial preferences cannot be the sole determinant in employee development. Career counselling and discussions at performance appraisal time will help ensure that the employee's voice is heard. While organizations cannot promise lifetime employment, competition for leadership talent is so intense that high-potential employees must be given a reason for staying with an organization (Caudron, 1996).

An added benefit of listening to employees is the opportunity to customize the development plan. Employees are very aware of their strengths and weaknesses and their preferred learning styles. One employee might suggest that she could learn decision making by being given a leadership role; another might prefer a seminar on decision making.

By creating a process that invites employee participation, succession managers are more likely to gain employee commitment to and ownership of the plans. We turn now to a discussion of the limitations of succession management.

◆ ◆ ◆

SUCCESSION MANAGEMENT'S SOFT SPOTS

So far, we have discussed the many benefits of succession management and introduced a way to manage succession effectively. However, there are challenges to the implementation of a succession management program; these challenges include the creation of an elite corps of employees, the managerial risk encountered in spotlighting the best employees, the perennial problem of selection bias, and finally, the very human inability to predict the future.

ELITISM

Management development programs, particularly if they support the training of selected employees for specific senior positions, may lead to the perception that there is an elite group on the one hand and the "unwashed masses" on the other. There are several advantages to preparing a limited number—a select group of the elite—including the reduced costs of training. However, many managers fear that by publicly identifying those who will be promoted, a cadre of "crown princes" will be created. Those who are on the list (and expect to be the next vice-president) may coast in their careers, as they know that their contribution has already been recognized and the reward is in the near future. The organization, too, may relax and not invest sufficiently in the further development of these promotable employees. A bigger problem will occur (and it happens frequently) when the one on the chart is not chosen to be the successor. At that point, the person who expected to be the "winner" feels publicly humiliated and will either leave the organization or not fully support the new candidate. Sometimes, things do not happen as quickly as first thought. As Prince Charles, another crown prince, will testify, sometimes the manager never dies or departs, leaving the heir apparent to wait forever.

There are several ways that employees can be "demotivated" by succession planning. The attitudes of the elite may create discontent among other employees with uncertain futures. Suppose the successors were identified on organizational charts and these charts were made public. Those not on the successors list may consider leaving the organization for another where their career prospects are brighter. Managers may ignore the development of other employees who, with some training and assignments, would become likely contenders.

These disadvantages—the demotivating effects on those not chosen, the disappointment and withdrawal if the employee's succession plans are not realized—have resulted in about two-thirds of companies not telling employees that they are on a fast track (Joinson, 1998). By not telling employees this, companies risk having employees leave the organization for one that offers better opportunities, and they also risk having to groom someone who may not want the job. (However, most employees realize their special status through the frequency of their promotions, assignments, and training.) Employers must avoid promises such as "you will become CEO in five years"; such promises are an implicit contract that may be judged to be binding.

Does identifying many successors solve these problems? Surely competition between successors will ensure that the best candidate wins by trying harder and demanding better training. Furthermore, if one successor does not develop to the potential that was anticipated or quits the organization, then others are willing and ready But there are problems with this approach. One is that candidates might sabotage each other, by not sharing important information or by raiding key employees to improve their own track records. As well, many might engage in managing impressions and performing for short-term results in order to be evaluated more highly. This strategy does not encourage team playing, which is a force in organization culture.

There is no easy solution to these problems. At NCR, the management development plan is labelled Project 64K because it is meant for all 64,000 employees, not an elite group. At Johnson & Johnson, the focus is on the top 700 managers (Fulmer, 1997).

RISK OF THE SPOTLIGHT

Another problem with succession management is that executives may be reluctant to shine the spotlight on their most talented employees. Such executives may fear that if they identify their top performers, then other units may grab these talented employees, necessitating the onerous task of finding and developing other talented employees. A related fear is that by suggesting that the managers have developed their own replacements, they will be replaced sooner than desired. However, managers have to know that this talent represents an organizational resource, not a departmental hidden asset. An effective succession program would force managers to identify backfill candidates. Ask these managers, "Who can do your job?" If they are unable to provide names, then ask, "What can I expect to be different next year?" This question leads to a developmental action plan (Beeson, 1998). A manager who does not identify and develop talent is like a high school coach who plays the most senior players to win this year's game with no thought of winning games in the years that follow.

Highly developed professionals and managers make good recruitment targets for competitors, suppliers, and even customer organizations. Increased attrition is a risk, especially if the job offers are attractive. Should companies not develop employees and thereby avoid this risk? The riskier proposition might be to not develop managers and then be unable to find them on the open labour market when the company badly needs their skills.

SELECTION BIAS

Leaving the identification and development of the next generation of managers in the hands of the current one often leads to a "similar to me" selection bias. Managers have a tendency to select as their successors those who seem similar to themselves and who work in styles that are comfortable: the heirs apparent fit in, they look like the rest of the family members. Despite decades of employment equity, most key executives-in-waiting are white males.

UNPREDICTABLE FUTURES

Organizational careers are no longer guaranteed, if indeed they ever were. However, there seems to be a greater state of uncertainty and chaos, and even those who have given exemplary service are subject to layoffs and job loss.

Organizational executives are not psychic; they cannot predict the future accurately. There is a tendency to clone the incumbent executives and to plan the future as a continuation of the present. But as Wayne Gretzky says, "Pass the puck, not to where the player is, but to where he is going to be" (Lear, 1998). This is the challenge for organizations—determining where the play is going to be.

These kinds of problems may be the reason that only 42 percent of companies surveyed by the American Management Association in 1998 had a formal succession plan to replace the CEO (Silverman, 1998). After a decade of restructuring, many organizations saw no point in planning for the future when survival and downsizing occupied all their thoughts. Now that growth is a primary objective for many companies, succession management is increasingly on the agenda, as can be seen in the situation at Air Canada.

◆ ◆ ◆

SUCCESSION MANAGEMENT AT AIR CANADA

The following material was based on a discussion in November 1998 with J.W. Aldham, manager of organization and HR planning at Air Canada. In this case study, the steps in succession management are applied in the real world.

1. LINK SUCCESSION MANAGEMENT WITH STRATEGIC GOALS OF THE ORGANIZATION

During the early 1990s, Air Canada was in a survival mode primarily due to the economic recession. The HR planning role was to restructure the organization and downsize from 2500 managers in the early 1990s to 1200 in 1997. Managers were released through a combination of early retirements, buyouts, and terminations. The strategic goal was survival.

In 1992, Hollis Harris was brought in as the new CEO, and his goal was to return the airline to profitability. The board of directors also wanted to ensure that there were strong successor candidates for the CEO position and for the next levels of management. The board gave Mr. Harris a strong mandate to build management strength. A key focus was succession planning at the executive level. One of Mr. Harris's first steps was to supplement the internal team by bringing in a few key outsiders to fill the senior management positions and achieve a balance of internal and external resources. Lamar Durrett, one of the outsiders, replaced Mr. Harris as CEO in 1996.

2. IDENTIFY THE COMPETENCIES NEEDED

The second phase was to identify internal candidates. Branches were asked to think of their business and the issues that would arise in the future. They were asked if the business would change significantly and, if it did, would they then have the skills needed.

Identifying the requisite competencies was a particularly difficult area of succession management. Core competencies were identified but were not used systematically to select the high-potential employees. Jim Aldham admits that predicting the skills of the future is the weakest part of succession management. Air Canada is creating a program to do this more effectively on the next round, in two years.

3. IDENTIFY THE HIGH-POTENTIAL EMPLOYEES

A significant number of employees with growth potential had left the organization in the massive restructuring of the 1980s and early 1990s. As Jim Aldham says, "In hindsight, we should have been more selective about who went out the door. But we were losing a $1 million a day; we were in survival mode. A lot of grey-haired experience went out the door, and we were left with very bright people with limited managerial experience."

Managers were asked to identify three candidates who would be their potential successors and to rate them as "A: ready now," "B: ready in 18 months," or "C: ready with development." The managers discussed these candidates with their executives. The executives then presented their lists to other executives in a group session. The purpose of these discussions was to validate the branch's perception of potential and to obtain other potential candidates (i.e., in a cross-functional approach). Both senior executives and the board of directors approved the succession plans. Unlike most organizations, Air Canada went a step further, using the succession management process as a vehicle to assess all employees. Thus, they also identified the following:

Reassignments: These were employees who needed to be reassigned to other jobs either because they were in the wrong job, given their skill sets, or because they needed a different experience for developmental purposes after staying in one job too long.

Supply gaps: These were positions for which immediate backfills were not available. At the senior level, these positions were key to the success of the organization and needed to be protected from gaps in succession. Managers were asked to develop an action plan including steps for rectifying this replacement problem.

Marginal contributors: The employees whose performance was below standard and would be monitored for eventual improvement or termination were identified as marginal contributors.

Developmental requirements: These were employees who needed development opportunities to become more effective for current and future positions.

Expatriate candidates: Employees who had been moved to assignments in Europe and then brought back to more senior positions at Air Canada were considered expatriate candidates. These employees were assigned special status because of the huge expense involved in their relocations and the fast development curve they experienced as global managers.

There remained the issue of identifying high-potential employees (for management positions) among the 21,000 nonmanagement employees. Could they be they identified through self-nomination, that is, by applying for posted jobs?

4. DEVELOP THE HIGH-POTENTIAL EMPLOYEES

In the delayered Air Canada (where 50% of the managerial jobs were eliminated), there was little opportunity for employees to acquire managerial skills, although their functional skills were well developed. Therefore, the emphasis now is on the rapid development of managerial bench strength. The company has several methods for doing this:

> *Developmental assignments: The candidate is given a special task on a team or is given an assignment to develop a part of a new venture such as Star Alliance.*

> *Corporate learning: This method entails training courses, workshops, and seminars. An example of one such training program is the International Airline Management Training program, in which employees are given the opportunity to run a fictitious company on the verge of bankruptcy. The team, composed of employees from various functional areas, has to save the company and present their action plan to a fictitious board of directors.*

> *Job shadowing: This method involves a junior employee trailing a senior employee from another branch on an informal and as-needed basis. The goal is to expose the junior employee to other functions. Job shadowing may lead to a job in that other branch.*

5. MEASURE THE RESULTS

Air Canada has monitored the results of this new foray into succession management. The company measured the degree to which the plan identified high-potential employees, marginal contributors, reassignments, senior positions with no backfill, developmental positions, and new hires. They tracked the stock of people and the flow of these people through the organization via promotions, resignations, retirements, and so on.

◆ ◆ ◆
SUMMARY

In this chapter, we defined succession management and contrasted it with succession planning. The five-step model of effective succession management includes these steps: (1) align succession management plans with strategy; (2) identify the skills and competencies needed to meet strategic objectives; (3) identify high-potential employees; (4) provide developmental opportunities and experiences through promotions, job rotations, special assignments, formal training and development, and mentoring and coaching; and (5) monitor succession management. The employee's role in the process must be considered. The limitations of the succession management process include the creation of an elite corps of employees, the managerial risk incurred by spotlighting the best employees, the possibility of selection bias, and the difficulty of predicting the future. The Air Canada case study showed how the succession management process can be applied.

EXERCISES

1. Compare a traditional model of succession planning with the emerging model of succession management.

2. Based on the information contained in this chapter about the five steps of succession management, prepare a survey or a structured interview. Visit several large employers in your area and, using the survey as an interview guide, try to determine which of the succession management steps best characterizes each company.

3. Do you plan to align your career goals and developmental experiences with your employer's goals and needs? If so, how will you do this? If not, why not?

References

Beeson, J. 1998. "The CEO's Checklist." *Across the Board* (June): 41–42.

Belcourt, M., and A.M. Saks. 1998. "Benchmarking Best Training Practices." *Human Resource Professional* (December 1997/January 1998): 33–41.

Belcourt, M., A. Sherman, G.W. Bohlander, and S. Snell. 1998. *Managing Human Resources*, 2nd Canadian ed. Toronto: ITP Nelson.

Borstwick, C. 1993. "Eight Ways to Assess Succession Plans." *HRM Magazine* 38, no. 4: 109–114.

Campion, M.A., L. Cheraskin, and M.J. Stevens. 1994. "Career-Related Antecedents and Outcomes of Job Rotation." *Academy of Management Journal* 37, no. 6 (December): 1518–1525.

Caudron, S. 1996. "Plan Today for an Unexpected Tomorrow." *Personnel Journal* (September) 40–45.

Chereskin, L., and M.A. Campion. 1996. "Study Clarifies Job Rotation Benefits." *Personnel Journal* (November): 31–38.

Church, E. 1998. "New-Style CEOs Follow Zig-Zag Path." *Globe and Mail* (February 20): B23.

Dahl, H.L. 1997. "Human Resource Cost and Benefit Analysis: New Power for Human Resource Approaches." *Human Resource Planning* 11, no. 2: 69–78.

Drucker, P. 1998. "Management's New Paradigms." *Forbes* (October 5): 152–177.

Dutton, G. 1996. "Future Shock: Who Will Run the Company?" *Management Review* (August): 19–23.

Eichlinger, B., and Ulrich, D. 1996. "Are You Future Agile?" *Human Resource Planning* 11, no. 2: 30–41.

Fulmer, R.M. 1997. "The Evolving Paradigm of Leadership Development." *Organizational Dynamics* (Spring): 59–72.

Hall, D.T. and J.E. Moss. 1998. "The New Protean Career Contract: Helping Organizations and Employees Adapt." *Organizational Dynamics* (Winter): 22–37.

Horwitt, L. 1997. "It's Your Career: Manage It." *Network World* (March 17): 39–43.

Joinson, C. 1998. "Developing a Strong Bench." *HRM Magazine* (January): 92–96.

Klein, A.L. 1996. "Validity and Reliability for Competency Based Systems: Reducing Litigation Costs." *Compensation and Benefits Review* 28, no. 4 (July/August): 31–37.

Lawler, E.E. III. 1994. "From Job-Based to Competency-Based Organizations." *Journal of Organizational Behaviour* 15: 3–15.

Lear, R. 1998. "Making Succession Succeed." *Chief Executive* (March): 14.

Leibman, M., R. Bruer, and B.R. Maki. 1996. "Succession Management: The Next Generation of Succession Planning." *Human Resources Planning* 19, no. 3:16–29.

Lentz, S.S., and S. Wacker. 1997. "Career Development in an Uncertain World."

Unpublished paper presented at the Human Resource Planning Society Symposium, Ithaca, New York.

Martinez, M. 1997. "Prepared for the Future." *HRM Magazine* (April): 80–87.

Nowack, K.M. 1994."The Secrets of Succession." *Training and Development* (November): 49–54.

Pieperl, M., and Y. Baruch. 1997. "Back to Zero: The Post-Corporate Career." *Organizational Dynamics* (Spring): 7–22.

Silverman, E. 1998. "Gone Awry." *Human Resource Executive* (February): 42–44.

Walter, G. 1996. "Corporate Practices in Management Development." *Conference Board*, Report No. 1158-96-RR. New York: Conference Board Inc.

III

Strategic Options
and
HR Implications

10

Downsizing and Restructuring

This chapter was written by Professor Terry H. Wagar,
Department of Management, Faculty of Commerce,
St. Mary's University, Halifax, Nova Scotia.

◆ ◆ ◆

CHAPTER GOALS

Employee layoffs! Restructuring! Business closures! Select any major newspaper and see if you can avoid reading a story about downsizing. This chapter provides a discussion of a number of key issues relating to downsizing and restructuring. After describing the downsizing phenomenon and providing a definition of downsizing, we explore why organizations engage in downsizing. Considerable attention is paid to the downsizing decision, the impact of downsizing on the survivors and the organization, and the components of an effective downsizing strategy. The chapter concludes with an overview of the linkages between downsizing and HRM issues. After reading this chapter you should be able to do the following:

1. Appreciate the importance of defining "downsizing."
2. Be familiar with the complexity of the downsizing decision.
3. Recognize the need to address concerns of both the victims and survivors of downsizing.
4. Be aware of the consequences of downsizing.
5. Understand what downsizing strategies are effective in enhancing organizational performance.
6. Comprehend the concept of the "psychological contract."
7. Develop an awareness of the importance of HRM in managing the downsizing process.

◆ ◆ ◆

THE DOWNSIZING PHENOMENON

In the 1990s, organizations have become obsessed with reducing the workforce and operating in a "lean and mean" fashion. However, there is growing evidence that a number of firms have become too "lean" and downsizing has cut into the muscle of the organization. Furthermore, a number of the reductions have been characterized as "mean"—destroying the lives of victims of cutbacks and leaving a demoralized and frightened group of "survivors." In today's environment, downsizing and restructuring are critical components of HR planning.

Until recently, the focus in organizations has been on growth or the "bigger is better" syndrome. As a result, managers charged with developing a downsizing strategy often had little experience in effectively managing the HR planning process and very little guidance from the management litera-ture. While the past decade has seen a considerable volume of articles on downsizing and restructuring, the suggestions they contain often are based on a single experience, are not supported by research, and frequently are in conflict. For instance, should cuts be targeted or across the board? Will the firm's stock price increase or decrease when the firm announces a major lay-off or restructuring? Should an employer carry out all of the cuts at once or stage them in over a period of time?

Downsizing is not simply a Canadian phenomenon. Organizations around the world are striving to improve their competitive position and respond to the challenges of a global economy. Furthermore, downsizing is not restricted to the private sector—governments intent on trimming large deficits have been reducing public service employment in dramatic ways, and cutbacks in traditionally secure industries such as education, health care, and government have become very common in the past five years.

◆ ◆ ◆
A DEFINITION OF DOWNSIZING

It is important to clarify what is meant by the word *downsizing*. Managers and academics use it to mean a number of different activities: some exam-ples of words used as synonyms for downsizing include building-down, de-hiring, de-recruitment, reduction in force, resizing, and rightsizing (for a summary of words used to describe downsizing, see Box 10.1). Obviously, it is difficult to understand the effect of downsizing if we do not understand clearly what it means.

Cameron (1994, p. 192) has defined downsizing in the following way:

> *Downsizing is a set of activities undertaken on the part of management and designed to improve organizational efficiency, productivity, and/or competitiveness. It represents a strategy implemented by managers that affects the size of the firm's workforce, the costs, and the work processes.*

Cameron identifies three types of downsizing strategies:

■ *Workforce reduction:* Typically a short-term strategy aimed at cutting the number of employees through such programs as attrition, early retirement or voluntary severance packages, and layoffs or terminations. While a number of these approaches allow for a relatively quick reduction of the workforce, the problem is that their impact is often short-term, and, in many instances, the organization loses valuable human resources.

■ *Work redesign:* Often a medium-term strategy in which organizations focus on work processes and assess whether specific functions, products, and/or services should be changed or eliminated. This strategy, which is frequently combined with workforce reduction, includes such things as the elimination of functions, groups, or divisions; the reduction of

---

BOX 10.1 EXAMPLES OF WORDS USED TO DESCRIBE DOWNSIZING

Axed	Rationalized
Building-down	Reallocated
Chopped	Rebalanced
Compressed	Redeployed
Consolidated	Redesigned
Declining	Reduction-in-force
De-grown	RIF'd
De-hired	Redundancy elimination
De-massed	Re-engineered
De-recruitment	Reorganized
De-staffed	Reshaped
Disemployed	Resized
Dismantled	Resource allocation
Displaced	Restructured
Downshifted	Retrenched
Downsized	Rightsized
Fired	Slimmed
Involuntarily separated	Slivered
Personnel surplus reduction	Streamlined
Ratcheted down	Workforce imbalance correction

Source: These examples are taken from various sources including Cameron, K. 1994. "Strategies for Successful Organizational Downsizing." *Human Resource Management* 33: 189–211; and Moore, M. 1996. *Downsize This.* New York: Harper Perennial.

bureaucracy; and the redesign of the tasks that employees perform. Since some planning is required, this strategy takes somewhat longer to implement and gets away from the problem of the organization simply doing what it always has done but with fewer people.

It is possible to prioritize the work of the organization based on its business strategy. In carrying out this task, it is important to examine more carefully the work activities within the business. Work can be classified into four categories: (1) competitive advantage work—core work processes; (2) strategic support work, which assists in completing competitive advantage work; (3) essential support work, which is not a source of competitive advantage but must be completed if the firm is to continue to operate (e.g., completing tax or zoning forms); and (4) non-essential work, which does not add value and is not required for the firm to operate but continues to be done because of past organizational practices (Dalton et al., 1996). The elimination of non-essential work often produces significant benefits for the organization.

■ *Systematic change:* Long-term strategy characterized by changing the organization's culture and the attitudes and values of employees with the ongoing goal of reducing costs and enhancing quality. By its very nature, this strategy takes considerable time to implement. The thrust of the strategy is to consider downsizing as an evolutionary part of an organization's life with the goal of continuous improvement—employees assume responsibility for cutting costs and searching for improved methods and practices. Because of the human and financial commitment to this strategy, the impact on the organization's bottom line is rarely immediate and consequently, the approach is less than appealing to firms that focus on short-term profits or budget goals.

◆ ◆ ◆
HOW COMMON IS WORKFORCE REDUCTION?

One issue that comes up regularly involves how common workforce reduction is in Canada. In a national study of major Canadian organizations conducted in 1992, Wagar (1997b) found that 53 percent of respondents had permanently reduced the workforce over a two-year period. Wagar (1996) also found that 32 percent of employers in a 1993 Atlantic Canada study and 61 of respondents in a study of major Canadian workplaces reported reducing the workforce over a two-year period.[1]

When we look at the size of the workforce reduction, we are not talking about a small percentage of employees losing their jobs. Among organizations reducing the workforce in each of the three studies, the average reduction was between 14 percent and 18 percent of the workforce. Similarly, when investigating how the workforce reductions were carried out, combining the results from the three studies reveals that about 30 percent of the reductions were by attrition, 15 percent by voluntary severance or early retirement, and 55 percent by layoffs.

◆ ◆ ◆
WHY DO ORGANIZATIONS DOWNSIZE?

There are several reasons why organizations decide to downsize the workforce. Some of the factors most commonly mentioned include the following:

- Declining profits
- Business downturn or increased pressure from competitors
- Merging with another organization, resulting in duplication of efforts
- Introduction of new technology
- The need to reduce operating costs
- The desire to decrease levels of management
- Getting rid of employee "deadwood"

Simply put, many organizations engage in downsizing because managers believe that cutting people will result in reduced costs (with costs being more predictable than future revenues) and improved financial performance. In addition, labour costs are often seen as more amenable to adjustment relative to other expenditures (such as capital investment) incurred by organizations (Adamson and Axmith, 1983). While executives often perceive that reducing the number of people in the organization will lead to lower overhead costs, reduced bureaucracy, better communications and improved decision making, increased innovative activity, and higher productivity, there is mounting evidence that workforce reduction programs often fail to meet their objectives, as has been observed by Cascio (1993, p. 100):

> *Study after study shows that following a downsizing, surviving employees become narrow-minded, self-absorbed, and risk averse. Morale sinks, productivity drops, and survivors distrust management.*

There are some organizations that drastically reduce the workforce and employ a severe reduction strategy despite increasing demand and a favourable competitive environment. This development, which has been observed by Tomasko (1990) and mentioned by HR managers in personal interviews, may be due to a variety of reasons including a decision to follow the lead of other firms engaging in cutback management and an increasing awareness of the need to operate in a lean and mean fashion.

Although blue-collar and service workers have been the target of downsizing and restructuring efforts for years, middle managers are also under severe attack and vulnerable to downsizing. Based on interviews with 250 managers in eight companies, Heckscher (1995) concluded that the assault on middle managers was not due primarily to increased competition and technological advancement but to dramatic changes in the employment relationship. Organizations are moving away from a hierarchical structure and an ethic of paternalism to an environment of empowerment, independence, and mobility, with organizational loyalty being replaced by the professionalism of management.

◆ ◆ ◆
THE DOWNSIZING DECISION

For many organizations, going through a downsizing is a very painful and difficult experience. A 1994 article in *Business Week* profiled Robert Thrasher, executive vice-president at Nynex and the individual responsible for cutting 16,800 jobs. While he would prefer to be considered a change agent, he has been labelled the "corporate assassin." In speaking about downsizing, Thrasher commented (Byrne, 1994: 62):

> *This is tough, ugly work. The stress is palpable. I'm vilified throughout the company ... that's a tough thing to carry around.*

Too often, organizations embark on a downsizing program without careful consideration of whether there are feasible alternatives to downsizing. Study after study reveals that many downsizings are not well planned, frequently ignore the linkage between downsizing and the strategic direction of the organization, and underestimate the impact of downsizing on the organization and its human resources.

ALTERNATIVES TO DOWNSIZING

Downsizing can be a costly strategy for organizations to pursue, and, as a result, it is desirable to investigate whether alternatives to downsizing exist. In a number of instances, organizations discover that pursuing different alternatives to downsizing may eliminate the need to reduce the workforce or allow for a less severe downsizing strategy.

Some of the alternatives include (1) cutting nonpersonnel costs (e.g., through energy conservation, planned capital expenditures, leasing of capital equipment, reductions in travel or club memberships), (2) cutting personnel costs (e.g., through a hiring freeze, job sharing, a reduction in work hours, reduced benefits, wage concessions), and (3) providing incentives for voluntary resignation or early retirement (Adamson and Axmith, 1983). While this list is not complete, it emphasizes the need to consider other ways to manage costs within an organization.

TYPES OF DOWNSIZERS

It is possible to identify three different approaches to downsizing (Mentzer, 1996):

1. *Rational approach:* This is also known as the economic or common sense approach and is based on the notion that senior executives make rational, logical decisions. An organization that is flabby and inefficient must cut costs to improve its competitive position and ultimately increase profits.

2. *Asymmetric or hysteretic approach:* This involves delaying the downsizing decision because senior management fails to observe objectively what is happening in the organization. Because of their close involvement and high level of attachment to the firm, senior managers may be unable to evaluate critically what is happening and what changes are needed.

3. *Institutional approach:* This approach is based on the premise that organizations, when confronted with change, may adopt a strategy of copying other firms. This may lead to the view of downsizing as a fad that is being adopted by organizations because it is the popular thing to do.

INPLACEMENT AND OUTPLACEMENT ISSUES

In examining the downsizing decision, it is necessary to consider both inplacement and outplacement issues (Latack, 1990). *Inplacement* refers to a career management approach aimed at reabsorbing excess or inappropriately placed workers into a restructured organization, while *outplacement* focuses on the provision of a program of counselling and job search assistance for workers who have been terminated. In making career management decisions, organizational decision makers may opt for an inplacement program or termination with outplacement.

PLANNING FOR DOWNSIZING

Assuming the organization has decided to embark on a downsizing strategy, planning is essential (Adamson and Axmith, 1983). Some key issues include the following:

- Determining how many people will lose their jobs.
- Determining who will be let go. For example, will the decision be made on the basis of seniority, performance, or potential?
- Determining how the reduction will be carried out. For example, to what extent will the organization use attrition, early retirement or voluntary severance programs, and layoffs or termination? It is possible to consider the approach to workforce reduction from the perspective of the employee. As indicated in Table 10.1, the approaches to workforce reduction vary in terms of the degree of protection to employees and the cost to employers.
- Determining the legal consequences. For example, organizations often ignore or are unaware of legal requirements when downsizing the workforce. Some areas of law to be aware of include the law of wrongful dismissal, employment standards legislation, human rights legislation, trade union law, and existing collective agreement provisions.

TABLE 10.1 APPROACHES TO WORKFORCE REDUCTION

Workforce Reduction Approach	Examples	Degree of Protection to Employee	Implementation Time
Attrition	Hiring freeze	High	Slow
Voluntary redeployment	Early retirement Voluntary buyout Work sharing		
Involuntary redeployment	Transfer Demotion Imposed job sharing		
Layoff with assistance	Retraining Job counselling Advance notice		
Layoff without assistance	Termination No advance notice No severance	Low	Fast

Source: Adapted from Greenhalgh, L. A. Lawrence, and R. Sutton. 1988. "Determinants of Workforce Reduction Strategies in Declining Organizations." *Academy of Management Review* 13: 241–254.

- Designing current and future work plans. This issue represents a key challenge for the organization and is frequently neglected.

- Implementing the decision. Implementation includes such elements as severance payments, outplacement counselling, the communication of the termination decision, the timing of the decision, security issues, and communications with remaining employees.

- Performing follow-up evaluation and assessment. Although this step is critical, it is often ignored in many organizations.

ADJUSTING TO JOB LOSS

Workers who have lost their job frequently experience tremendous pain. As well, job loss can be very difficult for family members (see Box 10.2). A number of organizational interventions and practices have been identified as helping previously employed workers adjust to job loss and secure new employment (Feldman and Leana, 1994). They include:

- Advance notification of layoffs, which gives employees time to deal with the reality of job loss and seek future employment

- Severance pay and extended benefits, which provide an economic safety net

- Education and retraining programs, which give individuals time to acquire marketable skills

- Outplacement assistance to inform employees of new job opportunities and to improve their ability to "market" themselves

- Clear, direct, and empathetic announcement of layoff decisions

- Consideration of HR planning practices that represent alternatives to large-scale layoffs.

◆ ◆ ◆
THE "SURVIVORS" OF DOWNSIZING

While we see media accounts of people rebounding from downsizing and starting a new life for themselves, the reality is that for many individuals, the pain of being downsized is very severe. The impact on family life, career plans, and personal esteem are devastating and the social costs can be enormous.

What about the survivors of a downsizing? How do employees that remain with an organization react? A typical response is described by Lee (1992, p. 18):

BOX 10.2 PARENTS' JOB INSECURITY AND CHILDREN'S WORK BELIEFS

Does the job insecurity of parents influence the work beliefs and attitudes of their children? Three researchers at Queen's University collected data from undergraduate students, their mothers, and their fathers in seeking to answer this question.

The results of the study indicated that children who observed their parents experiencing layoffs and job insecurity were able to perceive that insecurity and develop negative work beliefs that in turn predict their work-related attitudes. In other words, family stressors result in negative consequences for children.

Source: Adapted from Barling, J., K. Dupre, and C. Hepburn. 1998. "Effects of Parents' Job Insecurity on Children's Work Beliefs and Attitudes." *Journal of Applied Psychology* 83: 112–118.

The initial anger and pain are often followed by fear and cynicism. Stress, bred of uncertainty and the necessity of doing more with less, sky-rockets. Trust in the company and its management plummets. Employees who remain spend their days juggling more work and avoiding anything that approaches risk taking or innovation.

PERCEPTIONS OF JUSTICE

Perceptions of fairness and equity play a key role in understanding how survivors of a downsizing react to the experience. In examining the survivors of downsizing, three types of justice warrant consideration (Armstrong-Stassen, 1993):

- *Procedural justice:* This focuses on the procedures (or "decision rules") used to determine which employees will leave or remain with the organization.

- *Interactional justice:* This addresses the type of interpersonal treatment employees receive during the implementation of the downsizing decision.

- *Distributive justice:* This deals with the fairness of the downsizing decision. For example, responses from employees may include feelings of guilt after seeing co-workers lose their jobs, support for the downsizing decision as necessary for the firm, or feelings of unfairness and concern that further layoffs may place their own job in jeopardy.

SURVIVOR REACTIONS

There is considerable evidence that downsizing may produce a number of dysfunctional behaviours among the employees who remain with the organization. Some of these impacts, which have been documented by Mone (1994), are as follows:

- *Negative attitudes and behaviours:* In a number of downsizings, employees who retain their jobs report increased job insecurity, fear, stress, and burnout. They may also experience lower self-confidence and self-esteem, reduced job satisfaction, and lower commitment to the organization. Not surprisingly, these factors may lead to increased turnover, absenteeism, and lateness.

- *Reduced performance capabilities:* There is growing evidence that it is not necessarily the poor performers who leave the downsized organization. Of particular concern to organizations is the fear that the best employees will leave, since quality workers are more attractive to other firms. This result, which has been experienced by several organizations, undermines the HR activities of the organization.

- *Lower organizational productivity:* Negative employee attitudes and behaviour, in conjunction with lower performance capabilities, may destroy or markedly harm team activities and result in lower productivity.

Few studies have focused specifically on managers' reactions to downsizing. One recent exception is a study by O'Neill and Lenn (1995), interestingly entitled "Voices of Survivors: Words That Downsizing CEOs Should Hear." The authors conducted interviews with middle managers who had survived a downsizing in their organization (a large financial services firm). The managers were trying to come to grips with what happened, attempting to figure out their new roles as change agents and mentors in the new organization, and struggling to make sense of what had happened. Among the emotions that emerged were the following:

- *Anger:* For instance, one manager stated, "Stop telling us to work smarter. Show us how… Stop blaming us! We've been loyal to the company. We've worked hard and did everything we were told" (O'Neill and Lenn, 1995: p. 24).

- *Anxiety:* Comments included "We don't know who we are anymore." "We talk about empowerment, but we've still got shackles on people. We have to go to senior managers for permission" (O'Neill and Lenn, 1995: p. 25).

- *Cynicism:* There is often very little trust in upper management.

- *Resentment:* Employees frequently compare their rewards with those of others, and even small symbols of inequity trigger emotional responses.

- *Retribution:* There is a need to redress past problems and then move on with the business of improving the new organization.

- *Hope:* While negative feelings often dominate in a downsizing environment, there are occasional voices of hope and expressions of a desire to enhance quality and productivity and rebuild the organization. However, those who are hopeful also believe it is essential that organizational structures not get in the way of rebuilding the organization.

◆ ◆ ◆
FINANCIAL PERFORMANCE AND DOWNSIZING

Do organizations that have reduced their workforces perform better than other firms? This is an important question—one would anticipate that organizations engaging in downsizing expect that their financial performance will improve.

While some analysts suggest that downsizing will improve the value of a firm's stock, investors generally respond negatively to the announcement of a layoff, particularly if the reduction is due to financial factors or involves a large-scale permanent cutback of employees (Worrell et al., 1991). Announcements of plant closings also are typically associated with negative stock price reactions, cutbacks in asset acquisition and dividend growth, and decline in productivity (Gombola and Tsetsekos, 1992).

A study of the financial performance of Fortune 100 firms revealed that firms engaging in layoffs continued to perform much more poorly than organizations not laying off employees (DeMeuse et al., 1994). Similarly, a recent study in Canada revealed that shareholders generally reacted negatively to announcements of layoffs, particularly when a large percentage of the workforce was let go (Ursel and Armstrong-Stassen, 1995).

Two recent studies shed more light on the relationship between downsizing and financial performance. Mentzer (1996) found no consistent relationship between downsizing and profitability in his study of major Canadian firms. However, there is some U.S. evidence supporting the position that improved return on assets and common stock may be related, at least in part, to the downsizing strategy employed by the organization (Cascio et al., 1997). Firms following a "pure employment" downsizing (a workforce cutback of at least 5% but little change in plant and equipment expenditure) did not outperform other firms in their industry. However, "asset downsizers" (firms that cut at least 5% of the workforce accompanied by a decline of at least 5% in expenditures on plant and equipment) generated higher returns relative to other industry competitors.

◆ ◆ ◆
CONSEQUENCES OF DOWNSIZING

There is growing evidence that many downsizing efforts fall well short of meeting organizational objectives. Moreover, many workforce reductions are carried out with little strategic planning or consideration of the costs to the individuals and the employer (Cascio, 1993; Cameron, 1994). More often, job cuts represent a short-term reaction to a much more complex problem. While senior executives often focus on financial issues during a reorganization, the benefits of restructuring frequently fail to transpire if HR issues are not carefully thought out and resolved appropriately.

Despite the guilt associated with permanently reducing the workforce, a growing number of firms are willing to downsize and are discovering that workforce reduction can lead to many unwanted consequences (Tomasko, 1990). Some of these consequences include the high human costs, psychological trauma experienced both by those let go and the survivors, reduced employee commitment, lower performance among employees due to job insecurity, greater attention by management to the downsizing process while ignoring customer and client needs, loss of valuable employees, a shift from innovation to protection of one's turf, lower morale, and potential litigation by employees who believe that they are victims of discrimination.

Cameron (1994) reports on a Wyatt study of firms that have engaged in downsizing. In several instances, participants indicated that the downsizing failed to meet organizational objectives. Among the findings were that only 32 percent had increased profits, 22 percent had increased productivity, 17 percent had reduced bureaucracy, 14 percent had improved customer satisfaction, 9 percent had improved product quality, 9 percent had enhanced technological advances, and 7 percent had increased innovation. While based on U.S. data, these findings appear to be representative of a number of downsizing efforts.

SOME RECENT CANADIAN EVIDENCE

Using data from a survey of almost 1300 major Canadian organizations, Wagar (1997a) examined the relationship between permanent workforce reduction and a number of organizational outcomes. Employers experiencing a workforce reduction were more likely to report that expenses had been cut as low as possible and that the organization was better able to control operating expenses. In addition, employers experiencing a workforce reduction perceived that the downsizing had a negative impact on the firm's reputation. Furthermore, the downsizing firms were more likely to perceive problems relating to financial performance.

The most dramatic results were found when investigating employee relations issues. For eight of the nine "people outcomes" examined in the study, there was a strong relationship with permanent workforce reduction. Organizations engaging in employee cutbacks were more likely to experience negative outcomes with regard to employee resistance to change, employee morale, employee perceptions of top management, conflict within the organization, turnover, job insecurity, stress among managers, and credibility among top management.

Workforce reduction has a more immediate impact on the people in the organization—the effect on performance and efficiency outcomes may be more long-term. However, the degree to which this poses a problem is open to question. If a single organization acting alone decided to engage in workforce cutbacks, the employees would have the option of seeking alternative employment; however, in an economy in which several firms are downsizing, frustrated employees have few alternative employment opportunities and survivors may be unwilling to engage in negative behaviour for fear that they would lose the jobs they currently hold (Cappelli, 1995). Still, firms that have not treated employees well may encounter difficulties in attracting and keeping quality employees when the demand for workers is high.

◆ ◆ ◆
EFFECTIVE DOWNSIZING STRATEGIES

Some organizations are not lean and mean, and downsizing may be an appropriate strategic response. However, cutting the number of people in an organization is not a "quick fix" remedy; prior to embarking on any workforce reduction effort, firms should carefully consider the consequences. Considerable care and planning must go into the decision, and the reasons for the reduction must be effectively communicated to employees. Organizations tend to focus on workforce reduction while ignoring the critical aspects of redesigning the organization and the implementation of cultural change (Cameron, 1994). In addition, managers frequently have little experience or training with regard to downsizing and restructuring.

From a strategic perspective, an important decision involves answering such questions as these: Should we downsize? When should we do it? How should we do it? The focus should be on *rightsizing*, which involves establishing a shared vision of the organization and a clearly stated strategy supported by management, understood by employees, and involving a sense of "ownership" by members of the firm (Hitt et al., 1994).

It is critical that the HR department play a very active role in the early stages of formulating a downsizing strategy. There is evidence that negative outcomes associated with downsizing could be mitigated by increased communication and employee participation and systematic analysis (in advance) of tasks and personnel requirements (Cameron, 1994). In addition, senior management must take an aggressive, visible, and interactive role in formulating the downsizing strategy. However, the identification, development, and implementation procedures should involve the employees. In many instances, the identification of inefficiencies and areas where improvements are possible is best left to employees, who typically are in a better position to make such judgments (DeMeuse et al., 1994).

STRATEGIC DOWNSIZING

Why do so many workforce reduction programs fail to meet expectations? More than half of the organizations engaging in downsizing had no policies or programs to address problems associated with cutting human resources, and several organizations failed to anticipate the dramatic impacts workforce reduction has on the work environment, employees, customers, and clients. Furthermore, many downsizing efforts were not carefully thought out or integrated as part of the organization's overall strategic plan (American Management Association, 1994).

In a number of instances, organizations embarking on a downsizing strategy are also going through considerable organizational change. As indicated in Table 10.2, there are several change issues to be considered by organizations seeking to remain competitive in today's economy.

An effective downsizing is dependent on comprehensive planning for change; proper communication of the plan; credibility of the organization with employees, customers, suppliers, and other stakeholders; and consideration and compassion for both employees who are terminated and those remaining with the organization (Ford and Perrewe, 1993). Moreover, firms engaging in downsizing typically focus only on workforce reduction aspects of the strategy and ignore the more time-consuming but critical strategies of

TABLE 10.2 ORGANIZATIONAL CHANGE AND DOWNSIZING

Characteristic	Old Approach	New Approach
Organizational structure	Functional specialization	Matrix/cross-functional teams
Operational focus	Internal (production)	External (customer/client)
Decision making	Top down	Bottom up
	Centralized	Decentralized
Response to change	Slow	Fast
Communication	Downward	Multidirectional
Career paths	Hierarchical	Lateral/diagonal
Recognition	Individual	Teamwork

Source: Adapted from Mathys, N., and E. Burack. 1993. "Strategic Downsizing: Human Resource Planning Approaches." *Human Resource Planning* 16: 71–85.

redesigning the organization and developing a systematic strategy predicated on massive cultural change within the firm (Cameron, 1994). Research in both Canada and the United States indicates that while almost all organizations engaging in downsizing focus on the first component (workforce reduction), only about one-half make some attempt at work redesign and less than one-third implement a systematic change strategy.

Mishra and Mishra (1994) compared the effect of the three downsizing strategies (workforce reduction, organizational redesign, and systematic change) on two performance outcome measures (cost reduction and quality improvement). They found that the workforce reduction strategy was negatively related to organizational performance while the organizational redesign and systematic change strategies were associated with improved performance. In other words, firms that simply focus on reducing the number of employees typically will find the results fail to meet organizational objectives. Moreover, mutual trust between employees and senior management plays an important role in the success of organizational redesign and systematic change strategies. The creation of a culture of trust is essential prior to embarking on a downsizing strategy.

Bruton, Keels, and Shook (1996) examined one hundred Fortune 500 companies. They found two factors that distinguish effective and ineffective downsizers:

■ Better performing firms cut back not only on the number of people but also on the firm's asset size. In other words, they concentrated on fewer lines of business but typically did not cut employee wages—rather, the strategy was to focus on core areas of competency. In short, strategically focusing the firm is extremely important.

■ For a firm in trouble, cosmetic changes will not produce the results necessary to allow the company to survive and improve performance. It is critical that the downsizing strategy match the needs of the particular organization.

EFFECTIVE AND INEFFECTIVE DOWNSIZING STRATEGIES

A number of studies have pointed out downsizing strategies and practices that do not work. For instance, Hitt, Keats, Harback, and Nixon (1994) identify nine ineffective downsizing practices (most of which have been identified in other studies):

1. Offering voluntary early retirement programs
2. Instituting across-the-board layoffs
3. Eliminating training programs
4. Making personnel cutbacks that are too deep
5. Placing survivors in jobs for which they lack the necessary skills and hoping that they will learn by experience
6. Emphasizing employee accountability instead of employee involvement
7. Expecting survivors to "row harder"
8. Implementing layoffs slowly in phases over time
9. Promising high monetary rewards rather than careers

In his studies of Canadian organizations, Wagar (1996) investigated organizations that had downsized with the goal of identifying what practices distinguished successful and unsuccessful workforce reduction efforts. Five key issues associated with more successful downsizings were as follows:

1. *An expressed higher commitment to job security:* A number of successful organizations met with survivors of workforce reduction and assured

them that they were an important component of the restructured organization.

2. *An ideology based on progressive decision making and a culture that focuses on human resources:* Again, organizations with these attributes were overwhelmingly more likely to have higher economic performance and overall employee satisfaction scores. A progressive decision-making ideology is characterized by participative decision making, explanations of proposed changes to those affected, open channels of communication, and employee input into the decision-making process.

3. *An entrepreneurial spirit within the organization:* Organizations that performed better after a workforce reduction were more likely to underscore the importance of both innovation in the development of new products or services and the presence of an entrepreneurial culture.

4. *Investment in training, new technology, and a quality management/customer/client focus:* While there is often a tendency to cut training and investment in new technology, organizations with lower investment in these two areas tended to be less successful in their workforce reduction strategies. Similarly, moving away from a focus on quality and the customer leads to a number of negative consequences.

5. *The manner in which the workforce reduction was carried out:* While there was little evidence that aspects of the severance arrangement provided to employees who were let go was associated with enhanced performance, the results indicated that more successful reductions were characterized by the following:

   - The reasons for the reduction were clearly explained to employees.
   - The employees perceived that the cuts were necessary.
   - Employee input into the decision-making process was fair.
   - The methods used to select which employees to let go were communicated to employees.
   - Employees perceived that the assistance provided to workers who were let go was fair.
   - Cuts were targeted rather than across the board.
   - Downsizing was part of the strategic management process.

The role of communications in the downsizing decision cannot be overemphasized. It is important to (1) attend to rumours, (2) provide survivors with available information on the downsizing, (3) ensure that survivors are aware of the new organizational goals, (4) make expectations clear, (5) tell survivors that they are valued, and (6) allow time for grieving (Dunlap, 1994). Box 10. 3 contains a summary of some key points of effective downsizing.

BOX 10.3 SOME KEY ISSUES IN EFFECTIVE DOWNSIZING

Approach

Envision downsizing as a long-term strategy.

Treat the organization's human resources as assets.

Develop early warning signals to identify HR needs.

Establish HR planning systems that focus on redeployment of the organization's human assets.

Prepare in advance for downsizing.

Downsizing Strategy

Formulate strategy based on the future mission of the organization and its core competencies.

Communicate in a direct, honest, and empathetic manner with employees.

Involve employees in the design and implementation of worker assistance programs.

Carefully consider the impact of downsizing on employees, the organization, customers, and the community.

Cooperate with relevant organizations, agencies, and institutions (such as labour unions, government agencies, community groups, and educational institutions).

Ensure that organizational leaders are visible, accessible, and interacting with the individuals affected by downsizing.

Smooth the transition for employees losing their jobs by providing safety nets (such as advance notice of layoff, severance pay, outplacement counselling, and job skills training).

Don't neglect to evaluate the impact of the downsizing strategy.

Source: Adapted from Cameron, K., S. Freeman, and A. Mishra. 1991. "Best Practices in White Collar Downsizing: Managing Contradictions." *Academy of Management Executive* 5: 57–73; Feldman, D., and C. Leana. 1994. "Better Practices in Managing Layoffs." *Human Resource Management* 33: 239–260; Wagar, T. 1996. "What Do We Know About Downsizing?" *Benefits and Pensions Monitor* 6: 19–20, 69.

SUMMARY OF BEST PRACTICES

Cameron, Freeman, and Mishra (1991) developed a list of six best practices in downsizing firms:

1. Downsizing should be initiated from the top but requires hands-on involvement from all employees.
2. Workforce reduction must be selective in application and long-term in emphasis.
3. Special attention should be paid both to those who lose their jobs and to the survivors who remain with the organization.
4. Decision makers should identify precisely where redundancies, excess costs, and inefficiencies exist and attack those specific areas.
5. Downsizing should result in the formation of small, semi-autonomous organizations within the broader organization.
6. Downsizing must be a proactive strategy focused on increasing performance.

HRM ISSUES

A critical issue revolves around the impact of downsizing on an organization's HRM initiatives. In light of the growing evidence that HRM practices do matter and are related to organizational performance (Betcherman et al., 1994; Huselid, 1995, Becker and Gerhart, 1996), it is essential that any downsizing decision be made with consideration of the impact on HRM initiatives.

MANAGING THE CHANGING PSYCHOLOGICAL CONTRACT

An important part of the employment relationship is the *psychological contract* (those unwritten commitments between employers and employees). Over the past decade, the psychological contract between employers and employees has changed dramatically. Historical notions of job security and rewards for loyal and long service to the organization have, in many instances, been replaced by ongoing change, uncertainty, and considerable shedding of employees (Mathys and Burack, 1993). Associated with such developments are the considerable pain, stress, and hardship inflicted on employees, including both workers who have lost jobs and those survivors who remain with an organization.

A number of organizations try, as part of their HR planning and development activities, to hire from within the firm (where possible). Such organizations develop internal labour markets in which new employees are hired at specific "ports of entry," and other positions are filled through internal transfers and promotions. Historically, employers and employees often had an implicit contract that was based on the notion that there was a mutual commitment by both employers and workers to long-term employment, and job hirings were viewed as "implicit contracts" in which employees are given certain assurances regarding security of wages and employment. However, such contracts have been radically altered or have ceased to exist in many organizations.

THE "NEW DEAL" IN EMPLOYMENT

In recent years, many organizations have been unwilling to promise job security and continued employment to loyal, senior employees. Rather, a new employment arrangement between employees and a number of employers is emerging. This "new deal" has been described in the following way (O'Reilly, 1994, p. 44):

> *You're expendable. We don't want to fire you but we will if we have to. Competition is brutal, so we must redesign the way we work to do more with less. Sorry, that's just the way it is. And one more thing—you're invaluable ... We're depending on you to be innovative, risk-taking, and committed to our goals.*

What does this mean for employees? In many organizations, we have moved away from the expectation of lifetime employment (Cappelli, 1995). Rather, workers should prepare for a "multiorganizational career" and recognize that it is highly unlikely that they will remain with the same organization throughout their working lives.

While nonmanagerial employees have been the victims of downsizing for years, the trend toward cutting huge numbers of managers is a recent phenomenon. However, the massive cutbacks of management personnel are more than simply a response to competitive pressure or to the introduction of new technology. They demonstrate that we are experiencing a dramatic change in the employment relationship characterized by a movement away from paternalism and a community of loyalty to the new order of "community of purpose," which focuses on completion of the task or mission rather than on loyalty to the organization (Heckscher, 1995).

ALTERING THE PSYCHOLOGICAL CONTRACT

How does an organization go about changing the psychological contract with its employees? There are two different approaches that may be taken (Rousseau, 1996):

- *Accommodation:* This approach involves working with the existing contract and changing parts of the agreement over time. For example, there may be a change in hours of work, job duties, or benefits. While this approach is preferable in a number of instances since workers do not experience dramatic changes, it requires a positive relationship between the employer and employees.

- *Transformation:* This approach involves establishing a new employee mindset and requires workers to *radically* change the old way of doing things. Examples include moving from individual to team-based work or learning to operate new technology. According to Rousseau (1996), there are four steps in implementing transformational contract change:

    1. *Challenge the old contract:* An organization that wants to introduce major changes to the employment contract and yet still retain valued employees needs to provide solid reasons for the changes. Without effective communication and trust, workers simply are not going to buy into the changes.

    2. *Prepare for change:* This involves creating credible signs of change (that is, that the organization is committed to change and is going to follow through), reducing losses associated with change (such as loss of authority, emotional distress, and increased uncertainty), and estab-

lishing transition structures (such as phased-in change or the setting up of task forces to help employees adjust to change).

3. *Generate the new contract terms:* It is critical that managers communicate the new expectations and secure employee acceptance of the terms.

4. *Live the new contract:* Organizations must make it clear that the old contract is over and there is no going back. Too often, managers send mixed messages to employees who then may try to cling to the old agreement. Training for all organization members is critical.

DOWNSIZING AND "HIGH INVOLVEMENT" HRM

Although it has taken some time, a growing number of organizations are introducing programs such as total quality management or continuous quality improvement, self-managed work teams, joint labour-management committees, and incentive compensation. However, a number of these same firms have also undertaken (or are planning to undertake) large-scale restructurings. From the perspective of the employee, these strategies appear to be in competition—if human resources are so valuable and worthy of development, why is the organization getting rid of its assets? Management credibility is destroyed since employees view the notion of progressive HRM practices as diametrically opposed to the shedding of workers—employee involvement and empowerment programs require employee attachment and commitment while downsizing programs focus on organizational detachment (DeMeuse et al., 1994).

When considering the implications of downsizing from an HRM perspective, DeMeuse, Vanderheiden, and Bergmann (1994) identify six key issues:

1. The shifting of responsibility for employment security away from the organization to the employee

2. The paradox of laying off some employees while simultaneously hiring from outside to match employer needs and employee skills

3. Movement from traditional hierarchical career paths to ones in which promotions may be lateral

4. The development of training programs so that employees and managers are able to survive and function at a high level in the new workplace

5. Compensation packages with a larger component consisting of variable pay

6. A focus on the learning organization and continuous improvement.

HR experts have a considerable role to play in downsizing and restructuring (Mone, 1994). Some considerations are as follows:

- Advising on restructuring the organization (including work groups, teams, departments, and so on) to maximize productivity and retain quality performers.

- Developing skill inventories and planning charts to evaluate the impact of a downsizing on HR needs and projected capabilities.

- Communicating the downsizing decision effectively.

- Evaluating the downsizing program after completion. This includes an assessment of who left the organization and who remains. Some key issues include job design and redesign, worker adjustment to change, the need for employee counselling, organizational communication, and a review of the appropriateness of HRM policies and programs (such as training, compensation and benefits, orientation of employees into the "new" organization, etc.).

LABOUR RELATIONS ISSUES

Practitioners in unionized organizations often face additional challenges when participating in the restructuring process. In any downsizing involving a union, it is critical that management representatives *read* the collective agreement—while this should go without saying, in many instances practitioners do not follow this advice. The collective agreement often outlines the procedures to be followed in the event of a reduction of bargaining unit employees. Of particular relevance are clauses addressing notice period requirements in the event of a layoff and provisions dealing with seniority.

There has been a movement in labour relations toward greater cooperation between labour and management and the emergence of new employment relationships. However, changes in managerial attitudes and behaviours are necessary if cooperation between labour and management is going to succeed—unfortunately, many downsizing programs have destroyed positive labour relations programs. Securing commitment to joint labour–management initiatives is, not surprisingly, very difficult when an organization is also cutting the number of employees. It remains to be seen how true cooperation can exist when the job security of employees is threatened.

By way of example, union leaders frequently report that joint committees and employee involvement programs are designed to get workers to make suggestions that increase productivity at the cost of job security. Although a positive labour climate is often associated with favourable organizational outcomes, achieving such a climate is very difficult, and several good relationships have been destroyed when firms embark on a program of cutting jobs.

◆ ◆ ◆
SUMMARY

HR planning plays an important role in the development and implementation of an effective downsizing strategy. The "job for life" approach has been radically changed in the past decade, resulting in a number of new challenges for both employees and employers. It does not appear that the downsizing phenomenon is over, and, consequently, HR professionals must have a solid understanding of how to manage the downsizing process.

There is considerable evidence that many downsizings fell far short of achieving the goals that senior management expected. In a number of organizations, downsizing was followed by lower morale, greater conflict, reduced employee commitment, and poorer financial performance. Moreover, many downsizings were carried out without considering the strategic objectives of the organization, and many employers failed to assess how downsizing would affect its victims, surviving employees, the organization, customers, or society. Managing human resources in a time of cutback management presents several unique challenges to the HRM professional.

E X E R C I S E S

1. Discuss the following statement: "Downsizing is unavoidable. Firms that want to survive and prosper in the global economy need to engage in downsizing strategies."

2. Interview three classmates, friends, or family members who are presently working. Ask them to describe their perception of the psychological contract that exists between the organization and its members.

3. Severance and notice requirements vary among jurisdictions. Use the Internet to discover the requirements that apply in your province.

4. Meet with an HRM professional or a senior management official whose organization has gone through a downsizing. Ask the individual to describe the downsizing strategy employed by his or her organization. Consider Cameron's three downsizing strategies of workforce reduction, work redesign, and systematic change. To what extent did the organization use any or all of these strategies?

E N D N O T E S

1. In a 1997 study of more than 600 Canadian organizations, the author found that 59 percent of Canadian organizations had permanently reduced their workforce over the previous two years (thus suggesting that the downsizing phenomenon is not over yet).

References

Adamson, B., and M. Axmith. 1983. "Managing Large Scale Staff Reductions." *Business Quarterly* 48: 40–52.

American Management Association. 1994. *1994 AMA Survey on Downsizing: Summary of Key Findings*. New York: AMA.

Armstrong-Stassen, M. 1993. "Survivors' Reactions to a Workforce Reduction: A Comparison of Blue-Collar Workers and Their Supervisors." *Canadian Journal of Administrative Sciences* 10: 334–343.

Becker, B., and B. Gerhart. 1996. "The Impact of Human Resource Management on Organizational Performance." *Academy of Management Journal* 39: 779–801.

Betcherman, G., K. McMullen, N. Leckie, and C. Caron. 1994. *The Canadian Workplace in Transition*. Kingston: IRC Press.

Bruton, G., J. Keels, and C. Shook. 1996. "Downsizing the Firm: Answering the Strategic Questions." *Academy of Management Executive* 10: 38–45.

Byrne, J. 1994. "The Pain of Downsizing." *Business Week* (May 9): 60–63, 66–69.

Cameron, K. 1994. "Strategies for Successful Organizational Downsizing." *Human Resource Management* 33: 189–211.

Cameron, K., S. Freeman, and A. Mishra. 1991. "Best Practices in White Collar Downsizing: Managing Contradictions." *Academy of Management Executive* 5: 57–73.

Cappelli, P. 1995. "Rethinking Employment." *British Journal of Industrial Relations* 33: 563–602.

Cascio, W. 1993. "Downsizing? What Do We Know? What Have We Learned?" *Academy of Management Executive* 7: 95–104.

Cascio, W., C. Young, and J. Morris. 1997. "Financial Consequences of Employment-Change Decisions in Major U.S. Corporations." *Academy of Management Journal* 40: 1175–1189.

Dalton, G., L. Perry, J. Younger, and W. Smallwood. 1996. "Strategic Restructuring." *Human Resource Management* 35: 433–452.

DeMeuse, K., P. Vanderheiden, and T. Bergmann. 1994. "Announced Layoffs: Their Effect on Corporate Financial

Performance." *Human Resource Management* 33: 509–530.

Dunlap, J. 1994. "Surviving Layoffs: A Qualitative Study of Factors Affecting Retained Employees After Downsizing." *Performance Improvement Quarterly* 7: 89–113.

Feldman, D., and C. Leana. 1994. "Better Practices in Managing Layoffs." *Human Resource Management* 33: 239–260.

Ford, R., and P. Perrewe. 1993. "After the Layoff: Closing the Barn Door Before All the Horses Are Gone." *Business Horizons* (July/August): 34–40.

Gombola, M., and G. Tsetsekos. 1992. "The Information Content of Plant Closing Announcements: Evidence from Financial Profiles and the Stock Price Reaction." *Financial Management* 21: 31–40.

Heckscher, C. 1995. *White Collar Blues: Management Loyalties in an Age of Corporate Restructuring*. New York: Basic Books.

Hitt, M., B. Keats, H. Harback, and R. Nixon. 1994. "Rightsizing: Building and Maintaining Strategic Leadership and Long-term Competitiveness." *Organizational Dynamics* 23: 18–32.

Huselid, M. 1995. "The Impact of Human Resource Management Practices on Turnover, Productivity, and Corporate Financial Performance." *Academy of Management Journal* 38: 635–672.

Latack, J. 1990. "Organizational Restructuring and Career Management: From Outplacement and Survival to Inplacement." In G. Ferris and K. Rowland, eds., *Research in Personnel and Human Resources Management*. Greenwich, Conn.: JAI Press.

Lee, C. 1992. "After the Cuts." *Training* 29: 17–23.

Mathys, N., and E. Burack. 1993. "Strategic Downsizing: Human Resource Planning Approaches." *Human Resource Planning* 16: 71–85.

Mentzer, M. 1996. "Corporate Downsizing and Profitability in Canada." *Canadian Journal of Administrative Sciences* 13: 237–250.

Mishra, A., and K. Mishra. 1994. "The Role of Mutual Trust in Effective Downsizing Strategies." *Human Resource Management* 33: 261–279.

Mone, M. 1994. "Relationships between Self-Concepts, Aspirations, Emotional Responses, and Intent to Leave a Downsizing Organization." *Human Resource Management* 33: 281–298.

O'Neill, H., and J. Lenn. 1995. "Voices of Survivors: Words That Downsizing CEOs Should Hear." *Academy of Management Executive* 9: 23–34.

O'Reilly, B. 1994. "The New Deal: What Companies and Employees Owe One Another." *Fortune* (June 13): 44–52.

Rousseau, D. 1996. "Changing the Deal While Keeping the People." *Academy of Management Executive* 10: 50–59.

Tomasko, R. 1990. *Downsizing: Reshaping the Corporation of the Future*, 2nd ed. New York: AMACON.

Ursel, N., and M. Armstrong-Stassen. 1995. "The Impact of Layoff Announcements on Shareholders." *Relations Industrielles* 50: 636–649.

Wagar, T. 1997a. "Organizational Outcomes and Permanent Workforce Reduction: An Exploratory Analysis." *Research and Practice in Human Resource Management* 5: 1–15.

_____. 1997b. "Factors Affecting Permanent Workforce Reduction: Evidence from Large Canadian Organizations." *Canadian Journal of Administrative Sciences* 14: 303–314.

_____. 1996. "What Do We Know About Downsizing?" *Benefits and Pensions Monitor* 6: 19–20, 69.

Worrell, D., W. Davidson, and V. Sharma. 1991. "Layoff Announcements and Shareholder Wealth." *Academy of Management Journal* 34: 662–678.

11

International HRM

This chapter was written by Professor Sharon Leiba-O'Sullivan, Department of Management, Faculty of Commerce and Administration, Concordia University, Montreal, Quebec.

◆ ◆ ◆
CHAPTER GOALS

This chapter develops the idea that international assignments are more likely to succeed when HR managers (1) align their HR activities with the international strategic objectives of the firm and (2) recognize that managing people at a distance introduces an extra level of complexity to most HRM functions. The chapter starts with what may, in a sense, be regarded as the HR planning part of international HRM, introducing the variety of strategic business objectives that firms might have for using international assignments, and then presenting a brief overview of the different kinds of international assignments that can be created to meet those objectives. Next, the discussion turns to international staffing and includes a review of criteria for expatriate success, cross-cultural KSAs, and strategic decisions that must be considered in the areas of expatriate recruitment and selection. The third section addresses the topic of cross-cultural training, including how and when training should be provided to maximize cross-cultural adjustment. The question of how to evaluate your international assignee's performance is addressed in the next section, regarding international performance appraisals, and the fifth section addresses the costly question of international compensation. The sixth section explores issues in long-term international career development, including the management of repatriation and the strategic advantage of using your returnee's international expertise. Finally, various strategic issues in international labour relations are reviewed.

After reading this chapter you should be able to do the following:

1. Understand how international assignments can play a role in making or breaking a firm's growth.

2. Recognize the tradeoffs among different approaches to expatriate staffing.

3. Recognize the kind of selection techniques that might help to predict expatriate success, and recognize the advantages of collecting KSA data well in advance of the need to fill an international position.

263

4. Understand the rationale behind testing for expatriate trainability.

5. Recognize the various methods of cross-cultural training, as well as their advantages and disadvantages.

6. Be able to discuss the strategic issues involved in appraising and compensating expatriate performance.

7. Recognize the significance of having a long-term career development plan for expatriate employees, and of having the international assignment represent a key step in a broader plan of job rotation.

8. Recognize the potential cross-cultural adjustment problems that employees returning from international assignments might experience and be familiar with ways that a firm can minimize these problems.

9. Recognize critical strategic issues that may arise when employing labour from around the globe.

♦♦♦
INTERNATIONAL HR PLANNING

As discussed in the introductory chapter, HR planning typically involves the following steps: projecting HR supply, forecasting HR needs, and comparing forecasted needs with projections of supply. The basic purpose of HR planning is to identify the number and kinds of employees needed to fill vacant positions within the firm. However, as was also noted in that chapter, the new model of HR planning demonstrates that it is also essential to integrate these forecasting and analysis techniques within the broader context of the firm's business strategy and to be aware of your firm's strengths and weaknesses.

When the strategic plan is made in tandem with the forecasting activities of HR planning, firms will be more likely to have sufficient lead time to properly conduct the next step (i.e., to plan the policies and programs that will help to get employees ready to perform the tasks required by these new positions). That is, the firm will have sufficient lead time to conduct a thorough recruitment campaign, identify selection predictors to use, and fully train the incoming employees—all of which must typically be done before employees assume the responsibilities of their position. If the business strategy is generally one of growth, but the timing and scale of that growth remain unclear to HR executives, firms might find themselves without sufficient lead time (see Box 11.1). This could lead to hasty, and potentially very costly "hiring" decisions as opposed to well thought out "selection" decisions.

Although the content of the strategic objectives may differ between the domestic and the international context, the importance of HR managers' close involvement remains critical. For this reason, it is helpful to consider the kinds of international strategic objectives that may be likely to create a need for international assignments.

INTERNATIONAL STRATEGIC BUSINESS OBJECTIVES

Firms typically proceed to grow their operations into the international realm in several distinct phases (Dowling et al., 1994). At each phase, different strategic objectives exist, and each of these holds planning implications for international HRM (Ondrack and Leiba-O'Sullivan, 1998).

Firms that are starting to internationalize usually begin by exporting goods abroad as a means of seeking new markets (Phatak, 1989). Although an export manager may be assigned to control foreign sales, exporting is often handled by middle people (e.g., export agents or foreign distributors). So, at this point there is really very little demand on the HR department to conduct staffing activities any differently.

As the firm develops expertise in the international market and as the foreign market grows in importance for the success of the organization, a sales subsidiary is typically set up (Dowling et al., 1994). Employees working in this kind of subsidiary will have a range of tasks. Most will be concerned with developing the foreign market by selling to foreign nationals. Depending on the scale of the operations, one or more managers may be required to manage the sales force (Briscoe, 1998). This is where the inter-

---

BOX 11.1 INTERNATIONAL HR PLANNING

Dr. Stewart Black, co-author of *Global Assignments*, makes this observation:

> *Most international assignments are made in haste, like knee-jerk reactions, when a job is created in a foreign country, but there is no host national to fill it ... the time a human resources manager has to pick an individual is limited. Sometimes it's a matter of hours. Rarely is it longer than a few weeks.*

Source: Ioannou, L. 1995. "Unnatural Selection." *International Business* (July): 54–57.

national HR planning function becomes strategically interesting. The firm needs to assess the feasibility of staffing the subsidiary with host-country nationals (HCNs)—individuals from the subsidiary country who know the foreign cultural environment well—or with parent-country nationals (PCNs)—individuals from headquarters who are highly familiar with the firm's products and services, as well as with its corporate culture. Until managers gain a clear understanding of the labour market surrounding the subsidiary, they may find it easiest to start with PCNs as both sales force and sales management, and then gradually train HCNs to take over the sales function. As upper management is considering whether the risks involved in loosening control (e.g., hiring even a few lesser-known HCNs) will exceed or be exceeded by the risks involved in sending many costly expatriates (i.e., PCNs) abroad, HR managers should remain closely involved. Otherwise, they may not be able to train or properly select staff in time to meet the deadline for getting the subsidiary up and running. Box 11.2 illustrates the lead-time concerns created by complex international strategic business objectives.

Many firms then proceed from having a sales subsidiary to having an international division (a foreign plant involved in production) (Phatak, 1989). This may be done to avoid barriers to trade (e.g., import tariffs), to exploit cheap labour, or to take advantage of government incentives. International divisions tend to be the central point for all of the firm's international activities, and, as such, they are typically maintained separately from the firm's other divisions. Although a combination of both HCNs and PCNs may be employed in various positions (not just sales anymore!) in the subsidiary, *management* will usually consist entirely of PCNs, and a senior executive at headquarters will usually manage the division from headquarters. The HR planning task here will be to ensure that the right number of PCNs will be available who are thoroughly familiar with the firm's culture, as well as highly skilled from a managerial standpoint (especially a cross-cultural communication standpoint).

As the firm grows larger, it typically seeks to standardize and diversify its production efforts (Dowling et al., 1994). The strategic response is often the fourth phase of internationalization: the global product/area division (Neghandi, 1987). A product-based global structure is typically used if the firm's growth strategy is through product diversification; an area-based structure will be preferred if its growth strategy is through geographical expansion. In either case, the key strategic planning and major policy decisions will be made at headquarters to preserve a consistent, worldwide perspective on the firm's activities (Stopford and Wells, 1972). However, the HRM responsibilities will typically become more decentralized (Pucik, 1985): Corporate HR will remain responsible for PCNs classified as expatriates, while a subsidiary-based HR department will be established to manage local employees. The HR planning focus at corporate HR becomes that of identifying (staffing) or preparing (training) expatriates who can develop both a good understanding of the subsidiary's strategic needs and a good rapport with the HCNs. The selected expatriates must not only be able to demonstrate loyalty to headquarters (e.g., communicate headquarter's intentions to locals and

BOX 11.2 INTERNATIONAL ASSIGNMENTS

According to Carla Joinson, a recent Windham International and U.S. National Foreign Trade Council report, *Global Relocation Trends 1996 Survey*, estimates that 300,000 U.S. expatriates are on assignment at any given time. Responding companies reported a solid trend toward more international assignments, with 64 percent predicting expatriate growth.

According to the United Nations, the most transnational firm on the planet is Canadian: Thomson Corp. has the greatest percentage of foreign assets (a minimum of $4.5 billion [US]), foreign sales, and employment based outside a company's home country. Also on the list are Montreal's Seagram Corp., at number 13, and Alcan Aluminum Ltd., at number 15. Canadian direct investment abroad now equals 84.7 percent of the offsetting foreign investment here in Canada.

The reasons cited for the growth in international assignments vary. Colgate-Palmolive, for example, is using expatriates to shorten the delivery time of products to market. AT&T is sending Americans on long-term assignments to impart its home-grown corporate culture. Other firms send PCNs abroad only long enough to enable them to hire and train locals to replace them. Chevron Corp., for example, begins with as few American expatriates as possible; they then quickly turn the operation over to host-country employees.

Regardless of the specific objective for the international assignment, the implications of this growth in international assignments for HR managers are clear: As Jo-Anne Vaughn, a consultant with Global Human Resource Services Ltd. of Bethesda, Maryland, observes, "You don't want to be writing your international HR policy when the first guy's already on the plane."

Source: Joinson, C. 1998. "Why HR Managers Need to Think Globally." *HR Magazine Focus* (April): 3–7; Kidd, K. 1997. "Outward Bound: Canadian Firms Quietly Conquering the World." *Globe and Mail Report on Business Magazine* (Autumn): 8; Solomon, C.M. 1994. "Staff Selection Impacts Global Success. *Personnel Journal* (January): 88–101.

report back to headquarters about local goings-on), but must also have the skills needed to negotiate with headquarters on behalf of the subsidiary's strategic needs.

The fifth phase of internationalization is the truly global organization structure (Dowling et al., 1994). In this phase, internationalization may take on many forms (e.g., the matrix, the mixed structure, the transnational, the heterarchy, the network structure), each of which represents further variations in degrees of control and autonomy between headquarters and subsidiary. The term *subsidiary* may, in fact, be a misnomer in some cases as subsidiaries may take on global coordination for some business activities and subsidiary roles for others (Hedlund, 1986). A common thread linking all of these forms is the increased need for informal controls such as corporate identity, together with a need for greater communication skills and a broader international perspective on the part of expatriates. Expatriates must be aware not only of their own subsidiary's role and that of headquarters, but also of the role(s) played by the firm's other subsidiaries as well. Third-country nationals (TCNs), individuals from one subsidiary country assigned to work in another subsidiary country, are highly attractive staffing prospects at this phase of internationalization due to their experienced perspective on the firm's international activities (Briscoe, 1998). Consequently, HR managers in such organizations must plan to ensure that these more complex HR competencies are met, whether they be in the form of PCNs, TCNs, or HCNs.

There is yet another broad form of internationalization—interfirm linkages in the form of alliances (e.g., strategic alliances, cooperative ventures, collaborative agreements, or joint ventures). International HR managers conducting HR planning in such organizations should recognize that alliances that demand more interaction among the partners require international managers with greater cross-cultural negotiation and communication skills than alliances that demand less interaction (Cascio and Serapio, 1991; Schuler and van Slujis, 1992).

Not all internationalizing firms will progress through these states chronologically; moreover, those that do may proceed at varying speeds (Dowling et al., 1994). The key point for HR planners to recognize is that although expatriates (in the form of PCNs, for example) are used throughout many of the phases, the duration and job descriptions of the expatriates' international assignments will vary according to the nature of the assignment, as will the extent of cross-cultural and managerial training needed prior to departure. International HR executives who are not plugged into the strategic directions of the firm will often have to react, rather than act proactively, in the face of changing international HR needs.

For these reasons, Dowling, Schuler, and Welch (1994) advised that top management give the personnel department accurate forecasts of staffing needs in foreign subsidiaries. The HR department, for its part, should ensure that the expatriate selection and training processes begin early in a manager's career so that the organization can develop a pool of internationally oriented managers.

EVALUATION OF EFFECTIVENESS OF INTERNATIONAL HR PLANNING

The effectiveness of international HR planning can be evaluated according to at least three criteria: (1) the lead time the firm has available to fill a position, (2) the firm's accuracy in estimating the time it will take to fill the position, and (3) the appropriateness of the kinds of international assignees selected for the particular kind of business strategy identified.

◆ ◆ ◆

INTERNATIONAL STAFFING

The strategy is set, the kinds of assignments have been identified, and now we need to look for bodies to fill the roles. The international staffing process involves reviewing job descriptions to identify job specifications (KSAs) for the position, recruiting for the position, using validated predictors to select qualified personnel to fill the position, and evaluating the effectiveness of the recruiting and selection functions. Doesn't this process sound exactly the same as the process involved in staffing domestic assignments? To some extent, yes. However, there are a number of additional strategic staffing issues that are unique to international contexts. These are discussed below.

CRITERIA FOR CROSS-CULTURAL EFFECTIVENESS

We need to begin by defining the "targets" (criteria) that we will be planning to hit with our "arrows" (the instruments we use as selection predictors). Then we'll work backward to describe what we know about these arrows (and the issues surrounding them). Finally, once our archery game is all set up to identify a top-performing international assignee, we'll discuss our options for sources of recruitment (e.g., HCNs, PCNs, and TCNs).

Cross-cultural effectiveness is typically defined in terms of cross-cultural adjustment and performance. The two approaches most commonly used to measure cross-cultural performance are as follows: (1) performance evaluations—reports of the expatriate's performance on the job, defined in terms of goal accomplishment (examples here would include the extent to which sales targets are met, market share growth is achieved, HCNs are trained within a targeted timeframe, etc.) and (2) early returns—reports on whether the expatriate returns home earlier than expected from the assignment and prior to completing the objectives of that assignment (Mendenhall and Oddou, 1985; Black and Mendenhall, 1990; Parker and McEvoy, 1993).

Recent reports conducted by the National Foreign Trade Council in Washington, D.C., and St. Louis-based SRI Selection Research International estimate that the direct costs of a failed foreign assignment can range from $250,000 (US) to $500,000 (US), depending on the country or region of the world (Mervosh and McClenahan, 1997). Moreover, this estimate often does not even include the cost of securing a replacement, the loss of morale and business opportunities at the foreign subsidiary, and the blighting of someone's career who probably should not have been given the assignment (Ioannou, 1995). What do these findings imply? Cross-cultural performance is one target you really want to hit accurately and consistently.

Cross-cultural adjustment, the other aspect of expatriate effectiveness that is common to all international assignments, is often defined as the absence of cultural shock (Mendenhall and Oddou, 1985; Black and Mendenhall, 1990; Parker and McEvoy, 1993; Oberg, 1960). Generally speaking, cross-cultural adjustment represents the degree of comfort that the expatriate experiences in the cross-cultural context. People can experience cross-cultural adjustment along three different dimensions: (1) work adjustment, which refers to emotional adjustment with respect to job responsibilities, supervision, and performance expectations; (2) general living adjustment, which refers to emotional adjustment with respect to housing, food, shopping, and so on; and (3) interaction adjustment, which refers to emotional adjustment with regard to dealing with people from different cultures, including adjustment to socializing and speaking with HCNs both on and off the job.

Cross-cultural adjustment and cross-cultural performance tend to go hand in hand (Ruben and Kealey, 1979; Earley, 1987; Black and Mendenhall, 1990). Ones and Viswesvaran (1997, p. 80) said the following:

> *With regard to both early returns and expatriate job performance, ... adjustment is a determinant variable. As such, adjustment is not an end in itself, but rather a part of a process that allows the expatriate to be able to focus on and carry through the tasks of the job that s/he has been sent to perform.*

For these reasons, firms that seek to maximize expatriate performance should also seek to maximize cross-cultural adjustment. Amazingly, many firms neglect to consider this (see Box 11.3).

CROSS-CULTURAL KSAs

Now that we've got our targets, let's consider the arrows that are available to us. Many different KSAs have been identified as being helpful for minimiz-

---

BOX 11.3 INTERNATIONAL SELECTION

A study conducted jointly by the National Foreign Trade Council of New York, a nonprofit organization created to promote export expansion, and Selection Research International, a St. Louis-based management consultancy, found that formalized international selection procedures are remarkably absent among many of the most globally oriented U.S. multinationals (Ioannou, 1995). The survey elicited responses from only 52 of the 1000 U.S. corporations surveyed, a low response rate by anyone's estimation. One executive at a Fortune 500 firm admitted later, "Frankly, we were too embarrassed to reply; we have nothing in place." Among the responding companies, most failed to carry out any psychological testing of managers destined for foreign locales. They relied instead on the views of line managers and HR staffers, who may often have little knowledge of the business and social culture into which the potential expatriate was about to be dumped. Moreover, only 8 out of the 52 companies even identify the well-known core personality traits and competencies that make for successful expatriates. Despite the finding that half of the managers posted abroad fail, and that 80 percent of those failures are due to the inability of the manager or his or her family to adjust to the new culture, the responding companies indicated they select expatriates entirely on the basis of the technical requirements of the job and the immediate business needs of the company.

Source: Ioannou, L. 1995. "Unnatural Selection." *International Business* (July): 54–57.

ing the likelihood of maladjustment in lengthy international assignments. These include cultural knowledge, stress management skills, conflict resolution skills, communication skills, extraversion, and cognitive flexibility (Mendenhall and Oddou, 1985; Walton, 1990; Black and Mendenhall, 1990; Abe and Wiseman, 1983; Parker and McEvoy, 1993). Several authors (e.g., Black and Mendenhall, 1990; Mendenhall and Oddou, 1985) have simplified the above lengthy list into three dimensions of cross-cultural competencies: (1) self-maintenance competencies, which refer to the capability to substitute sources of reinforcement when necessary and deal with alienation and isolation; (2) relationship competencies, which refer to the capability to develop and maintain relationships with HCNs; and (3) perceptual competencies, which refer to the capacity to understand why foreigners behave the way they do, to make correct attributions about the reasons or causes of HCNs' behaviour, and to correct those attributions when they prove to be incorrect.

Research is still needed to identify which of these competencies is most important under different international assignment conditions (Leiba-O'Sullivan, 1998). In the meantime, reference to this three-dimensional framework can at least provide us with a general roadmap for the kinds of KSAs that organizations should seek when recruiting international assignees.

PREDICTORS ISSUE: SOME DILEMMAS

You may have noticed that the above list of KSAs refers to a mix of specialized knowledge, interpersonal skills, and personality characteristics. A challenge facing international management researchers has been that the instruments used to measure these various KSAs have had low reliability and validity (Phatak, 1989). A related challenge has been that instruments that were found to be valid and reliable in one culture did not necessarily have the same psychometric strength in others (Gertsen, 1989).

Recently, some advances have been made toward globally valid measures of many psychological characteristics (e.g., in the form of Costa and McCrae's [1992] Big 5 personality inventory), and these have been tested with expatriates to some extent (e.g., Ones and Viswesvaran, 1997). Biodata instruments, which have shown high reliability and validity in domestic contexts (Childs and Klimoski, 1986; Mael, 1991), may also prove promising for international contexts. Still, considerably more empirical research appears to be needed before the use of such instruments becomes widespread for international selection. Not surprisingly then, most firms appear to be relying on domestic performance appraisal results alone, which tend to be light on cross-cultural competencies, if they are even addressed at all (Dowling et al., 1994).

One observation that may help speed things along is that organizations need to be clear about what they are trying to predict from the instruments. Leck and Leiba-O'Sullivan (1998) have shown that some KSAs might be better predictors of expatriate success while others might be better predictors of expatriate failure. To date, international management researchers have not attempted to differentiate among the KSAs in this manner. Yet, according to this theory, organizations that are using success-relevant predictors will observe greater criterion validity when they are trying to predict successful outcomes than when they are trying to predict outcomes of failure. (Conversely, organizations using failure-specific predictors may observe greater criterion-related validity when trying to predict outcomes of failure.)

Although further research is needed here before firm conclusions can be made, this issue of targeting the right criteria with the right instruments is worthwhile for international HR managers to keep in mind. International HR managers seeking to run their international selection activities in a proactive manner may benefit by validating instruments for their own organizational context and maintaining employees' test results in their files to facilitate rapid assignment as business needs arise.

OTHER STRATEGIC ISSUES IN INTERNATIONAL SELECTION

Trainability Issue

Research so far appears to have presumed that cross-cultural training (CCT) is the panacea for most expatriate ills (Leiba-O'Sullivan, 1998). Yet, it is quite possible that some individuals are simply more cross-culturally adaptable than others, and that, accordingly, CCT will have a more positive effect on them. Other researchers have also observed that there is a synergistic relationship between selection and training (Wexley and Latham, 1991). If you select someone who is "ready to hit the ground running," then you are less likely to need to invest costly training dollars in that person. Therefore, the question of selecting for trainability is an important one.

Trainability refers to an individual's ability to acquire certain skills to a desired level of performance (Tannenbaum and Yukl, 1992). Preliminary conceptual research on expatriate trainability (e.g., Leiba-O'Sullivan, 1998) has observed that the various cross-cultural KSAs may be classified according to their stable properties (e.g., personality) versus their dynamic properties (e.g., knowledge, skills). Put simply, we may be able to gain incremental success in our selection efforts if we select expatriates who possess a minimum level of the stable characteristics (e.g., extraversion) because such individuals may be better able to acquire the interpersonal skills (e.g., developing and maintaining relationships with culturally different others) that contribute to that success. Further empirical research is needed here as well before firm conclusions may be made.

Cultural Distance Issue

The particular destination to which we're hoping to send the selected expatriate has also been argued to be an important consideration in expatriate selection. More specifically, most theorists have agreed that the cultural distance between the expatriate and his or her host country contributes to the likelihood that the expatriate will experience culture shock (Dowling et al., 1994; Mendenhall and Oddou, 1985). This perspective has implied that selecting expatriates according to their cultural similarity to the host country would increase the likelihood of success overseas.

However, an interesting recent study has suggested that this may not always be the case. Sometimes a country that appears culturally very similar to the expatriate's own (e.g., Canada when compared to the United States) can actually prove to be more challenging. O'Grady (1994) coined the term "psychic distance paradox" to describe the experience of expatriates who underestimate the distance between one's own culture and the culture of an apparently similar host country.

Therefore, a good general rule for international HR managers is not only to consider the KSAs that might be necessary for adaptability to that specific country (based on the cultural norms of that country), but also to inquire about prior experience with that country's HCNs in particular. More realistic expectations can be established in the form of a realistic job preview during the staffing process and in the form of CCT (which will be discussed in the next section).

Legal Issues

The third complicating strategic constraint in international selection concerns legal issues. International HR managers working in Canada should keep in mind, when conducting international selection, that Canadian organizations are covered by human rights legislation. Therefore, although it may seem simpler to send a male on certain international assignments (e.g., to Saudi Arabia), to send an employee of a specific ethnic background to a subsidiary location of that person's particular background, or to send a single employee to almost any international assignment (due to the widely reported negative impact of unhappy trailing spouses on expatriate adjustment abroad), doing so could leave the firm open to charges of discrimination. Firms doing business internationally must, therefore, come up with creative ways to meet both business objectives and legal constraints. Box 11.4 illustrates a potentially contentious legal situation, and shows how one Canadian staffing manager handled it.

RECRUITMENT FOR INTERNATIONAL ASSIGNMENTS

In the domestic context, one of the key strategic decisions in recruitment is the internal recruitment versus the external recruitment decision. This two-option decision has a three-option parallel in the international domain. Three types of employees (PCNs, TCNs, and HCNs) each have their own strategic advantages and disadvantages, some of which were addressed briefly in the HR planning section (e.g., strategic business needs for control versus decentralization). This section will approach the issues from more of an HR per-

---

BOX 11.4 LEGAL ISSUES IN INTERNATIONAL STAFFING

David Banks, president of Resource Professionals, has recruited finance managers, internal auditors, computer programmers, geologists, marketers, lawyers, and even doctors, for countries such as Qatar. He noted that medicine is one of the few areas for which conservative Muslim countries such as Qatar specifically recruit women. Iqbal Ali, managing director of Petro Staff International, finds he has to spend time explaining baffling cultural differences. For example, many Muslim countries require visa applicants to state their religion on the application form. Leaving the space blank or writing "atheist" can result in being denied a visa. The concepts of atheism and agnosticism are anathema to most Muslims, recalls Ali. He recounted an instance when the manager of a company in the Middle East refused to interview a candidate who wrote atheist on his visa form. After Ali explained the sensitivity involved, the candidate rewrote his application filling in Christian. His interview was granted.

Source: Lorenz, A. 1998. "Globe Trotters." *Oilweek* (February 2): 18–21.

---

spective and will briefly introduce some training and compensation implications of each approach.

Suppose your firm is opening a new plant in France. Do you staff the management positions with PCNs, TCNs, or HCNs? According to Dowling, Schuler, and Welch (1994), there are advantages and disadvantages to each approach.

If you choose to staff the management positions in your subsidiaries entirely with PCNs (what these researchers term an ethnocentric approach), then you have the advantage of having employees who are well versed in your company's needs and norms but the disadvantages of (1) having employees who may be unfamiliar with the cultural norms of the host country (including norms of supervision), (2) potentially blocking HCNs' career progression within the firm, and (3) the considerable costs of relocating many employees abroad.

If you choose to staff the management positions in your subsidiaries entirely with their respective HCNs (a polycentric approach), then you have the advantage of using employees who are familiar with the host-country culture. However, the disadvantages are that (1) the employees may be less familiar with your firm's own operations, (2) the PCNs at headquarters may lack sufficient understanding of the subsidiary's needs, and (3) corporate strategy for the subsidiary may suffer as a result.

As a third option, you may choose to staff the management positions in your subsidiary with TCNs as well. This is usually part of a geocentric or regiocentric approach, which seeks, for the most part, to place the best-qualified person in the position, regardless of the nationality of that person. With this approach, you would have the following advantages: (1) you would be using employees who may be more familiar with the host-country culture than your PCNs would be (if, that is, the TCNs come from a proximal nation, such as Switzerland) but whose loyalty will be to the firm (rather than to the host country per se); (2) the relocation costs would be lower than for PCNs; (3) you would be allowing employees from the various subsidiaries to move to other subsidiaries, and perhaps even to headquarters, thereby enhancing career development opportunities; and (4) TCNs positioned in headquarters, be it regional or corporate headquarters, would have the opportunity to interact with PCNs, thereby improving the corporation's understanding of the subsidiaries' needs and vice versa. However, this mixed approach would also involve several disadvantages: (1) you would be using employees who will still be considered cultural outsiders, so some degree of cross-cultural preparation may still be required; (2) unless the TCNs have worked for your company before, in another subsidiary, they will also suffer from a lack of knowledge of the corporate culture; (3) because the use of TCNs is often part of a strategy that entails the use of employees from many nationalities (including HCNs and PCNs), the overhead for expatriate relocation across the entire firm will be considerable; and (4) if you are using TCNs to the exclusion of HCNs, you may create the same blocked career advancement problem that occurs when PCNs are used in this manner.

There is no single correct solution. The ideal response will depend on the particular strengths and weaknesses of the firm, including the time available to conduct a thorough recruitment effort and to select and train the employees appropriately. The response will also depend on the particular constraints imposed by the host country. For example, as Dowling, Schuler, and Welch (1994, p.88) note, "many newly developing countries in Asia and Africa require MNCs [multinational corporations] to commit themselves to extensive training of HCNs before PCN employees are given work visas." The important thing to remember here is that any well thought out approach that reflects corporate strategic objectives will likely improve your firm's odds of success far more than would the use of an ad hoc approach.

EVALUATION OF EFFECTIVENESS OF INTERNATIONAL STAFFING

Evaluation of the firm's international staffing activities could proceed very much as in the domestic domain (e.g., examine validity coefficients for the predictors used). As noted earlier, certain predictors may be more indicative of expatriate success than failure (and vice versa). Therefore, to get the most accurate picture, it would be helpful to use the appropriate criteria for the predictors that are being used. Evaluation of international recruitment efforts could also be done in a manner similar to evaluation of domestic recruitment. Specifically, yield ratios per cost of recruitment source could be analyzed (e.g., number of expatriates yielded per internal posting, number of HCNs yielded per use of recruitment agency in the host country).

◆ ◆ ◆
CROSS-CULTURAL TRAINING (CCT)

We've picked our international assignee, and we're getting ready to give him or her some frequent flyer mileage. International HR's next step is to consider providing CCT prior to departure for the international assignment to minimize the likelihood of culture shock.

Tung (1981) observed that many different forms of CCT exist: (1) area studies programs that include environmental briefings and cultural orientations; (2) culture assimilators—essentially multiple choice questions about cultural characteristics (each answer choice has a paragraph associated with it, describing why that answer was correct or incorrect; until the right answer is picked, the reader is asked to read the paragraph and then return to the question for another guess); (3) language training; (4) sensitivity training (which could include role-playing exercises and behavioural modelling videos designed to raise awareness of cultural differences in behaviour); and (5) field experiences, such as visits to the restaurants of the target nationality or actual visits to the host country itself.

In terms of the effect of CCT on cross-cultural adjustment and performance, the international CCT literature has shown that any form of CCT is better than no CCT at all (Black and Mendenhall, 1990), ranging from the least effective CCT programs that take an information-giving approach (those, such as lecture-based area briefings, with negligible experiential activity) to more effective methods (e.g., behavioural modelling videos or case studies that offer vicarious learning) to the most experiential forms (e.g., training based on role-playing and immersion in the form of field experiences). Tung (1982) described the more experiential methods as being more "rigorous" (i.e., having a greater degree of trainee involvement). Box 11.5 illustrates the information-giving approach adopted by Hewlett-Packard.

Should the most rigorous forms of CCT always be used? Not necessarily, according to some researchers (Mendenhall et al., 1987; Tung, 1981). They suggest that the degree and duration of CCT provided should be a function of both the duration of the foreign assignment and the cultural distance between the expatriate and the foreign culture.

Although researchers have been calling for firms to conduct more formalized CCT for years now, many firms still fail to heed this call (Feldman, 1989; McEnery and Des Harnais, 1990). Part of the problem could be a lack of coordination with HR planning activities: many firms find that expatriates

BOX 11.5 CROSS-CULTURAL TRAINING

Motorola Inc., the telecommunications equipment and semiconductor manufacturer, reports that it outsources its two-day, cross-cultural expatriate training program. The tab? About $4000 (US). Hewlett-Packard Co. (HP), a computer and electronics firm, based in Palo Alto, California, that has expatriates in about 40 countries, puts approximately 1200 employees annually through an outsourced training program that also involves their families. The bill for each employee? Also around $4000 to $5000 (US). According to Ted Hitchcock, HP's international program manager for corporate relocations, "The three-day program includes general sessions packed with historical and cultural information, and targeted training for the employee and family. Employees receive special training in the business practices of the countries to which they are assigned. There are also children's sessions where they talk about their feelings about going to another country, and a section where spouses' special interests are addressed. Most countries won't allow expatriates' spouses to work, but the spouses do have other interests. We use cross-cultural training as an opportunity for candidates to deselect themselves. The training gives them an understanding of what it's like living in the country and working there. [And] then they can say, 'You know, this isn't right for us' because of the family situation or whatever reason."

Source: Mervosh, E.M., and J.S. McClenahan. 1997. "The Care and Feeding of Expats: In the Intensely Competitive World of Business, There's No Such Thing as Too Much Preparation." *Industry Week* (December 1): 69–70.

are often selected quickly (Mendenhall et al., 1987), which precludes a lengthy training process. In that case, one option that could be considered is some combination of on-the-job training and mentoring at the host-country site (Katz and Seifer, 1996). This could be provided by other expatriates at the host-country site or by HCNs.

EVALUATION OF CCT

It is important to evaluate reactions, learning, behaviour, and results for all training programs, regardless of the specific content of the training program (Alliger and Janak, 1989). In the case of a CCT program, the reactions could be gathered immediately after the program is completed and at various key points along the U-curve of adjustment (Black and Mendenhall, 1991) that occurs after entry into the new environment (e.g., after four, eight, twelve, and sixteen months). The learning measures could be gathered both before and after departure and could be conducted in the form of knowledge tests or self-efficacy reports (i.e., measuring the degree of confidence in reacting in appropriate ways in the host culture). Finally, the behaviour could be based on feedback from HCNs, and the results could include a variety of performance-related criteria (e.g., performance levels achieved, completion of the assignment without returning early).

◆ ◆ ◆
INTERNATIONAL PERFORMANCE APPRAISALS

The plane has landed; the expatriate has now been busy on the assignment for a while. How are things working out? When discussing international performance appraisals, we need to return to the stages of internationalization and the objectives underlying international assignments at each of these stages. Looking at these various stages, we find that two broad categories of expatriate assignments exist: technical/staff specialist and managerial (Dowling et al., 1994). The technical/staff specialist may play one of three kinds of roles (Hays, 1974): (1) structure reproducer (e.g., building a marketing framework, implementing a financial reporting system, or establishing a production plant, all of which are essentially replications of the individual's previous work experience in another part of the company), (2) troubleshooter (e.g., someone sent abroad to handle a specific technical problem, such as a computer database failure), and (3) operational element (i.e., someone who fulfils a technical/staff need that may be unique to that subsidiary). The managerial expatriate may perform technical/staff specialist roles as well (usually at a low- or mid-level managerial position) or may hold a higher level managerial position, such as being the general manager of the entire subsidiary itself.

As mentioned in the section on staffing (when we were discussing the criteria for evaluating the staffing function), performance criteria will vary according to the particular international assignment under consideration. In the next section, this point will be discussed in greater detail.

CRITERIA FOR INTERNATIONAL ASSIGNMENTS

Expatriates working as technical/staff specialists may also serve a managerial function, in which case managerial criteria (e.g., supporting or developing staff) will be appropriate (Dowling et al., 1994). However, operational/technical criteria (e.g., the troubleshooter's rate of solving problems) will often take on a more strategic importance. Accordingly, the operational/technical specialist will be evaluated according to more strategic criteria: at this higher level, expatriates are akin to managers of strategic business units who may be evaluated on the basis of their unit's performance (Dowling et al., 1994).

This may sound straightforward, after all, the job has objectives, and the objectives become criteria for evaluation. But, in the international realm, several additional environmental factors combine to make the choice of criteria significantly more complex than they would first appear.

One such factor is the extent of interaction that the position requires (Dowling et al., 1994). A troubleshooter or structure reproducer position in one context may demand greater interaction with HCNs than would a similar position in another context. For example, a computer specialist charged with the task of resolving a computer database problem may have relatively greater isolation when performing the task than would, say, a marketing manager charged with establishing a local distribution network. The greater the amount of interaction demanded, the greater the extent to which performance is contingent on the expatriate's cross-cultural skills. Expatriates hired in operational element positions may face a different kind of challenge. Such individuals, particularly those with managerial responsibilities, will often be faced with tasks that may both be novel and require considerable interaction with the environment. Such cross-cultural contextual factors will need to be incorporated into the performance targets set (either as criteria, or as a moderator of the level at which other targets are set). Otherwise, the set of criteria used may not be truly valid in terms of content.

Expatriates sent abroad to serve as upper-level managers, such as the general manager of a subsidiary, are often evaluated on the basis of the subsidiary's bottom-line results. But how comparable are these results internationally? Differences in accounting systems and financial reporting across countries can often lead to misinterpretation of results (Dowling et al., 1994). For example, as Garland, Farmer, and Taylor (1990) note, Peruvian accounting rules count sales on consignment as firm sales. Can this measure of sales performance be reliably and fairly used as an indicator of successful performance if none of the firm's other subsidiaries count their sales figures in this way?

Another complicating factor is the volatility of the foreign labour market. If labour costs are high in a particular host country (e.g., Hong Kong) but not in any of the other countries in which the firm's subsidiaries operate, is it fair to penalize the general manager operating in the country with high labour costs for lower returns due to costs that are beyond his or her control? Or, if the skill level of HCNs is fairly low, but the host-country government requires the firm to employ a minimum percentage of locals in their operations, can the resultant lacklustre productivity levels (as compared to other subsidiaries of the firm) be justly blamed on the general manager?

In addition, telecommunication and transportation infrastructures are severely lacking in many host countries, which adds to the time inefficiencies (and hence, costs) of doing business in these places (Dowling et al., 1994). Sometimes the infrastructure may exist, but it may operate in a way that is thoroughly foreign to the expatriate. Performance may be fairly slow until the expatriate has reached a more advanced level in his or her learning curve regarding "the way things are done around here" (i.e., in the host country). All of the above must be taken into consideration when setting target levels for performance.

INSTRUMENT AND SOURCE OF APPRAISAL

Everything we know about performance appraisals says that measuring observable behaviour (e.g., using behaviourally anchored rating scales, also known as "BARS") is the most valid and reliable means of assessing performance. So, what do we do when we can't observe the employee's performance directly?

For the general manager of a subsidiary, bottom-line financial results, with targets set in accordance with the environmental considerations mentioned above, are usually the way to go. Consequently, management at headquarters will usually conduct the performance appraisal of general managers.

For other levels of expatriates, however, evidence of performance may not be so easily measurable from afar. One suggestion often recommended in both such cases is to have both host-country supervisors and home-country supervisors perform the appraisal (Dowling et al., 1994). This is one way to get at the observable behaviours that can often make or break performance outcomes (e.g., how one communicates with HCNs). In such cases, standardized instruments such as BARS can be used.

Finally, if the expatriate is a manager, host-country employees and home-country employees may report directly to him or her. In this case, 360-degree feedback may be a helpful means of safeguarding the developmental needs of HCN employees who report directly to supervisors who may be either temporary (e.g., in the case of expatriates on short assignment who are supervising HCNs) or physically distant (e.g., in the case of expatriates whose subordinates are abroad in the home country).

EVALUATION OF INTERNATIONAL PERFORMANCE APPRAISALS

The effectiveness of domestic performance appraisals can be evaluated in terms of a number of criteria. These include (1) the extent to which performance is improved following the provision of specific, objective, and timely feedback; (2) employees' satisfaction with the performance instrument and the way the judgment is reached (e.g., objectivity, content validity, timeliness); and (3) the degree to which the appraisal is informative regarding how present performance can contribute to future career development.

International performance appraisals can be similarly evaluated, subject to, once again, the environmental and cultural constraints noted above. First, the expatriate can be surveyed regarding his or her satisfaction with the appropriateness of the appraisal form and method. (Even better, be proactive: involve the expatriate in the setting of the performance objectives right from the start! This will help to ensure their perceived appropriateness, and the objective-setting discussion will give the expatriate a much clearer understanding of the specific cultural and environmental challenges facing successful completion of the assignment.) Second, assess whether changes in post-assignment performance occurred in the desired direction. Third, survey expatriates as to their satisfaction with the career development aspect of their performance-review discussions. Box 11.6 illustrates how Pepsi-Cola International has incorporated both judgmental and developmental components into their international performance appraisals.

◆ ◆ ◆

INTERNATIONAL COMPENSATION

Would you move from Canada to Shanghai for a work assignment if it wasn't completely clear that you would be (1) compensated at least on par with your home-country salary and (2) given some incentive for uprooting yourself (presuming, that is, that you don't have overseas relatives with whom you're dying to room for three years)? Some people might go just for the adventure. Many would prefer to be assured of a fair, bottom-line reward for this relocation. International compensation policies generally presume that a fair reward is a concern for most people.

BOX 11.6 INTERNATIONAL PERFORMANCE APPRAISALS

Pepsi-Cola International has operations in over 150 countries. The company has developed a global performance appraisal system that focuses on motivating managers to attain and maintain high standards of performance. Their performance appraisal system consists of five feedback mechanisms, which help to ensure consistency of administration while permitting modification to suit cultural differences: (1) instant feedback, (2) coaching, (3) accountability-based performance appraisals, (4) development feedback, and (5) an HR plan. The important thing is that the mechanisms be followed, not how the mechanisms are followed. For example, in Asia, feedback will be given instantly, but never in public. Thus, in practice, the successful delivery of instant feedback requires some adjustment to local cultures.

Sources: Fulkerson, J., and R.S. Schuler. 1992. "Managing Worldwide Diversity at Pepsi-Cola International." In S.E. Jackson, ed., *Human Resource Management Approaches for Effectively Managing Workforce Diversity*. New York: Guilford Publications; Schuler, R.S., J.R. Fulkerson, and P.J. Dowling. 1991. "Strategic Performance Management and Management in Multinational Corporations." *Human Resource Management* 30, no. 3: 365–392.

In the domestic realm, the objectives of any compensation program are to attract new employees, to motivate existing employees at the minimum cost possible, and to ensure that the compensation management process is perceived to be fair and equitable to all employees. The objectives of international compensation are similar. In this case, however, the focus is on attracting employees to international service and on balancing perceptions of fairness among the three categories of employees discussed earlier (PCNs, HCNs, and TCNs). To do so, multinational firms must ensure, at the very least, that employees aren't financially penalized for leaving to take up the international assignment.

THE INTERNATIONAL COMPENSATION PACKAGE

Expatriates and their families will usually incur the following categories of cash outlays (Dowling et al., 1994): (1) goods and services (food, personal care, clothing, household furnishings, recreation, transportation, and medical care); (2) housing (major costs associated with the employees' principal residence); (3) income taxes (payments to federal and local governments for personal income taxes); (4) reserve (contribution to savings, benefits, investments, education expenses, social security taxes, etc.); and (5) shipment and storage (major costs associated with shipping and storing personal and household effects). Employees working in any particular subsidiary may come from a multitude of countries; consequently, the first three of these outlay categories are where the greatest discrepancies can arise if the firm does not take careful action.

The multinational firm has several choices to make regarding how to cover these expenses. For example, salary can be paid at the home rate versus the local rate or in the home currency versus local currency. Ceilings can be established for payment of certain expenses (or certain expenses can be completely prohibited if excessive). The expatriate candidate should be informed of these ceilings in advance. The firm can also alter the combination of the package according to its direct and indirect compensation components to alleviate the effects of tax discrepancies across borders (Bishko, 1990). Finally, benefits such as home leave allowances (trips home) are commonly offered (Editorial, 1990).

By having a policy for the firm's strategic approach to international compensation, the firm will increase the likelihood that the above choices will be made in a fairly consistent manner and that there exists some incentive to go international. As Anderson (1990) explains, three common policy options typically are considered: (1) a home-based policy, (2) a host-based policy, and (3) a region-based policy.

The home-based policy approach links the expatriate's and TCN's base salary to the salary structure of the relevant home country. For example, a Canadian executive transferred to Mexico would have his or her compensation package based on the Canadian base salary level rather than that of the host country, Mexico. The advantage is that this policy (1) creates equity with home-country colleagues and (2) can be cheaper when some home countries have lower wages than the host country (e.g., if a Mexican employee was stationed in a Canadian subsidiary for a while). The key disadvantage is that international staff performing the same function in a given subsidiary may be paid at different base salaries merely due to an accident of birth location. This option can become particularly problematic when the expatriate has been bouncing around from subsidiary to subsidiary over many years and no longer identifies himself or herself as a birth-country national. Box 11.7 illustrates how Coca-Cola has adapted its home-based compensation policy to minimize the morale costs of preferential treatment.

The host-based policy approach links the base salary to the salary structure in the host country but retains the home-country salary structure for

BOX 11.7 INTERNATIONAL COMPENSATION

According to Carl Presley, director of compensation at Coca-Cola, the company has given international service workers a United States based compensation package. This means they're paid according to U.S. benchmarks rather than changing salaries for each geographical move they make. The workers pay hypothetical income taxes based on a calculation of what they'd pay if they were working in the United States. The company then pays the foreign taxes, taking any tax credits the employees might get. In this way, the company ensures that there is no preferential treatment for going into one part of the world for international service versus another. (If an expatriate is in a particularly difficult area, however, he or she might receive an environmental allowance in recognition of the difficulties of that location.)

The international workers' compensation packages also include such compensation-related benefits as housing allowances, cost-of-living differentials, and education costs. Expatriates in the program may receive home leave, which allows them to return home if they wish for a certain period to renew their ties with friends and family. Finally, to further ensure equity within the international ranks, the company also has a worldwide job evaluation system. The same positions in different parts of the world are accorded the same internal value.

Source: Anfuso, D. 1994. "Coca-Cola's Staffing Philosophy Supports Its Global Strategy." *Personnel Journal 73*, no. 11: 116

other international supplements (e.g., cost-of-living adjustment, housing, schooling, and other premiums). The one advantage of this approach is that it attracts PCNs or TCNs to a higher-paying location. Disadvantages are that it does not eliminate inequities between PCNs and TCNs unless the home-country supplements are phased out over time (something which would apply primarily to expatriates who are unlikely to be repatriated to their country of origin).

Finally, the region-based policy compensates expatriates working in their home regions (e.g., Canadians working in North America) at somewhat lower levels than those who are working in regions far from home. This approach has the advantages of (1) providing incentives for distant foreign relocation and (2) allowing significant cost savings, since those stationed in neighbouring countries will not receive the same premiums as those travelling farther away, and so it remains a promising option (Dowling et al., 1994).

EVALUATION OF INTERNATIONAL COMPENSATION

Recall that the objectives of international compensation were to (1) minimize costs, (2) maximize the motivation of the expatriate to be productive overseas, and (3) maintain equity (as much as possible) among the HCNs, PCNs, and TCNs working at each subsidiary. If expatriates (be they PCNs or TCNs) feel sufficiently compensated that they don't return early from the assignment or slacken productivity level while abroad, then that can be taken as a good sign. Giving them incentive payments in return for exemplary performance would be an additional sign that the compensation scheme is working. However, expatriates ideally should be advised about tax and investment strategies so that they are not shocked beyond belief upon returning home and encountering inflationary circumstances as well. Thus, *re*patriates' assessments can be another good indication of international compensation success. Finally, if the costs of expatriate compensation are spiralling out of proportion to the estimated financial returns for the international assignment itself, then the ceiling on certain categories of expenses or the overall staffing strategy may need to be reassessed (e.g., it may be time to consider moving toward use of HCNs, who often will cost less due to the lack of relocation expenses involved) (Anderson, 1990).

◆ ◆ ◆

INTERNATIONAL CAREER DEVELOPMENT

Two issues are of great importance for the long-term career development of the expatriate employee. The first is to regard the international assignment as merely one step in an overall career development plan. The second is to ensure that the next step (i.e., the expatriate's subsequent assignment) makes good use of the KSAs developed internationally, as these will serve as a source of competitive advantage to the firm.

TREATING THE INTERNATIONAL ASSIGNMENT AS A JOB ROTATION

To truly treat the international assignment as merely one step in an overall career development plan, one must consider the issues and principles involved in job rotation in general (Nicholson, 1984; Pinder and Schroeder,

1987). More specifically, the employee should remain on the rotation long enough to attain a level of proficiency that enhances context-specific knowledge and self-efficacy. The rationale for this is as follows.

If one of the objectives of the expatriate's assignment is to acquire technical skills that are available only in the subsidiary, then ample time should be allowed for the expatriate to develop these skills; similarly, if an objective of the assignment is to learn, from headquarters, how the organization works, then ample time should be allowed for this. The point is that removing the employee from the assignment prior to some degree of mastery being achieved may be detrimental to his or her self-efficacy (and, hence, to the actual expertise you sought to cultivate in the first place because self-efficacy is closely related to performance outcomes of various kinds) (Gist et al., 1989; Gist et al., 1991). The bottom line is this: Consider the learning curve and the time required to achieve proficiency in the assignment.

Still, to fully regard the international assignment as part of a long-term career development process, a plan must be in place for the expatriate's return to the home country (presuming, that is, that the PCN is to remain a PCN and not become a TCN). This, unfortunately, is where a lot of organizations fall short, and it has led to what has become known as the "repatriation issue."

THE REPATRIATION ISSUE

It is somehow expected that one will encounter culture shock when moving to another country. That one might experience culture shock upon return from abroad is usually not a concern. Yet, research (Welch et al., 1992) suggests that the "big picture" of the cross-cultural adjustment process is that it is not just a U-curve process (i.e., the high of the post-arrival honeymoon, the low of the cultural shock experience, and the eventual regained high of adjustment and mastery), but rather a W-curve process, with the last "V" of the "W" happening in the form of "reverse culture shock" on return to the home country (Black et al., 1992).

It has been argued that reverse culture shock upon repatriation leads to several serious consequences for the employee and the organization. First, prior to the return home, the employee may become anxious at the thought of having no appropriate position to return to; this anxiety can affect productivity abroad and work adjustment shortly after repatriation (Black and

Gregersen, 1991). Second, the employee may become dissatisfied with his or her standard of living upon return, having become accustomed to the special status that accompanied the expatriate position (Black and Gregersen, 1991). Third, co-workers may not be interested in hearing about the repatriate's experiences—lots of things have gone on in their own lives over the last few years, and they've had their own preoccupations and focus (Harvey, 1982). Fourth, the repatriate's job may not make as much use of internationally acquired KSAs as it could (Beck, 1988; Tung, 1988). In this case, "ought of sight, out of mind" is the operative phrase (Dowling et al., 1994). Box 11.8 illustrates how this attitude can create "perpetual expatriates" and deprive a firm's headquarters of badly needed international competencies.

Fifth, and perhaps more serious, is that there is a high rate of turnover among repatriates, ranging from 20 percent to 25 percent for U.S. repatriates (Adler, 1991); comparable figures are not available for Canadian repatriates. Clearly, making the most of the repatriate's internationally developed KSAs and letting the soon-to-be-repatriated individual have a clearer idea of what's in store will go a long way toward minimizing these negative consequences.

BOX 11.8 ONCE ABROAD, ALWAYS ABROAD?

A 1997 survey conducted jointly by Berlitz International, Inc., HFS Mobility Services, and the SHRM Institute for International Human Resources made some interesting observations regarding the way international careers are being managed. More than 400 mostly male (84%) international transferees from 80 corporations representing 52 countries participated in the survey. The majority of participants (52%) who responded had completed their assignments abroad in the last six months. Eighty-six percent of those surveyed indicated that they felt international career planning was an essential service. Seventy-four percent of international transferees were not offered the chance to discuss how the experiences gained abroad would be used after repatriation. Nearly half the respondents felt their organizations did not understand the skills and experiences they had acquired during the international assignment. Interestingly, 61 percent of those surveyed still expressed interest in another international assignment (perhaps in response to the lack of a suitable position in the home country).

Source: Berlitz International, Inc., HFS Mobility Services, and the SHRM Institute for International Human Resources. 1997. "1996–1997 International Assignee Research Project: Identifying the International Transferee's Expectation Levels for Support Services."

MAKING THE MOST OF YOUR REPATRIATE'S INTERNATIONAL KSA'S

There are a number of ways to incorporate KSAs acquired internationally into the repatriates' subsequent career development. The repatriate could serve as a mentor or formal trainer to future expatriates or provide input into the CCT process by recounting critical incidents experienced abroad. (This could have the benefit of giving the repatriate an appropriate forum in which to discuss his or her experiences.) Alternatively (or as well), the repatriate can apply his or her understanding of the subordinate's needs by eventually serving as a long-distance supervisor to other expatriates. Another option is for the expatriate not to be repatriated but instead to join the cadre of permanent international employees and remain an expatriate for the duration of his or her career, rotating from subsidiary to subsidiary. The precise effects of these various options on repatriate satisfaction and turnover require empirical investigation. Box 11.9 provides anecdotal evidence of how consideration of the repatriation issue proved to be effective for the Welcome Foundation. Some suggestions for how these options can be evaluated are given below.

EVALUATION OF INTERNATIONAL CAREER DEVELOPMENT

The success of the international career development effort can be evaluated in a number of ways. First, productivity levels and absenteeism can be assessed shortly prior to the scheduled return to the home country. Second, rates of expatriate turnover at various intervals shortly after the return to the home country can be assessed. Last but not least, expatriate job satisfaction

---

BOX 11.9 AN EFFECTIVE REPATRIATION POLICY

Michael Maher, the forum chairman and international HR director of the Welcome Foundation, says that Welcome has 47 locations around the world and 36 nationalities on expatriate assignments. In 1994, the company developed a new policy for its returning employees, treating assignments as effective organizational solutions without neglecting the employees whom they regard as a group resource. Maher said communication was given a high priority. Expatriates were given more information and more support on returning home. The new policy optimized management skills and led to fast and effective decision making. As a result, 87 percent of those who had been posted abroad reported being happy to go again.

Source: Hodges, C. 1995. "Planning Is Key to Successful Expatriation." *People Management* (March 9): 18.

can be assessed, and repatriates can be queried about specific aspects of their international assignment and the repatriation process that could have been managed better.

♦ ♦ ♦
INTERNATIONAL LABOUR RELATIONS

Knowledge of the types of unions that exist in a country (i.e., the union structure) and the rate of unionization in that country can be critical to international HR managers. This is because union activities can influence what HR practices may be implemented and how implementation may proceed. In short, such knowledge can influence international HR strategy.

This section will begin by reviewing the types of unions and give some examples of the rate and structure of unionization in various countries. Next, because labour relations practices may be applied differently in different countries, *even when* similar union structures exist, the second part of this section will review how specific functional areas of HR (e.g., staffing, compensation) may need to be altered when operating in various international unionized environments.

TYPES OF UNIONS AND VARIOUS NATIONAL APPROACHES TO UNIONIZATION

At least four types of unions can be identified (Katz and Elsea, 1997): industrial, craft, conglomerate, and general. Industrial unions represent all grades of employees in an industry; craft unions are based on skilled occupations across industries; conglomerate unions represent members in more than one industry; and general unions are open to all employees in the country. This diversity of types of unions can be found to varying extents in different countries (Katz and Elsea, 1997). For example, Canada's union structure is industrial, craft, and conglomerate. In Australia, the United Kingdom, and the United States, all four types of union structures exist, although the United States has white-collar unions as well. Germany's union structure is primarily industrial and white collar, and Norway's is both industrial and craft. Japan's union structure consists of enterprise unions.

In addition to the diversity in types of unions, nations vary in their rates of unionization (Katz and Elsea, 1997): The United States has the lowest unionization rate, at 17 percent. Japan's rate is slightly higher, at 29 percent. Canada's unionization rate is tied with Germany's, at 38 percent. Australia's rate is 46 percent, while the United Kingdom's is 52 percent. One of the highest rates of unionization exists in Norway, where it is 65 percent.

Differences in union structure and rate of unionization suggest differences in the influence of unions in a host country. This, in turn, suggests differences in the way HR managers will need to conduct their labour relations activities. To complicate matters further, the *level* at which labour relations activities take place also varies somewhat from country to country. For example, in Canada, labour relations activities are primarily aimed at peacefully preventing or settling grievances and collective industrial disputes while considering the well-being of the public (Katz and Elsea, 1997). Such activities, which seek to involve all parties concerned in decisions affecting basic workers, rights (e.g., the right to organize, to bargain collectively, and to strike to provide for adequate wages, working conditions, and the existence of a fair distribution of wealth that the workers help to create), occur primarily between firms and their unions. In Japan and in the United States, labour relations activities have also developed as the domain of individual business (Katz and Elsea, 1997). In contrast, in most of the European Union (EU), the negotiation of collective agreements has been treated as a matter external to the firm (Katz and Elsea, 1997): In Germany, the law has dictated union involvement in management of the enterprise through codetermination (i.e., the representation and participation of workers on corporate boards of directors). Indeed, sometimes even one-third of the board of directors consists of workers. In the United Kingdom, industrial democracy takes the form of shop-floor activities, which serve to provide an intermediate level of bargaining between labour and management. International HR managers need to be aware of these variations in methods of labour relations activity as they seek to employ HCNs.

INFLUENCE OF UNIONS ON INTERNATIONAL HRM STRATEGY: SPECIFIC ISSUES FOR INTERNATIONAL HR MANAGERS

Awareness of practical differences in labour relations, while laudable, is by itself insufficient. International HR managers need to translate this awareness into practice. Labour relations activities can constrain MNCs' abilities to influence wage levels (perhaps even to the extent that labour costs become noncompetitive) (Katz and Elsea, 1997). Such activities may also limit the ability of MNCs to vary employment levels at will and may hinder or prevent global integration of the operations of the MNC (Katz and Elsea, 1997).

Accordingly, international HR managers must devise strategies to improve the fit between their labour relations activities and the external environment. Strategic compensation might be limited in countries with strong governmental or union wage interference. Firms operating in such countries may need to find other ways of maintaining low costs. Staffing may be affected in countries that limit the firm's ability to implement redundancy programs (Katz and Elsea, 1997). In such countries, worker retraining may be important due to the economic necessity to cross-train and retain workers to adapt to environmental and technological changes affecting the firm rather than lay off workers (Katz and Elsea, 1997). In short, the presence of unions need not be disastrous for the international firm, rather, the wise international HR manager will simply learn the constraints posed by the local union conditions and devise an effective strategy to plan accordingly.

◆ ◆ ◆
CAREERS IN INTERNATIONAL HR

Has the topic of international HR captivated your imagination? If so, you're not alone. The good news is that the need for international HR specialists is increasing along with the growth in international assignments. Box 11.10 reviews some of the trends and issues that may be of interest to you if you are interested in a career in this area.

◆ ◆ ◆
SUMMARY

This chapter has addressed many of the strategic issues and decisions that must be taken into consideration in the context of managing international employees. As you are probably well aware by now (from all the "empirical research is needed" comments), a surprisingly large amount of research is still needed in this area. Future research will need to confirm under exactly which conditions (e.g., the types and duration of assignments, the types of cultures) certain practices would be most effective. In the meantime, however, organizations seeking to grow their businesses internationally would do well to do the following: first, recognize the strategic decision issues inherent in managing the HR function in an international context and second, strive to make these decisions in ways that take into account their firm's strategic

---

BOX 11.10 OUTSOURCING AND CAREERS IN INTERNATIONAL HR

Thinking about a career in international HR? Recent surveys say the demand may be increasing, particularly for employment within international HR services firms. According to a Society for Human Resource Management 1996 press release, a 1996 survey on expatriate HR program outsourcing was conducted jointly by Windham International (a global relocation consulting firm with headquarters in New York City), the National Foreign Trade Council in the United States, and the Institute for International Human Resources (a division of the Society for Human Resource Management). The survey included 313 respondents representing 280 companies (with a total of 6 million employees and 63,000 expatriates). Four percent of respondents (senior HR professionals and managers of international relocation programs located in the United States and Canada) indicated that their firms now outsource expatriate program administration. However, 17 percent indicated that their companies are exploring the outsourcing alternative for expatriate programs. A majority of respondents (56%) said that outsourcing will be a long-term trend. The most commonly outsourced services are tax preparation (81%), cross-cultural training (49%), and work permits/visas (46%). Among services being considered for future outsourcing, the most often cited ones were compensation administration (19%), cross-cultural training (17%), and total program administration (17%). The main reasons cited for this trend were to enhance expertise (54%), improve quality (49%), reduce staff (49%), streamline the process (41%), and reduce costs (41%). An early example of this trend was that of Ernst & Young and PHH Relocation, companies that joined forces in October 1995 to create a strategic alliance to provide multinationals with the complete array of services needed for employees on international assignments.

According to Olivier Maudier, international HR manager at Walt Disney World, those seeking international HR careers need to be prepared for a few surprises. They need to upgrade any weak areas, such as negotiation skills, and then quickly acquire country- or region-specific knowledge and skills about laws and the political system. Rita Bennett, managing partner of Bennett Associates, adds that they will need to be prepared to handle myriad practical matters as well, such as visas and work permits; currency, housing, schools, and medical care; language and cross-cultural training; and evacuation insurance, taxes, and compensation.

Sources: Editorial. 1995. *International Business* (October): 14; Joinson, C. 1998. "Why HR Managers Need to Think Globally." *HR Magazine Focus* (April): 3–7; Society for Human Resource Management. 1996. Press release (October 15).

objectives rather than in ways that neglect the added complexity that the international context brings.

Some obvious omissions from this chapter include the strategic and ethical issues related to assisting expatriates and their families with relocation counselling. There is, however, a growing body of literature on these subjects, and the reader is encouraged to pursue research in these areas.

E X E R C I S E S

1. Go to the library and collect current articles about five companies in one functional area of international HRM. Articles can be found in journals such as *International Executive, Personnel, Human Resource Management,* and other practitioner journals in HRM. Summarize these articles. Then, compare and contrast the practices used by these companies with the kinds of principles and issues raised in this chapter. Do the companies appear to be successful at what they are trying to do? Do they appear to be adhering to the prescribed theoretical approaches for managing these international HR functions? Comment on the similarity and differences between practice and theory. If real-life companies are not managing in the ways that are recommended by theory, then which deviations from the text theory appear to be having the greatest impact, and what is it about the firm and its particular circumstances that appears to be causing certain deviations to be more significant than others?

2. Pick a well-known multinational and identify the countries in which it has subsidiaries. Next, compile a short (10-page) CCT module that will prepare PCNs from the multinational to successfully adjust to the host-country culture of one of the firm's subsidiary countries. Using both pre- and post-tests, have your classmates evaluate the module in terms of its impact on their self-efficacy for interacting with HCNs from that culture.

   Here are some Web sites that might help you with your presentation:

   ■ Expatriate Forum:
   www.expatforum.com

   Provides information and services for expatriates and international business executives. Includes a cost-of-living index for over 40 countries.

   ■ Embassy Contacts:
   www.embpage.org
   Provides addresses and other information about consulates around the world.

- Expatriate Exchange:
  www.expatexchange.com
  Offers good information on two forums: a tax and finance forum and an international career page. Publishes a monthly newsletter from the Middle East. The focus is primarily for Americans working abroad.

- Taxi's Electronic Newspapers:
  users.deltanet.com/users/taxicat/newsstand.html
  This site lists and has links for online newspapers from around the world.

- Research:
  www.conference-board.org
  A powerful research organization supported by leading companies. The Conference Board's Web site contains lots of information regarding the latest research and thinking on all types of business issues, including a special council focus on HRM.

CASE: AN INTERNATIONAL CAREER MOVE

John Markham is a biochemist who now works as a manager with Drugs From Bugs (DFB), an innovative international pharmaceutical firm. John has been with DFB for the past 10 years. He is married and has two children (a daughter in high school and a son in kindergarten). His wife Anya is a certified general accountant who works for a major accounting firm in the Toronto area. Their combined household income amounts to $150,000. The president of DFB has asked John to become the managing director of DFB's operations in Israel. The government there has just offered a number of incentives to international pharmaceutical firms that make Israel a highly desirable location in which to operate.

John is keen on growing the business in Israel, but he has concerns about his future with the company. He has heard that life in Israel can be fascinating but also quite difficult for someone who has never lived outside Canada.

John has received a memo from Anne Monty, DFB's vice-president of HR: "John, I hear there are quite a few good Web sites about Israel. You might want to check them out. Meanwhile, I have asked the Israeli Tourist Board to forward some material to you. Are you free for lunch next week? I look forward to hearing your thoughts. Cheers, (signed) Anne."

Discussion Questions for the Case

1. Discuss the various issues that John should be concerned about regarding the transfer.
2. What additional information should John seek from the HR department?
3. Suggest the types of financial and nonfinancial incentives that DFB might offer to John to induce him to accept the transfer.
4. Using the material discussed in this chapter, what issues should DFB consider when setting John's performance objectives for the international assignment?

References

Abe, H., and R.L. Wiseman. 1983. "A Cross-cultural Confirmation of the Dimensions of Intercultural Effectiveness." *International Journal of Intercultural Relations*, 7: 53–67.

Adler, N.J. 1991. *International Dimensions of Organizational Behavior*, 2nd ed. Boston: PWS-Kent Publishing.

Alliger, G.M., and E.A. Janak. 1989. "Kirkpatrick's Levels of Training Criteria: Thirty Years Later." *Personnel Psychology* 42: 331–342.

Anderson, J.B. 1990. "Compensating Your Overseas Executives, Part 2: Europe in 1992." *Compensation and Benefits Review* (July/August).

Beck, J.E. 1988. "Expatriate Management Development: Realizing the Learning Potential of the Overseas Assignment." In F. Hoy, ed., *Best Papers Proceedings, Academy of Management 48th Annual Meeting* (August 1988). Anaheim, Ca.: 112–116.

Bishko, M.J. 1990. "Compensating Your Overseas Executives, Part I: Strategies for the 1990s." *Compensation and Benefits Review* (May/June): 33–34.

Black, S., and H.B. Gregersen. 1991. "When Yankee Comes Home: Factors Related to Expatriate and Spouse Repatriation Adjustment." *Journal of International Business Studies* 22, no. 4: 671–694.

Black, J.S., and M. Mendenhall. 1991. "The U-Curve Adjustment Hypothesis Revisited: A Review and Theoretical Framework." *Journal of International Business Studies* (2nd Quarter): 225–247.

_____. 1990. "Cross-cultural Training Effectiveness: A Review and a Theoretical Framework for Future Research." *Academy of Management Review* 15, no. 1: 113–136.

Briscoe, D.R. 1998. "What Matters Most: Integrating Business and HR Strategies in the Selection of International Assignees." Paper presented at "What Matters Most in the Management of Expatriates," a symposium chaired by D. Ondrack at the annual meeting of the Academy of Management, San Diego, Ca.

Cascio, W.F., and M.G. Serapio. 1991. "Human Resources Systems in an International Alliance: The Undoing of a Done Deal?" *Organizational Dynamics* (Winter): 63–74.

Childs, A., and R.J. Klimoski. 1986. "Successfully Predicting Career Success:

An Application of the Biographical Inventory." *Journal of Applied Psychology* 71: 3–9.

Costa, P.T., and R.M. McCrae. 1992. *Revised NEO Personality Inventory [NEO-PI-R] and NEO Five-Factor Inventory [NEO-FFI] Professional Manual*. Odessa, Fla.: Psychological Assessment Resources, Inc.

Dowling, P.J., R.S. Schuler, and D.E. Welch. 1994. *International Dimensions of Human Resource Management*, 2nd ed. Belmont, Ca.: Wadsworth Publishing Company.

Earley, P.C. 1987. "Intercultural Training for Managers: A Comparison of Documentary and Interpersonal Methods." *Academy of Management Journal* 30, no. 4: 685–698.

Editorial. 1990. "Trends in Expatriate Compensation." *Bulletin to Management* (October 18): 336.

Feldman, D. 1989. "Relocation Practices." *Personnel* 66, no. 11: 22–25.

Garland, J., R.N. Farmer, and M. Taylor. 1990. *International Dimensions of Business Policy and Strategy*, 2nd ed. Boston: PWS-Kent.

Gertsen, M. 1989. "Expatriate Selection and Training." In R. Luostarinen, ed., *Proceedings of the Fifteenth Annual Conference of the European International Business Association*. Helsinki, Finland: 1251–1280.

Gist, M.E., C. Schwoerer, and B. Rosen. 1989. "Effects of Alternative Training Methods on Self-Efficacy and Performance in Computer Software Training." *Journal of Applied Psychology* 74: 884–891.

Gist, M.E., C.K. Stevens, and A.G. Bavetta. 1991. "Effects of Self-Efficacy and Post-Training Intervention on the Acquisition and Maintenance of Complex Interpersonal Skills." *Personnel Psychology* 44: 837–861.

Harvey, M.G. 1982. "The Other Side of Foreign Assignments: Dealing with the Repatriation Dilemma." *Columbia Journal of World Business* 17, no. 1: 52–59.

Hays, R. 1974. "Expatriate Selection: Insuring Success and Avoiding Failure." *Journal of International Business Studies* 5, no.1: 25–37.

Hedlund, G. 1986. "The Hypermodern MNC—A Heterarchy?" *Human Resource Management* 25, no. 1: 9–35.

Ioannou, L. 1995. "Unnatural Selection." *International Business* (July): 54–57.

Katz, J.P., and S.W. Elsea. 1997. "A Framework for Assessing International Labor Relations: What Every HR Manager Needs to Know." *Human Resource Planning* 20, no. 4: 16–25.

Katz, J.P., and D.M. Seifer. 1996. "It's a Different World Out There. Planning for Expatriate Success through Selection,

Pre-Departure Training, and On-site Socialization." *Human Resources Planning* 19, no. 2: 32–47.

Leck, J.D., and S. Leiba-O'Sullivan. 1998. "What Matters Most: Selecting the Best or Eliminating the Worst?" Paper presented at "What Matters Most in the Management of Expatriates," a symposium chaired by D. Ondrack at the annual meeting of the Academy of Management, San Diego, Ca.

Leiba-O'Sullivan, S. In press. "The Distinction between Stable and Dynamic Cross-cultural Competencies: Implications for Expatriate Trainability." *Journal of International Business Studies.*

Mael, F. 1991. "A Conceptual Rationale for the Domain and Attributes of Biodata Items." *Personnel Psychology* 44: 763–792.

McEnery, J., and G. Des Harnais. 1990. "Culture Shock." *Training and Development Journal* 44, no. 4: 43–47.

Mendenhall, M., E. Dunbar, and G. Oddou. 1987. "Expatriate Selection, Training, and ÔCareer-Pathing': A Review and Critique." *Human Resource Management* 26: 331–345.

Mendenhall, M., and G. Oddou. 1985. "The Dimensions of Expatriate Acculturation." *Academy of Management Review* 10: 39–47.

Mervosh, E.M., and J.S. McClenahan. 1997. "The Care and Feeding of Expats:

In the Intensely Competitive World of Business, There's No Such Thing as Too Much Preparation." *Industry Week* (December 1): 69–70.

Neghandi, A.R. 1987. *International Management.* Newton, Mass.: Allyn and Bacon.

Nicholson, N. 1984. "A Theory of Work Role Transitions." *Administrative Science Quarterly* 29: 172–191.

Oberg, K. 1960. "Culture Shock: Adjustment to New Cultural Environments." *Practical Anthropology* 7: 177–182.

O'Grady, S. 1994. "The Psychic Distance Paradox." Paper presented at the 1994 annual meeting of the Academy of International Business.

Ondrack, D., and S. Leiba-O'Sullivan. 1998. "Staffing a New International Operation." Paper presented (by Ondrack) in the "Applied Research Track" at the annual conference of the Human Resources Professionals Association of Ontario, February. Toronto, Ont.: 18–20.

Ones, D.S., and C. Viswesvaran. 1997. "Personality Determinants in the Prediction of Aspects of Expatriate Job Success." In Z. Aycan, ed., *Expatriate Management: Theory and Research* 4: 63–92.

Parker, B., and G.M. McEvoy. 1993. "Initial Examination of a Model of

Intercultural Adjustment." *International Journal of Intercultural Relations* 17: 355–379.

Phatak, A.V. 1989. *International Dimensions of Management,* 2nd ed. Boston: PWS–Kent Publishing Co.

Pinder, C.C., and K.G. Schroeder. 1987. "Time to Proficiency Following Job Transfers." *Academy of Management Journal* 30, no. 2: 336–353.

Pucik, V. 1985. "Strategic Human Resource Management in a Multinational Firm." In H.V. Wortzel and L.H. Wortzel, eds., *Strategic Management of Multinational Corporations: The Essentials.* New York: John Wiley.

Ruben, B.D., and D.J. Kealey. 1979. "Behavioral Assessment of Communication Competency and the Prediction of Cross-cultural Adaptation." *International Journal of Intercultural Relations* 3: 15–47.

Schuler, R.S., and E.V. Van Slujis. 1992. "Davidson-Marley BV: Establishing and Operating an International Joint Venture." *European Management Journal* 10 (December): 428–436.

Stopford, J., and L. Wells. 1972. *Managing the Multinational.* London: Longmans.

Tannenbaum, S.I., and G. Yukl. 1992. "Training and Development in Work Organizations." *Annual Review of Psychology* 43: 399–441.

Tung, R.L. 1988. "Career Issues in International Assignments." *Academy of Management Executive* 2, no. 3: 241–244.

_____. 1982. "Selection and Training Procedures of U.S., European, and Japanese Multinationals." *California Management Review* 25, no. 1: 57–71.

_____. 1981. "Selecting and Training of Personnel for Overseas Assignments." *Columbia Journal of World Business* 16: 68–78.

Walton, S.J. 1990. "Stress Management Training for Overseas Effectiveness." *International Journal of Intercultural Relations* 14: 507–527.

Welch, D., T. Adams, B. Betchley, and M. Howard. 1992. "The View from the Other Side: The Handling of Repatriation and Other Expatriation Activities by the Royal Australian Airforce." In O. Yau and B. Stening, eds., *Proceedings of the AIB Southeast Asia Conference.* Brisbane, Australia.

Wexley, K.N., and G.P. Latham. 1991. *Developing and Training Human Resources in Organizations,* 2nd ed. New York: Harper-Collins.

12

Mergers and Acquisitions

♦ ♦ ♦
CHAPTER GOALS

This chapter examines the role that the HR function can play in mergers and acquisitions. We start by examining the reasons why organizations want to merge, how they merge, and the success rate of these mergers. Culture management is the key to successful mergers. Then we examine the impact of a merger on each HR function.

After reading this chapter, you should be able to do the following:

1. Understand the various types of mergers and acquisitions.

2. Explain why organizations merge and the methods used to achieve a merger.

3. Identify the financial and human effects of mergers.

4. Describe the issues involved in blending cultures.

5. Discuss how a merger affects HR planning, selection, compensation, performance appraisal, training and development, and labour relations.

♦ ♦ ♦
BIG IS BEAUTIFUL

Mergers and acquisitions (M&As) play a critical part in a corporation's survival, growth, and profit strategies. Big is beautiful is the belief. Abitibi-Price and Stone-Consolidated merged in 1997 to become Abitibi-Consolidated, the world's largest newsprint maker, with revenues of $4.1 billion. The number of mergers is rising. The dollar value of mergers and the average size of the typical transaction are also rising. The 1980s saw the emergence of billion-dollar M&As. In Canada, 1997 was a record-breaking year, with a $101-billion volume of transactions (McNish, 1998). The average value of a takeover in Canada was about $600 million, compared to $100 million a decade ago.

Before embarking on a discussion of the motives for mergers, readers are encouraged to become familiar with the terms used to describe them.

◆ ◆ ◆
DEFINITIONS

A *merger* is a combination of two corporations in which a new corporation arises and the previous ones cease to exist. Within mergers, there are three categories:

■ A *horizontal merger* is the merging of two competitors. The competitors combine to increase market power. These mergers typically are subject to review by regulators who fear monopoly power in the marketplace. The merging of Coles Books and Smithbooks to form Chapters is an example of two competitors uniting to achieve economies of scale and to withstand the attack from U.S. megabookstores.

■ A *vertical merger* occurs when a buyer and a seller (or supplier) merge to achieve the synergies of controlling all factors affecting a company's success, from the production of raw goods to manufacturing to distribution and retail sales. A fast-food restaurant, like McDonald's, might merge with a producer of French fries.

■ A *conglomerate merger* occurs when one company merges with another but the two companies have no competitive or buyer-seller relationship. In other words, they are in different businesses competing in different markets.

An *acquisition* is the purchase of an entire company or a controlling interest in a company. The purchase of Federated Department Stores by Robert Campeau is a highly public example. By purchasing Federated Department Stores for $6.6 billion, Campeau, a Canadian, became the fourth largest retailer in the United States.

A *consolidation* occurs when two or more companies join together and form an entirely new company. In this case, the assets and liabilities of both companies are taken on by the third company, usually after the original companies are dissolved. Burroughs and Sperry, two computer manufacturers, consolidated to form UNISYS. Three hospitals in Toronto—York Finch, Humber Memorial, and Northwestern General—merged in response to budget cutbacks.

A *takeover* occurs when one company seeks to acquire another company. Usually, a takeover refers to a hostile transaction, but it can mean a friendly merger, as well. A hostile takeover refers to the acquisition of a company against the wishes of its management. The management team campaigns actively to win the support and votes of more than 50 percent of the outstanding shareholders.

For the purposes of this chapter, M&As will be treated as one category, that of two companies joining together. Why do companies wish to join? The next section examines three motives for merging.

THE URGE TO MERGE

Companies merge for three reasons: strategic benefits, financial benefits, or the needs of the CEO or managing team.

STRATEGIC BENEFITS

The current boom in M&As is being driven by corporate strategy as firms try to protect or expand market share. Companies that have growth as a strategic objective can expand in many ways: leveraging present customers, opening new markets internationally, corporate venturing, and M&As. The first three are slower methods. Acquisitions of companies in different regions or serving different markets is much quicker than internal expansion. For example, CIBC Insurance acquired the Personal Insurance Company to expand quickly into the insurance business, where originally CIBC Insurance had a relatively minor market share.

Companies may acquire or merge with others to achieve complementarities. Different types of synergies can be achieved through M&As. (*Synergy* is a term taken from the physical sciences and refers to the type of reactions that occur when two substances or factors combine to produce a greater effect together than would result from the sum of the two operating independently. More simply stated, synergy can be described as two plus two equals five). *Operating synergy*, which usually is referred to as economies of scale (decreases in per-unit costs), is the cost reduction produced by a corporate combination. These gains are achieved by the spreading of overhead, the increased specialization of labour and management, and the more efficient use of capital equipment. Closely related to the economies of scale benefit is the economy of scope advantage. This is the ability of a firm to use one set of inputs to produce a wider range of products and services (Master, 1987). Banks, for example, would like to use their bank tellers (now called financial consultants) not only to do banking but also to do mortgage financing, insurance selling, and so on. Another type of synergy may occur when the acquiring firm believes that it can manage the target firm better and could increase its value. For example, a small firm may benefit significantly by using the larger firm's distribution networks and experienced management.

Companies may merge to give them access to new markets. For example, Air Canada was facing a domestic market that was mature, with little likelihood of growth. Therefore, Air Canada joined with several other carriers, including Thai Airways, Lufthansa, SAS, and United Airlines, to pool costs, revenues, and destinations. More importantly, the merger allowed Air Canada, Canada's largest airline, to serve foreign markets such as Asia and northern Europe, which it was forbidden to access under bilateral agreements.

Diversification may be another strategic motive. A company may wish to reduce its dependency on a market that is cyclical in nature to capitalize on excess plant or employee capacity. For example, a ski resort may acquire a water slide business in order to fill its hotel rooms and restaurants during the stagnant summer months. General Electric pursued this diversification strategy. Not wanting to depend entirely on electronics, the company became a diversified conglomerate by acquiring insurance businesses, television stations, plastics manufacturing businesses, credit card businesses, and so on over a 10-year period.

Companies may also wish to achieve the benefits associated with vertical integration and horizontal integration. *Vertical integration* refers to the mergers or acquisitions of companies that have a buyer–seller relationship. Such a move may assure either a dependable source of supply or control over quality of the service or product. For example, a company producing furniture might acquire a trucking company to ensure reliable shipping.

Horizontal integration refers to the increase in market share and market power that results from M&As of rivals. Western Canada's BC Telecom and Telus merged to become a stronger regional telephone company that was better able to compete against Bell Canada's launch of a new national company.

FINANCIAL BENEFITS

Organizations look to M&As to achieve some financial advantages. Among these are the following:

- Organizations expect to reduce the variability of the cash flow of their own business. An organization lowers its risk by putting its "eggs in different baskets." However, a counterargument suggests that executives cannot manage unrelated businesses and must focus on and protect the core business from competitive and environmental pressures. The suggested wisdom is to put eggs in similar baskets (Lubatkin and Lane, 1996).

- Organizations expect to use funds generated by their own mature (or cash cow) businesses to fund growing businesses. However, some experts argue that the advantages of using one division to fund another division may be risky in the long run (Lubatkin and Lane, 1996). Labelling one business in the portfolio a "cash cow" and another a "star" (see Chapter 13 for a detailed discussion of these labels) results in negative effects. Employees in the "mature" business may feel neglected, as resources are poured into the star, and may reduce their commitment to production and innovation. Management may misjudge which businesses have potential for market share increases and which do not. For example, most industry observers viewed the piano market as having slow or no growth. However, Yamaha saw the industry quite differently: the company looked worldwide for market share, saying, "Anyway, we are not in the piano business, we are in the keyboard business" (Hamal and Prahalad, 1989). Sometimes slow-growth, highly competitive industries offer stable (not risky) returns.

- There may be tax advantages to the takeover, which vary by country. Considerable tax losses in the acquired firm may offset the income of a parent company.

- Astute corporations may analyze the financial statements of a company and decide that the company is undervalued. By acquiring the company, and sometimes by merging it with the administration already in place, a company can achieve financial gains.

The overriding goal is to increase the shareholder's wealth.

MANAGERIAL NEEDS

Some argue that corporate life is a game, and managers love to play it. The theory here is that managers seek to acquire firms for their own personal motives, and economic gains are not the primary consideration (Roll, 1986).

This hypothesis may help explain why some firms pay questionably high premiums for their takeover targets.

One theory examines the "incentives" or payoffs to the CEOs if they engage in acquisition behaviour. Managers may pursue their personal interests at the expense of stockholders. For example, there is a positive correlation between the size of the firm and management compensation, and so CEOs can expect higher salaries for managing larger firms (Kroll et al., 1997). Other indirect incentives may include the prestige or status of owning larger firms or companies in fashionable sectors, such as the entertainment or sports sectors.

Another perspective examines the unconscious motives of CEOs. Robert Campeau's takeover of Allied Stores and Federated Department Stores has been subject to "armchair" analysis as he overpaid for his acquisitions and ultimately went bankrupt servicing the debt. Speculation on his motives ranges from the simple need to prove himself to complex theories espoused by psychoanalysts. But does the research support this perspective?

Most of the work in this area analyzes the role that a manager's unconscious desires or neuroses play in formulating corporate strategy or decision making (Kets de Vries, 1991). Some research is based on the intensive analyses used by therapists to explore motives. A few studies attempt to link personality characteristics, such as the need for power or self-confidence, with growth strategies (Rovenpor, 1993). One study found that the greater the ego of the acquiring company's CEO—as reflected in the CEO's relative compensation and the amount of media attention given to that CEO—the higher the premium the company is likely to pay (Zwieg, 1995). However, few studies arrived at helpful conclusions that would explain the behaviour of executives.

MERGER METHODS

How do companies merge? The process, in a friendly environment, is relatively simple. The management of one company contacts the management of the target company. Sometimes an intermediary is used, such as an investment banker or, in smaller firms, a colleague who makes an introduction. During the first tentative talks, the boards of directors are kept informed of the procedures, and ultimately, they approve the merger. Friendly deals can be completed quickly. Hostile takeovers become dramatic, with management pushing for "poison pills" and seeking "white knights" to protect themselves. (The term *poison pills* refers to the right of key players to purchase shares in the company at a discount—around 50 percent—that makes the takeover extremely expensive. *White knights* are buyers who will be more acceptable to the targeted company.) There is even a "Pac-Man" defensive manoeuvre, when the targeted company makes a counteroffer for the bidding firm.

◆◆◆
THE SUCCESS RATE OF MERGERS

Many studies have established that most M&As ultimately fail (Harshbarger, 1990; Cartwright and Cooper, 1992). Acquisitions of related businesses fare better than acquisitions of businesses unrelated to the parent business (Gaughan, 1996). The novice M&A management team does as poorly as the experienced team. Why? Perhaps because each merger is different, with different synergies and cultures.

Not only is the merged firm at risk, but the subsidiaries may also be at risk. There is some indication that a merger occupies so much management time, attention, and other resources that the original businesses are neglected. There are enormous challenges in joining two companies. The problems include integrating computer systems, eliminating duplication, re-evaluating supplier relationships, reassuring clients, advising employees, and reconfiguring work routines.

The success rate may also vary by sector and by size. The manufacturing sector, for example, differs from the service sector. In the manufacturing sector, much more is fixed, with capital investments already made, with technology controlling process, and with lower job skills. The service sector, in contrast, relies on social control mechanisms, which are highly subject to culture management. As such, the risk is greater with acquisitions in the service sector.

Size appears to influence success rates. A large firm can absorb a small firm in a relatively inconsequential fashion. The merger of two large firms generates more problems.

FINANCIAL IMPACT

For many reasons, the financial returns are rarely those that were envisioned. Sometimes, a premium price was paid, and the company is unable to service the debt or recover the investment. At other times, the forecasted economies of scale or complementarities are not achieved. The market may have changed, resulting in revised forecasts.

During the merger of two health care facilities in the United States, chaos was created in the resulting company by the collapsing of 525 branches into 350, the attempt to standardize the two facilities' computer systems, the termination of a tenth of the workforce, an attempt at a second acquisition, and the defence of the company against a barrage of law suits (Schonfeld, 1997). The result was that outstanding bills jumped 30 percent in one year, payment times increased from 109 days to 131 days, earnings were down substantially, revenues were less than those of previous years, and the stock price dropped.

Overall, studies by McKinsey & Co. reported that only 23 percent of mergers end up recovering the costs incurred in the deal, and about half of those analyzed by the American Management Association resulted in profit reductions (Fisher, 1994). Of 150 deals analyzed by Standard & Poor's, about half destroyed shareholder wealth (Zwieg, 1995). Most devastating of all for merger maniacs was the analysis that demonstrated that non-acquiring companies (i.e., those that made no acquisitions) outperformed acquiring companies on Standard & Poor's industry indices.

Many mergers fail because the buyer overextends itself financially (Kadlec, 1990). The buyer borrows heavily, and then must engage in cost cutting to service the debt. Assets are spun off, employee numbers are reduced, and the new company is left in a financial shambles.

Even if the overall financial picture of the merged company appears rosy, there are indications that different functional areas suffer. For example, a firm that has to use cash to pay for the debt incurred in acquiring another business now has less to spend on certain projects that can be postponed, such as research and development.

However, there are some winners, namely, the merger advisors. The Campeau-Federated Department Stores deal alone generated approximately $500 million (US) in fees for M&A advisory firms (Harshbarger, 1990). One billion dollars in profits was generated for these firms in 1988 alone, and about 50,000 people are employed in work directly related to M&As (Harshbarger, 1990).

IMPACT ON HUMAN RESOURCES

The real costs of a merger may be hidden, that is, not evident when analyzing financial records. Takeovers result in human displacement. The cost of losing the best sales rep, who either is anxious about her job or does not wish to work for the acquired company, cannot be measured in accounting terms. The time involved in replacing this employee with a new one, the orientation period—all represent costs to the employer. One survey established that one-third of companies reported an increase in turnover following a merger or acquisition (Knowles, 1989).

Another study showed that nearly half of the senior executives in large acquisitions leave within a year of the takeover (Kanter and Seggerman, 1986). Another study reported that from 1981 to 1986, as a result of acquisitions, a half million executives lost jobs that they had held for more than three years, and 30 percent were still unemployed two years later (Nulty, 1987). Add to this the thousands of jobs that are lost in the restructuring or downsizing of the merged companies. One study estimated that the U.S. economy lost 1 percent in gross national product (GNP) in 1986 because of the losses of hundreds of thousands of jobs (Heisler et al., 1988).

That is a national effect. The organizational effects are that it takes from 6 to 18 months for an organization to assimilate the effects of an M&A, and the productivity loss is estimated to be 15 percent (Knowles, 1989). The loss of employee productivity stems from many sources:

- Employees go underground, afraid to make themselves visible or do anything that may put their jobs at risk.

- Overt sabotage occurs when employees deeply resent the turmoil the merger is causing in their lives.

- Self-interested survival tactics emerge, include hiding information from team members to accumulate a degree of power (the employee feels that he or she is "the only one who really knows how things work around here").

- A resigned attitude appears, stemming from the belief that no amount of work will prevent one from being fired (Hollister, 1996).

But the real cost is to the thousands of employees who lose their jobs. Those who survive are affected in different ways. Most experience stress and anxiety, with the resultant loss of productivity.

To summarize, the feeling among those experienced in M&As is that, while mergers are forged for strategic and financial reasons, they succeed for human reasons. The next section examines what many consider to be the greatest challenge of M&As—the blending of corporate cultures.

◆ ◆ ◆
CULTURAL ISSUES IN MERGERS

In an effort to increase the probability that the merger will work, many are turning to the principal reason that they fail: the meshing of cultures. *Culture* is the set of important beliefs that members of a community share. These beliefs are often unspoken and are shaped by a group's shared history and experience. Culture can be thought of as the "social glue" that binds individuals together and creates organizational cohesiveness (Cartwright and Cooper, 1993). Cultures, growing slowly over time, are not easy to describe, and employees are often aware of their corporate culture only when they try to integrate with people from another organization that has a different culture.

It is estimated that one-third of all merger failures are caused by the faulty integration of diverse operations and culture (Shrivastava, 1986). The longevity of an organization's culture cannot be underestimated. Canadian Airlines International was formed by merging about half a dozen different airlines. A decade after the merger, employees still referred to themselves as veterans of Wardair or Canadian Pacific Airlines, that is, they retained their original cultures. Integrating two cultures is a difficult process. Early on, the merger executives have to decide if one company's culture will be grafted onto the other company's, or if the two cultures will merge to create a third culture.

In some cases, firms that are aware of the difficulties of merging cultures attempt to negotiate, in the form of a contract, many aspects in advance. The assignment of positions or the acceptance of a culture, such as one of empowerment, seems like good advance planning. But those who have been through this process liken it to a marriage (Kadlec, 1990). The couple may agree, in writing, on who will do the dishes and how many children they want, but the day-to-day living may be quite different, and the assumptions change over time. Recognizing this, some employees may choose to leave the corporation rather than endure the pain of culture mergers.

Anthropologists have something to say about the blending of cultures. According to researchers such as Berry (1990), there are four options open to those involved in M&As:

Assimilation: Assimilation occurs when one organization willingly gives up its culture and is absorbed by the culture of the acquirer or the dominant partner.

Integration: Integration refers to the fusion of two cultures, resulting in the evolvement of a new culture representing (one hopes) the best of both cultures. This form rarely occurs because the marriage is rarely one of two equals, and one partner usually dominates.

Deculturation: Sometimes, the acquired organization does not value the culture of the dominant partner and is left in a confused, alienated, marginalized state known as deculturation. This is a temporary state, existing until some integration or separation occurs.

Separation: In some instances, the two cultures resist merging, and either the merged company operates as two separate companies or a divorce occurs.

Merging two cultures is difficult. How can a rule-bound, bureaucratic organization such as the Bank of Montreal merge with the "cowboys" of the brokerage firm Nesbitt Burns? To complicate this issue, the acquiring company typically wants to retain the entrepreneurial spirit of the target company and to infuse this spirit into its own troops. Instead, the entrepreneur is squashed by the rules and rigid decision making of the parent company. For example, Novell purchased WordPerfect (currently owned by Corel) and managed to stifle the innovative talent they had bought.

The blending of cultures can take years. As in all organizational change programs, a process must be undertaken. The first step is to identify the differences, to ensure that employees are aware of the differences and can verbalize or label them. Is one company entrepreneurial and the other risk averse? Does one have programs of team building while the other rewards individual achievements? Later, we recommend that a team of "sprinters" be appointed to deal with urgent matters. Likewise, we suggest that a team of "long-distance runners" be appointed to address broad issues of mission statements, the creation of culture to achieve the strategic goals, and similar matters. Part of their mandate would be to measure current attitudes, solicit opinions, and give the employees a voice in the process.

Here is an example of how this is done. Two hospitals that merged had very different cultures, which did not blend. One had a culture of controlling employees, the other, a culture of growing employees (Riddell and Lipson, 1996). The hospitals began the culture blending process by conducting a comprehensive audit, using a paper and pencil diagnostic tool. The results were terrible, and the only positive finding was that *everyone* wanted a change. Two teams were appointed, one to change the culture of both hospitals to a culture of employee development and the other to help form this new culture.

Sometimes, cultural characteristics that are common to both merging companies can be identified. For example, two very different firms found out that they both placed top priority on customer service, and this common focal point became the link for their merger. Sometimes a superordinate goal can be created.

The formation of task forces or one-off projects has as a subgoal an integration goal. As is the case when warring nations are forced to fight together against an alien force, the ways in which two corporate cultures are more similar than different are apparent when a superimposed goal becomes the catalyst. American Express uses this technique regularly. Managers from merging firms work together on projects to develop new products or services, for which the merged firms can claim ownership. Besides integration, such projects have other benefits: they develop in-house talent, provide an opportunity to solicit broad perspectives, and facilitate transfers as the project ends (Koeth, 1985).

While all of this seems time-consuming, it may, in fact, save time in the longer term. Organizational change experts realize that time spent ensuring employee buy-in will speed implementation. If time is not spent ensuring that employees are committed to the changes, then employees will resist the changes.

Another approach is to "seed" the company with experienced managers who walk the talk and can facilitate the adoption of the new culture. However, just transferring personnel from one company to another may only increase the differences between them and promote subcultures or cliques. "Living together" before the marriage may also help ease merger shock. Japanese companies usually have worked on a joint venture or a collaborative project, designed to assess culture fit, before they acquire another company. Turf battles are a problem unless companies establish the new structure, including the reporting relationships, early in the merger process.

More radical measures may be necessary. Some companies force into early retirement or some other exit option employees who are opposed to the merger or cannot adapt to the new culture.

A more positive story is that of the merger of Lotus and IBM, discussed in Box 12.1.

◆ ◆ ◆
HR ISSUES IN M&A'S

Experts in HRM have much to say about increasing the success rate of mergers. The impact of a merger on HRM is discussed below in terms of the familiar functional areas of HR.

HR PLANNING

In a merger context, planning moves beyond the traditional concepts of HR planning for several reasons. HR planning in an M&A situation has several dimensions that are not part of the normal planning process outlined in Chapters 3 to 9.

BOX 12.1 THE BLENDING OF CULTURES

IBM and Lotus had agreed to merge, but many Lotus employees were worried about the impact of the IBM culture on the Lotus culture. Lotus employees were used to a culture known for its quality of life programs. Lotus had won awards for its willingness to accommodate the needs of its employees through spousal benefits programs, job sharing, allowing employees to work from home or at remote sites, on-site child care, summer camp programs, a lunch-and-learn wellness series, tuition reimbursements, and so on. Lotus employees were understandably worried that IBM would challenge these programs. But IBM was intrigued by the Lotus culture and chose to adopt Lotus's innovative approach to quality of working life. The result was that the Lotus employees who exited before the merger phoned a year later asking to be rehired.

Successful mergers may result from an analysis of the cultures. Each firm could identify its strengths, such as empowered employees, and the merged firm could attempt to retain this aspect and build on it. For example, in the Lotus-IBM merger, the senior manager of HR reports:

> What I've seen is that IBMers are intrigued by the Lotus culture and are trying to figure out how to bring some of it into their own company. What's been unique to Lotus is that IBM, in the past, has absorbed companies it has bought and found that total absorption can actually put people at risk. With us, it has tried to figure out what we do well that it could do better; it has tried to figure out in what ways to leave Lotus alone so that it retains its unique culture, and it has also tried to figure out how to leverage us so that the merged company can become stronger in the market.

These culture audits provide an objective means to identify differences, provide a basis for discussion, and track merger progress.

Source: Adapted from Frazee, V. 1996. "Winning Ideas Prove Timeless." *Personnel Journal* (November): 48–57.

---

1. The Contingency Plan

Strategic planners must be aware of the board of directors' interest in M&As. Based on this expressed interest, a contingency plan that can be implemented when a deal is in play should be prepared. The plan should identify the contact person and the merger coordinator, who should have received training in effective merger management. The contact person should develop a plan, similar to emergency plans developed for fires or gas leaks. The plan should outline the chain of command, methods for communicating, procedures to follow during a takeover, and negotiation skills training and media response training for the senior team, and should identify a transition team (Stuart, 1993). Some companies even keep lists of compatible white knights (in cases of being targeted for acquisition) and prepare lists of consultants who are experts in negotiation techniques or productivity enhancement methods.

2. HR Due Diligence

The second element of HR planning in an M&A situation is the need to conduct a due diligence review (Walker, 1992). From an HR perspective, the due diligence would include a review of the collective agreement, executive compensation contracts (particularly golden parachutes), and retirement and other benefit plan commitments. Sometimes, these liabilities (e.g., an enriched retirement plan) or obligations (e.g., an incentive plan) may kill the deal. Once the legal obligations have been thoroughly assessed, the level of employees' KSAs must be evaluated. The HR planning team would address the suitability of current management talent and cultural fit. A deal may be aborted if talent shortfalls are extreme or if the cultures are seriously incompatible.

3. Transition Team

A third dimension is the need to appoint a transition team. This team is necessary because of the urgency of the M&A situation and the information gaps and employee stress that characterize it:

- *Urgency:* Staffing decisions, such as terminating, hiring, evaluating, and training, become urgent. Planners don't have the luxury of planning in three-year periods, during which orderly succession proceeds as predicted. Job analyses must be conducted immediately to identify duplicate positions and new work processes. Soon after the merger is announced, decisions about the retention of employees and the reassignment of others have to be made and executed humanely. At the same time, marketable employees are finding jobs elsewhere and customers are re-examining their business relationships. The uncertainty impedes productivity and new business development.

■ *Information gaps:* While both companies may have excellent plans for employees and reams of documentation, these plans have to be adjusted to the merged needs. For example, the targeted company may have prepared succession plans for its finance department, but now most of these positions (and people) are redundant because the bidder may have its own finance department. Furthermore, the merged company may use its combined resources to seek businesses in new countries (with different financial reporting or tax laws), and neither of the merged companies has that expertise. Thus, the information accumulated to date may have to be updated rapidly and revised in light of the new needs. The loss of capable employees, those who are marketable and can easily find other jobs, also results in the need to update plans continuously during a merger. When Lotus merged with IBM, some sales representatives resigned immediately because they did not want to be absorbed into the IBM culture. When the Royal Bank and the Bank of Montreal announced their merger, bank employees immediately called headhunters, and other firms called the headhunters fishing for the talent that might be interested in leaving the uncertain environment of the merger (Gibb-Clark, 1998).

■ *Stress:* The moment that the companies go "into play," employees are stressed. They are aware of the traditional fate of employees in merged companies. Most employees realize that most positions are duplicated. A transition team, whose sole concern is HR issues in the merger, must be appointed. The transition team may be the most important determinant of merger success. The role and responsibilities of the transition team are outlined in Box 12.2.

The goals of the transition team are to retain talent, maintain the productivity (in terms of both quantity and quality) of employee performance, select individuals for the new organization, integrate HR programs (e.g., benefits, incentive plans), and take the first steps toward the integration of cultures.

As the transition team is handling the urgent matters, the HR planners can undertake the revisions necessary to prepare HR plans. Employee skills inventories must be updated and succession plans revised. If the business enters new sectors and they require new labour pools, these labour pools have to be identified and the need for them assessed. Employment equity data has to be revised and, perhaps, resubmitted to the relevant agencies. Based on the revised strategic plans, the HR department must revise and align its HR plans and produce a new forecast for HR requirements.

BOX 12.2 THE TRANSITION TEAM

Senior vice-presidents of HR, who have had a lot of experience in mergers, recommend that a transition team be appointed to deal with the concerns of employees in mergers. These vice-presidents cite the need to deal with employee stress before the stress renders employees incapable of working. In addition, it is known that employees who have access to information about their future are less likely to begin a job search and leave the organization. Communication is critical, and employees should be the central focus of communication efforts. The transition team should be composed of employees from both companies and union representatives (if there is a union in either company).

Here are some elements of a good merger management process:

- *A formal announcement:* When a merger or acquisition is announced, the CEO should issue a statement containing the following items of information:

   The rationale for the merger, that is, its intended benefits

   General information about both companies

   Information about changes in the corporate name and structure, particularly changes in key management positions

   Plans for employee reductions

   Plans for recognizing and working with the union

   Plans for changes in products or services

   Detailed information about changes in benefits, or the date for decisions about such changes

- *A merger hotline:* When Inland Gas purchased Mainland Gas, creating BC Gas, the company immediately set up a hotline so that employees could call the vice-president of HR and ask direct questions. E-mail and voice mail make the management of this process easier.

- *A newsletter or Web page:* Experts agree that the formation of communication channels must be swift and all communication must be honest.

SELECTION

Retention and reduction, paradoxically, are two critical areas that must be addressed immediately. Duplicate positions and redundant employees must be terminated while highly qualified employees in critical positions must be motivated to stay. The first critical question is, How many employees does the merged company need? The answer is not to eliminate the most jobs possible in an attempt to operate a lean and mean corporation; the result would be work overload and stress. The answer may lie in benchmarking statistics. Increasingly, HR professionals are developing benchmark data, by sector. For example, one merged hospital, which employed six full-time workers per occupied bed, reduced the number of employees to match the benchmark of four full-time workers per occupied bed (Riddel and Lipson, 1996).

Reductions might be necessary. The dismissal process can be heartbreaking, as is described in one merger case (Schonfeld, 1997). In the rush to terminate quickly, some employees were notified by voice mail or e-mail or in hurried and short meetings with strangers. A supervisor was forced to fire three of his employees before being fired himself. His termination was particularly difficult to understand, as his performance reviews were excellent. As wave after wave of salespeople were laid off, customers became confused about their contacts. Departing employees took advantage of this and went to the competition, taking the business relationships with them.

Chapter 10 covers this aspect of restructuring in detail. A number of decisions need to be made immediately. Employees will want to know if they will be offered employment in the merged company; if not, they will want to know what the severance packages contain. If jobs are offered, can employees choose not to accept them? For those wary of the new owner or who fear being dumped once the sale closes, will there be a safety net? For those who are terminated, will assistance such as financial planning, job relocation, and career planning be offered? Will benefits continue for a short adjustment period? One organization, which could not promise job security to its employees, did promise to position them for work in the new organization or outside of it (Riddell and Lipson, 1996). This pledge was kept. Employees were trained, at organizational expense, for other positions. Part of the training included seminars in which employees were taught to be responsible for their own development and were given assistance to develop a survival kit called "Making Me Marketable." Jobs were reanalyzed to focus on basic skills. For example, the job specifications for a patient care technician stated that a high school diploma was required, but a review showed that certain skills, but not a high school diploma, were needed to do the job. Managers used their contacts and networks to assist departing employees. Employees were encouraged to work on cross-functional teams to expand their horizons and skills. The result was that productivity did not diminish dramatically, as occurs in most mergers. Furthermore, the downsizing and exodus were orderly, lessening the stress on remaining employees. The culture was changed, and employees were rewarded.

Those who stay with the newly acquired or merged company face several fates:

- *Demotion:* Under the new organizational structure, some employees are given less responsibility, less territory, or fewer lines due to amalgamation.

- *Competition for the same job:* Some companies force employees to compete for their old jobs by having to apply as new candidates for a position.

- *Termination*: If not successful in the competition, employees are then let go. Sometimes, the acquiring firm waits until it can obtain its own appraisal of employee capabilities and has a chance to determine fit.

The survivors have adjustments to make, and these are detailed in Chapter 10. Like employees involved in a restructuring, the survivors of a merger are dealing with their loss of identity as the company changes, a lack of information and the resultant anxiety, a lack of protection from adverse effects over which they have no control, the loss of colleagues, and a change in their jobs (Walker, 1992). Those remaining with the corporation will need to know about compensation plans.

COMPENSATION

Incentive plans have to be aligned to support the merger strategy. But consideration can be given to incentives to make the merger work. BC Gas gave each employee 50 free shares and introduced an attractive stock purchase plan to promote commitment in the new company (Kadlec, 1990).

In a merger, a major issue for the HR department is the integration of benefit plans. Which company's plan should be adopted? Employees obviously wish for the most favourable benefits, but organizations are concerned with cost. When benefits are removed or reduced in the integration of companies, employees may experience loss of morale. Thus, for employees who stay with the organization, the resolution of the benefits package may affect their decision.

The best resolution of this problem would be to conduct a cost–benefit analysis of the benefits, package by package. For example, child care centres or health and wellness centres may seem to be costly benefits. But, if the number of sick days and mental health days taken is reduced or employee turnover is diminished, then the benefits may outweigh the costs. Pension concerns will be high. Although there are regulations governing certain pension credits, different approaches to pension plan transfers must be analyzed as variances can run into the millions of dollars.

For employees who are being terminated, retaining certain benefits during the months or years after the merger may be a humane way to soften the adverse effects of the merger. Companies may wish to offer extended medical and dental coverage, modified retirement plans, and some counselling to deal with unemployment and with career plans.

PERFORMANCE APPRAISAL

During a merger, employees undergo stress and productivity can be expected to drop. Focusing on long-term goals may be difficult and so short-term goals should be substituted. Business is not as usual. The role of the manager may change from one of supervisor to one of coach. Employees may play it safe and may require constant positive reinforcement for the work they do accomplish under the new house rules.

Performance appraisals for development purposes may have to redone. The merged company may be larger or engaged in different businesses, allowing for more or different promotion paths and developmental experiences. Employee intentions and aspirations under the new regime will have to be redocumented.

Stress levels may necessitate a relaxation of the rules and more counselling and coaching. Personal problems (such as financial or marital difficulties), rather than performance problems, may surface as the stress begins to affect employees.

TRAINING AND DEVELOPMENT

Once the strategic plan has been developed, an inventory of the KSAs needed to align with the strategy should be undertaken. Information based on previous needs analyses may have to be revised in light of the new strategy, which may create new jobs.

Managers and peers may need some additional training in the role of coach and counsellor. Every employee might benefit from stress reduction or relaxation programs. Developmental programs, such as overseas assignments or executive exchanges, or long-term educational opportunities may be put on hold while the new organization establishes long-term plans.

LABOUR RELATIONS

Unionized employees are covered by a collective agreement, which is a legally binding document. Typically, these agreements set out the conditions under which job changes must occur. Various issues will need to be considered. For example, will unionized employees continue with the same working conditions and benefits, as negotiated, or will the contracts be renegotiated? At a minimum, the collective agreements must be read to determine what provisions exist for job security and what the notification periods are for layoffs and terminations. Merger experts say that unions should be informed and involved from the outset of the merger so that they can make valuable contributions.

As you can see, HR plays a pivotal role in the success of M&As.

◆ ◆ ◆

SUMMARY

The focus of this chapter was on the HRM implications of M&As. The reasons for mergers were outlined, as were various methods for achieving a merger. The financial and human results of mergers were discussed. Culture, the area that experts say is the most important predictor of merger success, received special attention. The chapter ended with a discussion of the impact of a merger on each of the functional areas—HR planning, selection, compensation, performance appraisal, training and development, and labour relations.

E X E R C I S E S

1. Outline the strategic and financial benefits of a merger.
2. Describe all the effects that a merger may have on employees. What can management do to lessen the more negative effects of a merger? What can employees do to protect themselves when they start to hear rumours of a merger?

CASE: THE CITY OF TORONTO—COURAGE IN THE FACE OF CHAOS

On January 1, 1998, the new unified city of Toronto was created out of the cities of Etobicoke, North York, Toronto, York, East York, and Scarborough and the municipality of Metropolitan Toronto. Few mergers have attempted to integrate seven organizations. The goal was to integrate the policies, practices, and systems of municipalities as large as Toronto (with a staff of 11,000) and as small as East York (with a staff of 430) and to achieve savings from the overlapping of administrative and staffing costs of the seven municipalities. Toronto is now the fifth largest city in North America, with 2.5 million residents. Its budget of $6 billion and staff of 26,000 are larger than those of several Canadian provinces. More than 800 municipal staff from all seven jurisdictions worked on the integration project, developing a vision, a mission, and a governance structure. About 70 percent to 95 percent of departmental budgets are for staffing costs.

An important position, particularly in the merger process, was that of the executive director of Human Resources and Amalgamation, a position that was filled through an internal and external search. Brenda Glover, formerly the HR commissioner of the city of Etobicoke, was chosen for the position of executive director. Ms. Glover had the critical task of designing an HR strategy that would accomplish the integration in a seamless fashion by building a new vision and culture. She noted, "If HR was not organized, then the rest of the city is in chaos. The first goal is to have all people in place."

Ms. Glover discussed the staffing, labour relations, compensation, benefits, and culture issues in this very large public sector merger:

Staffing: An HR transition team focused first on staffing. On January 1, 1998, only six new employees were working for the merged city. The goals, which were met, were to have separation programs ready by February 1, all HR directors in place by March 1, and all managers in place by April 1. Every municipal employee had the opportunity to compete for the "new" jobs, his or her former job, and jobs two levels down. Within one year, from March 1998 to March 1999, the HR department had posted 900 jobs, and an average of 12 candidates competed for each job. The priority was to hire internally, but the HR staff also looked at 16,000 résumés from external candidates during this period.

About 10 percent (or 2500) jobs were to be eliminated. Attrition and voluntary exit packages were the primary basis for workforce reduction. Those facing termination were given counselling, retraining opportunities, incentive programs for early retirement, and assistance in the job search process.

Labour relations: The seven cities operated with 56 collective agreements. The unions were given time to work through their members to determine who would be the bargaining agent. It might have been faster to force the Labour Relations Board to make this decision, but urgency was subordinated to longer-term issues of trust and collaboration.

Compensation: Working with the seven municipalities, the transition team developed an interim salary schedule. It had problems. In hindsight, a compensation consultant should have been hired to design a completely new salary schedule. There were significant integration problems, such as the case of two people who were doing the same job for which one employee was earning $20,000 more than the other.

Benefits/payroll: The goal was to harmonize the benefits and move from seven systems to one benefits policy. This was not easy, as the new city wanted to achieve savings and rationalize benefits whereas employees rarely want to give up their "rights" to achieved benefits. So, the decision made was to go neither to the lowest nor the highest, but to benchmark, creating a new standard.

Culture: Mergers generally occur between two partners, and cultural issues are a challenge. Imagine a merger between seven partners. Here are some of the cultures, without naming names, that had to be harmonized:

> City A: Cheap, fiscally prudent; has meagre compensation and resources; has a history of downsizing and little job security
>
> City B: Politically correct; an advocate for change
>
> City C: Bureaucratic, process oriented
>
> City D: Quick, entrepreneurial, rich; does little research or analysis; has good job security

As could be predicted, early encounters were filled with comments such as, "I am from Etobicoke, and we think..." or "The way we do things..." The goal was to create new values and a new mentality that was not welded to old ways of doing things.

Lessons Learned

When asked what she would have done differently, Ms. Glover mentioned several lessons learned:

1. *Communication:* "We had Web sites, brochures, hotlines, everything to inform employees about emerging policies. But we found that unless and until a policy impacts an employee personally, it is not heard or absorbed. So we found we were answering the same

questions over and over again. We learned that timing, frequency, and repetition are very important."

2. *Training:* "It became obvious very early that the transition team needed skills, and employees needed unique skills to integrate the seven municipalities. For example, the move to City Hall required new skills, such as enhanced project management. We should have realized this earlier."

3. *Profile:* Mergers in the public sector are particularly difficult because they tend to be high profile, and many of the merger decisions are made public. For example, the separation packages, which had to be approved by Council, were leaked to the press before there was time to inform employees.

4. *Services:* The integration was accomplished in such a way that the public saw no disruption in services. As Ms. Glover states, "Not one heartbeat was missed in service, even when management was in chaos, with some managers leaving and others coping with loss of [employees] and organizational memory. The frontline employees deserve a lot of credit."

What was done right? Ms. Glover reports, "No merger works without a sense of urgency. We met deadlines. We balanced urgency against fairness. We had to create teams, which is a slow process, while balancing the need to deal with immediate issues. We communicated, with lots of meetings, updates, answering questions personally. But a merger presents incredible opportunities to create a culture, handpick staff ... basically a blank sheet to do things right."

Discussion Questions

1. Compare the process used by the city of Toronto with the prescriptions for an effective merger as outlined in this chapter.
2. What do you see as the differences?
3. Would you have handled the merger of the cities any differently?

References

Berry, J.W. 1990. "Social and Cultural Change." In H.C. Triandis and R.W. Brislin, eds., *Handbook of Cross-cultural Psychology* 5. Boston: Allyn & Bacon.

Cartwright, S., and C.L. Cooper. 1993. "The Role of Culture Compatibility in Successful Organizational Marriage." *Academy of Management Journal* 7, no. 2: 57–70.

_____.1992. *Mergers and Acquisitions: The Human Factor.* Toronto: Butterworth-Heinemann.

Fisher, A. 1994. "How to Make a Merger Work." *Fortune* 129, no. 2 (June 24): 64–66.

Gaughan, P.A. 1996. *Mergers, Acquisitions, and Corporate Restructuring.* New York: John Wiley & Sons.

Gibb-Clark, M. 1998. "Let the Head Hunting Begin." *Globe and Mail* (January 27).

Hamel, G., and C. Prahalad. 1989. "Strategic Intent." *Harvard Business Review* 3: 73.

Harshbarger, D. 1990. "Mergers, Acquisitions, and the Reformatting of American Businesses." In D.B. Fishman and C. Cherniss, eds., *The Human Side of Corporate Competitiveness.* Newbury Park, Ca.: Sage Publications.

Heisler, W.J., W.D. Jones, and P.O. Benham Jr. 1988. *Managing Human Resource Issues.* San Francisco: Jossey-Bass.

Hollister, M. 1996. "Competing Corporate Cultures Can Doom Acquisition." *Human Resource Professional* (January/February): 7–10.

Kadlec, R.E. 1990. "Managing a Successful Merger." *Business Quarterly* (Autumn).

Kanter, R.M., and T.K. Seggerman. 1986. "Managing Mergers, Acquisitions, and Divestitures." *Management Review* (October): 16–17.

Kets de Vries, M.F.R. 1991. "Introduction: Exploding the Myth That Organizations and Executives Are Rational." In M.F.R. Kets de Vries and Associates, *Organizations on the Couch: Clinical Perspectives on Organizational Behavior and Change.* San Francisco: Jossey-Bass.

Knowles, L.L. 1989. "How to Manage a Merger." *Canadian Manager* (Winter): 20–22.

Koeth, B. 1985. "Expressly American: Management's Task Is Internal Development." *Management Review* (February): 24–29.

Kroll, M., P. Wright, L. Toombs, and H. Leavell. 1997. "Form of Control: Determinant of Acquisition Performance and CEO Rewards." *Strategic Management Journal* 18, no. 2 (February): 85–96.

Lubatkin, M.H., and P.J. Lane. 1996. "Psst—The Merger Mavens Still Have It Wrong." *Academy of Management Executive* 10, no. 1 (February): 21–39.

Master, L.J. 1987. "Efficient Product of Financial Services: Scale and Scope Economies." *Federal Reserve Bank of Philadelphia* (January/February): 15–25.

McNish. J. 1998. "Takeover Binge Expected to Sweep Canada." *Globe and Mail Report on Business* (January 29).

Nulty, P. 1987. "Pushed Out at 45— Now What?" *Fortune* (March 2): 26–34.

Riddel, A., and F. Lipson. 1996. "Bankrupt Hospital Lands on Its Feet." *Personnel Journal* (August): 83–86.

Roll, R. 1986. "The Hubris Hypothesis of Corporate Takeover." *Journal of Business* 59, no. 2 (April): 197–216.

Rovenpor, J.L. 1993. "The Relationship between Four Personal Characteristics of Chief Executive Officers and Company Merger and Acquisition Activity." *Journal of Business and Psychology* 8, no. 1 (Fall): 27–55.

Schonfeld, E. 1997. "Have the Urge to Merge? You'd Better Think Twice." *Fortune* (March 31): 114–116.

Shrivastava, P. 1986. "Postmerger Integration." *Journal of Business Strategy* (Summer): 65–79.

Stuart, P. 1993. "HR Actions Offer Protection during Takeovers." *Personnel Journal* (June): 84–95.

Walker, J. 1992. *Human Resource Management*. New York: McGraw-Hill.

Zwieg, P.L. 1995. "The Case against Mergers." *Business Week* (October 30): 122–130.

13

Business Strategies

CHAPTER GOALS

Corporate strategies focus on long-term survival and growth. Business strategies concentrate on the best way to compete in a particular sector. Numerous prescriptive models assist business managers who want to compete by being the lowest-cost producer, and others who might want to compete by offering the best-designed product in the sector. Each of these approaches means that HR managers will use different HR programs to select, train, and motivate employees to help business managers achieve their goals. The purpose of this chapter is to describe these choices and to propose that HR practices be aligned with business strategy to achieve the business results desired.

After reading this chapter, you should be able to do the following:

1. Define business strategy and discuss how it differs from corporate strategy.
2. Discuss three approaches to business strategies: the Boston Consulting Group approach, the Miles and Snow approach, and Porter's generic competitive strategies.
3. Explain HR's role in a business that competes by using a low-cost provider strategy by discussing six areas: HR planning, selection, compensation, training, performance evaluation, and labour relations.
4 Outline HR's role in a business with a differentiation strategy.
5. Discuss why firms with more than one business strategy need more than one HR strategy.

The next section introduces the concept of the business strategy and differentiates it from corporate strategies.

◆ ◆ ◆
BUSINESS STRATEGY

Corporate strategies are concerned with questions such as these: Should we be in business? What business should we be in? Business strategies are concerned with questions such as these: How should we compete? Should we compete by offering products at prices lower than those of the competition or by offering the best service?" Business strategy is concerned with how to build a competitive position, with the best way to compete in that line of business. Businesses compete for customers, as the wars between Bell Canada and AT&T have shown so clearly. Businesses try to demonstrate to the customer that their business is better because they have lower prices or more innovative services than their rivals.

Business strategy is all about means and ends. Business strategies focus on the best ways to compete in a particular sector. Organizations try to become (or remain) competitive based on a core competence, which can be defined as a specialized expertise that rivals do not have and cannot easily match. Wal-Mart's core competence is inventory management, resulting in low prices. Wal-Mart competes on the basis of low cost. Holt Renfrew competes on a service basis, giving customers products designed to differentiate them from other people.

Business strategy is the action plan for managing a single line of business. It is entirely possible that there be one corporate strategy and many business strategies. For example, the overall corporate strategy for the Bank of Hong Kong might be to maximize profits, but the business strategy for its bank business might be to provide a unique kind of banking, and for its insurance business, to be the low-cost provider of insurance. There is one corporate strategy, but two business strategies.

The next sections link HR strategy with business strategy.

◆ ◆ ◆
HR ALIGNMENT WITH BUSINESS STRATEGY

HR strategies are about making business strategies work. HR planning must support the implementation of corporate and business strategies. Senior managers must focus on issues such as these: What are the HR implications of adopting a strategy? What are the internal and external constraints and opportunities? As is implied by these two questions, the concept of reciprocal independence between strategic planning and HR planning is integral to implementation.

Thus, a firm engaged in strategic planning will review those HR programs that will assist or block the achievement of the chosen strategy. Skill shortages or personnel retention, discussed in Chapters 6 and 7, are just two

HR issues that will affect strategy implementation. We want to expand that range of options, and describe how six different HR functional areas have to be designed to match business strategy. An organization must examine the HR practices and resources needed to implement each strategy.

In the next section, we will describe three popular approaches to understanding business strategies. (Note that no one has developed generic strategies for not-for-profit organizations, so this discussion focuses on private, for-profit firms). We will spend some time describing these models because HR professionals are expected to understand the language of business and to be able to discuss HR programs in a strategic sense. This exposure to strategic models and terms will enable HR practitioners to participate more fully during strategic discussions. We wish to introduce the models and terms used by managers in business. Then HR managers will be able propose or defend HR programs in ways that other managers will understand.

◆ ◆ ◆
MODELS OF BUSINESS STRATEGIES

There are three popular models for analyzing businesses: the Boston Consulting Group model, the organizational types model proposed by Myles and Snow, and Porter's five forces model.

BOSTON CONSULTING GROUP MODEL

Organizations with multiple businesses need a technique for analyzing the strategies of the different business units. The most frequently used method is portfolio matrix analysis. In this method, indicators such as industry growth rate, market share, long-term industry attractiveness, and competitive strategy or stage of product/market evolution are placed on a graph. One popular matrix is that developed by the Boston Consulting Group (BCG) (Thompson and Strickland, 1995). Figure 13.1 illustrates the grid; industry growth rate is on the vertical axis and relative market share is on the horizontal axis.

To place a business unit on the grid requires some analysis. For example, to position a firm on the high end of the industry growth rate, the firm must be competing in a sector in which the growth rate is around twice the real GNP growth rate, plus inflation. In other words, the industry is growing faster than the economy as a whole.

FIGURE 13.1 The BCG Growth Share Business Position

Relative Market Share

		High (above 1.0)	Low (below 1.0)
Industry Growth Rate	High	Stars	Question marks
	Low	Cash Cows	Dogs

Then, to position a firm on the horizontal axis, one analyzes the business's market share in comparison to the market share held by the largest competitor in the sector. For example, if Reebok has 20 percent of market share, and Nike has 30 percent, then Reebok's relative share would be 2:3. (Market share is measured in unit volume, not dollars.)

An analysis of the grid follows:

Stars: Stars are found in the upper left-hand quadrant. These businesses offer excellent profit and growth opportunities, and parent companies will pour cash into expanding them. In some cases, stars can generate enough cash to fund their own expansion. Microsoft does this better than most companies.

Question marks: Businesses in the upper right-hand quadrant of the matrix are labelled question marks or problem children. This is because the industry growth rate suggests lots of opportunity, but the firm has a limited market share and does not seem to be capitalizing on the opportunity. The questions to be asked are these: Does the firm have the strength to compete? Does the parent company have the cash (or resources) to make it competitive? The firm is left with two options: divest or invest and expand aggressively.

Dogs: Dogs, found in the lower right-hand quadrant, have no potential and cannot generate enough cash to fortify and defend themselves. Profits are marginal in an industry where competition is tough, and so the strategy is almost always "close," through harvesting, divesting, or liquidating. Eaton's is the most recent example of a major retailer divesting in a brutally competitive market where margins are thin.

Cash cows: Cash cows are firms with a relatively high market share in a low-growth market. This type of business typically generates more cash than is needed to grow or reinvest. The strategy is a defensive one: keep the cow healthy to subsidize the stars or deal with the problem children. In this case, the HR strategy remains constant, depending on what has made this firm a cash cow. It may be profitable because its products are less expensive than those of competitors or its services are unique in the industry.

Another way of understanding business strategy is by grouping organizations into types based on how they approach businesses in stable or turbulent environments.

MILES AND SNOW'S ORGANIZATIONAL TYPES

This approach to examining business strategy was proposed by Miles and Snow (1978). They identified four organizational types:

Defender: The defender type competes in a relatively stable and predictable environment and pursues low-cost operations, focusing on efficiency through standardized jobs, formalization, and centralization. A manufacturer of toasters would fall into this category.

Prospector: The prospector operates in a dynamic environment. Innovation and adaptation are critical to success. Any company operating in the telecommunications sector, such as Clearnet, would exemplify this organizational type. Such companies achieve innovation and adaptation through heavy investments in research and development, through organic structures that are highly decentralized to allow for rapid and intelligent responses to the changing environment. These companies are roughly similar to Porter's low-cost provider and differentiator types.

Analyzer: Miles and Snow's third type, the analyzer, is a combination of the defender and the prospector, attempting to achieve efficiency with an interest in new markets and products. These companies scan competitors' actions and react promptly by developing better ways to get products to market. The Bay, in its attempt to outmanoeuvre Wal-Mart, is a good example of a company with this strategy.

Reactor: The reactor type of company has no apparent strategy, and, indeed, Miles and Snow see it as an imperfect type that lacks a consistent response to changing conditions. Research has shown that reactors are always ineffective, lending support to our earlier contention that an organization with a strategy is better off than one without one (Smith et al., 1989).

Finally, we introduce a model that has received a lot of recognition in the field of strategic management.

PORTER'S MODEL

Michael Porter (1985) made a major contribution to the field of strategic management by grouping the many ways in which organizations can compete into five generic competitive strategies:

Low-cost provider strategy: The goal here is to provide a product or service at a price lower than that of competitors while appealing to a broad range of customers. Fast-food businesses use this strategy almost exclusively. The cheap hamburger is consumed by a range of customers from toddlers to seniors. This is a good basic product with few frills. A company competing on this basis searches continually for ways in which to reduce costs.

Broad differentiation strategy: An organization employing this strategy seeks to differentiate its products from competitors' products in ways that will appeal to a broad range of buyers. The company employing this strategy searches for features that will make their product or service different from that of competitors and that will encourage customers to pay a premium for it. Thus, Burger King will introduce the Whopper, with "frills" for which people will pay an extra dollar.

Best cost provider strategy: The goal here is to give customers more value for the money by emphasizing a low-cost product or service and an upscale differentiation. The product has excellent features, including several upscale features, that are offered at low cost. East Side Mario's offers hamburgers, but offers them on a plate, with extras such as potato salad, served by a waiter in a fixture full environment.

Focused or market niche strategy based on lower cost: The goal here is to offer a low-cost product to a select group of customers. Red Lobster uses this approach, selling fish and seafood at reasonable prices to a narrow market segment that likes this type of food.

Focused or market niche strategy based on differentiation: Here, the organization tries to offer a niche product or service customized to the tastes and requirements of a very narrow market segment. For example, Black and Blue is a very expensive restaurant that specializes in steaks and permits cigar smoking, thus appealing to the older, usually male, business customer.

Under Porter's schema, business strategy concerns itself with the product and market scope. What particular goods and services are to be provided? What distinguishing features or attractive attributes will characterize these products and services? Typical product characteristics include cost, quality, optional features, durability, and reliability. Market dimensions refer to the target market population characteristics of size, diversity, customer buying patterns, and geographic regions.

To illustrate the alignment of HR programs with business strategy, we focus on Porter's model and discuss two strategies: the low-cost provider strategy and the differentiation strategy. Although Porter recognized the importance of HRM, and even concedes that, in some firms, HRM holds the key to competitive advantage, he did not delineate any specific practices that can be aligned with business strategy. We will attempt to fill this gap and provide one of the few "recipes" for using HR strategies to support a business strategy. The next section explores the HR strategies that should align with the business strategy of the low-cost provider.

◆ ◆ ◆
HR ALIGNMENT WITH THE LOW-COST PROVIDER STRATEGY

A firm competing on cost leadership attempts to be a low-cost provider of a product or service within a marketplace. The product or service must be perceived by the consumer to be relatively comparable to that offered by the competition and to have a price advantage. McDonald's uses this approach, as do Zellers and Timex.

Buyers are price sensitive, and businesses appeal to this price consciousness by providing products or services at prices lower than those of competitors. Survival is the ultimate goal, but organizations price low to gain market share (by underpricing competitors) or by earning a higher profit margin by selling at the going market rate. This strategy requires the company to balance the delivery of a product that still appeals to customers with not spending too much on gaining market share. McDonald's could deliver a cheaper hamburger, but would it have any taste? McDonald's could underprice its competitors, but it may risk its survival by going too low. The key is to manage costs down every year.

The adoption of a low-cost provider strategy by a firm has immediate implications for HR strategy. Costs are important, and labour costs are carefully controlled. Efficiency and ideas for controlling costs are paramount. The implications of a low-cost provider strategy for five key components of HR are discussed below, but first we start with the job description of a typical employee working in a company competing as a low-cost provider.

THE EMPLOYEE

To keep wages low, jobs have to be of limited scope so that the company can hire people with minimal skills at low wages. The job requires highly repetitive and predictable behaviours. There is little need for cooperative or interdependent behaviours among employees. The company directs its efforts at doing the same or more with less and capitalizing on economies of scale. For example, in 1987 Toyota produced about 3.5 million vehicles a year with 25,000 production workers, the same number of workers it employed in 1966 when it produced only 1 million vehicles (Schuller and Jackson, 1987). Toyota achieved what low-cost providers want—an increase in productivity and reduced output cost per employee. Doing more with fewer employees is the goal of most organizations with a low-cost provider strategy.

Risk-taking behaviour on the part of the employee is not needed, but comfort with repetitive, unskilled work is necessary. Customers, like those at McDonald's, are "trained" not to make idiosyncratic requests (such as a "medium-rare hamburger" or "hot mustard"), and so no unique response system is required. Employees are not expected to contribute ideas.

Another way to cut costs is to eliminate as many of the support or managerial layers as possible. The impact of cutting costs in this way is that employees may have to do more with less, make more decisions, and so on, which would require more skilled employee. Alternatively, the jobs could be so tightly designed that little supervision is required, thus saving costs. Substituting technology for labour is another way to save costs. Let us now look at five HR functions that will facilitate the personnel work at a low-cost provider organization.

HR PLANNING

At the entry level, succession planning is minimal, ensuring only the feeder line to the next level. Outside labour markets are monitored to ensure that entry-level people are in adequate supply. The availability and use of fringe workers—those who are retired, temporarily unemployed, students, and so on—is part of the planning strategy, particularly if the employment market is offering better opportunities to the normal supply of low-skilled workers.

At the executive level, succession management assumes the same importance as in other organizations.

SELECTION

Recruitment is primarily at the entry, or lowest, level and is from the surrounding external labour market. Recruitment is by word of mouth, and application forms are available on-site, thus saving the costs of recruiting in newspapers. Most other positions are staffed internally through promotions from within. Thus, career paths are narrow.

COMPENSATION

A low-cost provider strategy includes lower wages and fringe benefits. Beyond the legal minimum pay requirements, firms with this strategy carefully monitor what their competitors are paying in the local labour market. These firms' strategy tends to be a lag strategy, where they attempt to pay wages slightly below industry norms.

One way of achieving these lower costs is to outsource production to sites with lower labour costs. In the United States, this means moving production from high-wage states, such as New York, to low-wage states, such as New Mexico. In Canada, wages are highly similar across provinces, so firms analyze wage rates in countries such as India, which pay employees substantially less for similar productivity. Outsourcing has also meant moving the work from highly unionized plants, where workers make $20 or more an hour, to non-unionized smaller sites, where workers are paid slightly more than the minimum wage.

Cost reduction in wages can also be achieved through the use of part-time workers, who receive no fringe benefits. Canadian organizations pay around 30 percent in fringe benefits, and the saving gained by using part-time workers is substantial among large employers. Food franchises employ part-time workers almost exclusively to reduce labour costs.

Pay for performance, such as incentive compensation that is linked to productivity, rewards individual effort. Group rewards are based on explicit, results-oriented criteria and the meeting of short-term performance goals.

It is important to note that innovative compensation schemes may produce a competitive advantage. Programs designed to reduce labour costs, such as outsourcing or using part-time workers, can easily be imitated by competitors, and so may produce no long-term competitive advantage. However, an innovative compensation scheme that cannot be duplicated by rivals may provide a competitive advantage. For example, in an arrangement between the Great Atlantic and Pacific Tea Company (A&P) and the United Food and Commercial Workers (UFCW), workers took a 25-percent pay cut in exchange for cash bonuses. If the store's employees could keep labour costs at 10 percent of sales by working more efficiently or generating more store traffic, they would receive a cash bonus of 1 percent of store sales. This arrangement resulted in an 81 percent increase in operating profits. However, unions were opposed to the spread of this practice, and so A&P's rivals in the low-margin food business were unable to reduce their labour costs in the same way (Schuller and Jackson, 1987). Any incentives for performance would reward cost savings, or improvements in efficiency, as this example shows.

TRAINING

Training is minimal, as few skills are required. Any training is based on increasing efficiency in the present job, or specialization for the current position. Such training is fast and inexpensive. McDonald's can train a new hamburger flipper or cashier in under an hour. There is little to no investment in the long-term development of the employee, nor in the acquisition of skills for jobs other than the current one.

The training staff is lean, with the organization relying on outside suppliers. However, most training takes place on the job in the form of direct instruction from or coaching by the supervisor. The jobs are so narrow in scope, so repetitive in nature, that little need for training exists.

PERFORMANCE EVALUATION

Short-term results, with explicit and standardized criteria, are used for evaluating an employee's performance. The feedback is immediate and specific. Individuals are held accountable only for their own behaviour or results, not for that of the team or the company (Ulrich, 1991). Only the supervisor provides input for the performance evaluation. Forms are kept to a minimum, and rating is done against check marks. Feedback, if based on a performance review, tends to be one way, with little opportunity for the employee to debate the results or receive developmental feedback. Results are used for consideration for promotion.

LABOUR RELATIONS

Low-cost providers try to prevent the formation of a union because they feel that unions drive up wages. Unions find low-cost providers, such as McDonald's, difficult to unionize because employees work shifts and part-time hours. Furthermore, employees quit often, and many low-cost providers absorb turnover rates of 300 percent annually as a cost of doing business. High turnover has the primary advantage of keeping compensation levels low.

Box 13.1 describes how one company aligns its HR strategy with its low-cost provider business goal.

Now that we have an idea of how HR programs align with a low-cost provider strategy, let us examine how different these programs would be under a differentiation strategy.

◆ ◆ ◆

HR ALIGNMENT WITH THE DIFFERENTIATION STRATEGY

In most markets, buyer preferences are too diverse to be satisfied by one undifferentiated product. Firms providing features that appeal to a particular market segment are said to compete on a differentiation strategy. A firm competing on the basis of a differentiation strategy will offer something unique and valuable to its customers. Mercedes, Polo Ralph Lauren, Rolex,

BOX 13.1 COST REDUCTION AT UNITED PARCEL SERVICE

United Parcel Service (UPS) employees 152,000 people to deliver parcels in an extremely competitive sector where "a package is a package." UPS profits by keeping costs low. How does it do this?

Its key is to manage labour costs. UPS starts by simplifying and standardizing the work to optimize efficiency. Early in the company's history, management used time and motion studies to measure the time each UPS driver spent each day on specific tasks. The engineers then changed some of these tasks to improve worker effectiveness, thus leading to work standards. Additionally, workers were less tired at the end of each day. Workers engage in repetitive tasks, requiring little participation in decision making. More than 1000 industrial engineers—experts in work efficiency—continue to monitor the work. The unionized workers earn about a dollar more than drivers at other companies and gain employment security if they perform at acceptable levels.

The cost reduction strategy through work process refinements enables UPS to gain a competitive advantage in a service sector, that of overnight delivery, that is relatively undifferentiated.

Source: Adapted from Schuller, R.S., and S.E. Jackson. 1987. "Linking Competitive Strategies with Human Resource Management Practices." *Academy of Management Executive* 1, no. 3: 207–213.

and Hewlett Packard's scientific instruments divisions are firms that compete successfully by charging a price premium for uniqueness. The primary focus is on the new and different. Observation, experience, and market research will establish what buyers consider important, what has value, and what they will pay for these features. Then the firm can offer a product or service that commands a premium price, increase unit sales within this niche, and gain buyer loyalty among those who value these features. The extra price outweighs the extra costs of providing these features.

A firm can differentiate itself from its competitors in many ways:

- Having quality products
- Offering superior customer service
- Having a more convenient location
- Using proprietary technology
- Offering valuable features
- Demonstrating unique styling
- Having a brand name reputation

These different features can be anything. Common examples show some firms competing on service (Four Seasons Hotels), on engineering design (BMW), on image (Polo Ralph Lauren), on reliability (Bell), on a full range of products or services (Procter & Gamble), on technological leadership (Corel), and on quality (Honda).

Most of the time, these competitive advantages are combined, such as by linking quality products with proprietary technology and superior customer service, thus providing the buyer with more value for the money. The key in this strategy is to provide the differentiation that is perceived to be of value to customers while keeping costs down. For example, a slice of lemon in a glass of ice water delivered to the table is an obvious way to differentiate the restaurant, but at low cost. After-dinner mints are less expensive than valet parking, but may be equally appreciated by diners.

The firm spends its time and money trying to determine those features that are difficult or expensive for its rivals to copy. Differentiation leads to more profits, and longer-lasting competitive advantage, when the differences are based on technical superiority, product quality, and comprehensive customer service. Buyers value these, and competitors cannot imitate them quickly or easily.

A differentiation strategy calls for innovation and creativity among employees. HRM is affected in fundamentally different ways in organizations that want to use employees' brains, versus their limited (mainly manual) skills, in the low-cost provider strategy.

Again, the starting point for aligning HR programming with a differentiation strategy is the employee.

THE EMPLOYEE

Organizations competing on a differentiation strategy require in their employees creative behaviour, a long-term focus, interdependent activity, and some risk taking, as well as an ability to work in an ambiguous and unpredictable environment. Their employees' skills need to be broad, and employees must be highly involved with the firm (Shchuler, et al., 1988). Organizations encourage employees to make suggestions, through both informal and formal suggestion systems, for new and improved ways of doing their job. Employees at Corning Canada Inc., for example, submit their suggestions to their supervisors, who review them formally and give feedback directly to the employee. Contrast this with the traditional suggestion box, which many employees view as a recycling bin because of the lack of timely feedback.

To encourage innovative behaviour, 3M has an informal policy of allowing employees to "bootleg" about 15 percent of their time on their own projects. Job classifications are flexible.

HR PLANNING

In a company that has a differentiation strategy and that recognizes that people are the key to competitive advantage, HR planning is taken very seriously. For example, at Sumitomo Metals in Japan, the business planning group reports to HR because the company understands that identifying what needs to be done is less difficult than planning how to do it.

Succession management is critical as employees would have to possess many attributes to move ahead in the organization. Thus, a strong emphasis on developing skills for the future is part of the promotion policy. Investments in career moves, training, and developmental experiences are substantial. Long-term job security and reciprocal loyalty are the norm.

SELECTION

Companies with a differentiation strategy need employees who have a broad range of skills and the ability to learn from others. An innovative atmosphere requires employees who are self-motivated and do not require a great deal of supervision. Employees are selected for their abilities to think creatively, to be flexible in work attitudes, and to be able to work in teams.

COMPENSATION

Compensation plans affect employee behaviour more directly than most HR practices. For example, Drucker describes a compensation scheme he implemented at General Electric in which pay for performance was based only on the previous year's results. As such, for 10 years, GE lost its capacity for innovation because investing in innovation affects expenses and decreases profits, so everyone postponed spending on innovation (Rutliagano, 1986).

Compensation is carefully designed in firms that have a differentiation strategy. Pay rates may be slightly below average market rates but may offer substantial opportunities to increase those base levels through incentive pay. Pay for performance is a large part of the compensation package and will be dependent on individual, group, and corporate results. These results are a combination of process and financial criteria and are set in advance, usually on a yearly basis.

There is more choice about the mix of components of compensation. Individuals may receive salary, bonus, or stock option incentives. Box 13.2 shows how one company designed its compensation package to reward flexible and innovative behaviour.

Internal equity is of greater concern than equity with the external market. Egalitarian pay structures are associated with greater product quality (Cowherd and Levine, 1992). Nonmonetary rewards also play a larger role in HR strategy in these types of firms. At Honda, the team that designs a unique transportation vehicle is awarded a trip to Japan.

TRAINING

Training is part of the differentiation strategy, and companies with this strategy have a strong training team. The focus of training is on both skills and attitudes. Process skills, such as decision making, the ability to work in teams, and creative thinking, are emphasized as much as skills needed for the current job.

The training itself is seen as an opportunity to generate new ideas and procedures (Ulrich, 1991). Indeed, customers and cross-functional teams might be included in the training program.

Developmental experiences are encouraged. The value of working in another division or another country is recognized and encouraged. Employees receive promotions or other job opportunities based, partially, on their willingness to undertake training and their track record in learning.

PERFORMANCE EVALUATION

In a company with a differentiation strategy, performance appraisal is not based on short-term results but instead on the long-term implications of behaviour. Processes that are deemed to lead to better results in the long term are rewarded. Thus, companies encourage and appraise attitudes such as empowerment, diversity sensitivity, and teamwork in an effort to build future bottom-line outcomes. Working beyond the job is encouraged, not punished. Failure is tolerated, although management tries to distinguish between bad luck and bad judgment or stupidity.

Evaluation tends to be based on a mixture of individual and group (and sometimes corporate) criteria. Thus, an individual might be evaluated on his

---

BOX 13.2 LINKING HR STRATEGY TO BUSINESS STRATEGY AT FROST

Frost, Inc. is a manufacturer of automobile parts with sales of over $20 million. The company was dependent on one product (overhead conveyor trolleys) in one sector (the automobile industry), and the president was concerned about the company's vulnerability in this cyclical industry. Attempts to design, build, and sell other products failed. The president set out to correct this problem, stating, "We had a single-purpose machine, and single-purpose people." He needed flexibility and a long-term orientation from his personnel.

To increase identification with the long-term survival of the company, Frost gave each worker 10 shares of the closely held company. Employees were able to participate in a share purchase plan and a corporate profit-sharing plan. This accomplished the goals of increasing employee commitment to the organization and promoting a long-term focus.

Then, the president set out to restructure the rest of the compensation package to improve innovation. A balance was needed between rewards for results (productivity) and rewards for process (manufacturing). Quarterly bonuses were given for productivity, but managers also were able to tap into a "celebration fund," which rewarded employees' significant innovative behaviour. Additional soft rewards of dinner with the president or weekend holidays for the employee and his or her spouse were used to reinforce innovative processes. Executive perks were eliminated to demonstrate the egalitarian nature of the innovative climate, and all employees had access to corporate information (except payroll) through terminals placed throughout the plant.

Frost paid employees to learn new skills, both through the company training programs and from outside vendors. Only those who had developed additional skills were eligible for advancement.

Source: Adapted from Schuller, R.S., and S.E. Jackson. 1987. "Linking Competitive Strategies with Human Resource Management Practices." *Academy of Management Executive* 1, no. 3: 207–213.

---

or her ability to achieve results and to work as a member of the team, the group's performance might be measured against established quotas, and the company would be evaluated in terms of its overall financial performance.

Three-hundred-and-sixty-degree evaluations, that is, appraisals that include input from employees, functional experts, peers, and so on, are the norm. Organizations in the service sector are more likely to include customers as sources of input for performance appraisal (Jackson and Schuller, 1992).

LABOUR RELATIONS

Any structure or process that reduces the capacity to be innovative and flexible is difficult to tolerate. Traditional unions, with rigid collective agreements, are encouraged to work collectively toward a new union-management relationship. The union-management relationship is characterized by shared information such as open books, shared decision making about best approaches, and shared responsibility for solving problems as they arise.

It seems feasible to design HR policies to match strategy, but what happens when an organization has more than one business and more than one business strategy? We attempt to answer that question in the next section.

◆ ◆ ◆
HR STRATEGY BY DIVISION

Firms with more than one business strategy are likely to have more than one approach to HR strategy. The challenge is to treat employees across divisions in an equitable fashion while motivating different behaviours that align with the divisions' strategies or functions. For example, General Electric might adopt HR practices that support innovation in the research and development branch while adopting policies that support low costs in the manufacturing branch. But, to achieve equity, employees in both branches would have the same employee benefits.

Similarly, an employee could expect to be exposed to different HR practices within his or her career, even within one firm. Flexibility in behaviour and diverse skill sets will be required from most employees. The basic prescription is to design HR programs that support business strategy.

The example in Box 13.3 shows how this is done.

Linking HRM strategy with business strategy can result in improved organizational performance.

◆ ◆ ◆
SUMMARY

This chapter defined business strategy and contrasted it with corporate strategy. Three models of business strategies were outlined: the Boston Consulting Group model, Miles and Snow's organizational types, and Porter's model. Two generic business strategies, the low-cost provider strategy and the differentiation strategy, were discussed in more detail. The implications for HRM policies and practices in organizations that practise these strategies were outlined in six areas: HR planning, selection, compensation, training, performance evaluation, and labour relations.

BOX 13.3 HRM STRATEGY AT THE BANK OF MONTREAL

The Bank of Montreal is one of the 10 largest banks in North America, with billions of dollars in assets and more than 33,000 employees around the world. The bank's overall corporate goal is to perform better than the competition by achieving an above-average level of profitability and return. The Bank of Montreal aims to be a high-quality, low-cost provider of financial services.

The HR department's role was to provide the support necessary to achieve this strategy. The HR strategy designed to do this had four goals: to be the employer of choice, to invest in the development of employees, to develop committed employees, and to place a high value on a learning culture. A number of programs were started to reach these goals, including flexible work arrangements, a diversity drive that included targets, an Institute for Learning, incentive pay, and a career management process using a call centre called the Possibilities Centre.

Over seven years, from 1990 to 1997, net income doubled, return on equity moved from 14.6 percent to 17 percent, and earnings per share increased by 72 percent. During this time, the Bank of Montreal received the following awards: the 1994 Catalyst Award for its advancement of women, the 1995 Vision Award from Human Resources Canada for efforts to create a diverse workforce, annual citations as the best company in Canada for HRM, and, in 1997, the Optimas Award for outstanding achievements in HRM.

Source: Adapted from M. Gonzalez. 1997. "Synchronized Strategies." *Journal of Business Strategy* (May/June): 9–11.

EXERCISES

1. Distinguish between corporate strategies and business strategies.
2. Identify two companies working in the same sector, such as the education or hospitality sectors. (Hotels, restaurants, and schools are good choices.) Compare and contrast the HRM practices of a company using a low-cost provider strategy with one using a differentiation strategy. For example, contrast the MBA schools at Queen's University with those at the University of Athabasca. Determine their strategies and discuss what implications they have on selection, performance evaluation, and training of both faculty and staff.
3. Using the Internet, find articles about the strategies of the Bay, Zellers, and Wal-Mart. Can you identify their business strategies? Talk to someone in the HR department of these companies or to a departmental store manager. Do their HR practices differ in any way? Then, go to a retailer that competes on a differentiation strategy, such as Harry Rosen or Holt Renfrew. Determine the differences in how they do HRM.

References

Cowherd, D.M., and D.I. Levine. 1992. "Product Quality and Pay Equity between Lower-Level Employees and Top Management: An Investigation of Distributive Justice Theory." *Administrative Science Quarterly* 37: 302–320.

Jackson, S.E., and R.S. Schuller. 1992. "HRM Practices in Service-Based Organizations: A Role Theory Perspective." *Advertising Services Marketing Management* 1: 123–157.

Miles, R.E., and C.C. Snow. 1978. *Organizational Strategy, Structure and Process.* New York: McGraw-Hill.

Porter, M. 1985. *Competitive Advantage.* New York: Free Press.

Rutigliano, A.J. 1986. "Managing the New: An Interview with Peter Drucker." *Management Review* (January): 38–41.

Schuller, R.S., and S.E. Jackson. 1987. "Linking Competitive Strategies with Human Resource Management Practices." *Academy of Management Executive* 1, no. 3: 207–219.

Schuller, R.S., S.A. Youngblood, and V.L. Huber, eds. 1988. *Readings in Personnel and Human Resource Management,* 3rd ed. St. Paul, Minn: West Publishing.

Smith, G. S., J.P Guthrie, and M. Chen. 1989. "Strategy, Size and Performance." *Organizational Studies* 10: 63–81.

Ulrich, D. 1991. "Using Human Resources for Competitive Advantage." In R.H. Kilman and I. Kilman, eds., *Making Organizations Competitive.* San Francisco: Jossey-Bass.

IV

Looking Back and Looking Ahead

14

Program Evaluation

◆ ◆ ◆
CHAPTER GOALS

Aligning HRM practices and policies with organizational goals is the beginning of the strategic HR planning process. Seeing whether these policies and practices worked is the end of one cycle in the planning process. HR professionals need to know how their programs and policies are doing.

After reading this chapter, you should be able to do the following:

1. Understand the importance of measuring the effectiveness of HRM activities.

2. Outline five aspects of HRM that can be evaluated using the 5C model for measuring effectiveness: compliance with laws and regulations, client satisfaction, culture management to influence employee attitudes, cost control of the labour component of the budget, and the contribution of HR programs.

3. Discuss methods of measurement, such as cost–benefit analysis, utility analysis, and auditing techniques.

4. Identify the challenges in measuring HR activities.

◆ ◆ ◆
THE SCORECARD

Corporate scorekeeping is the control that allows organizations to make the adjustments necessary to reach their goals. The scorecards produced by this process tell an organization if customer satisfaction is rising or declining or if sales in Manitoba are higher per capita than sales in Ontario.

The scorecard, with its measures of key indicators, focuses managers' and employees' attention on what is important to the organization. Focusing on desired results increases the ability to attain the results. Scorecard measures allow us to make judgments about the relative effectiveness of various policies and practices, just as baseball scores and records allow fans to track the success of sports teams.

The model of strategic HRM planning outlined in Chapter 1 called for the measurement of the success of the plan. The tracking of sales or customers enables organizations not only to measure progress, but also to pinpoint weaknesses and identify gaps. Just as organizations keep scorecards on their financial effectiveness, so too must the HR department track the effectiveness of its programs.

◆ ◆ ◆
THE IMPORTANCE OF EVALUATING HRM

An article in *Fortune* magazine (Stewart, 1996) called for the abolition of the HR function, arguing that HR managers are unable to describe their contribution to value except in trendy, unquantifiable, and "wanna-be" terms. The author also proposed that efficiencies could be increased by outsourcing legislated activities (such as payroll and equity) and returning "people" responsibilities to line managers. His exact words were, "Blow up the HR department." Senior executives who read *Fortune* were left wondering, Does HR make a difference? Does it add value? Clearly, until HR managers can talk about the contribution and value of HR activities in the numbers language of business, the HR department and the HR profession will be vulnerable to destructive proposals such as the one in the *Fortune* article.

Increasingly, the HR department is being treated like other operational units, that is, it is subject to questions about its contribution to organizational performance. In the simplest terms, HRM must make a difference; if it doesn't, it will be abolished. Decision makers within organizations view HR activities, such as training courses, as expenses. They view results as value. Measurement of the HR function is critical for improving both the credibility and the effectiveness of HR. If you cannot measure contribution, then you cannot manage it or improve it. What gets measured gets managed, and improved.

Business is a numbers game. Some surveys have shown that HR practitioners, while familiar with some numbers (such as the number of people employed in the organization), can't always recite other key numbers (such as the sales volumes, market share, profit levels, and rates of return for their organization). When asked to assess their contribution, most HR professionals describe it in such terms as "number of training courses" or "new hires." They do not provide numbers for outcomes. They say things such as, "120 people attended the training course" and never "the training courses resulted in a 15 percent improvement in customer satisfaction."

RESISTANCE

Some HR managers resist measuring their work. They argue that HR activities cannot be measured, since outcomes such as employee attitudes or managerial productivity are impossible to calibrate meaningfully or precisely. They assert that they cannot control the labour market. But the finance department cannot control the inflation rate, and the marketing department has little control over product quality, and yet each of these departments measures its activities and is accountable for results.

Very few organizations measure the impact of HRM. Only 20 percent of firms surveyed in Quebec (Dolan and Belout, 1997) and in the United States (Cashman and McElroy, 1991) formally evaluated their HR departments. Interest in measuring HR is growing slowly, fuelled by business improvement efforts across organizations, by attempts to position HR as a strategic partner, and by the need for objective indicators of success to accompany the analysis of HR activities. When introducing a new compensation scheme or training program, the proposer will have to be prepared to justify costs with predicted results, expressed in the numbers language of business. We will show you how to do this later in the chapter.

RATIONALE

Determining the quantitative impact of HR programs is so important that the Society for Human Resources Management, the largest HR association in the United States, has designated *HRM impact* as a top research priority and is funding research in this area.

There are six compelling reasons for measuring HRM effectiveness:

1. Labour costs are most often a firm's largest controllable cost.

2. Managers recognize that employees make the difference between the success and failure of projects and organizations.

3. Organizations have legal responsibilities to ensure that they are in compliance with laws governing the employer-employee relationship.

4. Evaluations are needed to determine which HR practices are effective because, at this point, managers and HR professionals cannot distinguish between a fad and a valid change program (Dolan and Belout, 1997).

5. Measuring and benchmarking HR activities will result in continuous improvements.

6. Audits will bring HR closer to the line functions of the organization (Huselid, 1994).

The next section describes the areas in which HRM departments can be evaluated.

◆ ◆ ◆
THE 5C MODEL OF HRM IMPACT

Senior managers, investors, customers, and HR professionals themselves make judgments in many ways about the effectiveness of the HR function. The numerous areas that are judged can be grouped into five clusters—the 5 Cs of evaluating HRM: compliance, client satisfaction, culture management, cost control, and contribution.

COMPLIANCE

Senior management depends on HR expertise to ensure that organizational practices comply with the law. Many HR departments were started because of the need to record compliance with employment standards, such as hours worked and overtime payments. Legislation dealing with the employer-employee relationship is increasing. The areas of safety, health, employment equity, and industrial relations are all highly regulated. Indeed, some people estimate that 20 to 30 percent of the increase in the salaries of HR professionals is due to the need to trust someone with the responsibility for compliance.

Highly publicized cases of safety violations in which board members of industrial organizations have been fined hundreds of thousands of dollars or threatened with jail serve as another wake-up call. Other public cases that have cost organizations not only the expense of fines but also loss in business have occurred because managers have been held responsible for the sexual harassment of their subordinates. HR can make a difference by ensuring that managers and employees comply with the law, thus saving the company legal costs, fines, and damaging publicity.

CLIENT SATISFACTION

As noted above, many organizations are tracking their success by measuring customer satisfaction or soliciting input on client complaints and attitudes. These measures have been found to predict financial performance, on a lagged basis. This means that if employee morale drops, management can expect to see customer satisfaction levels drop in about six months.

Stakeholders are important. Stakeholders are those people who can influence or must interact with the HR department. External clients of HR are candidates for positions, suppliers of HR services such as technology, and government regulators. Internal clients include employees grouped by occupation, union leaders, and managers.

Managers are turning to customer or stakeholder perceptions of the HR department for input about the effectiveness of HR performance. This approach stems from earlier efforts in total quality management and tries to reconcile the gaps between client expectations and levels of satisfaction. The bigger the gap, the less effective the HR department. This qualitative approach surveys stakeholders, such as managers and unions, about their perceptions of the effectiveness of the HR function. "Keeping the customers happy" has important political reverberations for the HRM department, as "clients" such as the CEO control the purse strings and the authority to approve HR policies and programs.

Advantages of Measuring Client Satisfaction

The advantages of measuring client satisfaction with the HR department include the following (Tsui 1987; Dolan and Belout, 1997):

- Measuring customer satisfaction reminds the HR department that it is indeed a "service" that must deal with the expectations of its clients. The clients, in turn, use assessment criteria that are important to them, such as response time and helping them to meet their goals.

- Surveying clients about their unmet needs increases the credibility of the HR function.

- Initiating and managing change by surveying stakeholders before, during, and after a change program increase the possibility that the HR department will understand the clients' perceptions, identify resistance to change and thereby overcome such resistance, and prove that the change program meets its goals.

Methods of Measuring Client Satisfaction

Information can be gathered from clients in several ways.

Informal Feedback Stakeholder perceptions can be obtained informally, as part of the feedback process, whenever the HR professional is undertaking an assignment or completing a routine task such as filling a position. People can simply be asked if they are satisfied with the service.

Informal feedback is of limited use, however, for several reasons. Line managers may be reluctant to give honest feedback face to face; an individual HR officer may not be able to see patterns in the feedback as there is no method for measuring the frequency of problems; and HR professionals have little incentive to report negative feedback to superiors in the organizational hierarchy. For these reasons, a more systematic method must be developed to identify gaps in the performance of the HR department.

Surveys Surveys can be used to solicit feedback confidentially, anonymously, and from a larger number of stakeholders. One approach is to list the HR activities, such as selection, and ask specific questions about them, such as questions about satisfaction with the time it takes to fill a vacant position. Some questions that might be included in such a survey are shown in Box 14.1.

Another survey, developed by Ulrich (1996) in his book *Human Resource Champions*, asks managers to rate the quality of the various roles that HR plays in strategy formulation. Box 14.2 contains a sample of the questions used in this survey.

Managers could be asked to list the chief strengths and principal weakness of the HR department. Line managers could be asked questions about what the HR department has been doing particularly well or particularly poorly, what it should not be doing, how it could contribute more effectively, and so on (Rothwell and Kazanas, 1988).

Critical Incident Method In the critical incident method, clients are asked to describe a situation in which the HR department provided assistance that was particularly useful, the consequences of this help, and why it was seen as

---

BOX 14.1 SAMPLE OF A CLIENT SURVEY

To what degree do you find the HR department cooperative?

How would you rate the quality of service given?

To what degree are HR employees available to deal with problems?

Do you have confidence in HR advice?

How would you rate the effectiveness of HR solutions?

What is your opinion on processing time?

To what extent does HR understand the needs of your department?

Overall, how satisfied are you with the HR department?

---

helpful. Similarly, they are asked to describe a situation in which the assistance was not at all useful, and why. Clients' responses help the HR department identify issues and services that affect unit effectiveness.

Problems with Measuring Client Satisfaction

Measuring client satisfaction is not without its weaknesses.

High Expectations of Clients The goal of surveying clients is to identify gaps between client expectations and client satisfaction. If the clients in one business unit have extremely high expectations, then their dissatisfaction scores will also be high, even though the level of HR service is constant across units. The temptation on the part of the HR department might be to promise or commit to less in terms of programs so as to appear to have performed better.

Conflicting Expectations Another problem occurs when different stakeholders have competing or conflicting expectations. The employee group may desire extensive counselling (a nurturing role) from the HR department, while senior managers may be concerned about maximizing productivity per employee (an efficiency goal). One group will be dissatisfied because it is difficult for the HR department to be both nurturing and efficient.

Professional Affiliations Furthermore, gaps between expectations and performance may occur because HR professionals are more closely tied to the norms and values of their profession than to the norms of managers or line operators (King and Bishop, 1991). For example, line managers may value how fast a job is filled, while the HR professional may value the creation of a valid selection test. In other words, the HR professional may be trying to do what is right in the profession ("validate the selection test"), rather than what managers consider important ("just hire someone fast").

BOX 14.2 HR ROLE ASSESSMENT SURVEY

Please rate your satisfaction with the HR department on the following items* (1=low; 5=high):

HR helps the organization accomplish business goals.

HR participates in the process of defining business strategies.

HR makes sure that HR strategies are aligned with business strategies.

HR effectiveness is measured by its ability to help make strategy happen.

HR is seen as a business partner.

*Selected items that measure the strategic role of HR.

Source: Ulrich, D. 1996. *Human Resource Champions.* Boston: Harvard Business School Press.

Whatever the problems with the client satisfaction approach, the important message is that the viability of the HR function depends to a large extent on stakeholder perceptions of value and effectiveness. These must be measured and managed.

CULTURE MANAGEMENT

Highly effective organizations seek to influence employee attitudes through the development of an appropriate culture that will support optimum performance. (Remember that culture can be defined as the set of important beliefs that members of a community share—"the way we do things around here.") Executives carefully monitor cultural programs (such as that of empowerment) through attitude surveys of employees. The results of these surveys can then be linked to the objective results of the department.

The assumption underlying the culture management model is that HR practices can have a positive influence on employee attitudes, which in turn influences their performance.

Attitudes, in an organizational context, can be defined as perceptions or opinions about organizational characteristics. Some examples include the attitudes expressed in these statements: "I think that management expects too much for the resources it gives me" or "I feel that I can talk to management about any problems I am experiencing." The most frequently measured attitude in the organization is job satisfaction. This multidimensional attitude is composed of attitudes toward supervisors, colleagues, pay, promotions, and the work itself. The interest in job satisfaction stems from a belief that a highly satisfied employee will be more productive (Chaiken and Stangor, 1987). A satisfied employee will more likely come to work, give more effort, and choose more effective job performance strategies if he or she expects to receive intrinsic or extrinsic rewards (Vroom, 1964). The research supports the proposition that attitude affects behaviour. (A number of studies have examined the relationship between employee attitudes and outcomes as diverse as absenteeism, tardiness, work performance, and strikes. See Goodman et al., 1988, and Zimbardo et al., 1990, for reviews of this literature). For example, bank tellers were surveyed about their intrinsic satisfaction, organizational involvement, and intrinsic motivation. Their on-the-job behaviour was measured by counting absences, turnover, and teller balancing shortages. The study demonstrated that more positive attitudes correlated with lower costs (Mirvis and Lawler, 1977).

Organizations should pay attention to employee attitudes and should attempt to manage the culture to improve individual and organizational performance.

COST CONTROL

Traditional organizations continue to see personnel as an expense. The labour component of the production process in service organizations, such as universities and government departments, is an organization's single largest expense. This cost represents up to 85 percent of the expenses in white-collar organizations. HR practices can reduce labour costs by reducing the workforce while attempting to get the same volume of work done with fewer employees.

HR departments can reduce expenses associated with employees in at least two other ways. The first is to increase the efficiencies of those working (i.e., achieve the same results at lower costs or faster speeds), and the second is to reduce the costs associated with behaviours such as absences or accidents that are, to some extent, under the control of the employee.

Increasing Efficiency

Efficiency is expressed in terms of the results achieved (outputs) in comparison to the resource inputs. Measures of efficiency include the following:

- Time (e.g., average time to fill an opening, process a benefits claim)
- Volume (e.g., the number of people interviewed to fill a job, the number of requests processed per employee)
- Cost (e.g., cost per training hour or per test)

HR managers should measure these resource inputs, and then attempt to improve the measurements—examples of which are listed in Box 14.3—over time or across units. The use of benchmarks is critical in comparing one organization's efficiency ratios against the best in the field. Data revealing a cost per hire of $500 or turnover rates of 15 percent are meaningless without relevant comparison points. For example, a turnover rate of 15 percent among senior executives indicates a problem; a turnover rate of 15 percent in a fast-food restaurant is very low.

The ratios generated must be interpreted and analyzed by comparisons made over time, across departments, and against the benchmarks of best practices. These benchmarks allow the HR manager to make the following

BOX 14.3 EXAMPLES OF EFFICIENCY MEASURES

Cost

Ratio of compensation expense to total operating expense

Benefit cost per employee covered

Ratio of benefits expense to total operating expense

Processing costs per benefit claim

Administration costs per benefit claim

Cost per training day

Cost per trainee per program

Volume

Number of training days

Number of interviews per selection

Ratio of filled positions to authorized positions

Percentage of employees with formal performance evaluations

Percentage of designated employees

Response Time

Time between requisition and filling of position

Time to process benefits

Time from identifying a training need to program

Time to respond to requests by category

kinds of statements: "The cost per hire is $500, which is $50 less than last year and $60 less than another company. That shows that we are doing a better job than we did last year and than other HR departments."

These efficiency measures must be managed with effectiveness in mind. Conceptually, it is possible to reduce training costs to zero, but the performance of employees would suffer in the long run. Therefore, most companies add a qualifier to the ratio when judging efficiency. For example, the cost per trainee might be amended to read "cost per trainee where performance improves at the same rate" (Walker and Betchet, 1991).

Cost of Employee Behaviour

The costs of absenteeism, turnover, and occupational injuries and illnesses can all be measured, benchmarked, and managed. Any introductory textbook in HRM will describe how to measure these factors and will provide prescriptions for reducing the costs related to them. To control the expenses associated with employees, organizations should carefully track and compare the rates of absenteeism, turnover, and occupational injuries and illnesses.

Box 14.4 provides an example of how a smoking cessation program for employees can result in cost savings.

In keeping with the trend to view employees as investments, and not just as expenses, the next section examines how organizations measure the return on this investment.

CONTRIBUTION

Unless HR can demonstrate its impact on the bottom line, it will continue to be seen as "overhead," as a department that grabs resources while contributing nothing. Many executives feel that it is time that the HR department identifies and evaluates its contribution, as other departments are expected to do.

The thesis underlying the contribution model is that HRM practices shape the behaviour of employees within an organization, and thus help the organization achieve its goals. In other words, the effective management of people makes a difference to how well an organization functions. Research has shown that HR practices can affect organizational performance in measurable ways. Studies have established that sophisticated and integrated HRM practices have a positive effect on employee performance: they increase knowledge, skills, and abilities, improve motivation, reduce shirking, and increase retention of competent employees. These best practices have a direct and economically significant effect on firm financial performance.

BOX 14.4 THE COSTS OF SMOKING

Decades of research have established that smoking is addictive, and that it is a health hazard. The costs to society of smoking include those associated with health care and income loss. The costs to organizations include those associated with absenteeism, medical care, morbidity and premature mortality, insurance, loss of on-the-job time, property damage and depreciation, maintenance, and passive smoking effects. It is estimated that about 35 minutes a day are lost to smoking, resulting in 18.2 lost days per year per employee. Smokers are absent three more days per year than nonsmokers. Furthermore, each smoker increases by about one-fifth the expenses incurred by nonsmokers (through involuntary smoke inhalation). If an employer were to forbid smoking for a year, the total cost saving per employee per year would, it is estimated, be around $3000 dollars (US).

Source: Adapted from Cascio, W.F. 1991. *Costing Human Resources: The Financial Impact of Behaviour in Organizations,* 3rd ed., Kent Series in Human Resource Management. Boston: PWS Kent.

How HR Contributes to Organizational Performance

Empirical studies have established some important findings:

- Fifteen percent of a firm's relative profit can be attributed to HR strategy (Huselid, 1995).

- HR systems can affect a firm's market valued by $15,000 to $45,000 per employee (Davidson et al., 1996; Huselid and Becker, 1995, 1996).

- HR can affect the probability of survival of a new venture by as much as 22 percent (Welbourne and Andrews, 1996).

- HR can improve the knowledge, skills, and abilities of a firm's current and potential employees, increase their motivation, reduce shirking, and enhance retention of quality employees while encouraging nonperformers to leave the firm (Jones and Wright, 1992).

- An increase in sophisticated HR practices of one standard raises sales per employee by an average of $27,000 (US) for one year, increases profits by $3,814 (US) per employee, and decreases turnover by 7 percent (Huselid, 1995). The advantages to employees of these high-performance firms may be higher wages and benefits and greater job security.

- Investments in HRM do pay off: proactive firms that plan for future labour needs and make investments in recruitment and selection for the job at the outset are rewarded with higher labour productivity. Firms that systematically develop their employees receive a productivity payoff (Koch and Gunter-McGrath, 1996).

We will look now at two ways of measuring contribution: financial measures and measures of managerial perceptions of effectiveness.

Financial Measures

Survival Private or for-profit organizations can measure a dramatic indicator of success: survival. This is a zero sum index. If the company survives, that is, does not go bankrupt or cease business, then the organization is a success. Survival is the first measure of effectiveness, and the contributions of HRM practices should be judged against this life-or-death index. Welbourne and Andrews (1996) tracked the survival rates over five years of new organizations listed on the stock exchange, and found that HR practices were associated with this ultimate measure of a firm's performance. This crude measure is not satisfying for most business people, however, because it doesn't give relative measures of success. (Teachers who give a pass or fail, rather than an A, B, C, or D grade, leave the same sense of dissatisfaction among students.) Most employees desire a relative measure and will even ask, "How am I doing compared to the others?" at performance evaluation interviews. The most common measures of business success provide these points of comparison, which allow judgments to be made across divisions, companies, and even sectors. They are the bottom-line measures such as profits.

Profits or Return on Investments All companies track sales, or revenues, return on investments (ROI), return on equity (ROE), expenses relative to sales, and other financial ratios. These indices measure the relative success of an organization in meeting its goals. Any HRM practice that contributes to these measurements would be endorsed by senior management. Measuring the impact of HRM investments in training or performance appraisal allows HR professionals to use the same language (e.g., basic costs, ROI) as other corporate units and provides a rational way of making decisions. Box 14.5 illustrates how this might work.

There are some limitations to financial analyses. They capture certain immediate aspects of performance, but they do not capture managerial perceptions of effectiveness.

Measures of Managerial Perceptions of Effectiveness

Sometimes financial measures are not available to researchers who are studying privately owned organizations, and sometimes financial measures are not appropriate for publicly owned companies. It is meaningless to talk about government departments in terms of profits, for example. Therefore, other measures have been sought. One method is to ask managers to assess their organization's performance relative to the performance of industry competitors (Delaney and Huselid, 1996). Despite the biases that could be introduced into such a measure, these perceptions have been found to correlate positively with objective measures of firm performance (Dollinger and Golden, 1992; Powell, 1992). The principal advantage of using a perceptual measure, such as this one, is the ability to compare profit-seeking firms with public organizations.

Templer and Cattaneo (1995) argue that organizational effectiveness is not easily defined. Measures beyond survival and those discussed above may include the following: the achievement of one group's political objectives at the expense of a competing interest group and the adaptation of an

BOX 14.5 RETURN ON INVESTMENT EXAMPLE

A chain of quick-service stores found that customers were demanding higher quality services. The stores had problems recruiting and selecting job applicants who were qualified to provide such service. The company decided to use tests to aid the store managers in the selection decision. A test was designed to identify the most qualified applicants, based on their skills and capabilities. The cost to design, implement, and validate the test was $1.135 million (US). After one year, each store that used the test had increased profits by an average of $10,000. If every store used the test, this would mean increased profits of $47 million a year. Thus, the ROI on the $1.135-million investment was 4000 percent.

Costs

Validation of test	$105,000
Implementation	$40,000
Ongoing test administration and scoring (per year)	$990,000
Total costs	$1,135,000

$$\frac{\text{Cost of test (\$1,135,000)}}{\text{Benefit of test (\$47,000)}} = \text{ROI} = 4000\%$$

Source: Neely-Marinez, M. 1997. "Strategies for Successful Business Partners." *HRM Magazine* (January): 1–4.

organization to its environment (which obviously contains an element of the survival measure).

The measure that supersedes all of these may be one of goal optimization (Steers, 1997). Templer and Cattaneo (1995) combined these various perspectives to conclude that "an effective organization is one in which the behaviour of employees contributes towards the attainment of organizational goals and enables the long-term adaptation of the organization to its environment," that is, survival and effectiveness.

Which is the best measure of HRM performance? Managers will choose whichever of the 5C measures meets their needs for information. Some will require measurement of all the 5 Cs; others will focus on one important indicator, such as cost control. A debate about the best approach is presented in Box 14.6.

We have examined five areas in which HR practices and policies should be tracked. Now we turn to an examination of the various approaches to measuring the effectiveness of HR policies, practices, and programs.

◆

BOX 14.6 BALANCE OR FOCUS?

The Balanced Scorecard: Analog Inc.

Analog Inc. manufactures computer chips for cellular phone, military, aviation, and communications applications. Analog executives believe that a corporate scorecard should be balanced. Therefore, they monitor not only financial performance numbers such as those for gross profit, but also softer indices such as employee satisfaction and the time it takes to get a new product to market. The underlying assumption of the Analog executives is that if the key drivers are managed, the bottom-line results will follow. Their argument against focusing on just financial indices is that the numbers only describe history, that is, where a company has been, not where it is going or its potential. So Analog monitors many indices.

The results? Analog's revenues have doubled over five years to $1.2 billion (US), and profits rose from 3 percent of sales to 19 percent, resulting in a quadrupling of the share price. The company's senior managers assert that these results would not have been attained by examining only the financial indices.

The Focused Scorecard: Shell Inc.

Shell Inc., an oil and gas company, employs 21,000 employees and generated $29.2 billion (US) in revenue in 1996. Senior managers at Shell argue that the balanced scorecard confuses the issue and that measurements must be made, but these measurements must be purely financial, such as revenue growth and ROI. Historically, Shell employees saw their company as a technology company and did not excel at managing the corporate wallet. So, with the new business model focusing on one or two financial indicators, they moved the corporate culture from building things to creating value. This focus serves as a financial beacon that supports decision making more rigorously than before.

The results? Shell improved the time to go from discovery of oil and gas to production from four years to one year. Since implementing this focused model, net income jumped 25 percent and revenue 20 percent in one year. Shell executives believe the purely financial approach is responsible for these results.

Source: Kurtzman, J. 1997. "Is Your Company Off Course: Now You Can Find Out Why" *Fortune* (February 17): 128–130.

◆ ◆ ◆

APPROACHES TO MEASURING HRM PRACTICES

This section outlines a number of quantitative and qualitative approaches to measuring the impact of HRM policies and practices. Most of these methods use numbers, which can measure the impact of HRM in the language of business: costs, days lost, complaints, and so on. We will examine the most important of these approaches: cost–benefit analysis, utility analysis, and audits.

COST–BENEFIT ANALYSIS

HRM activities, such as the process of selecting employees, cost money. Most organizations absorb the costs of these activities without conducting analyses to determine benefits. Cost-benefit analysis examines the relationship between the costs of a program and its benefits.

Costs included in these calculations are classified in several ways. *Direct costs* are those that are used to implement the program, such as the cost of selection tests or training materials. *Indirect costs* are those that an organization absorbs, such as the trainee's time away from work. Indirect costs are often unrecognized, and sometimes are not included in cost–benefit analyses. Box 14.7 contains an example of a cost–benefit analysis.

Most programs can be subjected to a cost–benefit analysis if hard data is available, or the value of a program can be estimated from soft measures such as supervisors' estimates of productivity.

UTILITY ANALYSIS

Senior managers are often faced with decisions about the most effective programs. For example, to motivate employees, should HR managers implement a leadership training program or a pay-for-performance program for new supervisors? To hire the best candidate, should HR managers use peer interviews or the new selection test? HR managers would have much to gain if they were able to estimate if program A provided a greater return than program B. The training director, for example, could argue that grouping 100 managers in a classroom for training is more expensive and less effective than teaching them via an interactive software program.

A tool that calculates, in dollar terms, the costs and probable outcomes of decisions would assist HR managers in making choices between programs. Utility analysis is such a tool. It is a method of determining the gain or loss to the organization that results from different courses of action. Faced with a decision, managers could use utility analysis to help them choose the strategy that produces the outcomes the organization is seeking (Brealey and Myers, 1988). This method measures the utilities (gains and losses) by using behavioural or cost accounting procedures. It seeks to quantify, in dollar terms, the value of improvements in HR activities, particularly selection. In

◆

BOX 14.7 MEASURING THE CONTRIBUTION OF HRM PRACTICES

A wholesale produce company hired, and then fired, seven ineffective sales representatives over a two-year period. The company calculated the costs of these actions.

Costs

Training	$493,738
Recruiting	30,100
Management time to train and terminate	25,830
Lower profits and higher waste due to poor performance	1,612,000
Total costs	$2,161,668

The HR department interviewed line managers to develop a profile of the ideal sales representative and identified twelve critical success factors. Then the company's HR department developed a solution involving three types of training:

■ Behaviour-based interview training for managers

■ A PC-based training program for newly hired sales representatives to accelerate performance readiness or weed out those who didn't meet the standards

■ Performance counselling training for managers so that they could learn to discuss performance problems and ensure that trainees accepted responsibility for their own learning and performance

The costs to implement these three programs were $15,400 (development and attendance costs).

The savings that resulted from this solution were then calculated.

Savings

Cost of the problem	$2,161,668
Cost of the solution	− 15,400
Total savings	$2,146,268

The cost–benefit ratio is as follows:

$$\frac{\$2,146,268}{\$15,400} = 139:1$$

Source: Adapted from Burrows, D.M. 1996. "Increase HR's Contributions to Profits." *HR Magazine* (September): 103–110.

utility analysis, which is an extension of cost–benefit analysis, the costs and benefits of alternative solutions to a problem are calculated and compared. The decision maker then can use the quantitative data that results from utility analysis to choose the alternative with the highest net value. Box 14.8 provides an example of how utility analysis can be used to reach a decision.

Utility analyses have been used in various studies. Selection using assessment centres instead of first-level management assessment was found to have a utility, over four years, of about $12,000 (US) in improved job performance per manager (Cascio and Ramos, 1986). However, the computations involved are beyond the competencies of most managers. If you are interested in knowing more about this topic, see Cascio (1991) for a detailed treatment of decision making using utility analysis.

AUDITS

Audits should be conducted periodically to ensure that HRM objectives are being met. An audit can help identify gaps between actual and expected or desired results. Audits may be conducted on functions or policies. For example, the training function can be examined in terms of the percentage of pay-

---

BOX 14.8 AN EXAMPLE OF UTILITY ANALYSIS

Utility analysis is statistically complex but can be illustrated by the following simple example.

An organization has a choice between two types of selection procedures (or can use neither). The utility of a selection procedure is the degree to which it results in a better quality of candidate than would have been selected if the selection procedure not been implemented. Quality can be measured in terms of tenure (Did the employee selected using the selection procedure remain with the organization at least one year?) or performance (Did the new employee rate above average in performance after one year?) or other objective outcomes (Did the employee sell more accounts or process more files?). The costs of using procedure one (an ability test), procedure two (peer interviews), or the usual selection method (or base rate) of managerial interviews are calculated. Then, the benefits of the candidates chosen under each of the three methods are determined. If tests resulted in higher performing candidates but cost more that the performance increase is worth, then the tests have little utility. If peer reviews result in greater performance at no greater cost, then peer reviews have great utility.

Source: Blum, M.L., and J.C. Naylor. 1968. *Industrial Psychology: Its Theoretical and Social Foundations*, rev. ed. New York: Harper-Row.

◆

roll spent on training, training dollars spent per employee, profits per employee, training costs per hour, and so on. The results of these examinations can be compared to comparable figures for other organizations. For example, in Canada, organizations spend about $800 per employee on training, and each employee receives about seven hours of training a year (Belcourt and Wright, 1996). These benchmark statistics can be used as guidelines. If statistics are available on the best-performing companies, then organizations can attempt to match those figures. For example, if the best companies train fifteen days a year, then this would be the figure to try to match.

Audits can also be performed on policies. In an audit, managers may simply be asked if they understand and apply company policies.

Managers may be asked to complete surveys about their understanding of what constitutes sexual harassment. For example, a manager may be asked to respond "yes," "no," or "uncertain" to the following question:

Do these behaviours constitute sexual harassment?
1. *A manager calls female subordinates "sweetie" and "honey."*
2. *A male employee uses vulgar language, but it is not overheard by female employees.*

Behaviour Costing Approach

Another auditing approach is the measurement of employee attitudes on the assumption that attitudes, such as those about job satisfaction, ultimately determine performance. This approach is called the behaviour costing approach. Behaviour costing is based on the premise that attitudes are indicators or predictors of subsequent employee behaviours (Mervis and Lawler, 1977). These behaviours have financial impacts on organizations. Building on Vroom's (1964) expectancy model of behaviour, the behaviour costing approach states that attitudes such as satisfaction will affect performance outcomes. Using surveys developed by experts, organizations such as the Canadian Imperial Bank of Commerce (CIBC) measure employee attitudes semiannually, tracking satisfaction scores. These organizations use the results of such surveys to discuss areas of dissatisfaction with employee groups and to identify solutions that will improve these areas. These organizations are committed to this process because they believe that attitudes are tightly linked with customer satisfaction and, ultimately, with profits.

Audits can be conducted by internal personnel or external consultants. Internal auditors have the advantage of knowing more about the organization and being trusted by the staff supplying the information. However, external auditors may be more objective, have greater numbers of outside references or benchmarks, and are more likely to convey bad news to management. Despite these advantages, 97 percent of companies use internal auditors (Segal and Quinn, 1989)

Obviously, the results obtained from audits can be compared with benchmarks obtained from previous years, with other organizational units, or even with other companies.

MEASURING THE WORTH OF EMPLOYEES

Many company presidents say, "Employees are our greatest assets," or, as the president of Dofasco said, "Our product is steel; our strength is people." What do they mean? There have been attempts to measure the worth of employees by counting them and then attempting to put a number value on their knowledge. These methods are discussed in the appendix to this chapter. Our focus is not on measuring the worth of employees, however, but on measuring the effect of organizational practices and policies.

Readers interested in a fuller description of measuring HR effectiveness should consult *Research, Measurement and Evaluation of Human Resources* (Saks, 1999).

The measurement of HR effectiveness is not easy. The next section outlines some of the difficulties faced by those attempting to track HR effectiveness.

◆ ◆ ◆
CHALLENGES IN MEASURING THE IMPACT OF HRM

Measuring the effectiveness of HRM practices has been widely viewed as a progressive step in the development of HRM as a profession and the positioning of HR as a strategic partner at the boardroom table. But, in fact, most organizations do not undertake this evaluation because the measurement of HRM activities is not easy and the problems in measurement are difficult to resolve. Let us look at some of the problems that arise when we attempt to measure the impact of HRM practices.

APPLICABILITY OF BEST PRACTICES

No single best practice works in every situation. Some companies, such as banks, consist of many different companies, including insurance companies, discount brokerages, and venture capital firms, all with unique characteristics. Therefore, the HRM policies and practices that affect performance in the bank may hinder performance in the venture capital arm. The environment and culture of the parts of the larger company are very different. For example, the routine transaction work of the bank lends itself to compensation systems based largely on base salaries, while the entrepreneurial, risk-taking nature of the venture capital firm cries out for incentive-based pay.

Furthermore, organizations and business units may have different strategic goals. The goal of the financial sector is to maximize ROE, while the goal of the Department of Immigration is to survive in the political arena and perhaps optimize the number of immigrants. Within a single organization, the goals of one business unit may be to maximize market share (at the expense of profit), while another unit is attempting to maximize profit. These differences lead to the conclusion that the impact of HRM must be measured against unit goals, not against some generality such as growth or profits.

SEPARATION OF CAUSE AND EFFECT

The perennial problem in measuring the impact of HRM practices is separating causes and effects. For example, does a profitable company share its profits with employees through bonuses; or does the possibility of earning a bonus make employees more productive and their companies more profitable?

Associated with the lack of confidence in the explanation of causal links between specific HRM practices and organizational performance is the observation that the culture of an organization may explain more than a specific HRM practice. The day-to-day norms of an organization may influence employee behaviour more than any specific practice. For example, if an organization is deeply committed to valuing employees, then the day-to-day actions of all managers have more powerful effects than a stand-alone program such as 360-degree feedback.

ATTITUDES ABOUT MEASURING THE IMPACT OF HRM

HR professionals may ask, What's in it for me? Measuring the impact of HRM is time-consuming, difficult, and costs money, and, once done, the HR professionals may be blamed if the results aren't good.

However, researchers, and even managers, are arguing that these challenges should not be used as an excuse never to measure the effectiveness of HR practices. Without an objective estimation of the value of the HR role, the HR professional risks being marginalized at the strategy table.

◆ ◆ ◆

SUMMARY

This chapter attempts to close the loop in the strategic HR planning process. When managers implement a plan, they need to know if the plan was successful. This chapter outlined the rationale for measuring the impact of HRM, including such reasons as the need to prove the value of HR and to improve HR performance. We looked at the 5C model for measuring HR effectiveness in five areas: compliance with laws and regulations, client satisfaction, culture management, cost control, and contribution. Having decided what to measure, we turned to an explanation of how to measure the impact of HRM. Methods included cost–benefit analysis, utility analysis, and audits. The challenges of measuring HR effectiveness were discussed.

E X E R C I S E S

1. The president of your company has said, "I see no value in having an HR department. Let's get rid of it. We can outsource payroll and benefits. Anything else, like training, can be arranged by each manager." You, as the vice-president of HR, want to save the department (and your job!).

    Prepare a report, describing areas in which the HR department does (or can) make a difference to the company.

2. We all know that being able to prove that a program is effective is a good way to ensure continued funding. List the ways that you might prove that a training program for supervisors is good for the organization. List some reasons why most HR managers would not want to measure the effectiveness of this training program.

3. A company wishes to increase the sales performance of its staff. It has been

determined that for each $15 product sold, the company makes $5 in profit.

Currently, employees, who are paid $20 an hour, sell an average of four products an hour. A consultant is persuading the company to purchase a four-hour training course. The consultant guarantees that sales capacity will increase by 25 percent and that the effect will last one year (50 weeks of selling time, assuming an eight-hour day). The cost of the course is $400 per employee.

Should the company buy the training course for its ten sales representatives? Conduct a cost–benefit analysis to determine the answer.

References

Belcourt, M., and P. Wright. 1996. *Performance Management through Training and Development*. Toronto: ITP Nelson.

Boudreau, J.W. 1991. "Utility Analysis in Human Resource Management Decisions." In M.D. Dunnete and L.M. Hough, eds., *Handbook of Industrial and Organizational Psychology*, 2nd ed., Vol. 2. Palo Alto, Ca.: Consulting Psychologists Press.

Brealey R., and S. Meyers. 1991. *Principles of Corporate Finance*, 3rd ed. New York: McGraw-Hill.

Cascio, W.F. 1991. *Costing Human Resources: The Financial Impact of Behaviour in Organizations*, 3rd ed., Kent Series in Human Resource Management. Boston: PWS Kent.

Cascio, W.F., and Ramos, R.A. 1986. "Development and Application of a New Method for Assessing Job Performance in Behavioural/Economic Terms." *Journal of Applied Psychology* 71: 20–28.

Cashman, E.M., and J.C McElroy. 1991. "Evaluating the HR Function." *HR Magazine* (January): 70–73.

Chaiken, S., and C. Stangor. 1987. "Attitudes and Attitude Change." *Annual Review of Psychology* 38: 575–630.

Davidson, W.N. III, D.L. Worrell, and J.B. Fox. 1996. "Early Retirement Programs and Firm Performances." *Academy of Management Journal* 39, no. 4 (August): 970–984.

Delaney, J.T., and M.A. Huselid. 1996. "The Impact of Human Resource Management Practices on the Perceptions of Organizational Performance." *Academy of Management Journal* 39, no. 4: 949–969.

Dolan, S.L., and A. Belout. 1997. "Assessing Human Resource Effectiveness: The Emergence of the Stakeholder Approach." *HRM Research Quarterly* 1, no. 1 (Spring).

Dollinger, M.J., and Golden, P.A. 1992. "Interorganizational and Collective Strategies in Small Firms: Environmental Effects and Performance." *Journal of Management* 18: 695–715.

Goodman, P.S., and E.D. Darr. 1996. "Exchanging Best Practices through Computer Aided Systems." *Academy of Management Executive* 10, no. 2 (May): 7–19.

Goodman, P.S., R. Devadas, and T.L. Griffith-Hughson. 1988. "Groups and Productivity: Analyzing the Effectiveness of Self-Managing Teams." In J.P. Campbell and R.J. Campbell, eds., *Productivity in Organizations*. San Franscisco: Jossey-Bass.

Huselid, M.A. 1995. "The Impact of Human Resource Management Practices on Turnover, Productivity, and Corporate Financial Performance." *Academy of Management Journal* 38: 635–672.

____. 1994. "Documenting HR's Effect on Company Performance." *HR Magazine* 39, no. 1: 79–85.

Huselid, M.A., and B.E. Becker. 1996. "Methodological Issues in Cross-Sectional and Panel Estimates of the HR–Firm Performance Link." *Industrial Relations* 20: 245–259.

____. 1995. "High Performance Work Systems and Organizational Performance." Academy of Management meeting, Vancouver.

Jones, G.R., and P.M. Wright. 1992. "An Economic Approach to Conceptualizing the Utility of Human Resource Management Practices." In K. Rowland and G. Ferris, eds., *Research in Personnel and Human Resources Management*, Vol. 10. Greenwich, Conn.: JAI Press.

King, A.S., and T.R. Bishop. 1991. "Functional Requisites of Human Resources: Personnel Professionals' and Line Managers' Criteria for Effectiveness." *Public Personnel Management* 20, no. 3 (Fall): 285–298.

Koch, M.J., and R. Gunther-McGrath. 1996. "Improving Labour Productivity: Human Resource Management Policies Do Matter." *Strategic Management Journal* 17, no. 5 (May): 335–354.

Mirvis, P.H., and Lawler, E.E. II. 1977. "Measuring the Financial Impact of Employee Attitudes." *Journal of Applied Psychology* 62, no. 6: 1–8.

Powell, T.C. 1992. "Organizational Alignment as Competitive Advantage." *Strategic Management Journal* 13: 119–134.

Rothwell, W.J., and H.C. Kazanas. 1988. *Strategic Human Resources Planning and Management*. Englewood Cliffs, N.J.: Prentice-Hall.

Saks, A.M. 1999. *Research, Measurement and Evaluation of Human Resources.* Toronto: ITP Nelson.

Segal, J.A., and M.A Quinn. 1989. "How to Audit Your HR Programs." *Personnel Administrator* 34, no. 5: 67–70.

Steers, R.M. 1997. *Organizational Effectiveness: A Behavioural View.* Glenview Ill.: Scott, Foresman.

Stewart, J. 1996. "Blow Up the HR Department." *Fortune* (January 15).

Templer, A., and R.J. Cattaneo. 1995. "A Model of Human Resource Management Effectiveness." *Canadian Journal of Administrative Studies* 12, no. 1: 77–88.

Tsui, A.S. 1987. "Defining the Activities and Effectiveness of the Human Resource Department: A Multiple Constituent Approach." *Human Resource Management* (Spring): 35–70.

Ulrich, D. 1996. *Human Resource Champions.* Boston: Harvard Business School Press.

Vroom, V.H. 1964. *Work and Motivation.* New York: Wiley.

Walker, J.W., and T.P. Bechet. 1991. "Defining Effectiveness and Efficiency Measures in the Context of Human Resource Strategy." In R.J. Niehaus and K.F. Price, eds., *Bottom Line Results from Strategic Planning.* New York: Plenum Press.

Welbourne, T.M., and A.O. Andrews. 1996. "Predicting the Performance of Initial Public Offerings: Should Human Resource Management Be an Equation?" *Academy of Management Journal* 39, no. 4 (August): 891–919.

Zimbardo, P.G., E.B. Ebbesen, and C. Maslach. 1990. *Influencing Attitudes and Changing Behaviour,* 3rd ed. New York: McGraw-Hill.

Appendix

HR ACCOUNTING METHODS
THE HUMAN ASSET ACCOUNTING APPROACH

The *human asset accounting approach* attempts to use accounting principles, such as those used to calculate the historical costs or replacement costs of assets, to put a value on the worth of an organization's human assets. The models used in this approach measure the investment made in employees, treating them as capitalized resources, in economic terms.

- *Historical costs model:* The historical costs model of accounting measures the investment in employees (Cascio, 1991). The investment consists of the costs of acquisition, training, orientation, informal coaching, and experience and development. These costs are amortized over the expected working lives of individuals. Those expenses incurred with employees who left the company (the un-amortized costs) are written off. This approach has the advantages of being relatively objective and consistent with the accounting treatment of other assets, thus allowing comparisons. Critics of this approach complain that this method is seriously flawed because the assets are not saleable, and, therefore, there is no independent check of valuation. Estimating costs of informal training and experience is too subjective a process. Allowances have to be made for the changing value of the dollar. The main problem is that the process measures only costs and cannot distinguish between two employees: both may have cost the organization the same dollar amount in acquisition and training, but one may be an outstanding performer and the other a minimally effective worker.

- *Replacement costs model:* This model measures the cost of replacing an employee as an estimate of market value. The cost includes recruitment, selection, compensation, training, and orientation (Flamholtz et al., 1988). This model is unsatisfactory for several reasons. Although substituting replacement cost for historical cost provides an updated valuation, the actual opportunities to do these calculations are limited. Most organizations have limited turnover, particularly at senior levels, and so building a complex human asset formula into the accounting system would not be worthwhile. Furthermore, a badly managed HR department that incurred abnormal expenses in recruiting or selection might overestimate the cost of replacing an employee (Steffy and Maurer, 1988). A highly sophisticated system of staffing, orientation, and training would also generate high replacement costs, but the measure of the value added by exceptional employees would not be part of the accounting process.

■ *Present value of future earnings model:* This model measures contributions, not costs. The organization tries to determine what an employee's future contribution is worth today by calculating future earnings, adjusted for the probability of an employee's death (Lev and Schwartz, 1971). Contribution is calculated by the compensation paid to an employee. Probability of death is estimated using mortality tables. The problem with this model is that it assigns a value to the average worker, rather than to an individual. No investment in individual employees, for example, in training, is taken into account, and yet this training investment should have a payoff in future contributions.

These three models of human asset accounting value employee service at gross book value (the original investment expenses), net book value (the original investment minus depreciation), and economic value (the anticipated financial return on the investment) (Cascio, 1991). These models, however, have not been accepted either by HR professionals or by researchers for many reasons.

Limitations of Human Asset Accounting Models

As can be seen, the main problem with human asset accounting models is their failure to take into account employee effectiveness. They tend to measure only inputs, such as costs incurred in acquiring and training employees, and not outputs, such as employee productivity. Secondly, who is the best judge of employee worth—the employee, the manager, or the HR department? Another major problem is the cost and difficulty of obtaining this data. The most recent trend is to measure the intellectual capital—the brainpower—of employees in the hope of measuring actual and potential contributions.

INTELLECTUAL CAPITAL APPROACH

The productivity of most organizations entering the 21st century is highly dependent on the intellectual capabilities of their employees. The software, communications, educational, and medical sectors, which provide 79 percent of all jobs, owe their success to the knowledge of their employees (Quinn et al., 1996). McKinsey and Co. estimate that by the year 2000, 85 percent of all jobs in North America will be knowledge based. What is intellect and how is it measured?

Intellectual capital can be thought of as intellectual material (knowledge) that can be formalized, captured, and leveraged to produce a higher valued asset (Stewart, 1994). Intellectual capital can be seen as employee brainpower, some of which is described in skills inventories and patent lists.

Quinn and his colleagues (1996) described and ranked the importance of this intellectual capital:

1. Cognitive knowledge (know what)
2. Advanced skills (know how)
3. System understanding and trained intuition (know why)
4. Self-motivated creativity (care why)

Employers pay premiums for smart workers. In the United States, men with postgraduate degrees earn incomes 130 percent higher than men who never finished high school (Quinn et al., 1996). The pay gap between men with these different levels of education has doubled since 1980. Companies like Scandia and Dow Chemical are struggling to identify, describe, and measure these intellectual assets in order to manage them. The chief financial officer for Northern Telecom states, "As a technology company, much of our ability to differentiate ourselves from our competitors depends on being able to market new product solutions more quickly than anyone else. For this, we rely on our intellectual capital" (Edwards, 1997).

Intellectual assets have characteristics highly distinct from other assets. First, intellectual assets grow with use. Anyone who has gone back to school or completed a training course realizes that the learning of new knowledge, and its application, leads to even greater knowledge and a motivation to acquire more. Intellectual capital can be shared, and cannot be depleted. Sharing it results in increased feedback, acquisition of new knowledge, and modifications and adjustments to current knowledge. Some organizations, such as Arthur Andersen Worldwide, link via e-mail 82,000 employees in 360 offices in 76 countries, allowing the posting of problems on bulletin boards. They feel this taps dormant capabilities of employees and expands energy and solutions to problems.

Issues in Measuring Intellectual Capital

Experts in this nascent field estimate that the intellectual assets of an organization are worth three to four times the tangible book value. A common approach is to claim that the intellectual capital of a firm is equal to the difference between a firm's capitalized stock value and its book value. It is still very difficult to put a dollar value on the brain resources of employees. The Canadian Imperial Bank of Commerce (CIBC) tries to do so by counting employee skills (e.g., the ability to manage a portfolio of clients), which can be used to build a competency inventory. But as skills change, the dynamics of measuring them become difficult. Furthermore, most of this asset is left idle: observers and employees alike guess that only 20 percent of the knowledge available in their companies is used (Edwards, 1997).

Educational and medical institutions have measured intellectual capital for decades, relying on peer reviews (and publication records) for decisions about the worth of the faculty or professionals. Thus, first measures of intellectual capital include peer review, although in some cases, it may be done by colleagues working together on projects. Some organizations add another review level, that of customer or client evaluations of outputs (Quinn et al., 1996). Customers are asked to rank team participants on professional knowledge and specific project contributions, and on overall satisfaction with results. To supplement these human evaluations, some organizations add measures of efficiency and effectiveness, which normally are measured in business terms (e.g., costs, fulfillment time and accuracy, delivery times). Finally, some organizations track the intellectual assets created. CIBC charts the growth of intellectual capital by tracking the flow of knowledge among employees. The company counts, as indicators of intellectual capital, the number of new ideas generated, the number of new products created, and the percentage of income from new revenue streams.

The competitive advantage of intellectual capital is enormous. This asset cannot be traded or expropriated. Competitors fall farther behind because the top talent goes to organizations such as Microsoft to be part of a leading edge organization.

Many researchers have tried and failed to come up with a single, limited criterion to measure the worth of an organization's human resources. After reviewing the literature, Scarpello and Theeke (1989) concluded that the search should be abandoned, despite its attraction for managers making internal management and external investment decisions.

References

Cascio, W.F. 1991. *Costing Human Resources: The Financial Impact of Behaviour in Organizations*, 3rd ed. Kent Series in Human Resource Management. Boston: PWS Kent.

Edwards, S. 1997. "The Brain Gain." *CA Magazine* (April): 21–25,

Flamholtz, F.L.K., D.G. Searfoss, and R. Cof. 1988. "Developing Human Resource Accounting as a Decision Support System." *Accounting Horizon* 2: 1–9.

Lev, B., and A. Schwartz. 1971. "On the Use of the Economic Concept of Human Capital in Financial Statements." *Accounting Review* 46: 103–112.

Quinn, J.B., P. Anderson, and S. Finkelstein. 1996. "Leveraging Intellect."

Academy of Management Executive 10, no. 3.

Scarpello, V., and H.A. Theeke. 1989. "Human Resource Accounting: A Measured Critique." *Journal of Accounting Literature* 8: 265–280.

Steffy, B.D., and S.D. Maurer. 1988. "Conceptualizing and Measuring the Economic Effectiveness of Human Resource Activities." *Academy of Management Review* 13: 265–280.

Stewart, T.A. 1994. "Intellectual Capital." *Fortune* (October 3): 68–74.

15

Trends

CHAPTER GOALS

T he job is the constant factor in every chapter in this text. Therefore, it seems fitting that the final chapter highlights emerging issues about the job. We look at the disappearance of the good job and at the arrangements used to get the work done. Paradoxically, some good jobs still exist, and employers are scrambling to create strategies to retain employees in these high-value jobs. We then look at what you, as a free agent managing a career, might do to remain employable.

After reading this chapter, you will be able to do the following:

1. Discuss the changing nature of the job.
2. Identify the advantages and disadvantages of alternative work arrangements, including part-time work, flextime, telecommuting, contract work, and employee leasing.
3. List the benefits of outsourcing the functions of the HR department, and develop a set of guidelines for managing the outsourced functions.
4. Discuss the strategies that some companies are using to retain high tech and highly valued workers.
5. List the reasons why the traditional career management system is dying, and compare it to the emerging career management model.
6. Discuss the roles of the individual, the organization, and the professional association in career management.

We start with a look at the changing nature of the job.

◆ ◆ ◆
WHERE ARE THE GOOD JOBS?

Are jobs disappearing? Books with titles like *The Jobless Future* and *The End of Work* proclaim that the job is dead. The mantra of globalization and restructuring produces panic, the feeling that there are no jobs left. There are estimates that as many as 850 million workers worldwide are looking for work (Snyder, 1996). Are we facing a jobless future? Will technology do to the office employee what technology did to the farm labourer and the factory worker?

Will the job be replaced by guaranteed incomes, reduced hours, or irregular work periods? Will income tax be designed to distribute the wealth of those who are employed to those who are not so lucky? Will vouchers for school and community service be distributed to discourage people from looking for work?

The paradox in these glimpses of the future is that the data don't support the principal assumption, that is, that there are fewer jobs. Certainly in the United States, employment has been growing robustly for about two decades. The problem is not with the quantity of jobs, but with the quality of jobs. There seem to be fewer and fewer good jobs.

A good job can be described as one that provides a reasonably comfortable lifestyle. A comfortable lifestyle does not mean a Mercedes and a luxury condo and an annual vacation to an exotic locale; it means enough income to provide for survival above the poverty line. These jobs are hard to find.

Average wages have fallen in the United States, resulting in full-time employees earning less than the poverty wage. What does this mean to a comfortable lifestyle? More young people are living at home longer and are returning home after leaving home. In 1980, just 8 percent of people aged 25 to 34 lived at home; now 25 percent do. More households need two incomes to survive. In 75 percent of marriages, both parties work, compared to 33 percent just 30 years ago (Snyder, 1996).

To make ends meet, many people in the Canadian workforce turn to moonlighting, stringing together a series of part-time jobs and job contracts to earn a living. The number of moonlighters has tripled in the last twenty years, with 5 percent of Canadians holding more than one job (Mitchell, 1997).

One solution, proposed by John Kettle, a futurist, is to share work or reduce the number of working hours per person. If everyone worked shorter hours, employers would have to hire more people. Based on his calculations, he estimates that if the work week was reduced to 30 hours, unemployment in Canada would drop to 3 percent. Work would be guaranteed to virtually everyone who wanted to work. However, 94 percent of those employed do not want to work fewer hours for less pay (Gibb-Clark, 1997).

There is an increasing concern that jobs, and jobholders, are in the process of polarization. The lucky few will work in good jobs, with employment security, benefits, and good pay. The unlucky masses will work in various types of contingent employment, which is the focus of the next trend we discuss.

◆ ◆ ◆
ALTERNATIVE WORK ARRANGEMENTS

For the last 200 years, people have adjusted to a rhythm of work scheduled around a nine-to-five day and 50-week year. It is important to note that prior to the Industrial Revolution, people followed the rhythms of the seasons, not those of machines. Usually working for themselves or small firms, people worked on demand. During harvest seasons, the work day might extend to eighteen hours, while in the winter, there might be no work hours. Holidays were likely taken in periods when demands were less, and would consist of a few days off. Benefits were nonexistent. We may, in fact, be returning to "the good old days." Self-employed individuals will work extended hours as needed, work reduced hours when necessary or desired, and schedule breaks periodically. The job will flow from the work, not the work from the job.

A traditional job is considered to be one in which employees work about eight hours a day, five days a week, 50 weeks a year. Variations on this pattern occur with flextime, part-time, and contract work. Contingent workers are those who have a loose association with the organization. Included are temporary workers, at-home employees, and subcontracted employees, as well as part-timers. Estimates of the number of contingent workers range from 2 percent to 16 percent of the workforce, and others claim that a third of the labour force has a nontraditional relationship with employers (Larson, 1996). Part-timers form the largest part of the contingent labour force (Larson and Ong, 1994).

PART-TIME WORKERS

Part-time work is work of fewer than 35 hours per week (Levenson, 1996). (A temporary job provides work for only short periods and may be either full-time or part-time.) The number of people working part-time is difficult to estimate because many people hold two or more part-time jobs, which results in overestimates. Many of these workers are involuntary part-time workers, and, when offered a full-time job, will quickly accept it. We estimate that about 18 percent of the workforce works part-time (Lipovenko, 1997). However, we do know that about 50 percent of Canadian companies employ part-timers, who represent about 30 percent of their workforce.

FLEXTIME

The majority of employers now offer flextime. Flextime divides the work day into core hours (usually 10 a.m. to 3 p.m.), during which employees are required to work, and elective flexible hours. Some employees will work from 7 a.m. to 3 p.m., others from 10 a.m. to 6 p.m.

Do flexible hours—adjusting the hours to fit the personal needs of employees—have any benefits for organizations? According to one study, the answer is yes. First Tennessee National Corp. has conducted studies and generated data that established that flexibility has the following results: employees stay with the company twice as long as is the average at banks, saving $3 million (US) in turnover costs; these longer-term employees create 7 percent more customer retention; and profit gains are 55 percent more since flextime was implemented (Flynn, 1997). A study done by the Royal Bank of Canada after it had introduced a flextime work arrangement for its employees reported an increase in employee productivity, reduced stress, and an increase in job satisfaction (Yukich, 1997).

TELECOMMUTING

Employees no longer have to be at work to do their work. Telecommuting is the label given to work done by those who do at least part of their work off-site, usually in the home. Telecommuting has been described as moving the work to the worker (Grensing-Pophal, 1997). It has been estimated that for 60 percent of the workforce, location isn't critical to doing their job. Telecommuting employees work from home or in satellite offices, and do most of their work with technology: faxes, e-mail, voice mail, and so on. Distance staffing, which has been fuelled by technology, refers to an employment relationship in which an employee is not physically present in an office, on a regular basis, to do the work assigned.

While the telecommuting option has been available to employees (such as computer programmers or customer service representatives) working on independent projects, for a long time, the newest trend is to hire people who will never or rarely ever work at the company's headquarters. For example,

Northern Telecom was looking for a vice-president for global enterprise services, and the most qualified candidate refused to leave Philadelphia to move to Nashville. So, Northern Telecom moved the job to him. Working from home, he manages a staff of approximately 2,000 people. Recruiting is facilitated by the elimination of geographic restrictions.

The costs of relocation are saved, as well as the costs of providing and maintaining an office, usually in an expensive urban location. No transportation expenses are incurred, and thus, pollution is reduced. In Canada, it is estimated that the new century will show that nearly 1 million teleworkers are employed but are working from a remote office wired to the main office.

Trust and control are seen as two obstacles to the employment of more telecommuters. If managers cannot see workers working, how do they know they are working? The obvious answer is that results are controlled, not hours of work. Most employers have overcome these obstacles, and about 40 percent offer telecommuting as an employment option (Williams, 1996).

The main benefits of telecommuting are increased productivity due to reduced interruptions, distractions, and commuting time. Money is saved on gas and business clothing, and even by claiming taxable expenses such as heat and electricity for a home office.

About one-third of Canada's labour force works in these various contingent employment relationships. Most of them work this way because that is what the employer wants. The employer designs programs so that employment levels fluctuate according to work demands. But there is another type of worker with whom the employer has a different relationship. The focus here is not on keeping the worker at a distance, but on bringing the candidates in and keeping them happy.

CONTRACT WORKERS

The trend towards contract work has been accelerating. Employers do not want the high costs associated with benefits and outplacement of permanent employees. Furthermore, they want the flexibility of hiring exactly the kind of worker required, when needed, rather than undertaking the costs of training permanent employees for ever-changing jobs. Thus, employers will offer contracts of limited duration to employees who are needed to do specialized tasks. Employers responding to a survey indicated that the major reasons for hiring contract employees were to provide labour flexibility to meet demand fluctuations, to acquire specific expertise, to control head counts, and to fill in for absent employees and buffer core workers against job losses (Sunoo, 1996).

To employees, the benefits of contract work are mainly convenience and training. For those working part-time voluntarily, this arrangement allows them to manage their studies, child care responsibilities, or other vocational interests. Some contract workers see this arrangement as a way to increase their skills rapidly, rather than sit at the same desk doing the same thing all year long. One survey of several thousand temporary employees indicated that two-thirds learned new skills (Lynn, 1995). One-third said they liked the diversity and challenge of working on different assignments (Larson, 1996).

While contract workers generally receive lower pay, the principal disadvantage of this work arrangement is the lack of benefits. In Canada, Saskatchewan is the only province that requires employers to extend benefits to regular part-time workers. Some employers offer benefits as a way to increase the loyalty of part-time workers. But others are highly resistant to offering benefits because the money saved by not providing benefits is one of the key reasons to hire contingent employees. According to one survey, 95 percent of employers said that if they were required to provide benefits, they would take extreme countervailing measures. They said they would get rid of all part-time workers or get rid of benefits for all workers (Church, 1996).

White-collar contingent employees tend to make more money and may have more negotiating leverage. The demand for professional contingent employees gives them some power in negotiating their contracts, including benefits. Employers are being forced to provide benefits to attract and retain the best of the contingent workforce. Furthermore, when the temp agencies reach a critical mass of "permanent" part-time employees, they may start to consider a benefits package to attract potential candidates for their labour pool. But at this point, only about 8 percent of temporary employees receive health care coverage in the United States (Lynn, 1995), and in Canada, the figure is 6 percent (Church, 1996). Sometimes the court rules on these matters. For example, a court ruled that hundreds of temporary workers who were on contract to Microsoft were treated as regular employees, and, as such, were eligible for retirement benefits. (The employees were supervised on a daily basis, told when to come to work, and so on.) The courts also ruled that Microsoft could only avoid this problem by hiring people who were employees of an outside contracting firm (King, 1996).

EMPLOYEE LEASING

In response to such events, there is a trend toward professional employer organizations (PEOs). These organizations, of which 2,500 exist in the United States, manage all the day-to-day employment and administrative arrangements of the people working in other firms (Laabs, 1998). The number of leased employees is estimated to be about 2.5 million in 1996, up from 10,000 in 1984 (Laabs, 1998). PEOs lease employees and manage payroll, unemployment insurance, and workers' compensation, and will provide job descriptions, employee manuals, employee assistance programs, complaints resolutions, and so on. Clients can decide which service or administrative function they wish to buy. Small companies save money because the leasing organization can achieve economies of scale with benefits, recruiting, and other services.

However, there is increasing concern among employers about contract workers. Employers are reanalyzing the costs of contract workers, realizing that purchasing these skills results in costly mark-up rates. A second force slowing the use of contract workers is the realization that people who are not committed to the organization may not provide the kind of service or innovations that create sustainability in the long term.

Even the HR department is not immune to a rearrangement of its traditional jobs.

◆ ◆ ◆
OUTSOURCING HR FUNCTIONS

Outsourcing refers to a long-term contractual relationship for the provision of business services by an external provider. In other words, a company pays another company to do some work for it. Currently, outsourcing is being promoted as one of the most powerful trends reshaping management. However, organizations have always outsourced some functions. For decades, most organizations hired firms to operate their cleaning or restaurant functions. What is different now is the scale. Firms are outsourcing everything from information technology management to entire functions such as training. In

HR, the functions most likely to be outsourced are temporary staffing, payroll, training, recruiting, and benefits administration (McGlone, 1997). Surveys continue to show that most firms (nearly 80%) have outsourced parts of their HR function, with smaller ones outsourcing more often.

There are many reasons why organizations outsource HR functions. The first is to save money. Employers recognize that they cannot pursue excellence in all areas. Therefore, they decide to focus on their core competence, such as customer service or innovation, and move secondary functions, such as benefits administration, to firms in which these functions are a core competence. (Core work contributes directly to the bottom line; non-core work doesn't.) Economies of scale can be achieved when a firm concentrates on one area and provides this service to many corporations. A second driver of this trend has been technology. Much of traditional HR service has involved answering employee inquiries about benefits or making changes to employee files. These kinds of tasks can be handled easily by interactive voice responses or on-site kiosks. Reducing transaction time (the time it takes to handle a request) is another major reason why firms outsource. Quality improvement is cited as another benefit, as contracting firms do a better job. Another reason cited by some smaller companies is that they find the laws and regulations governing HR so complex that they decide to outsource to firms that have the specific expertise required.

Outsourcing must be subjected to a cost–benefit analysis. Can the contractor do a better job, faster, while maintaining service levels and meeting legislative requirements? How will this be measured?

Managing the outsourcing becomes critical. The work is managed by results, not necessarily by time expended to generate the results. The outsourced project or function might be clearly defined. If the terms are fuzzy, however, the contractor might be invited to brainstorm and help generate the guidelines and standards (Petrick, 1996). A relationship with the firm must be established to ensure that the outsourcer acts in the firm's best interests and has knowledge of its unique needs. References must be checked, just as they are when hiring any employee.

While smaller firms might outsource all HR functions, most large firms retain the critical components. They will never engage in 100-percent outsourcing for three reasons. As has been argued throughout this text, the HR function is so critical to the culture and strategic objectives of an organization that it must be closely managed by the organization itself. Secondly, situations arise that are impossible to predict and outsource, such as industrial relations disputes. Timeliness of response is crucial. The final reason is the lack of providers of total HRM services. The field of outsourcing is replete with hundreds of small companies specializing in market niches. One might do an excellent job of benefits counselling, another might specialize in employee assistance, but none can do everything from training to managerial succession to payroll. These competencies have to reside within the firm ("How to Outsource Personnel," 1997).

Now that companies have had some experience with outsourcing functions, there are hints that the process is not as cost effective and problem free as expected. Surveys have indicated that about 25 percent of companies are not satisfied with the vendor–client relationship, that costs are regularly higher than they would have been if the work had been done in-house (Laabs, 1998). The reasons for the cost overrides include system incompatibilities and client demands outside the standard vendor package.

To manage the outsourcing relationship, companies should follow these steps:

- Understand the strategic and tactical reasons for outsourcing—cost, expertise, or quality of service. Determine if the function is a core competence, which should remain within the company.

- Develop benchmarking levels for internal services.

- Establish a list of qualified vendors.

- Preselect a vendor, basing the selection on standards developed from benchmarks. Do a cost–benefit analysis to determine if providing the service in-house, as compared to using an external provider, meets the cost, expertise, or quality of service goals. If the external vendor adds value, move to the next step.

- Check vendor references.

- Do a pilot phase to test system compatibilities.

- Negotiate a contract with defined measurements and benchmarks.

- Monitor vendor performance.

After discussing the ways in which organizations manage to keep employees off the permanent payroll, it seems fitting to devote some space to a discussion of how organizations try to keep some employees.

◆ ◆ ◆
RETENTION

The previous section focused on keeping one type of worker in a temporary relationship. Now we examine how companies try to keep another type of worker from straying to other companies. This new class of worker, the technology employee, is highly educated and skilled in technologies. Unlike temporary and outsourced employees, these high tech workers enjoy substantial pay packages, paid vacations, retirement plans, and stock purchase options. All of these benefits are offered so that this worker will not only be attracted to a particular company but also, more importantly, will stay working for that company. Retention is the issue.

Holding onto talented employees is a critical issue for several reasons. The first is that certain workers are in short supply. Knowledge or high tech workers are the most frequently cited scarce labour, but, indeed, senior managers and specialists in many areas are also in short supply. Part of the reason for labour shortages is the demographic shift: the number of workers between ages 35 and 44 will decline by around 1 percent between the years 2000 and 2015 (Lowe, 1998). The labour market is shrinking. The baby boomers are retiring and there aren't enough replacement workers.

Another reason that retention is emerging as an issue is that employees are simply more mobile, less attached to the corporation. As employers have abandoned the concept of job security, so too have people abandoned the concept of job loyalty. Employees in demand are realizing there is an upside to not having a job for life: more interesting assignments and more money. There seems to be a shift to being loyal to the profession, not to the organization. How can companies keep their top talent?

As with any organizational problem, the first step is to realize there is a problem and pay attention to it. Many management consulting firms and large telecommunications companies are doing just that. They appoint someone responsible for talent retention, attraction, and development. Such people have titles like "Manager, Employee Satisfaction." These retention experts then develop retention programs that do the following:

■ Pay the best employees extremely well.

■ Hold line managers responsible for talent development.

■ Allow employees to change jobs within the company. These programs facilitate this process by allowing employees to try out new jobs without transferring officially out of their old jobs. If they like the new job, they can ask for an official transfer.

■ Offer benefits, such as dry cleaning, day care, shopping services, training, and bank accounts from which employees can draw money for their desired training. These benefits are kept flexible so that employees can choose those that match their lifestyle.

■ Reward long service. Companies can do this by offering stock options or pensions that pay out only after a certain time. For younger employees, some companies are offering to pay off their student loans if they stay for five years.

Some companies develop an employee value proposition (EVP) that will help attract and retain employees (Cliffe, 1998). They base this EVP on concepts that they have learned in customer attraction and retention. An EVP is a brand positioning aimed at employees so that the company will be seen as an employer worth working for, and all company messages sent to the labour market are compelling and consistent. Key employees seem to be attracted to companies that pose one of four brand positions (Cliffe, 1998):

■ A "winning" company, which is characterized by growth and development

■ A "big risk, big reward" company, which offers great potential for advancement and compensation

■ A "save the world" organization, which is attractive to those wanting a mission

■ A "lifestyle" company, where employees want flexibility and a good relationship with the boss

Besides positioning their companies, employers are also paying employees for referrals. Employees receive $100 for referring an entry-level employee, $3000 for a mid-level tech employee, and $10,000 for an executive (Caudron, 1996). Companies scan newspapers for downsizing announcements, hoping to pick off the best employees. Still other employers use telecommuting as an attractor and retainer, allowing employees to choose to work in the city that gives them the lifestyle they desire.

After a decade of viewing employees as surpluses to be discarded, it seems fitting to end this book by discussing how valuable employees are. The key message, whether we talk about labour surpluses or labour shortages, is that you should take care of your own career.

◆ ◆ ◆
THE FREE AGENT CAREER

We have all heard stories about the old career pattern: get a job and keep it for life, while slowly scaling the organizational ladder until you reach the top. This model of career management (climbing the ladder in a pyramid shaped organizational structure) is dated. Why? There are several reasons, some of which are the result of the economic slowdowns of the 1960s and 1980s.

■ To survive, organizations were forced to cut jobs drastically, which decimated the middle managerial ranks. This resulted in a flattening of the pyramid and far fewer rungs on the career ladder.

■ During the same period, millions of baby boomers were finishing school and entering the workforce, ready to assume the managerial positions they had all read about. But there were few managerial jobs. The boomer bulge was trying to push through a flattening pyramid, with fewer jobs available.

■ Coupled with this was a movement to run companies based on principles of core competencies, so that, to achieve efficiencies, any function that was not central to the survival of the organization was outsourced. Again, the result was fewer jobs in large organizations and fewer managerial positions.

■ The core employees who were left to run the organization had to develop different sets of skills to manage these external relationships and to work as members of newly empowered teams. These employees, witnesses to the brutal downsizing efforts of most companies in which even competent and loyal employees were terminated, developed a healthy distrust of corporate careers.

These changes have resulted in a change in the psychological contract that an employee has with the employer. The traditional employment contract with the organization was built on an implicit understanding that the employee would work hard, develop additional skills provided mainly by the employer, and, in return, would be promoted on a regular basis. At a minimum, the employer would reward the loyalty and efforts of employees with job security. This contract is dead. The new contract, transactional in nature, lists the responsibilities and rights of each party in the employer–employee relationship, and employees want this contract stated explicitly in writing. If loyalty to any organization still exists, it is to the professional organization, to a network of peers and to certifiable credibility that confers collegiality and respect. Table 15.1 contains a comparison of the two concepts of career management.

These changes have transformed our traditional concepts of career management. We will look at an emerging concept of career management, which is still searching for a label. It has been given various names in an attempt to distinguish it from the older concept of a career ladder, or of a career in a pyramid-shaped, hierarchical organization. Some of the names that have been tried include "the jungle gym," "the protean career" (Hall, 1996), "the networked career," and "the cellular." We will discuss the cellular career, as it contains many of the elements proposed by others writing about career management.

◆ ◆ ◆

THE CELLULAR CAREER

The concept of the cellular career, proposed by Allred, Snow, and Miles (1996), recognizes that the changes we discussed previously influenced the structure of organizations. These structural changes have resulted in work

TABLE 15.1 COMPARING TRADITIONAL AND EMERGING CAREER MANAGEMENT CONCEPTS		
Characteristics	**Traditional**	**Emerging**
Employment contract	Implicit	Explicit
Duration	Long-term	Short-term
Career responsibility	Employer	Self-directed
Career identity	Organization	Profession/occupation
Benefits	Focus on security	Focus on learning
Loyalty	To the organization	Profession, friends, family
Mindset	Inward, political	Outward, entrepreneurial
Development	Formal training	Work experiences
Career progression	Vertical	Horizontal
Employment stability	Job security	Employability
Career goal	Corporate success	Psychological success

Source: Adapted from Hall, D., and J.E. Moss. 1998. "The New Protean Career Contract: Helping Organizations and Employees Adapt." *Organization Dynamics* (Winter): 22–37.

being accomplished through teams of people, both inside and outside the formal organization. The organizational hierarchies with strict controls have been replaced by cells of skilled contract workers, whose talents are used as needed. Contract workers have to keep their skills current, but this is more easily accomplished because they have access to many job experiences, unlike bureaucrats in the traditional organizational form. These independent workers often accept assignments based solely on the possibility of learning or new experiences. Film projects and management consulting firms are the most common examples of this cellular organizational structure.

This new organizational form has resulted in a need for individuals to manage their own careers, professionally, while they network with others. The cellular organization created the cellular career. Why is the concept of the cell so applicable to careers? A cell possesses all the characteristics necessary to function independently but, when combined with other cells, can perform much more complex work. People can manage their careers by working independently, using their specialized skills. Doctors and lawyers have always done this but these independents can survive and prosper by joining forces with other "cells." The most fundamental shift in thinking about careers is the realization that careers take place outside organizations, rather than within organizations (Pieperl and Baruch, 1997). Thus, employees become free agents, and employers become facilitators. Their roles are discussed in the following sections.

ROLE OF THE INDIVIDUAL IN THE SELF-MANAGED CAREER

Candidates entering the labour market have to realize that the traditional concept of a long-term job in a long-term organization is no longer viable. Expecting a company to manage your career is risky. As free agents, self-managed professionals are responsible for finding work, educating and training themselves, arranging their own benefits and holidays, and negotiating compensation. Self-managed professionals in cellular organizations must ensure that they have the following competencies:

Technical skills: To be hired on any basis (e.g., contract, permanent, part-time), an individual must have some skills that employers want. As always, individuals will begin their careers with some kind of specialty, such as accounting or programming. Any additional skill, such as computer literacy or fluency in another language, will provide the competitive edge to obtain more lucrative or interesting contracts.

Self-management skills: These skills include the kinds of personal work habits and attitudes that employers value and that are necessary to continue in the self-managed career. Self-management skills include managing time, being ethical, wanting to learn, balancing work and family demands, keeping motivated, being adaptable, being flexible, and so on (Allred et al., 1996).

Collaborative skills: This is a broad category referring to a range of skills involved in dealing with others. As a first step, candidates must be able to market themselves and negotiate employment contracts. Once hired, relationship skills are needed to identify the organization's resources so that contract work is done efficiently and effectively with others in the network. The individual will establish a network of contacts, which will facilitate future job searches, and so will manage all relationships (e.g., those with suppliers, friends, classmates) with a view to the "exploitation" of these contacts.

◆ ◆ ◆
ROLE OF THE ORGANIZATION IN THE SELF-MANAGED CAREER

Just as individuals must adapt to changing career directions, so too must the organization adapt to managing employees' careers in a changing world. The organization can manage those with cellular careers in the following ways:

Managing the cells: The employing organization acts as a facilitating mechanism (Allred et al., 1996), to enable the free agents to work together effectively. The organization acts as a broker, linking people and assignments. The organization also brokers mentor relationships and even training and development opportunities.

Providing learning opportunities: Those candidates with valued skills will place a premium on keeping their technical skills current and will choose contracts that provide opportunities to learn. The employing organization will have to develop methods to identify a contractor's strengths and weaknesses so that the strengths can be used and training provided if necessary.

Providing interesting benefits: Employees will likely collude and form partnerships with other contractors to obtain those benefits traditionally supplied by employers (e.g., dental care, pension plans). Any employer that can offer nontraditional benefits, such as access to training, opportunities for international assignments, or language training, will be able to attract and retain valued employees. Furthermore, employers will be able to build a pool of people with the training and experience required for achieving organizational strategies.

However, despite this list, the organization's role in career management is being phased out, and the role of the individual's professional association is taking on a greater importance. The professional association to which an individual belongs can provide a range of services and benefits to its members. For example, the Human Resources Professionals Association of Ontario (HRPAO) provides the following member benefits and services: training courses, conference sessions on the most current trends in the field, job placement services, a magazine and newsletters, and networking opportunities.

We end this chapter and the book by focusing on you and your professional career. As an HR professional, you have the tools to scan the environment for career opportunities, to evaluate your competencies, and to prepare a developmental plan for achieving your career goals.

◆ ◆ ◆
SUMMARY

The concept of the job is changing. The current labour market is paradoxical in that organizations are simultaneously creating work arrangements so that they don't have to retain more workers than necessary and developing retention strategies to keep the employees they need. The alternative work arrangements that have been discussed are part-time work, flextime work, telecommuting, contract work, and employee leasing. A special section on the benefits and problems of outsourcing HR functions was included. Then, strategies for successfully retaining employees were discussed. The chapter concluded with a comparison of the traditional concepts of career management with emerging concepts, and a discussion of the roles of the individual and the organization.

EXERCISES

1. List the advantages and disadvantages of telecommuting. A good starting point is the Bell Canada Web site: www.bellglobal.com/business-solutions/teleworking.html. To find others, use a search engine such as Yahoo and search for "telework Canada."

2. For many years, you have been worried about finding and keeping a job. But the labour market is changing, and now employers are focusing on keeping key employees. List the kinds of things an employer could offer you to get you to join an organization and stay with it. Now, work with members of a small group in your class and compare your lists. Are there any differences between people's lists based on factors such as the people's previous work experiences, stage in life, or type of education?

3. Consult the Web site of the Council of Canadian Human Resources Associations (www.chrpcanada.com), and click on the Web site of your provincial HR association. List the services and benefits offered by your provincial association that might be useful to you as a self-employed HR professional. If you are employed, contrast this list with the kinds of career help your employer offers you. (If you are not employed, interview an HR professional within an organization to determine what career assistance his or her employer offers.) Does the professional association or the employer offer a better career management package? For what reasons? Are there gaps that you, as a career-minded individual, must fill through your own efforts and interests?

References

Allred, B.B., C.C. Snow, and R.E. Miles. 1996. "Characteristics of Managerial Careers of the Twenty-first Century." *Academy of Management Executive* 10, no. 4 (November): 17–27.

Caudron, S. 1996. "Low Unemployment Is Causing a Staffing Drought: Here's Your Survival Kit." *Personnel Journal* 75, no. 1 (November): 58–67.

Church, E. 1996. "Business Balks at Part-time Benefits." *Globe and Mail* (October 8): B13.

Cliffe, S. 1998. "Winning the War for Talent." *Harvard Business Review* 76, no. 5 (September/October): 18–19.

Flynn, G. 1997. "Making a Business Case for Balance." *Workforce* (March): 68–74.

Gibb-Clark, M. 1997. "Interest Wanes for Shorter Work Week with Less Pay." *Globe and Mail* (May 21): B12.

Grensing-Pophal, L. 1997. "Employing the Best People—from Afar." *Workforce* (March): 30–38.

Hall, D., ed. 1996. *The Career Is Dead: Long Live the Career.* San Francisco: Jossey-Bass.

King, J. 1996. "Court Ruling Spurs Look at Temporary Workers." *Computer World* 30, no. 44 (October 28): 8.

"How to Outsource Personnel." 1997. *People Management* (February 20): 40–44.

Laabs, J. 1998. "The Dark Side of Outsourcing." *Workforce* (September): 42–48.

Larson, J. 1996. "Temps Are Here to Stay." *American Demographics* 18, no. 2 (February): 326–333.

Larson, T., and P.M. Ong. 1994. "Imbalance in Part-time Employment." *Journal of Economic Issues* 28, no. 1 (March): 187–193.

Lavv, J.L. 1996. "PEOs Make HR Easier with Staff Leasing." *Personnel Journal* (December): 64–72.

Levenson, A.R. 1996. "Recent Trends in Part-time Employment." *Contemporary Economic Policy* 14, no. 4 (October): 78–90.

Lipovenko, D. 1997. "Growing Army of Part-timers Being Shut Out, Study Says." *Globe and Mail* (November 17): A3.

Lowe, G.S. 1998. "The Future of Work." *Relations Industrielles* 53, no.2 (Spring): 235–257.

Lynn, G. 1995. "The Future of Contingent Work." *Personnel Journal* 74, no. 4 (April): 54–55.

McGlone, J.R. 1997. "Outsourcing for Growing Companies." *HR Focus* (April): 10.

Mitchell, A. 1997. "Moonlighting Triples in 20 Years." *Globe and Mail* (July 1): A1.

Peiperl, M., and Y. Baruch. 1997. "Back to Square Zero: The Post Corporate Career." *Organizational Dynamics* (Spring): 7–22.

Petrick, A.E. 1996. "The Fine Art of Outsourcing." *Association Management* (December): 42–48.

Snyder, D.P. 1996. "The Revolution in the Workplace: What's Happening to Our Jobs?" *Futurist* (March/April): 8–13,

Sunoo, B.P. 1996. "From Santa to CEO—Temps Play All Roles." *Personnel Journal* (April): 35–44.

Williams, B. 1996. "Trends in Employment Patterns and Policies." *Public Management* 78, no. 8 (August): 24–25.

Yukich, K. 1997. "Learn to Use Flexible Staffing or Perish." *Canadian HR Reporter* (October 20): 32.

Index

◆

To the owner of this book

We hope that you have enjoyed Belcourt and McBey's *Strategic Human Resources Planning* (0-17-604893-6), and we would like to know as much about your experiences with this text as you would care to offer. Only through your comments and those of others can we learn how to make this a better text for future readers.

School _____ Your instructor's name _____

Course _____ Was the text required? _____ Recommended? _____

1. What did you like the most about *Strategic Human Resources Planning?*

_____

_____

_____

2. How useful was this text for your course?

_____

_____

_____

3. Do you have any recommendations for ways to improve the next edition of this text?

_____

_____

_____

4. In the space below or in a separate letter, please write any other comments you have about the book. (For example, please feel free to comment on reading level, writing style, terminology, design features, and learning aids.)

_____

_____

_____

Optional

Your name _____ Date _____

May Nelson Canada quote you, either in promotion for *Strategic Human Resources Planning* or in future publishing ventures?

Yes _____ No _____

Thanks!

You can also send your comments to us via e-mail at
college@nelson.com

PLEASE TAPE SHUT. DO NOT STAPLE.

TAPE SHUT

TAPE SHUT

FOLD HERE

Nelson

MAIL ➤ **POSTE**
Canada Post Corporation
Société canadienne des postes
Postage paid   Port payé
if mailed in Canada   si posté au Canada
Business Reply   **Réponse d'affaires**
0066102399   **01**

0066102399-M1K5G4-BR01

NELSON, THOMSON LEARNING
MARKET AND PRODUCT DEVELOPMENT
PO BOX 60225 STN BRM B
TORONTO ON M7Y 2H1

TAPE SHUT

TAPE SHUT